Prop. Dickerson

Dickerson/Hist. 27

W9-AFI-055

The American Social Experience Series
GENERAL EDITOR: JAMES KIRBY MARTIN
EDITORS: PAULA S. FASS, STEVEN H. MINTZ, CARL PRINCE,
JAMES W. REED & PETER N. STEARNS

Gullahs worshiping in Goose Creek Church. (Courtesy of the New-York Historical Society, New York.)

"A PECULIAR PEOPLE"

Slave Religion and
Community-Culture Among the Gullahs

MARGARET WASHINGTON CREEL

NEW YORK UNIVERSITY PRESS

NEW YORK AND LONDON

1988

Library of Congress Cataloging-in-Publication Data
Creel, Margaret Washington
A peculiar people : slave religion and community-culture among the
Gullahs / Margaret Washington Creel.
p.   cm. — (The American social experience series : 7)
Bibliography: p.
Includes index.
ISBN 0-8147-1404-8
1. Slaves—South Carolina.   2. Slaves—South Carolina—Religion.
3. Afro-Americans—South Carolina—Social life and customs.   4. Afro-
Americans—South Carolina—Religion.   5. Slaves—Sea Islands—
Religion.   6. Afro-Americans—Sea Islands—Religion.   7. South
Carolina—Social life and customs.   8. South Carolina—Religious
life and customs.   9. Sea Islands—Social life and customs.   10. Sea
Islands—Religious life and customs.   I. Title.   II. Series.
E445.S7C74 1988
306'.6'089960730—dc19   87-22698

For Minor Washington and
Beatrice Clark Washington

But ye are a chosen generation, a royal priesthood, an holy nation, a peculiar people that ye should shew forth the praises of him who hath called you out of darkness into his marvelous light.—I Peter, 2:9

This "conscription," together with its manner of execution has created a suspicion that the government have not the interest in the Negroes that it has professed. . . . were it not for the desire to still sympathise with this, as they call themselves—short minded—but peculiar people—I should . . . commit my charge to some person with a . . . sterner heart than my own—G. M. Wells to E. L. Pierce, May, 1862, Beaufort, South Carolina, in Ira Berlin, ed., *Freedom: A Documentary History of Emancipation, 1861–1867, Series II, The Black Military Experience* (Cambridge: Cambridge University Press, 1982), 50.

They are . . . suspicious and sensitive. They have not acquired . . . confidence in us . . . —they do not as yet, so realize that they have a country to fight for . . .—Edward L. Pierce to Maj. Gen. David Hunter, May 11, 1862, Beaufort, South Carolina, Ibid., 47.

Contents

Illustrations

Acknowledgments

My thanks to the University of California at Los Angeles for research support I have received in the past several years, through summer and sabbatical assistance. Funds from the Institute of American Cultures, College Institute Program, Faculty Career Development Program, and the Academic Senate were most generous.

In my search for information on the Gullahs I visited and had correspondence with many libraries. While investigations were not always fruitful, every library staff was helpful. I wish to thank the South Caroliniana Library, University of South Carolina; Southern Historical Collection, University of North Carolina; Methodist Church Archives, Wofford College; Baptist Collection, Furman University; Beaufort Township Library, South Carolina; South Carolina Historical Society; Historical Society of Pennsylvania; Library of Congress; Cornell University Library; Houghton Library, Harvard University; Historical Society of Wisconsin; Interlibrary Loan staff at the University of California at Los Angeles; and Oscar Sims, Social Science Bibliographer at UCLA.

I have received encouragement and suggestions from a number of people. My colleague Ruth Bloch read two important chapters of the manuscript and offered useful suggestions for rewriting. Daniel Littlefield of Louisiana State University read and commented on my chapter on the African slave trade and shared with me his historiographical knowledge of source material. Michael Mullin of California State University, Sacramento, read an earlier draft of the manuscript and offered perceptive comments. My colleague Gary Nash referred me to important source material and read an early version of the manuscript with much care and sensitivity. Many thanks to Professor Velma Pollard of the University of the West Indies, for sharing with me her impressive knowledge of linguistic patterns in the black diaspora. Discussions with Joseph Holloway of California State University, Northridge, concerning African influences among the Gullahs were productive and stimulating. Although our opinions differ, I believe we learned from each other, and we concur in the belief that there is still much to be uncovered regarding the African impact on African-American life, thought and culture. A special note of thanks to Peter Wood of Duke University. He read two versions of the manuscript and offered his expertise on the African-Carolina experience during the colonial era. Professor Wood's penetrating insights and suggestions lead to fruitful rethinking in a number of areas.

This study began as a dissertation under the direction of Professors Daniel H. Calhoun and Daniel Crowley at the University of California, Davis, and Professor Leon F. Litwack at the University of California, Berkeley. I am particularly grateful for Professor Calhoun's advice and encouragement during my years as his student, and for his continued belief in the worthiness of this subject. Professor Crowley's anthropological input was invaluable. More significantly, whenever the vastness and controversial nature of this project seemed overwhelming, I recalled his comment to me when I first embarked on the project: "You're on to something."

The enthusiasm, intelligence and perception of many of my graduate students in the antebellum history and Afro-American history seminars at UCLA was inspiring. In those courses we raised probing questions about religion, culture, community and politics which I hope have made this a better volume. My right hand in the project was Jill Marie Watts. As my research assistant for three years, Ms. Watts' library detective work went well beyond my expectations. For typing and word processing assistance I wish to thank Alesia Barbour, and UCLA's Central Word Processing Center, especially Nancy Rahn. While I received valuable comments, suggestions, and advice, I have also been selective in adhering to recommentations regarding the book. Thus I am fully responsible for any limitations contained herein.

Members of my family, as always, were a source of strength. My two children, James and Céleste Creel, never ceased to add color and zest to life. They accepted my preoccupation with unusual patience. My niece, Anita Louise Crawford, was a wonderful surrogate mother when needed, and she deserves my thanks and gratitude. My beloved aunt, Hattie Clark Harrison, who so much looked forward to publication of this book died this year before it went to press. Though we in her immediate and extended family miss her sorely, she is alive in us all. Her legacy of vitality, generosity, and love is a wellspring which continues to empower her "children" with fortitude.

On the professional and personal level, I owe much to Graham R. Hodges. He read the dissertation and the manuscript drafts with interest and thoughtfulness, offering ideas for improvement in my discussion of the colonial black experience and black participation in the War for Independence. Graham's impressive knowledge of these two periods as they affected blacks in the Northeast, informed my own evaluation of the Carolina situation. He was particularly helpful in alerting me to primary and secondary early American sources, from which much can be learned about black activities and the black-white counterpoint. Most of all Graham, thanks for many hours of listening, for cheerful encouragement, and for being a friend.

Finally, for my parents, words of thanks and acknowledgment in no way convey adequately how much is owed. I dedicate this book to them with love, respect, admiration, and gratitude.

List of Abbreviations

AHR	*American Historical Review*
AMA	American Missionary Association Papers
BC	Baptist Collection, Furman University, Greenville, S. C.
CAJ	*Christian Advocate and Journal*
HSSCC	Historical Society, South Carolina Conference, Methodist Church Archives, Wofford College, Spartanburg, S. C.
MMQR	*Methodist Magazine and Quarterly Review*
HSP	Historical Society of Pennsylvania, Philadelphia
SCA	*Southern Christian Advocate*
SCG	*South Carolina Gazette*
SHC	Southern Historical Collection, University of North Carolina, Chapel Hill, N. C.
SCHS	South Carolina Historical Society, Charleston, S. C.
SCL	South Caroliniana Library, University of South Carolina, Columbia, S. C.
SPGLL	Society for the Propagation of the Gospel, London Letters

Introduction

This study grew out of my interest in the sociohistorical relationship between community, religion, and resistance as these concepts affected African-Americans during slavery. My focus is limited to the Gullahs of South Carolina for several reasons. First, a monographic approach allowed for more in-depth interpretations and analyses of community, religion, and resistance. Second, the Gullah slave community's religious legacy has not had the historical treatment it deserves in the scholarship. Third, this community of slaves provides a significant model for studying African-American adaptive capacities and retention of traditional African provenance.

The notion of community used in this book presupposes that subjectively the term represents a sense of collectivity and togetherness, based on a definite pattern of essentially positive relationships, possibly changing over time, and a sense of mutual dependence. Objectively speaking, community occurs when a group of social actors are bound by responsibility, accountability, and compromises made in order to maintain organization and stability. Hence, on a rational level, for the closeness and security which community offers, it extracts loyalty, obedience, relinquishing of some individual freedom, and personal authority.[1] (And community has strong political connotations if viewed in this light.) Essential to a community's development is the culture of the people involved. There are various ways of defining culture. Here it refers to creative, adaptive, dynamic patterns of behavioral meanings, which are inherited and historically transmitted through rituals, symbols, and systems of communication that represent societal understanding, awareness, and conceptions of life. Community and culture are intricately connected. Grasping the significance of one can lead to meaningful analyses of the other: "community is a culturally defined way of life."[2]

The above methods of considering community-culture provide one foundation for understanding the direction of this book on the Gullah socioreligious experience. It is also a way of interpreting the link between the meaning of community among the Gullahs and one major group of their African foreparents. These African communities of the Windward Coast (today Sierra Leone and Liberia) were structured under the sacred and secular authority of two secret societies—Poro for men and Sande for women. Nearly all West African ethnic groups had secret societies, but most were not mandatory organizations like Poro and Sande. Instead they were associations of exclusivity or privilege. Nevertheless, the prevalence and structure of such societies suggest that they could, if reinforced by similar but new traditions, and servicable in a new ambiance, be *adaptively* retained. Thus this volume argues that some adaptive concepts of community (and aspects of spirituality) inherited from secret societies fused with Gullah interpretations of Christianity, becoming part of folk religion in the slave quarters.

The second major theme of this study—religion—is, as previously stated, engaged with the first. If community broadly organizes human social existence and social relations, religion as employed herein, is an integral component of community and culture. It provides powerful, persuasive belief systems, symbols, and images of cosmic order which act as realistic explications of human experience and/or the human condition. The sacred symbols embodied in a people's religious beliefs synthesize their ethos and world view. In addition to interpreting reality cosmologically, Clifford Geertz suggests that the "moods and motivations" produced by religious orientation cast a "lunar light" over a people's secular life.[3] This view provides a foundation for my treatment of Gullah attitudes toward life, death, and the supernatural. I argue that traditional African spiritual belief and cosmology, particularly that of the BaKongo and other Bantu peoples, found a significant niche within Gullah Christian practices and helped stage their folk religion. The strength and flexibility of some African spiritual customs, such as the use of sacred medicines, ancestor reverence, and beliefs about immortality facilitated merger into an African-Christian synthesis among the Gullahs.

Belief systems can be a source of interpreting social and psychological human processes, comprehending natural phenomena, or may recommend ways of dealing with reality. The Gullahs defined life in sacred terms, an inherited African legacy.[4] Their introduction to Christianity reinforced this sense of the sacred but also raised questions regarding contradictions inherent in the teachings. Slaves who organized the 1822 revolt attempt in Charleston, called the Vesey Conspiracy, based their right to rebellion on several principles, among which were certain Christian beliefs extracted from the Bible. Yet slave masters and clergymen used the same Bible (albeit different texts) to explain *their* "right" to keep blacks in bondage. Both groups' beliefs determined their interpretations of scriptures, reflecting diametrically opposed interests and attitudes. Furthermore, as the more isolated Gullahs became "Christians," their spiritual orientation continued to foster independent ways of thinking. This was demonstrated by the Gullah's spiritual autonomy, in the structuring of their community-culture, their sense of morality, and sense of themselves as a people.

In this volume, I have tried to strike a balance between "pure" religion (for its own sake, other worldly or transcendental) and applied religion (its functional or empirical use) because both were practiced among slaves who ultimately adopted Christianity. Yet evidence sometimes points to a cloudy qualitative difference between the two. Some Gullah slaves accepted Christianity at face value as presented by missionaries and masters. Most did not, but instead blended transcendental aspects of Christianity with the everyday, paramount reality of their human experiences and aspirations.

Awareness of the empirical impact of religious instruction, and in some cases the lack thereof, is important for understanding how and why folk religion flourished among the Gullahs. The religious instruction movement also provides a way of contemplating the reasons for Christian instruction on the part of whites. Almost from the beginning a few whites, despite much opposition, attempted to Christianize slaves. Some slaves responded warmly. Yet a concerted process of slave conversion among the majority of coastal Carolina slaves did not begin in earnest by whites until around 1830. Even then, the way was sometimes filled with pitfalls created by a reluctant master class and disinterested clergy. Furthermore, the culturally and geographically isolated black population, whose main spiritual tradition still rested on Africanity, showed only lukewarm interest for some time. Certainly there was exposure to Christianity before 1830—from acculturated, privileged blacks and occasional spiritually moved ministers and planters. Also the Great Awakening of the colonial era touched South Carolina even if it did not linger there for very long. And early Methodists actively tried bringing Christianity to the Gullahs, but were under bans of proscription as an antislavery denomination. Hence, prior to the movement begun by the Methodist Missionary Society in 1829, most slaves working in the fields received their "Christian" instruction from fellow slaves. When slaves accepted Christianity under Methodist and later Baptist tutelage, they embraced it selectively, fusing Christianity with African traditions to create Gullah folk religion. This religion was a means of explaining experiential reality for the Gullahs on sacred and secular levels. If community was the base or substance of Gullah life, spirituality (a more appropriate term, I think, than religion) was the superstructure upon which the foundation was posited.

The final area of investigation in my broadly considered three-tier thematic construct, is resistance—perhaps the most debated issue in the North American bondage experience. There is a tendency to interpret resistance in its strictest sense—as bloodletting or flight to freedom. These are obvious means of rebellion, and from the beginning, African-Carolinians were a restless, insurgent group. This study is a further comment on that spirit of resistance. Yet I primarily delve into what are in my opinion equally meaningful ways of analyzing resistance to enslavement. The Denmark Vesey Conspiracy denotes the end (as far as historical knowledge goes) of concerted efforts at black liberation among the Gullahs. The revelation of the Conspiracy and subsequent debates over the value of religious instruction (since the event was planned under the guise of religion) ushered in, paradoxically, a movement to convert the slave population in South Carolina. From outward appearances the Vesey Conspiracy marked the end of organized black resistance in South Carolina. This is the juncture at which I believe the question of resistance takes on expanded meaning. I attempt to demonstrate that resistance against white power and hegemony was conspicuous in the Gullahs' sense of cultural autonomy, authoritative, creative community-building, and their spiritual disengagement from the slaveocracy's version of Christian teachings. The means and methods of their accomplishment are viewed through the Gullah community and folk religion.

I have benefited greatly from the works of previous writers. W. E. B. DuBois was among the first to discuss elements of continuity between the African tradition and the "spiritual strivings" of African-Americans. He was also a pioneer in expressing the historic role and significance of black religion as a means of political protest. And Sterling Brown, another sage of African-American cultural thought, observed over forty years ago, that much could be learned of black life-style and values through studying the folklore of slaves. Brown, one of the earliest interpreters of black thought, viewed folktales, spirituals and narratives as historical documents that spoke "with convincing finality against the legend of contented slavery." Thus more recent scholarship on the slave community, from which my own work draws directly, is part of a tradition begun with the exploratory works of African-American writers of previous generations. Among current scholars, perhaps the most extensive elaboration of the importance of black culture as a means of delving into the black mind-set is provided by Lawrence Levine in *Black Culture and Black Consciousness*. Levine's seminal work provides an impressive continuum for probing black culture and black thought through analysis of slave folk beliefs, spirituals, and African-American fusion of the sacred and secular. Levine's general discussions of the significance of African traditions and behavior patterns among bondspeople is supported in the particular case of the Gullahs. He debates, as I do, the contention that slaves did not oppose bondage and he maintains that if historians cannot perceive the "sacred universe created by slaves as a serious alternative to the societal system created by southern slaveholders," it is perhaps the historians' problem and not the slaves'.[5]

My book is a regionally limited and more concentrated study involving only the period of enslavement. Levine's work permeates myriad areas of black thought, encompassing bondage *and* freedom, allowing for an emphasis somewhat different from mine and for a greater range of cultural and aesthetic treatment. Bondage takes up only two, albeit important, trend-setting chapters of *Black Culture and Black Consciousness*. My attention focuses on a full interpretation of one group's spiritual experience in a manner not previously explored. For instance, I see evidence of a strong New Testament ideology and outlook among the Gullahs as they embraced Christianity. Levine does not ignore this impact, but sees more Old Testament messages in general African-American consciousness.[6] Additionally, my work discusses the means by which slaves may have forged African sacred-secular traditions and offers explanations about *how* meanings of religious symbols and rituals related to social processes and community structure. Ultimately my study presents an amplification of rather than disagreement with most of Lawrence Levine's interpretations. Our methods are not always comparable yet our motivations seem to grow from similar concerns and lead to complementary conclusions—at least in terms of the bondage experience.

A pioneering and, for me, encouraging work on slave religion is Albert J. Raboteau's *Slave Religion: The "Invisible Institution" in the Antebellum South*. Raboteau writes that one purpose of his book was to provide a "rough sketch for further, more exhaustive examination" of slave religion.[7] Nearly a decade has passed since his book was first published. Slave religion, though considered the pillar of African-American culture, remains largely unexplored through historical scholarship (even Raboteau's background was in religious studies).[8]

Thematically, Raboteau's book and mine run parallel: the African heritage, slave conversion, religious life in the slave community, and the relationship of religion to resistance. Yet we treat these issues differently. In his early chapter entitled "Death of the Gods," Raboteau summarily states that certain factors "tended to inhibit the survival of African culture and religion in the United States." Whatever African influences remained, says Raboteau, are found in "spirituals, ring shouts and folk beliefs." In the case of Gullahs, and perhaps other slave communities, his two contentions seem contradictory.[9] Spirituals, the ring shout, and folk beliefs tell us most of what we know (at least from the Gullahs themselves) about Gullah religion. These cultural traits move us as close, perhaps, as we can come to understanding a *black Weltanschauung*, and they were intrinsic to Gullah religion. If we probe folk religion and culture, it leads to some general insights, as Levine demonstrated, about slave religion. I examine the manifestations and meanings (as symbols and rituals) of various elements of Gullah folk belief. Then I compare my hypotheses with African spiritualism, cosmology, and other beliefs. I do not argue for "survivals," a somewhat lifeless term implying passive existence. But I do argue for the presence of dynamic, creative, cultural trends of African provenance among the Gullahs, which they adapted to their concept of Christianity and integrated into New World black collective consciousness.

Raboteau and I both expend much energy on the slave conversion process because it is crucial to the black religious experience in America. On this issue we are probably in closer, though not complete agreement.

Christianity was capable, says Raboteau, of "producing a Christian social order based on the observance of mutual duty, slave to master and master to slave."[10] I found however, an abundance of literature on the "duty" of the former, but comparatively little on the "duty" of the latter. Certainly, a liberal attitude existed in the religious sector of the South—probably the only sector where such ideas could survive. Raboteau provides an excellent treatment of eighteenth-century religious activity. Early Methodism is the best, though not the only example of religious liberalism. The emergence of a few independent black churches is another. In the mid nineteenth-century Lowcountry, this tradition was to some extent epitomized by Methodist lay preachers who supplied the plantation missions.[11] As far as slaveholders and most regular clergy were concerned however, amelioration of bondage via religion was a minor consideration when compared to the influence of social control ideology. Raboteau seems to argue for balance between white conversion of slaves for moral and spiritual reasons and the use of Christianity to encourage docility and submission. That may have been true for the South in general. I do not ignore the white moral and spiritual imperative, but the weight of the argument in coastal South Carolina leans heavily toward the use of religion to encourage submissive personalities.

Raboteau understandably desires to "preserve the texture of slave testimony and to avoid forcing the experience reflected in that testimony into any preconceived theoretical framework."[12] I also try and conserve the historical reality of the black religious experience. However I saw important elements in the Gullah experience in need of interpretation and I sometimes practiced what some scholars have called imaginary reconstruction of historical facts.[13] When empirical data implied theoretical constructions or thematic conclusions I did not avoid hermeneutics. This is most obvious in the difference between Raboteau's and my treatment of two issues—religious life and rebellion. Our conclusions are, I think, somewhat similar. Our methodologies and discussions of operative, determining forces that explain these phenomena differ. Also (as is the case with Levine's work), our emphasis differs. One obvious explanation for this is that I am writing about a community, not the entire slave South. Yet contrasts go deeper than that. Raboteau sees a complex ambiguity in slave life and religious orientation which supports accommodation as well as rebelliousness, and which ultimately offered "freedom," and "transcendence" for the "individual."[14] Certainly among the Gullahs a range of responses to religion existed. But *particular* responses predominated and I emphasize these. Thus I structurally explore and interpret not only the spiritual experience, but religion as a *determining factor* in Gullah ideas of liberation, resistance-culture, and community organization. Although my book is primarily historical, it also addresses psychological, sociological, and anthropological issues. That apparently is not Raboteau's intention. Thus, thematic similarity between the two books is deceiving. Still, Raboteau's fruitful beginning furnished grounding for my study and hopefully, for others, in an area of black history worthy of and needing much more examination.

Two other scholars deserve mention here even though their major works are not directly on slave religion. My work has been influenced by Vincent Harding because he places the historical black experience in progressive-nationalistic, radical-protest, freedom-quest perspectives. His book, *There Is a River*,[15] is a poetic, apocalyptic historical message that *struggle*, more than "survival," permeated black motivations in the North and South, among slave and free. Harding's work is a statement that may ostensibly address a black popular audience.[16] Yet it is no less a significant contribution to the historical literature.

The late Herbert Gutman's *Black Family in Slavery and Freedom, 1750–1925* explores black cultural beliefs and behavior as well as examines the black family. And if black religion is one key to the nature of black life and culture, the black "family," despite historical (and present-day) assaults, is the other. Gutman analyzes the adaptive nature of black culture, specifically patterns of family cohesion. Yet researching familial associations involved investigating origins of marrying practices and ceremonies, belief systems, kin obligations versus decisions to flee, child-rearing practices, sexuality, and collective organization. Gutman is exceptional in inquiring into the African past and relating this to the above deterministic features of black culture.[17] No historian has made such frontal attempts to integrate specific aspects of Africanity into the historical functioning of the black family.

Eugene Genovese's *Roll, Jordan, Roll* set the tone for a more conservative view of slave life: slaves "accommodated" their bondage, masters were "paternalists" who exercised their "hegemonic" power with a sense of "duty" and "burden."[18] *Roll, Jordan, Roll* is a culminating achievement based on years of research and writing centered around issues related to the above concepts, and despite its conservative conclusions, is part of the essentially progressive "community-and-culture" historiography of the 1970s.[19] Genovese presents a dramatic, panoramic view of slave life and culture, engulfed in a Christian motif. Through abundant documentary evidence, he offers an engrossing but challenging (not to mention disturbing) exploratory interpretation of the Old South. Within these frameworks, Genovese introduces an international comparative method, a hemispheric perspective, discussions of work ethics, social relations, and rebellion—to name only a few themes of the book. The author's work has revitalized scholarship and debate on race, culture, class, and labor arrangements. The book has engendered both negative and positive controversy since its publication,[20] and one hesitates to add to the plethora of comments. Through all of the pro and con discussions, the profundity and general excellence of Genovese's scholarship remains. Still, any historian writing on slave life and culture, especially religion, will necessarily take a position on Genovese's major and even some minor precepts. My disagreements with the author, implicitly discussed throughout this book, are briefly stated here in general terms. Both Genovese and I recognize value in slave culture, seeing the central role of religion and spirituality. And we observe a developing nationalism. On the major points of "paternalism," "hegemony," and "accommodation" as he uses the latter term, our views differ. Among the Gullahs, and especially in the Sea Islands, paternalism was not a determining factor in master-slave relationships. Nor did paternalism, as Genovese maintains, prevent slavery from evolving into that "closed" system discussed by Stanley Elkins.[21] To enforce my argument, and to provide a fuller presentation of Gullah society, I discuss master-slave relationships (especially as they affect the religious sector) throughout this volume. Rather than paternalism, I see *slave folk religion* as an important determining factor in precluding the development of a "closed" system. Gutman saw the slave family as another foil to white authority. Slave religion also represents black denial of white cultural authority in the slave quarters. One cannot debate the political power of master over slave, and hegemony is one kind of power. However, consider hegemony on a cultural level. Gullah religion was a congealing force in cultural creativity and a sense of community. The contours of black spiritual organization embodied certain African beliefs, an African world view and selective Christianity. In some respects, Genovese would probably not disagree with this[22] (in fact my reading of his work as a graduate student some years ago inspired these considerations). Yet my examination of symbolic elements, behaviorisms, and rituals within Gullah culture lead to interpretations and conclusions different from Genovese's. The socioreligious connection that encouraged and helped fashion black life did not, among the Gullahs, rest "on a politically dangerous kind of individualism."[23] What Genovese interprets as conservatism and individualism, I see as forged resistance culture and group consciousness.

Slave religion had its individualistic tendencies. Yet on the positive side these enhanced a sense of personal dignity and self-esteem. Of course some slaves were involved mainly for spiritual, otherworldly gratification. But more significantly, religion was a support for community-building processes, collective strength, and solidarity. Life represented more than "endurance," "accommodation," or "survival," but an effective means of resisting the hegemonic trappings Genovese writes about. Genovese also sees Christianity as binding "master and slave together in universal communion,"[24] though contributing to their separation. *Communion?* It is doubtful that slaves accepted this psychic bonding. My evidence points to the contrary—to a people defending their collective spiritual separation and independence.

Genovese is confusing when he acknowledges the African heritage in the slave work ethic, dancing, cooking, and even housing, but maintains that "spiritual collectivism retreated before the advance of Christianity." In place of Africanity slaves "accepted Christianity's celebration of the individual soul," which became their "weapon of personal and community survival."[25] This "community" is a type of nationalism in its most conservative form—religious. It is a sort of knee-jerk reaction (this nationalism) that replaces true struggle or resistance and forces slaves into a Gordian knot with the planters pulling the strings. This nationalism confines slaves as willing social, psychological, and cultural dependents.[26] Without the input of resistance, this type of religious nationalism takes a conservative, nonprogressive emphasis. But among the Gullahs resistance to bondage on a number of levels remained a facet of black life. It is important to historical inquiry that the experiences of bondspeople be examined in terms they help define, as one does with other groups—slaveholders for instance. Otherwise one risks espousing a kind of retrospective cultural chauvinism. Why interpret the psyche of the slave through the ideology of the slave master? Or, how much can we learn about workers by studying them through management ideology?

Professor Genovese describes the slave South in prebourgeois or precapitalist terms, a theory other historians have adopted. One can see the convenience and appeal of this definition as a means of explaining social and economic relations. Paternalism is a prebourgeois ideology for the most part. Paternalistic, feudalistic, or signorial relationships characterize societies where political and religious structures are inextricably tied to their economies. There is less class cohesion, or class consciousness in prebourgeois societies because of the simplicity of production organization and the "self-sufficiency" of communities. Within such an historical period, the oppressed group supposedly never become *conscious* of the *true* economic driving forces behind historical movement. Nor are the oppressed *conscious* of their own victimization because class relations in these societies remain complex and concealed. This is a contrast to the stark simplicity of class interest and exploitation under capitalism.[27] Not all of the South, especially that which provides Genovese's model, fits the economic pattern. Plantations were largely dependent upon an international market for profit. They were not "self-sufficient" since other areas of the country and world supplied them with provisions and commodities of life-style. But the social pattern in prebourgeois society raises more interesting questions if applied to the bondspeople—the oppressed. Can we say that slaves were not *conscious* of their *oppression* (that they had only *false consciousness*)?[28] Slave testimony indicates otherwise, though not in the Marxist-Leninist sense. The wealth of masters and impoverishment of slaves is evidence of the "alienation" (lack of ownership of or equitable return for labor) of the "producers" (slaves) from their "commodity" (fruits of labor). Oppression and victimization were realized on the conscious level, but slaves' reaction to these forces needs to be measured less from a twentieth-century perspective.

As far as class relations being concealed, in the slaves' case under a web of paternalism and hegemony, the polarization between master and slave, especially when the latter was a field hand, was real. And of course Marx (who developed this analysis) was not referring to bondage, but to feudalism. In the latter case, relations may be less obvious because, among other things, peasants have a claim to the land they cultivate, race is not a factor, cultural differences are not as divisive, and in some societies,

the peasants and the lords were distant relations. Thus a system of pa-
tronage, dependency, and moralism could exist. But did slave masters
need to morally justify a system of exploitation against blacks? On the
individual level they occasionally did, especially with favored slaves. But
as a class, history indicates that in the final outcome, slaveholders had
no more moral imperative toward the slaves than capitalists have had
toward industrial workers.

Genovese's sources certainly point to contradictory aspects of bondage, most of which supports paternalism, conservative Christianity
practiced by slaves, and black accommodation. The complexity of his
argument and thoroughness of his research is food for thought, to say
the least. Where were paternalism and accommodation embraced by
blacks? John Blassingame wrote that if Stanley Elkins' "Sambo" existed
at all, he (or she) was probably a "big house" inhabitant.[29] Could the
same be said for the enslaved religious accommodationists if they existed
as a group? *Roll, Jordan, Roll* contains discussions of blacks in numerous
occupational roles and situations—from preachers to prostitutes, from
children to old folk. But it is difficult to find the workers in the fields—
those who perhaps represent the "beauty and power of the human spirit"
in ways that mammies, drivers, body servants, and artisans may not.
Our glimpse of field hands comes through only vaguely. Most social
actors in *Roll, Jordan, Roll* are white, or they are the "privileged" blacks,
more likely bearers and beneficiaries of accommodation, than people in
the quarters. Genovese implies as much about "life in the Big House."
But he eases out of the contradiction by asserting that no social stratification existed between field hands and house servants who identified with
white culture.[30] Thus we are left thinking these black "integrationists"
carried accommodation to the slave quarters and the field hands bought
it. Perhaps the author gives too much credit to the capacity of "big house"
and "favored" slaves to fashion their brand of "nationalism" and impose
it on the larger black population. I think at least two types of nationalism
developed—one from the slave quarters and one originating with the "favored" groups. In any case more studies are now taking a less monolithic
approach to slave society. Just as there were many Souths, there were
many slave communities, and their complexities await more examination. We know that slaves created communities. We are just beginning
to investigate the nature, structure, and stratification of these communities. Recent, more regionally focused works ask new questions, but also

seem to reinforce the 1970s "slave community" consensus to which previously mentioned (and many unmentioned) scholars contributed so pro-
lifically. Inherent in that consensus is the theme which on some level we
all agree: among African-Americans the oppression of bondage bred resistance and active, even if it was not always open, rebellion.

The primary methodologies used in structuring this book are comparative and dialectical. A comparative model is adopted because I wish to
demonstrate the relationship between African, white Protestant, and
Gullah worlds. Thus in Part I the African background is discussed. Here
I ask the reader's forbearance. This discussion of the African slave trade,
ethnic displacement, and the significance of the African socioreligious
legacy, is necessary because these relate to the entire thrust of the book
and because my theory regarding ethnic origins and African influences
will be controversial, yet I believe, sound in plausability.

I agree with Eugene Genovese that to some extent, "an understanding
of the slaves requires some understanding of the masters and of others
who shaped a complex slave society."[31] Part II, consisting of two chapters, begins my dialectic of black-white counterpoint and deals with South
Carolina up to the War for Independence. One chapter is devoted to
missionaries and masters. The next chapter, on the black religious experience, deals with the Great Awakening and that limited group who
laid a foundation for acculturation and black-to-black spiritual interaction. Part III continues the black-white counterpoint. Chapter 5 develops
concepts of black rebelliousness, and the period of the American War for
Independence is crucial. It represents a time of religious liberalism on
the one hand and black resistance on the other. Yet the ultimate outcome
of the new "republicanism" was retrenchment of old socioeconomic alliances and forces. The black response is rebellion. Immediate white reaction is repression. But on another level white "thinking men" believed
in a safer, possibly more successful method of dealing with black recal-
citrance. Chapters 6 and 7 analyze and narrate the movements, primarily
by Methodist laymen and Baptist planters, to convert the masses of Gullahs. These chapters also interpret Gullah responses to Christianity,
slavery, and life in bondage. In Part IV the counterpoint technique is
dropped. Throughout this book I attempt to present a picture of plantation life among Gullahs, as well as a view of slave religion and conversion. But Part IV is devoted fully to offering a presentation of Gullah
socioreligious culture in a collective setting. Chapters 8, 9, and 10 sug-

gest ways in which Gullahs interpreted Christianity, and how Africanity was integrated into Christianity, into attitudes toward life, death, and the supernatural. I do not argue for direct, fixed, or unchanging transmission of African religion and culture. Yet persistence of traditional beliefs, embedded in a recently created society, is not remarkable. Nor should we assume that traditional African customs and beliefs necessarily disintegrated before Christian and white cultural icons.[32] Still my aim is to demonstrate African-Gullah adaptability in their interaction with another major cultural form, and their capacity for change and meaningful continuity given the realities of new situations.

I rely heavily upon primary sources in this book, although my discussion on African culture and cosmology is an exception. Here the emphasis is on secondary material. This was necessary since I aim to fuse history and anthropology into ethnohistory. It was not always possible to obtain sources directly from the Gullahs. Yet I have tried to articulate their social history by using sources at least derived from the Gullahs. Thus, missionary reports and sketches, spirituals, folk practices and customs, diaries, church minutes, and similar types of records are used extensively. Sources which support interpretations and historical depictions of white attitudes toward religious instruction are also mainly primary. And whenever applicable and possible, I attempted to incorporate current historiographical trends into this study.

Prologue

The coastal region of the South Carolina Lowcountry, bounded on the
north by Georgetown and on the south by Port Royal and St. Helena
Sound, was the land of the Gullah slave population. Bordering on these
coastal lowlands, stretching out into the arms of the sea, halfway between Charleston, South Carolina and Savannah, Georgia are a fringe of
fertile islands. The largest of these islands are Port Royal, Paris, Ladies,
Hilton Head, and St. Helena.[1] Here indigo and the once famous long
staple cotton were cultivated by the most isolated Gullah slaves, who
also created and maintained a distinct, imaginative, and original African-
American culture. Because their isolation precluded direct exposure to
mass Euro-American influences, Sea Island Gullahs offer evidence of significant combinations of traditional retentions, American acculturation,
and intergroup socialization.

The name "Gullah" is generally believed to be a shortened form of
Angola. Africans from the Kongo-Angola region, Bantu-speaking peoples, were imported in large numbers during Carolina's early colonial
history.[2] As early as 1742, the *South Carolina Gazette* advertised for a
runaway slave called "Golla Harry." One of Denmark Vesey's cocon-
spirators, "Gullah Jack," was reportedly born in Angola. An entry of the
Charleston City Council for 1822 refers to "Gullah Jack" and his "Gullah
or Angola Negroes." The Vesey trial record, however, simply refers to
Jack as an African. Winifred Vass, in *The Bantu Speaking Heritage of the
United States*, points out that the ruler of the Mbundu nation in Central
Africa was called the Ngola, from which the Portuguese named the colony. Vass suggests that this name was used by Europeans to refer to

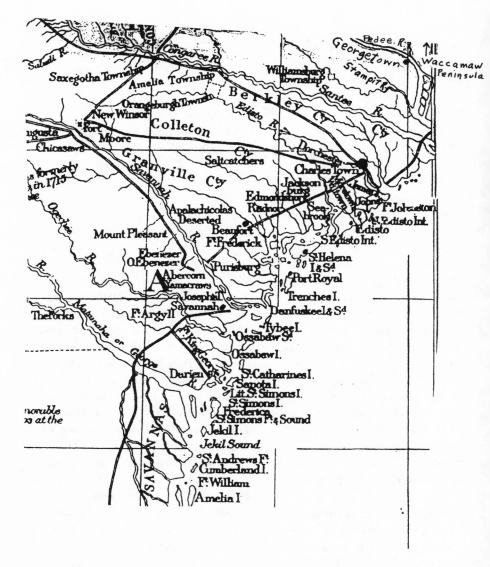

Map of the Sea Island Region. (From the South Carolina Historical and Genealogical Magazine, vol. 27, no. 4 [October 1926], 189.)

slaves from the Angolan ports.[3] Her theory implies an ethnic identification retained by BaKongo peoples.

Another theory also suggests that the name was group-initiated, yet from a different ethnic source. "Golla" was used in the eighteenth century while "Gullah" was a nineteenth-century term for slaves in the coastal region of South Carolina. A very large group of Africans from the Liberian hinterland were called Golas, sometimes spelled "Goulah." Chapter 1 discusses their importation into the Carolina Lowcountry and Georgia in large numbers during a period of rapid growth and settlement. One early twentieth-century white South Carolinian, Reed Smith, wrote extensively about Gullah dialect, maintaining that the term refers to the Golas of Liberia. His suggestion alone proves nothing. But further research demonstrates its plausibility, or at least the possibility of two complimentary original derivations. During the colonial era, Africans from the Windward Coast (Sierra Leone and Liberia) entered Charleston and heavily contributed to the coastal and Sea Island population. Golas and neighboring Gizzis (also called Kizzis or Giggis) were two of the largest African ethnic groups preyed upon by domineering Mende, Vai, Mandingas, and others. Methodist missionaries went to Liberia in the 1840s to convert the "Goulah nation." The spelling of Gullah and Goulah have obvious similarities. Additionally, missionaries were struck by "Goulah" Africans' use of English, as Northerners were by the Gullah speech. "The native Africans never use the personal pronoun of the third person feminine," wrote one missionary in 1843. ". . . it is always 'he, him.' " Similarly, Elizabeth Botume wrote of her initial incomprehension of the Gullah dialect during the Civil War, stating that her head grew "dizzy" trying to understand it. Worst of all for Botume was the confusion regarding family relations: "I never knew whether they were talking of boys or girls. They spoke of all as 'him.' "[4]

Even more interesting observations come from Lorenzo Turner's *Africanisms in the Gullah Dialect*.[5] There are a number of problems with Turner's study. Yet even critics admit that in a "fair number of instances the derivation and meaning found for a Gullah name are reasonably convincing."[6] Turner includes in his list of African words *gala (gola, gula)* which he takes to mean "Gullah, a dialect spoken by Negroes in coastal South Carolina and Georgia, one who speaks Gullah." He does not list an African homologue for *gala*, but defines its African equivalent as "gola (. . . gula, gura) a Liberian tribe and its language . . . also see ngola, a tribe in the Hamba basin of Angola."[7] Hence Turner allows for both possibilities in the origin of the term. Linguist P. E. Hair observes that, given this Gola association, it is curious that Turner found almost no Gola language terms. Hair has another insight. It is generally conceded that Turner may have exaggerated the amount of African influence in Gullah, but also that he "conclusively" demonstrated it had "more" 'Africanisms' than any other dialect in the United States. But, says Hair, it has gone unnoticed that "a remarkably large proportion of the 'Africanisms' cited by Turner came from the Sierre Leone region." Of the 3,500 words listed by Turner and used in Gullah, only 500 are "working vocabulary" terms with known meaning. Of the latter number, 350 are terms used in conversation. The Sierra Leone proportion is about 20 percent. Also, the shortest list is terms from Gullah stories, songs, and prayers. There are 85 such terms and 63 percent are Mende and 21 are Vai. Says Hair, "thus the Sierra Leone region makes virtually a clean sweep of this list."[8]

Of the 3,000 personal names with "suggested" derivations, Hair states that even here the Sierra Leone influence is prominent. He suggests that Turner missed other ethnic identifications of Windward Coast origin (Bullom, Limba, Kissi, and Gola for instance), because "no dictionary or informant was available."[9] This indicates a greater Upper Guinea influence than scholars have previously recognized. Most have concentrated on the Kongo-Angolan influence, as indeed from first appearances, does Lorenzo Turner.[10]

African-American slaves who inhabited the Georgia coast were called Geechees, but had essentially the same culture as Gullahs. Linguistically speaking, Turner uses both terms interchangeably. He lists *gisi* as Mende and defines it as "a language and tribe of the Kissy country (Liberia)." Both Golas and Gizzis shared the same cultural institutions—Poro and Sande—as indeed did the Mende, Vai, Bullom, and others over a wide geographical area. Today *Geechee* is a folk term, generally used as a provocation. In this context it means "country." The term is generally used between intimates in a joking manner, or intended as a challenge to fight.[11]

One final point on linguistic considerations regarding Gullah origins. Several Gullah personal names identified by Turner and listed with West African equivalents relate to Windward Coast secret societies. For example, Gullah *beri*, and *berimo* are listed as Vai. The former Gullah name refers to ". . . a branch of the society known as pora . . . a 'ceremonial

rite.' " For the latter Gullah name, Turner states ". . . a ceremony during which the male receives the national mark . . . and a new name, at
the same time being given certain instructions which he keeps strictly
secret. . . ." The Gullah name *pora* Turner determines is Mende, referring to "the great secret society of the men." Also, Turner's African
equivalent for the Gullah name *zo* is a Vai term, "the wearer of the mask
in the Sande Society." Among Windward Coast groups, secret society
leaders hid behind masks and the leaders were called *zo*.[12] Given the fact
that the above Gullah words are personal names rather than vocabulary
terms, one obviously views these relationships as speculative. Yet they
do point to Upper Guinea influence. These considerations, together with
observations made by P. E. Hair, indicate a strong ethnic influence in
South Carolina of peoples from the Windward Coast.

This suggested presence of Upper Guinea and Windward Coast influences qualifies rather than negates the BaKongo impact. Certainly early
colonial records indicate the overwhelming presence of Kongo-Angolan
groups. As far as linguistics go, Turner argues strongly for that impact.
Furthermore, some linguistic relationships noted for Windward Coast
groups can be made for BaKongo. For example, the Gullah *ndoko* is Bo-
bangi (KiKongo), referring to "a bewitching that is said to cause illness."
In KiKongo *ndoki* is a sorcerer, or witch. Also, the Gullah name *n'zambi*
is KiKongo for God. Yet how does one account for what Hair calls "the
extraordinary" prevalence of Sierra Leone terms in Gullah ritual and
working vocabulary? Undoubtedly both ethnic influences were significant. Moreover, the prevalence of Tshi names among Gullahs probably
indicates important Ashanti and Fanti presence, the first slaves to reach
Carolina as well.[13]

Brazilian scholar, Roger Bastide, points out that even in Portuguese
communities where Bantu peoples dominated the slave population, "only
a few traces of their religion survived. . . ." Perhaps Bastide makes too
fine a distinction between religion and magic. Taking a theme from Melville Herskovits, he acknowledges the continued significance of customs
related to death, funeral practices, and afterlife, but also maintains that
Bantu was the most susceptible of all African religions to "external influences." More recently, Robert Farris Thompson takes a more expansive
approach. In discussing the religion and art that "withstood the horrors
of the middle passage," Thompson argues for a strong BaKongo influence. He believes the BaKongo cosmogram was "too complex" to re-

main, but other elements of religion and ritual were not. Sacred medicine in the form of conjuration and healing is one example. According to Thompson "Nowhere is Kongo-Angola influence on the New World more pronounced, more profound than in black traditional cemeteries in the South. The nature of the objects that decorate the graves there . . . reveals a strong continuity . . . a restatement of the Kongo notion of the tomb as a charm for the persistence of the spirit. . . ." Thompson notes the strong sense of communion with ancestors among Kongo peoples and manifestations of this retentive element in the New World. Additionally, the BaKongo concepts of "bad magic" play a significant role in New World attitudes toward the supernatural.[14] All of these elements were part of Kongo sacred traditions. Thus, a complex pattern of convergence of at least two African cultural regions developed in coastal Carolina, creating a socioreligious community among the Gullahs.

Sea Island Gullahs received little attention in antebellum days. On the contrary, while as laborers they produced some of the world's finest cotton, Sea Island slavery was a very impersonal type of bondage. Most slaveholders did not directly oversee their plantations, nor live on the "unhealthy" Islands for more than a season. But the advent of civil conflict brought some immediate changes. Early in the war the Sea Island region was occupied by Northern forces, and widespread interest centered on these slaves whom the "aristocracy" left behind in their hasty flight. It was in the Sea Islands that the so-called "Port Royal experiment," supposedly a test of black initiative and valor, was tried.[15]

Northern reaction to the Gullahs was mixed. Not all of the "missionaries" who embarked on the Sea Island enterprise were convinced that efforts at "uplifting" Gullahs would succeed. "It is the opinion of all who know the South," wrote Arthur Sumner of Cambridge, Mass., from St. Helena Island, "that the negroes of these Sea Islands are the most degraded slaves South of Dixie's Line . . . a meaner, more ungrateful and unhandsome lot than those of our district I pray that I shall never see."[16]

Undoubtedly Northerners such as Sumner were completely unprepared to find such "foreign" and "pure" blacks, who had an initial suspicion about the motives of white people no matter what their political affiliation. Yet other Northerners felt differently about the Gullahs and grew to truly appreciate them. Their distinct form of speech was more than a separate dialect which linguists and folklorists later attempted to capture. To some whites, this language was a gifted, colorful, and picturesque form of expression, so original and peculiar to the Gullahs that it was beyond emulation. In 1863, David Thorpe, then a teacher on occupied St. Helena Island, wrote to his father-in-law, "Old John" Mooney, describing among other things, the force with which Gullahs used their limited vocabulary:

If you ask a man how he came from any place, he will say, "I took my foot." If you ask him about any work he has on hand, when he is to do it, he says, "I will strike in on that tomorrow and fight on with him till I get him done, den drop back on the next thing them is."[17]

Gullah musical ability was noted even in antebellum years. None who visited and wrote about the Sea Islands before or during the Civil War failed to comment on the rhapsodic tunes which the Gullah boatmen sang as their oars maintained a graceful, timely rhythm when striking the waters. And perhaps no one, except Gullahs themselves, was more stirred by the melancholy beauty of their "prayer-songs" than the Methodist missionaries who, after 1830, went among them to proselytize. But even a Northern skeptic like Arthur Sumner was moved by the musical power the Gullahs displayed, as indicated by his sublime description of July 4, 1862, on St. Helena:

We had a glorious celebration of the Fourth. All the negroes on this island were assembled, and marched in a melodious procession, bearing green branches, and singing "Roll, Jordan, Roll" down through the beautiful shady road by the old Episcopal Church. Around this picturesque building, in front of the platform they gathered in a great crowd under the moss-grown oaks, while our majestic gridiron waved above them. General Saxton and one or two others made brief remarks. The height of the festivities was music and dried herring.

Oh, I wish you and all my friends could have heard these Africs sing! I never listened to more impressive music than this. The singing was intrinsically good; the songs strange and beautiful and their swaying to and fro with the melody, seemed to have a sort of oceanic grandeur in it.[18]

The late nineteenth and early twentieth century brought a flurry of interest and writing related to the Gullahs which continued through the 1930s. Folklorists, linguists, anthropologists, musicologists, sociologists, and novelists began celebrating the Sea Island region as a quaint, mysterious, picturesque corner of America. Some of this literature remains useful. Most of the scholarship of the period badly needs placing in a more modern, sensitive perspective, because it is dated and full of the sociological bias reflected in the "white-to-black" method of interpreting African-American culture. Willie Lee Rose's *Rehearsal for Reconstruction*, written in 1964, is a fine work which demonstrates the early Reconstruction era and the problems African-Americans faced as new citizens. Yet Rose's book discusses the land question and Northern "missionaries" more than Gullah culture, which we only glimpse. More recently, Charles Joyner has written a historical recreation of the Gullah rice community, *All Saints on the Waccamaw River*. Using interdisciplinary techniques, Joyner offers a detailed reconstruction of daily life in this Georgetown District plantation society. Our works are similar in that we attempt to express historical appreciation of Gullah culture, and we make use of similar sources. Beyond that, our books differ considerably, especially in terms of focus, themes, structure, and style.[19]

All who went among the Gullahs were struck by the significance of religion in nearly every aspect of their social and cultural existence. Yet no writer has attempted to characterize or interpret, from a cultural perspective, the spiritual components of Gullah life. This study represents such an effort. It has been a thought-provoking, engrossing study of social cohesion. In addition to considerations of a historical nature, this book was embarked upon because of a deep, subjective interest in the Gullahs and their fascinating example of group identity, adaptability, and black resistance on a militant and cultural level. I hope the book offers a useful means of discerning, capturing, and understanding the phenomenon that characterized and gave vitality to their spiritual and communal life.

No event polarized public opinion on the issue of religious instruction of slaves in South Carolina more than the Denmark Vesey Conspiracy of 1822. This attempt by Charleston slaves to "make a desperate struggle to recover their rights" was planned in the large African Methodist Church in that city. The incident created two well-defined and opposing views regarding religious instruction. On the one hand, panic-stricken Carolinians insisted that religious instruction of the slaves cease altogether. Yet others calmly counseled that if religion played a role at all in the Conspiracy, it was either a misguided interpretation of Christianity, inspired by Northern clergymen infiltrating the South, or was the result of "superstitious," "primitive" notions taught by native Africans. Some within this latter group argued that not only was it the *duty* of planters and churchmen to convert slaves, but that a concerted program conducted by "Southern men with Southern principles," was the best insurance against slave insurrection. Both views gained adherents as 1831 brought Nat Turner's Rebellion, which went well past the planning stages and had an even clearer relationship to Christianity and biblical imagery. The Turner Rebellion made it seemingly more evident that measures had to be taken to avert disruption of the South's peculiar institution.[20]

Once frenzy over the Vesey Conspiracy had abated somewhat, the South Carolina Methodist Conference, supported by a few influential planters, became the first denomination to openly advocate religious instruction for slaves, and to actively engage in a program of plantation missions. Gradually, often begrudgingly, other churches followed. By 1845 support for religious instruction was a majority opinion in the state. By the end of the antebellum era many slaveholders credited Christian teaching with quelling a rebellious spirit in the slave quarters. Many planters who once doubted or were openly hostile to the benefits of Christian instruction viewed it as essential to plantation management. Clergymen and missionaries who took interest in the slaves' spiritual welfare extolled the success of the "great work." Churches prided themselves on overcoming planter opposition and criticism from Northern brethren. In their eyes the accomplishment was threefold: (1) a "veil of ignorance" was lifted from the spiritual cognizance of the bondspeople, (2) the Southern religious sector fulfilled its duty to God by saving black souls, and (3) the status quo was preserved by making slaves satisfied with their place in the social order:

In reviewing the history of this society [the Methodist Missionary Society] and its operation since its organization . . . it is a matter of no ordinary gratification to remember that we hold the honor of having been pioneers in the missions to the African race. It is likewise a source of peculiar and grateful satisfaction, that the progress of these labours instead of awakening fears as to their political effects, have, on the contrary, dispelled such apprehensions, and shown that the teachings of the gospel are in the highest degree compatible with our institutions, and afford additional security to the public peace. While our missionaries have been unfolding to the negro race the riches of the grace revealed in Jesus Christ and opening up to their faith and hope the glories of an eternal life, they have been likewise teaching from the same inspired record that the way to the attainment of that life is by obedience and fidelity, by contentment and holy living. Spurning the doctrines of a false philanthropy, they have been content with the truth of divine revelation, and acknowledge no "higher law."[21]

If the results of Christian instruction were measured by numbers of rebellions following Vesey and Turner, it could be said that insofar as status quo proponents were concerned, such instruction of bondspeople was eminently successful. Slaves appeared to accept Protestantism taught in a spirit purposely antithetical to their will to freedom. Emphasis was on authority, dependence on future rewards and punishments for suffering or wrongdoing on earth, and a profound inequality between master and slave. This seemed especially the case in the Sea Islands. There no widespread slave conspiracy or rebellion was known of, and Christianity appeared well entrenched by the time of freedom.

This study examines the Christian conversion process among the Gullahs in an effort to understand these slaves' interpretation of Christianity and the motives behind attempts to Christianize them. It is hypothesized that Gullah slaves of coastal Carolina used Christianity as an ideology with strong connotations supporting their sense of freedom. Early efforts to resist bondage, represented fusing Christianity with Africanity to provide a militant nationalism articulated by the black rebels of Charleston. Failure of that Conspiracy shook the Gullah community and may have facilitated a new adaptive structure in which slaves selectively employed Christianity in ways important to their own social existence. Slaves continued to oppose bondage, not with physical force, but by creating a strong, religious collective which shielded them from a sense of alienation. But their experiences were also based on an African world view and cultural structure though conceptually expressed in Christian terms. In the new religion, the slaves found some features reminiscent of their African socioreligious past. It also offered an explanation for their historical situation, which inspired currents of hope. On the Sea Islands, Gullahs partly used the moral teachings of Christ as a basis for community structure and organization. Yet they saw no contradiction in refusing to blindly internalize everything they were taught. Thus Gullahs did not trespass against their own moral sense or jeopardize their integrity as a people struggling against oppression. Their retention of an African world view enabled them to maintain an appreciation of life on a collective level, striving to preserve the group consciousness that was a main ingredient of African heritage. Hence Christian and African traditions helped shape the resistance culture and plantation commonwealth that evolved in the slave quarters. In this sense religious instruction of the slaves cannot be measured merely from the standpoint of its negative use as a conservative force, but rather in relation to its value to slave life, community, and the slaves' efforts to remain spiritually free.

The present study then elucidates the role of slave religion among the Gullahs. Slave folk religion, comparable to the elaboration of a new Sea Island dialect of English, facilitated and, to no small degree, made possible the cohesion of a New World culture, Gullah culture. The approach which is attempted here will naturally involve an examination of the slave trade, Christian conversion, and the heritage of West African socioreligious and philosophical traditions to the extent that they were serviceable in bondage.

PART I

The African Background

CHAPTER I

Gullah Roots

The majority of the tribes of the Upper Guinea Coast were active participants in the Atlantic slave-trade. . . . But the Mandingas, Susus and Fu-
las stood well to the fore—partly because of their own key role in the
slaving operations on the Upper Guinea Coast, and partly because they
succeeded in reducing many of the littoral peoples and the inhabitants of
the Futa Djalon to a state of vassalage, under the banner of Islam.*

But I must own to the shame of my own countrymen, that I was first
kidnapped and betrayed by my own complexion, who were the first cause
of my exile and slavery; but if there were no buyers there would be no
sellers.**

Ethnic Origins and Carolina Preferences

European traders divided the African shoreline into Upper and Lower
Guinea, although opinions differed on where the division occurred. In
this study Upper Guinea refers to the area from the Senegal River north,
called the Senegambia, to the Cross River south, termed the Slave Coast.
Lower Guinea is south of the Slave Coast, to the Kongo-Angola region.
Most Africans imported into South Carolina were taken from trading
stations in four areas of the Guinea Coast. From Lower Guinea Africans
mainly from the Kongo and Angola region comprised black cargoes destined for Charleston. From Upper Guinea they came from the land between the Senegal and Gambia Rivers, present-day Gambia; from the

---

*Walter Rodney, "African Slavery and Other Forms of Social Oppression on the Upper
Guinea Coast in the Context of the Atlantic Slave-Trade," *Journal of African History* 8, no.
3 (1966): 436.

**Ottobah Cugoano, *Thoughts and Sentiments on the Evils of Slavery* (London: Dawsons of
Pall Mall, 1969; repr. from 1787 ed.), 12.

Windward Coast, now Sierra Leone and Liberia; and from the Gold
Coast, presently the Republic of Ghana. Few African ethnic groups were
spared a tribute to slave coffles. Yet the littoral of the above areas and
inhabitants living about 200 miles inland provided the majority of black
cargoes destined for the Carolina coast.[1]

Gold Coast Africans were apparently the first black Carolinians. They
were preferred by West Indian adventurers who initially settled Carolina
and brought about 1,000 slaves with them. Often referred to as Coromantees (or Kromanti), after the coastal factory from which they were
first shipped, most of these Africans, generally Akan and Ashanti peoples, were sold into bondage by powerful, coast-dwelling Fanti. Famous
on West Indian plantations for their work habits, efficiency, and strength,
Akan-Ashanti groups were also said to possess the haughty spirit that
planters associated with rebelliousness. "The Coromantees are not only
the best and most faithful of our slaves, but are really born heroes,"
wrote the governor of the Leeward Islands in 1701. He added that:

there never was a rascal or coward of that nation, intrepid to the last degree.
. . . My father, who had studied the genius and temper of all kinds of negroes
for forty-five years . . . would say "no man deserved a Coromantee that would
not treat him like a friend rather than a slave."[2]

Men who made voyages to the Guinea Coast concurred with and often
fostered attitudes expressed toward Gold Coast Africans. John Atkins, a
ship's surgeon, considered himself an "authority" on Africans. "Slaves
differ in their goodness," he insisted, maintaining that "those from the
Gold Coast are accounted best, being cleanest limbed, and more docile
by our Settlements than others." But Atkins cautioned that Akan-Ashanti were also "more prompt to Revenge, and murder the Instruments
of their Slavery, and also apter in means to compress it."[3]

Charleston merchants paid particular attention to the source of black
cargoes. Although Gold Coast Africans sold at a premium, early Carolinian planters were forced to compete for them with West Indian sugar
producers who usually got first choice. Second in favor were Africans
from Angola. "We wish therefore you would send either to the Gold
Coast or Angola," wrote one Charleston factor. "And there will not be
this next Year Insuing Negroes Enough especially Gold Coast and Angola, for the Demand."[4] Peter Wood's study of blacks in colonial South
Carolina argues effectively for a preponderance, by 1740, of "salt water"

Angolans over other ethnic groups. According to Wood, the 1730s was
a time of massive slave importation and low natural increase. Over 50
percent of the slaves had been in the colony less than ten years, and
approximately 70 percent of the black population was originally from
Angola where the trade was mainly conducted by the Portuguese.[5]

The diversity of Portuguese slave-trading policy and their concentration on penetrating Africa's interior partly accounts for a paucity of records on their trade.[6] At any rate studies do indicate that while slave
traders were not usually compelled to go into the interior in the eighteenth century, they occasionally went as far as Mozambique, largely by
sea. Dieudonne Rinchon, a well-known French scholar and sometimes
apologist for the slave trade, provided evidence of the expanse of Portuguese activity:

Les esclaves exportés sont principalement des Ambundus, (Ovimbundu) des gens
de Mbamba et de Mbata, et pour le reste des Nègres due Haute-Congo achetés
par les Bamfumgunu et les Bateke du Pool [the Stanley Pool]. Quelques-uns de
ces esclaves viennet de fort loin dans l'in-térieur. Le capitaine négrier De-
grandpré achète à Cabinda une Négresse qui lui paraît assez familière avec les
Blancs, ou du moins qui ne témoigne à leur vue ni surprise, ni frayeur; frappé
de cette sécurité peu ordinaire, le négrier lui en demande la cause. Elle répond
qu'elle a vu précédement des Blancs dans une autre terre, où le soleil se lève dans
l'eau, et non comme au Congo où il se cache dans la mer; et elle ajoute en
montrant le levant *monizi monambu*, j'ai vu le bord de la mer; elle a été en chemin,
gonda cacata, beaucoup de lune. Ce récit semble confirmer les dires de Dapper
que parfois des esclaves du Mozambique sont vendus au Congo.[7]

Information provided by Rinchon's informant is supported by recent
scholarship. Long-distance trade routes in Central Africa were a direct
result of the emergence of Portuguese activity according to Jan Vansina.
Trade around the Stanley Pool touched a number of regional water net-
works. Slave recruitment extended as far as what is now Shaba Province
in Zaire. Furthermore, scholars investigating African retentions in Gullah dialect identify Ovimbundu, BaKongo, Mbundu, Mayombe, and others
as Bantu-speaking peoples who greatly contributed patterns of speech to
the Sea Island patois. With the exception of Mozambique(ans), most of
these people lived no more than 200 miles from the Coast.[8]

Ethnic characteristics as perceived by white Carolinians labeled Angolan slaves as "docile" and "comely" but not particularly strong. Hence
they supposedly made better house slaves than the presumably more
sturdy Gold Coast Africans. Bantu-speaking Africans were also consid-

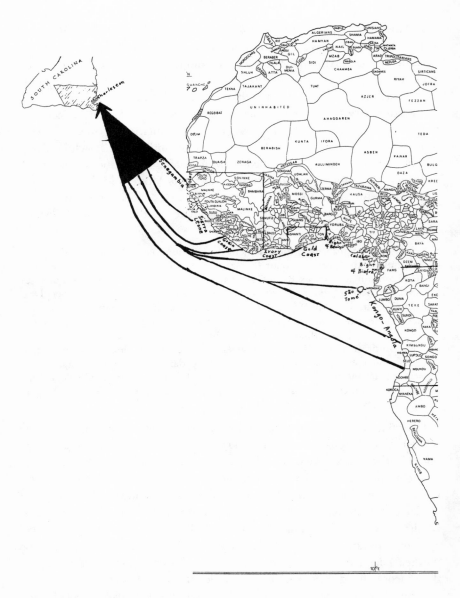

Cultural map of Africa.

ered especially apt at mechanical arts and trades. Categories related to temperament and labor capability were subjective, having more to do with need than reality. At a time when Carolina's economy was diverse and Africans were engaged in numerous occupations, perceptions may have suited availability. Yet the theory that Africans contributed skill and know-how to Carolina's early economy has much validity. In any case, events leading up to the Stono Rebellion of 1739 caused white Carolinians to alter their attitudes toward their servile population. The Bantu family of Africa was ethnically diverse, and from Angola to Mozambique contained a variety of physical types. Yet they possessed many common customs and values. In Carolina, cultural and linguistic homogeneity, coupled with mounting white repression, inspired a reputedly "docile" people to rebel against the "Instruments of their Slavery." Thus to Kongo-Angolans, Carolinians attributed still another adage—the tendency toward flight and rebellion.[9]

At the time of the Stono Rebellion, there were around 39,000 blacks and 20,000 whites in South Carolina. Fear and anxiety followed the uprising, culminating in a prohibitive duty on slave imports. During this nearly ten-year moratorium the trade was reduced to a mere trickle, bringing to a close what can be considered the first of three phases in the history of the African slave trade to the colony and the state.[10]

Cessation of the transatlantic slave trade found the majority of South Carolina's black laborers, between 80–90 percent, concentrated in parishes closest to Charleston. The sparsely settled Sea Island parish of St. Helena, located on the southern frontier, had only forty-two slaves in 1720. Even by the 1730s when settled parishes were bulging with Africans and rice shifted from a competing export to the primary agricultural concern, growth and settlement of the coastal frontier remained minimal. Given the preponderance of Kongo-Angolans in the slave population, most slaves in the Sea Island region were undoubtedly from this group. St. Helena Parish was close to Spanish territory and possible freedom. It was a congregating area for slaves, and a number of bondsmen from there were known to have been involved in the Stono Rebellion.[11] Naturally, as the Sea Islands developed, planters relied on their supply of country-born and more acculturated Africans to oversee labor operation on frontier plantations. Hence early African cultural influences of Akan-Ashanti and Bantu were present. During the next generation, following the slave trade moratorium, two developments added to African cultural patterns. These dual occurrences encouraged rapid settlement of the islands south of Charleston, and created labor demands that brought a resurgence of African importations, ushering in the second phase of the Carolina trade.

First was the geographical change of rice-producing areas. In the 1750s inland swamps, which since the 1720s had been utilized for rice cultivation, were gradually deserted in favor of tidal and river swamps. These were better suited for growing rice because soil was more fertile and irrigation was more easily conducted. This discovery opened the remaining coastal frontier to settlement. Workers were not only needed for rice cultivation but also to clear away dense woods and growth prior to planting. Memory of the Stono Rebellion notwithstanding, large-scale use of white labor was never seriously considered. Not only was such labor scarce and expensive, but tidal swamps were infested with malaria-carrying mosquitos, and the summers there were so hot and unhealthy that whites convinced themselves they could not endure such conditions.[12] Rather than relinquish dependency on African workers, South Carolinians altered their ethnic preferences.

The second factor responsible for renewed interest in forced black labor was the cultivation of indigo in the Sea Islands. Great Britain needed large quantities of indigo for its textile industry and encouraged indigo production in the colony. But despite the prospect of a guaranteed market, and even though indigo was found growing in a wild state in Carolina, no commercial possibilities were realized until 1748. The change was precipitated by a young Sea Island woman, Eliza Lucas (later Eliza Lucas Pinckney), who from 1742 to 1744 engaged in a series of experiments. She crossbred and developed the plant through seed selection and from a West Indian indigo maker learned the difficult process of properly extracting dye from the plant. Indigo grew well in the Sea Islands and soon became the most favored commodity with the British government. Next to rice, indigo was also the most bountiful source of wealth in the province, laying the foundation for many Sea Island fortunes while further enriching British textile capitalists. Commodity output of rice and indigo during this period of economic advancement was matched by heavy African importation. From 1740 to the eve of the War for Independence, South Carolina imported over 50,000 Africans into the colony.[13] This middle period of the slave trade provided the Sea Island region with numerically dominant African ethnic groups who strongly impacted Gullah religious culture and communal organization.

Strong preferences and equally fervent disdain for certain Africans continued to dominate Carolinian rationale, but Kongo-Angolans were no longer considered desirable. Instead, Africans from Senegambia were put on a par with those of the Gold Coast. Newspaper advertisements and private correspondence provide insight into this preference. The most influential Charleston factor was Henry Laurens. Carolina-born and British-educated, Laurens established himself as a successful merchant and planter in his early twenties. Laurens was a "particular friend" of Richard Oswald, a wealthy British merchant. Oswald owned the British slave factory on Bance Island in the Sierra Leone River. During the middle period of the trade (1750–1787), Laurens handled Oswald's Sierra Leone cargoes in Charleston for a 10 percent commission. Laurens was careful and methodical in preserving communications. His records reveal a sense of prevailing attitudes toward African origins. In one correspondence, Laurens urged a West Indian associate to send portions of his cargoes to Carolina where Africans who were "healthy and in good flesh would find a ready market." Laurens cautioned, however, that the quality of the slaves should be high, at least two-thirds of them men eighteen to twenty-five years of age and that "there must not be a Callabar (Igbo) amongst them. Gold Coast and Gambia are best, next to them the Windward Coast are preferred to Angolas. . . . Pray observe that our people like tall slaves best for our business and strong withal."[14]

Cargoes from the Slave Coast (Dahomey and the Ivory Coast) were rarely noted by Laurens or mentioned in newspaper advertisements. When ships from these areas did arrive, an explanation in the announcement was called for: "Just arrived in the ship Marlborough . . . 300 Negroes, directly from Whydah, a country greatly preferred to any other thru-out the West Indies and inferior to none on the Coast of Africa."[15]

Callabar Africans were shunned by Carolinians and consistently rejected by Laurens. "Callabar slaves won't go down when others can be had," Laurens warned a British merchant in 1755. That same year he also wrote to another correspondent discussing the deplorable conditions of the trade for Carolina merchants competing for Africans with West Indian planters. He asked for "stout healthy fellows . . . the country is not material if they are not from Callabar which slaves are quite out of repute from numbers in every cargo that have been sold with us destroying themselves."[16]

Among the many judgments Carolinians made about African ethnic groups—from supposed suicidal and melancholy tendencies of Callabars to the height and strength of Senegambians, one characteristic predominated: the desirability of purchasing slaves familiar with rice cultivation. Upper Guinea and especially Senegambia was visited by Europeans before North American settlement. Some Europeans settled on African coasts and along rivers leading inland. Daniel Littlefield has made a strong case for colonial Carolina preference being based on Africans' knowledge of rice cultivation.[17]

Early explorers were impressed with Upper Guinea Africans' knowledge of grain cultivation, particularly their rice staple. In the Gambia region, Africans engaged in large-scale planting operations of corn, pepper, grains, and nuts, as well as "superior" cotton and indigo. Present-day Liberia was first called the Malaguetta Coast by the Portuguese because the Africans there cultivated malaguetta pepper. This pepper supposedly prevented dysentery and was used to season food given to Africans during the journey to America known as the Middle Passage. Later the name Malaguetta Coast was dropped and the term Grain Coast was adopted. Before the end of the eighteenth century the Grain Coast was synonomous with rice producing and referred to as the Rice Coast. Following establishment of the slave trade, some Africans shipped to America had been employed previously at slave factories or in the homes of English businessmen residing on the coasts. These "castle slaves" were often skilled in trades and housekeeping, some even having knowledge of English. A Charleston newspaper provides an example:

230 choice Negroes . . . just arrived from Gambia . . . in perfect health, and have been inoculated for the smallpox on the coast. Among them are 20 young men and women with their children in families late servants of a person leaving Gambia R. Most of them can talk English and have been used to attend in a house and go in a craft, who will be kept separate in the yard.[18]

Of course most Africans possessed no rudimentary English and had no experience with white society. Their value was a long familiarity with planting and cultivation of rice and indigo, the quality of which was said to have surpassed that grown in Carolina. This meant that an extensive "breaking in" period and close agricultural supervision of "new" Africans was minimal. Thus while Upper Guinea Africans may have been preferred because they were tall and considered more manageable, evidence also suggests a more sound explanation: knowledge of agriculture made these Africans particularly sought after in coastal Carolina.

Hence, the middle period of the slave trade to Carolina which corresponds to the last half of the eighteenth century, is significant for obtaining additional impressions of African provenance in the coastal and Sea Island region, since this time span corresponded with vigorous economic growth in those areas. Aside from records left by merchants and factors, advertisements in the *South Carolina Gazette*, which, beginning in 1732, is an almost unbroken newspaper file, provide information on the trade. Announcements such as the following from 1756 usually mentioned and frequently emphasized the origin of cargoes:

To be Sold: on Wednesday . . . a cargo of fine Slaves just arrived in the ship St. Andrew . . . directly from the River Gambia [Wolof, Serer, Mandingo, etc.]; they are perfectly healthy, and have been so the whole passage.
Negroes chiefly from the same country as those which are brought from the River Gambia . . . from the factory in Sierra Leone [Mende, Temne, Vai, etc.] on the Windward Coast of Guiney, where said cargo was picked out of a large parcel.[19]

In the early nineteenth century the South Carolina up-country engaged in large-scale production of short staple cotton, creating a renewed demand for slaves. This brought on the third and final phase of African trading, from 1804 to 1808. The Kongo-Angola area mainly supplied up-country plantations as well as plantations in other states that refused to import. Percentage-wise then, Bantu-speaking peoples apparently comprised the majority of Africans imported to South Carolina. Yet it has generally gone unnoticed that Upper Guinea contributed heavily to the slave populations of the Sea Islands and surrounding coast. Africans of Senegambia figured most prominently in the slave trade to South Carolina prior to and immediately after the War for Independence. Closely following in imports were those of the Windward Coast. Together these two regions' captured inhabitants comprised a large majority of Africans brought to South Carolina even if we make allowances for the fact that Angolan ships were sometimes larger and sometimes brought more Africans to America.[20]

Thus, the middle period of the slave trade represented expanded economic enterprise in the Sea Islands where indigo dominated, and in the hinterlands where rice was almost exclusively cultivated. Africans brought into these areas where chiefly ethnic groups of Upper Guinea and were victims of the "holy war" conducted by Moslem Mandinga, Susu, and Fula peoples.

Moslem Jihad and Ethnic Displacement

European demand for slaves exacerbated a process of ethnic displacement already occurring in Upper Guinea. The mountains of the Futa
Djalon were a transitional point between Islamic Western Sudan and the
Upper Guinea Coast. The Futa Djalon massif was an irregular triangle,
the base of which began at the Upper Gambia River with the apex extending just north of present-day Sierra Leone. Mountainous country
extended south of the Futa Djalon so that a continuous range provided a
watershed from which a number of Upper Guinea rivers flowed, including the Senegal and the Niger. Previous to European coastal contact,
migration, population displacement, and assimilation, mostly the result
of efforts to spread Islam, affected geographical ethnic groupings and
patterns. Moslem Fula, Susu, and Mandingas occupied the Futa Djalon
with some non-Moslem ethnic groups, while other Sudanic groups continued west, settling beside peoples already inhabiting the coast. By the
time of Portuguese contact, non-Moslem coastal peoples were virtually
surrounded as well as somewhat infiltrated by a large semicircle of Moslem traders with a number of hinterland groups sandwiched in between
(in the rain-forest regions).[21]

In Senegambia Mandingas were the most powerful if not most numerous ethnic group and the first to meet Portuguese seamen in the fifteenth
century. Hence they began the barter in slaves, gold, and ivory in exchange for European goods. So-called pagans were the first victims of
the trade. By the time of British presence in the Gambia region, victims
included littoral groups such as Wolofs and to a far greater extent, Djolas. Other smaller, inland non-Moslem ethnic peoples such as the Pat-
charis in the Middle Gambia Valley, Baasaris in the Upper Valley, and
Bambaras were also mentioned in chronicles as contributing to slave coffles. In the seventeenth century the Wolof kingdom was located between
the Senegal River south to the Gambia River and extended inland. By
the eighteenth century some Wolof leadership accepted Islam while the
common people continued their traditional beliefs. Djolas were independent longtime residents of the coastal areas between the Gambia and
Cassamance Rivers and their communities spread a distance of one hundred
miles inland. Even at the leadership level Djolas physically resisted Mandinga dominance and Islamic religion. They were also among the few
groups who refused to be predatory participants in the Atlantic slave

trade. Djolas' simple manners and customs, loose tribal organization, and decentralized government made them easy prey for the European-backed, domineering, highly politically structured Moslem Mandingas. Thousands of Djolas filled the holds of British slave ships. Fulani inhabitants of the Gambia were, like Mandingas, followers of the Koran and by the sixteenth century were vassals of the latter. They planted crops, tended Mandinga cattle, leased their territory, and occasionally joined Mandinga merchants in wars against ethnic groups to procure slaves. Mandinga-Fulani interdependency probably goes farther than common religious ties to explain why large numbers of Fulani were not sold into slavery as compared with Djolas and Wolofs. Another large ethnic group of the Senegambia was the Seraculeh. They were actually a northern branch of Mandingas who engaged in slaving in the Upper River Division of the Gambia Valley.[22]

Besides obeying the Koran's edict to make war on "non-believers," black Muslim traders followed a custom of general acquisitiveness stimulated by European labor demands. Moslem Africans were enslaved for petty as well as major crimes and offenses. Walter Rodney has maintained that prior to the Atlantic trade most crimes were punishable by fines and few groups practiced capital punishment. The slave trade heightened rivalries and intensified a pattern of class exploitation.[23] This insight is supported by Francis Moore, a contemporary observer who remained on the Gambia River from 1730 to 1735. Moore noted that some Mandinga merchants journeyed inland and might not return with slaves for twenty days. But in referring to the littoral trade he observed:

Besides the slaves which merchants bring down, there are many bought along the river. These are either taken in war, as the former are, or else men condemned for crimes, or else stolen, which is very frequent. . . . Since this slave trade has been us'd all punishments are changed into slavery; there being an Advantage on such condemnations, they strain for crimes very hard . . . every trifling crime is punished in the same manner.[24]

Rulers and elites perpetrated the trade against the general population, often whether Islam was professed or not. Occasionally mistakes were made and a noble would be enslaved, as in the case of Job ben Solomon. He was a wealthy Fula of the Gambia region who crossed the river with a coffle of slaves that he intended to sell for his father. Ben Solomon was caught by Mandinga merchants and sold to a Captain Pike of the ship *Arabella*, the same person with whom ben Solomon had bartered for his slaves, although the two could not agree on a price. Job ben Solomon attracted attention in America because of his noble birth and knowledge of Arabic. He was sent to England and later returned to his native Gambia. Europeans made every effort to rectify such situations before the Middle Passage, if a local nobleman inadvertently fell into their hands. Fear of retaliation on the part of the black elite and a desire to protect trading interests dictated this policy.[25] Thus while Djolas, Wolofs, and smaller non-Moslem groups figured most heavily in the Senegambia slave trade during the eighteenth century, all of the major tribes of the region were represented in the slave marts.

In the Sierra Leone littoral, the Temne and Bullom were the largest and most powerful ethnic groups by the sixteenth century. Other peoples included the Baga and the Lokko. Moslems did not wield political or military dominance in this area of the coast in the sixteenth century. However, Portuguese arrival encouraged Moslem Susu and Fula to move closer to the sea. Most of this penetration was peaceful but at times conflicts flared and captives were sold to slaving captains. By the mid eighteenth century, the Susu had carved out a seaway at the expense of the Baga and rivaled Mandinga activity in the Upper Guinea trade.[26]

In the seventeenth century a new wave of Fulani and Mandinga Muslims began settling in the mountainous regions of Sierra Leone, intermingling with non-Moslem Susu and Fula. Initial peaceful contact gave way to violence and the invaders launched the Jihad of the Futa Djalon in 1726, pushing converted and non-converted Susu and their ethnic kinspeople, the Djalonkes, south and west. Hence on the coast, Susu presence was enhanced and speeded up by the coming of refugees from the Jihad, and Islam made inroads among the littoral ruling groups. The Futa Djalon refugees encroached upon the indigenous peoples and sold these "war" captives in the slave trade. The Mandinga contingent, interested primarily in slaves but dispersing their knowledge of Islam as well, backed Fula Moslems who were thrusting singly and in groups from the interior. The victims of Moslem Fula, Mandinga, and Susu traders were primarily the Limba, Lokko, and Gizzi; secondarily, the Kono and Kuranko. But Moslem forces also came to dominate the coastal Baga, Temne, and Bullom. Ultimately an Islamic base was established among the upper class and the Jihad of the sword was rarely necessary against them. Hence harrassment of the common people was practiced on both sides. Bullom and Temne often worked with Susu and Fula traders in supplying their own people, and placing Moslems in positions of authority and influence. Ruling groups became ideologically if not ethnically homogeneous.[27]

The result of the Jihad was a "prodigious" trade in slaves in the last half of the seventeenth century. Despite interruptions of the trade to North America caused first by European wars and later by the War for Independence, British and Yankee captains supplied Carolina planters with a large number of "war captives" from factories on the Sierra Leone littoral. While their numbers did not compare with those taken from the Gold Coast by the British, the latter were primarily destined for the West Indies. The Jihad largely created the "startling activity" of slaving on the Upper Guinea coast.[28] It also coincided with coastal Carolina's agricultural expansion and renewed labor demands peopling the Sea Island region with Africans from a common cultural circle.

Another large ethnic group falling within the present geographical boundaries of Sierra Leone and also heavily engaged in the slave trade was the Mende people. Mende were of Mandinga stock but not followers of Islam during the era of the Atlantic trade. They were a warlike people, pushing into occupied territories, killing local rulers, and enslaving villagers. In the eighteenth century Mende occupied a large section of the Sherbro hinterland. Although they remained inland throughout most of the slave-trading period, Mende traders frequented the coast. The Mende preyed upon some of the same groups victimized by Moslem traders. But they also spread havoc and influence into the hinterlands of the Malaguetta Coast, a present-day Liberia. There they sought slaves for European traders and for their own society which was dominated by this type of labor.[29]

Pre-European history of ethnic populations of the Malaguetta or Windward Coast has been largely overshadowed by the long, unsettling presence of black American colonizers since the beginning of the nineteenth century. Yet during the time of South Carolina's coastal expansion slave trading in this region was brisk. Linguistically speaking, people of the region, now called Liberia, can be divided into three groups. Among the lower coast were the Kru group or Kwa-speaking people consisting of the Kru, Bassa, De, and Grebo. Kru were seldom enslaved because they were reportedly so adverse to bondage that they committed suicide if escape was impossible. Actually Kru men were excellent sailors and both African and European traders depended on them to transport cargoes to waiting vessels on the lower coast. The second grouping was farther north and comprised the Mandingas or Mande-speaking people who were the Mandinga, Gbande, Mende, Vai, Kono, Buzi, Loma, Kpelle, Gio, and Mano. Within this group the Vai, Mende, and Mandingas dominated trade and most often infringed upon the liberty of their neighbors. The third group is perhaps most significant because so many of them made the Middle Passage. This group, the Gola, included Gizzis and Golas, and was of the Niger-Congo linguistic family encompassing Temne, Bullom, Fulani, and Wolof—widely separated peoples geographically. In the Malaguetta Coast region Gola and Gizzi were linguistically isolated on the northeast and northwest by Mande-speaking people.[30]

A process similar to what transpired in present-day Sierra Leone occurred in the Malaguetta Coast region of Upper Guinea. Warfare and movements of the Mende, Mandingas, and Fulani stimulated by the slave trade, created pressure situations for interior forest groups. Just as the Temne and Bullom were displaced by more aggressive groups, so was intensive Mandinga activity on the Malaguetta Coast evident by the seventeenth century. A commercial confederacy existed in which Western Sudanic goods were exchanged for slaves. The slaves were then sent to the coast through Vai and De middlemen. This created another series of wars in which Golas and Gizzis, inhabiting the interior northeast, were heavily involved. Golas and Gizzis struck back against Mandingas and Mende, but generally were no match for the two latter groups. Golas and Gizzis were in a state of almost continual warfare from the seventeenth century on. As slaving activity increased in the next century, Golas began stretching out to areas near Cape Mount and placing themselves under Vai and De protection. Other members of the Gola ethnic group moved out of the northeast where they had been heavily preyed upon. In both instances what began as small villages grew to become dominant towns. Hence while Gola numbers were being diminished in the northeast because of the slave trade, in regions near the coast they were thriving numerically. This led to conflict with Vai and De, the nominal rulers, and hence to more wars. The real source of conflict was control of trade. In the eighteenth century access to gunpowder, small arms, and cannon provided a new and more deadly kind of warfare, as well as extreme concentrations of power and wealth. A process of internal alliances and war within Gola chiefdoms and elsewhere created predacious conditions from the old Gola-Gizzi homeland in the interior to the heterogeneous coastal Mandinga confederacy.[31]

Golas never succeeded in wresting a settlement on the littoral from the Vai and hence had no direct commerce with European ships. Yet by the time of the first black American colonists' arrival in Liberia, Golas were a dominant group culturally and economically in the immediate interior. Prior to that however, they were, along with the Gizzi, the eighteenth century's major victims of the Atlantic slave trade in the region known as Liberia. They also succumbed to the defensive act of attacking and enslaving their own ethnic people. Gizzis were apparently transported in such large numbers that a river in Bullom territory was thusly named, although the Gizzi lived nowhere in that vicinity which was part of the Sierra Leone littoral. In 1778 it was reported that victims secured at Idolos, the factory near the Gizzi or Kizzi River, were in poor physical condition from having traveled great distances in slave coffles.[32]

The late Walter Rodney maintained that the scope of the Atlantic slave trade as conducted on the Upper Guinea Coast during the second half of the eighteenth century has not been fully appreciated and that the general level of trading from 1750 onward was high. Developments in South Carolina support his contention. During this period Africans arrived who transferred a medium of culture, communalism, and spirituality that assimilated with the existing African traditions, both of which necessarily adapted to Euro-American ambiance. Ultimately Africa's loss was America's gain. Still the history of the Atlantic slave trade remains a bitter memory, and the tragedy of it is poignantly revealed in the words of Professor Rodney:

The impression that African society was being overwhelmed by its involvement with the European economy was most strongly conveyed at points when Africans conceded that their slaving activities were the consequences of the fact that nothing but slaves would purchase European goods. Yet European consumer goods contributed nothing to the development of African production. Only the rulers benefited narrowly, by receiving the best cloth, drinking the most alcohol, and preserving the widest collection of durable items for prestige purposes. It is this factor of realized self-interest which goes some way towards explaining the otherwise incomprehensible actions of Africans toward Africans.[33]

In summary, I argue that in the Carolina Lowcountry there was an early cultural dominance of BaKongo peoples of Kongo-Angolan origin, followed by Upper Guinea Africans of the Senegambia and Windward

Coasts. Upper Guinea peoples coming to Carolina found a creolized black culture already adjusting and acculturating. But more significantly, the large numbers of African-born slaves, entrenched into a system of rice production, also reinforced the Old World heritage. The complex formation of African-American Gullah culture involved, in some ways, the concept of "hearth areas," that is, those who arrive earlier may have as strong an impact as latecomers of more numerical strength. This may explain the continued use of Tshi (Gold Coast) names from the colonial era through the Civil War. Still, it was the BaKongo influence that served as incubator for many Gullah cultural patterns, and superceded Akan-Ashanti impact. Yet BaKongo cultural antecedents did not smother the Upper Guinea contribution to African-American culture. Indeed, it appears that each major group left its presence, and the longevity of these influences depended on adaptability. Thus, the "Doctrine of First Effective Settlement"[34] is significantly altered in the case of the Gullahs.

CHAPTER 2

The Socioreligious Heritage

One of the most interesting problems of pre-colonial history is the relation of so-called secret societies to indigenous government. . . . Associations of this kind are prevalent . . . and are particularly numerous in the coastal area of rain-forest . . . including the Ivory Coast, Liberia, Sierra Leone. . . . They are not secret in any other respect. On the contrary, not only is the existence of these societies known . . . , but in many places the wide range of their activities makes them the dominant social force.*

In the case of a burial site, the coffin and the mound are the obvious containers; the soul of the deceased is the spark. In addition, . . . there are decorative objects that, in both Kongo and the Americas, cryptically honor the spirit in the earth, guide it to the other world, and prevent it from wandering or returning to haunt survivors. . . . The surface "decorations" frequently function as "medicines" of admonishment and love, and they mark a persistent cultural link between Kongo and the black New World.**

Upper Guinea Culture Circles

Just as the impact of the slave trade in the West Atlantic region of the Guinea Coast has been treated with relative disinterest, so also has this area's cultural homogeneity either been glossed over or dismissed as the result of recent intergroup contact and European administration. For purposes of study Upper Guinea is not particularly rich in documentation, nor did the societies there possess high degrees of political central-

---

*Kenneth Little, "The Political Function of the Poro," Part I, *Africa, Journal of the International African Institute* 35 no. 4 (October, 1965): 349.

**Robert Farris Thompson, *Flash of the Spirit: African & Afro-American Art & Philosophy* (New York: Vintage Books, 1984), 132.

ization. Moreover, community groups were usually not as large and territorial holdings not as extensive, as for instance those in the Niger Delta or Western Sudan. Hence the Upper Guinea, containing a multiplicity of ethnic entities, mixed kinship systems, and various languages has not received attention comparable to its significance. Yet early explorers, travelers, and traders were struck by what H. Baumann referred to as distinctive culture circles on the West African coast. Baumann referred to several regions, and his discussion applies to the Upper Guinea Coast, especially present-day Sierra Leone and Liberia. Here peoples historically had common cultural features, the most significant of which regulated the social, political, and to some extent economic life of the communities. These were secret societies with the Poro (or Beri) for men and the Sande (or Bundu) for women being almost universal, and, where they existed, always mandatory. The names sometimes varied but the influence and function of these societies was relatively uniform. The area of the "Poro Cluster" on the Central-West African Coast included the Lokko, Temne, Kono, Mende, Bullom, Krim, and the Limba ethnic groups in Sierra Leone. On the Malaguetta Coast (or Liberia), Poro and Sande groups included but were not limited to the Gola, Vai, De, Kpelle, Gizzi, Gbande, Belle, Loma, Mano, Gio, Ge, Sapa, Bassa, and Kru.[1]

In the sixteenth century, Portuguese traders referred to both male and female societies among Bulloms, observing similarities between various groups of people belonging to these associations. Affinity was so strong that traders viewed the people as one society, under the generic name of Sapi. Principal ethnic groups were Bulloms, Temnes, Limbas, and also some Bagas. They dressed alike, had the same system of justice, and understood each other. Unlike Western Sudanic groups, they had no political centralization, yet possessed social homogeneity through their common secret societies. The Portuguese considered the secret societies ways of training youth who reached puberty. There was a lengthy seclusion, secret training, bestowing of a new name, graduation, and celebration. Observers likened it to a convent procedure. Also, in the late seventeenth century, Dutch geographer Olfe Dapper reported on the multilingual quality of people on the Mesurado Coast under De control, in alliance with the Vai of Cape Mount. Among the languages listed were Temne, Mande, and Gola.[2]

British slave trader Nicholas Owen also witnessed manifestations of Poro society among the Bullom, even though group leadership was influenced by Islam. In 1746 he wrote:

There is a secret mistery that these people have kept for many ages or, as for what we know, since their first foundation of great consequence to the pace [peace?] of the country; it goes by the general name of Pora or Pora men. These men are marked in their infancy by their priests with three or four rows of small dints upon their backs and shoulders; any that has not these marks they look upon as nothing. The nature of this Pora is this: there is one among the rest who personates the devil or Pora and before they begin to rize him, as they term it, he hides him self in some convenient place within call and upon his priests shouting several times the word 'Wo Pon,' he in the bush answers with a terabal screetch several times. Whenever the woman or white man or any that's not Pora men hears, they immediately fly to the houses and shut the windows and doors. . . . The good of this Pora is to keep from quarrelling. . . .[3]

John Matthews lived in Sierra Leone for several years in the 1700s and also observed the workings of Poro:

This wise, political institution is desseminated through the country for the purpose of putting an end to disputes and wars, as the jealousy, pride, and irritability of the natives are such as will not suffer them even conscious of being the aggressors to make concessions. . . . This law is never used but in dernier resort and when it is in force, the crimes of witchcraft and murder are punishable by it.[4]

Hence certain functions of Poro-Sande were early discerned by Europeans. These secret societies introduced all members into adulthood. Initiates were isolated from the community for a period of years in a special place called the "sacred grove." In these "bush schools" social knowledge and instruction were imparted. Individuals were educated to their life's work; familiarized with tribal history and lore; and schooled in social conduct and behavior befitting their particular sex and station. For girls, household information, responsibilities as wives and mothers, their economic roles, medicinal knowledge, singing, and dancing formed the basis of their social introduction to womanhood. Boys learned how to build houses, to follow their choice of trade, how to make their own farms, tactics of combat and of hunting. Secrecy of bush activities was paramount on pain of death. Even in the twentieth century the resiliency of these associations, though greatly altered, still remains, and efforts to obtain eyewitness accounts are generally futile. In the old days, initiation was compulsory. Marriage, sexual relations, or holding of property was not possible for a non-initiate. Regardless of biological age, a non-initiate was not considered an adult nor allowed to hold any position of importance.[5]

While Poro and Sande represented transformation from childhood to citizenship, membership in these societies was clearly more than a puberty *rite de passage* or a course of training for various roles in community life. According to Kenneth Little, a specialist on the Mende Poro, those functions were secondary to the main one, "to impress upon the new member the sacredness of his duty to the Poro," and hence to the community. To this end a youth was subjected to a series of terrifying experiences and symbolically eaten by the Poro spirit—the devil—and reborn by the same spiritual force. What trader Nicholas Owen witnessed was the "devil" entering a village to "catch" boys for Poro. The marks he saw on initiates were not inflicted at birth, but part of the initiation operation, representing the devil's teeth. The devil Poro or Sande first devoured then released the initiate. Its capacity to do this deeply reinforced Poro-Sande power at an impressionable age. Each individual swore to uphold secrecy of the initiation process and to abide by Poro-Sande authority. Allegiance was no longer given primarily to parents and kin but to the secret society, the foremost arbiter. Thus social and political functions of Poro and Sande were implemented to fulfill collective and societal goals. These regulatory processes, in the form of social control, were deterrents to deviant social behavior and arbitrary power. The Poro Council was supreme, and this inner circle called "palavar" to discuss and rule on all important events. They stopped village quarrels, tried and condemned social criminals, intensified holiday spirit on great occasions, and gave permission to declare war. While a chief was the nominal civil ruler, real power was in the hands of the Poro Council, consisting of senior members of both societies who could even depose a chief.[6]

The Poro sign was a spiral of ferns which reportedly still holds sway today in parts of Sierra Leone and Liberia. It represented a powerful prohibition, bringing sickness and death to those who ignored its ban. The spiral of ferns regulated economic affairs, setting rules about fishing, farming, trading practices, and price standards. Thus the secret society functioned as the primary psychological and physical coercive agent for the common good. However, the institution's power was derived from its affinity with the spirits and from other supernatural manifestations. Poro was law. Poro was order. And Poro came from God.[7]

No aspect of West African life was truly secular and Poro-Sande sociopolitical power symbolized relationships between the sacred and the temporal. The foundation of Poro-Sande prerogative was mystical in nature, and the institution was "made by God, not by man." Thus Poro-

Sande spiritual significance was pervasive. Spirits dwelled in the sacred grove. Among them were ancestral spirits, bush and water spirits, spirits of associations, and Poro-Sande spirits, all with particular functions. Ancestral spirits, for example, explained life after death, were concerned with family and the larger group's well-being, and were protectors. Water and bush spirits, the nature category, imparted special knowledge and punishments. They were approached by medicine specialists, fortune tellers, or those specially versed in spirit communication. Association spirits represented such specialized organizations as the leopard or snake society, and were ancillaries of Poro and Sande, deriving power from the spirits they personified. Poro-Sande spirits, of which the "bush devil" was most important, were worldly representations of supernatural forces, personifying the will of "God" and mysteries of life. While other spirits in the pantheon were of the unseen world, Poro-Sande spirits represented the supernatural sphere, as well as earthly manifestations of supernatural power. All spirits remained hidden behind masks. The Poro and Sande leader's identity was an especially guarded secret. The leader's authority was intergroup, and his or her standing was recognized even in distant chiefdoms where a language barrier existed. Bush initiates were taken from several surrounding villages, adding to the strength of communal regulation. Also, a Poro or Sande member's status was recognized from group to group, creating solidarity and a fraternal spirit that superceded immediate kinship ties. A Poro-Sande founder was considered holy and immortal. Their death was kept secret by the society's inner circle of elders while another prepared to fill the place. The leader was buried in the sacred house in the grove. Thus strength and authority of Poro-Sande were not challenged because of a change in leadership.[8]

Hence, one aim was spirit control, mainly through ceremony, ritual, meditation, medicine, and exclusive contact. Essentially, "the Poro may be thought of as an attempt to reduce the pervading spirit world to an organization in which man might contact the spirit world and interpret it to the people, where men became spirits and took on godhead."[9] Additionally, meeting spirits in the bush, living and communicating with them symbolized control over the natural and supernatural environment. The spiritual seclusion also symbolized restraint over one's self by suspending elements of fear and individualism considered harmful to the community. The initiate's capacity to withstand the sacred bush experience and uphold its secrets extended functionally into the secular realm.

Society was organized around allegiance to and belief in the power of Poro and Sande. Reverence for the symbolically sacred led to obedience, accountability, and respect for what was generally its identical secular arm, the Poro Council.

The exact origin of Poro and Sande can probably never be determined. But Golas claim responsibility for the Poro's spread in their region. Vai tradition and that of other neighboring tribes confirm this point of view. Furthermore, Dutch geographer Dapper reported in 1686 that the "great priestess of Women society," residing in Gola country, came to administer to the Vai and De towns. The other theory of origin revolves around Sierra Leone groups. Temne people claim they borrowed the institutions from the Bullom, and the Portuguese observed the practices among the latter. Yet the Mende also claim to be the originators, and have historically had a very strong Poro-Sande. Possibly the institutions were introduced by the Bullom-Gizzi, early neighbors of the Gola, and when the Gizzi people of the south were overrun by and incorporated into the Mende group, they introduced Poro and Sande to the Mende. As neighbors of the Gola, Gizzi people shared the same linguistic background and other cultural traditions. Additionally, the Mende also overran the Gola and sold many into slavery. Hence, discussion comes full circle back to the Gola people. Even today, the most intensive and oldest presence of Poro and Sande is among Gola and Mende groups, as well as Moslem Vai.[10]

Further evidence for secret societies being of Gola origin stems from the interesting belief that the male Poro evolved after the female Sande. In precolonial times Gola society was matrilineal. "We were ruled by women and looked to our mothers," stated a Gola informant. In the beginning was Sande, a woman's society which governed, and was the custodian of ritual and of the spiritual powers necessary to defend ancestral interests. The initiation and training of women was a central task involving the entire community. And into these days of "peace and perfect order" came terrible wars, but women resisted the men's mobilization for defense. Thus the men invented a forest monster—the "Great Spirit of Poro" (a mask form) which frightened the women. This spirit provided men with the power to wrest control of the country, take away the sons, teach them the art of war and of politics, and to enforce loyalty exclusively among males, via the secret bush initiation. In these ways, the Gola defeated their enemies and became a great people. Yet a compromise of sorts was reached. Sande remained a force and the two societies shared sacred and secular governance. But Sande power was diluted and divided, symbolized by their initiation period being shorter than Poro's. By the time of European contact, Golas were a patrilineal people whose greatness had long since waned. In any event, both institutions were adopted by many ethnic groupings with decentralized structures of governance and administration.[11] And the historical importance of Golas in spreading Poro and Sande, coupled with their numerical contributions to slave coffles, provides food for thought regarding their previously ignored significance in coastal Carolina.

Basically then, bush initiation emphasized and reinforced traditional ways of life, a sense of camaraderie and societal bonds extending over a large area, transcending familial, clan, or ethnic barriers. The bush experience was a shared memory instilling loyalty, bonds of attachment, and unity that neither Christianity nor Islam could destroy even today. In Central West Africa allegiance toward the secret society was based on the institution's supernatural power, which was used to establish law, authority, accountability, security, and social cohesion in the community. Nearly all Africans brought to America came from groups where some type of initiation process was practiced, which further reinforces the argument for tenacity. Yet none contained the distinctive structurally inclusive elements of Poro and Sande with its compulsory ritual, social, political, economic, educational, and hierarchical framework. Poro and Sande influence, like most of traditional West African existence, suffered and was abused greatly because of the traffic in slaves. The power of Poro, rather than remaining a cementing force became, in many cases, an instrument of abuse.[12] Nevertheless, it was for many previous generations the foundation of social and spiritual organization among Upper Guinea ethnic groups. Once slave trading ceased, secret societies resumed much of their past significance. Poro and Sande existed before Europeans came and remained after the colonization of Sierra Leone and Liberia. In Africa these institutions withstood over three centuries of barbarous slave trading on the coasts. They survived the disdainful circumspection of black and white colonizers and repelled the narrow-minded indoctrination of black and white missionaries. Because so many ethnic groups from Poro-Sande traditions were transported to the Lowcountry and perhaps elsewhere, conceivably *some* of the more adaptive and useful elements of these institutions might remain, despite the trauma of capture, the long march, and the Middle Passage. Later discussion on Gullah folk religion will offer interpretations of how functional and ritualistic features of Poro-Sande Societies specifically, and other initiation rites generally, may have merged with Gullah versions of Christianity. This was especially apparent in that Gullah folk religion served as a cultural and community building force and a means of instilling individual self-worth among bondspeople.

Religion and Order in Traditional Society

Both Islamic and traditional African religions, similar to Christian spiritual belief, adhered to a kind of monotheism. For non-Moslem Africans the Supreme Being or Sky God had many names. Akan-Ashanti referred to God as *Onyame*. Bantu peoples called God *Nzambi*. Among the Mende God was *Ngewo* and to the Gola *Daya*. The Supreme Deity was generally considered omniscient, omnipotent, and creator of all life. God represented the highest values—kindness, justice, sincerity, and mercy. Thus in African perceptions, God was no fomenter of mischief or ill will. Unlike Jehovah, God was not to be feared, and no prayers needed to be offered. Evil came from other sources, not the Creator. Although God was not accorded worship through libation and was invisible, allegiance was rendered, and the Deity's ultimate power over humans was recognized. "Nzambi possesses us and eats us," or "he is gone, Nzambi has willed it," were central themes in some BaKongo proverbs and songs.[13]

Belief in afterlife was integral to traditional African religion. But Africans did not view the future world with fear, nor, as in Christianity, as a place of dispensations for rewards and punishments in a strict sense. In this land of the dead where life continued, there was no sickness, disease, poverty, or hunger. But underworld inhabitants retained the positions of their earthly hierarchy. Death was a journey into the spirit world, not a break with life or earthly beings. The idea of the perpetuity of life through time, space, and circumstance was common to African religious culture, and the complexity of this belief system is typified by BaKongo cosmology and concepts of the four moments of the sun. Using the sun through its course around the earth, the BaKongo pointed out the four stages which make up one's life cycle: (1) rising—meaning birth, beginning, or regrowth, (2) ascendency—meaning maturity and responsibility, (3) setting—implying death and transformation, (4) midnight, indicating existence in the other world and eventual rebirth. Life was a continuum and the sign of the four moments of the sun symbolized "spiritual continuity and renaissance" via its spiral journey. The crossing of the four solar moments, spacially like a Greek cross and similar to the Christian cross, was not introduced to the BaKongo by early Christianity. Long before the arrival of Europeans, this geometric statement, the Kongo Cruciform, adorned funerary objects and in other ways reflected BaKongo aesthetic perceptions of their relationship to the world. Robert Farris Thompson and Joseph Cornet have brilliantly demonstrated this through BaKongo visual traditions in Africa and the New World.[14]

Belief that one's spirit consciously existed after death was also common. "New" Africans, once they learned English, found reinforcement in Christian principles taught by white ministers, that everyone possessed a soul, apart from one's human form, with its own destiny. In certain ways African concepts were more complicated. Mende believed that each mortal had a *personality-soul*, or spirit existence, where the "vital force of the individual resided." This *personality-soul* left the flesh at death and took on full spiritual form. One who was a good person in earthly life continued as a good *personality-soul*. Those who led an evil life likewise became demonic as well as immune to antiwitch medicines. Golas and other neighboring groups referred to the soul as the "heart" which also stood for the mind. One's actions were directed by the "voice of his heart" which persuaded and guided individual behavior. Each living being possessed two hearts—one good and one bad—each trying to influence the other. Death destroyed the body but did not affect the soul, or "heart." The dead would awake, arise, and join their departed relations and friends at a common place of abode. A further example of immortality is provided by Akan tradition. Akan peoples believed that each person's guiding spirit, the *okra*, departed at death, indicating completion of earthly destiny. The *okra* returned to God to justify its existence on earth, but was also capable of appearing again in spirit form among the world of the living. The *okra* was considered the real self—in a sense, one's conscience—and was thus responsible for human behavior whether good or evil.[15]

Bantu peoples probably had the most elaborate and complex system of afterlife beliefs which were central to their religious traditions. Humans were double beings, consisting of an outer and inner entity. Each entity in turn had two parts. One part of the outer being, the shell, was visible. At death it was buried and rotted. The second part was invisible and could be "eaten" by bad medicine, *kindoki*, but helped by good medicine, *minkisi*. The inner being's two parts were both necessary for continued existence. One signified personal life and although expressions differed among groups, there was commonality in meaning. Some Bantu peoples expressed the personal entity as *kivuumunu* (breathing). Other expressions were *mwela* (breath), *kiini* (shadow), *moyoo* (life), *mpeeve* (spirit, wind) and *nsala* (soul or principle of life). *Kivuumunu* was the agent of life and breath, hidden and protected from black medicine. Death could not destroy it. The second part of the inner being, the *belly*, was different. It took food which had to be provided for the entity to continue living. Both contributed to continued existence, one through breath and the other through nourishments. In the world of *mpemba* (land of all things white), the dead, via powers commensurate with the goodness of their previous earthly life, were expunged of earthly acquired impurities and reentered the world as reincarnated spirits (in grandchildren) or as immortal *simbi* spirits.[16] Notions of the afterlife practiced by BaKongo peoples and their neighbors and reinforced by similar beliefs among other Africans parallel some Gullah "Christian" ritualistic customs of death and burial, as discussed in a subsequent chapter.

Spirits of the deceased ancestors constituted the largest group of religious intermediaries in African cosmology. They were bilingual in a sense, speaking the language of humans and that of the spirits and God. Still they remained a part of the human family, returning to share meals occasionally and appearing to certain elder members of the household. The living dead knew the needs and desires of their clan members and had access to channels of communication with God. The spiritual status and availability of the living dead facilitated their being approached more than God for concerns of life and for protection. The importance which departed members of the family occupied in African spirituality has been termed "ancestor worship." But modern African writers have denounced this phrase, first introduced by Herbert Spencer. These scholars insist that communion with deceased members of the family (via prayers, honorific offerings, interpretation of dreams and unusual events) was not "worship" but symbolic fellowship, respect, and veneration.[17]

Ancestor reverence was basic to Bantu belief systems perhaps because of the significance of lineage and kinship to societal structure and governance.[18] The absence of mandatory secret societies as a means of maintaining corporate linkage and community loyalty points up the significance of kinship and lineage in a monarchial system such as that practiced by peoples of the Kongo region. Clan loyalty was paramount. If *Nzambi* ruled, reproved, and in the final analysis ordered the world according to divine design, ancestors superintended, rewarded, and welcomed the dead into their subterranean village. Ritually, BaKongo spiritual behavior was concatenated to ancestor devotion, not to *Nzambi*, though the spirit world consisted of forces unleashed by *Nzambi*. Among the most powerful of these were deceased elders of the clan, called *bakulu*—white spirits who roamed the earth (in woods, streams, and villages) and resided in the subterranean "world of no evil." Vital to ancestor reverence was the belief that discarnate human spirits maintain interest in their people after passing to the unseen society where they guard traditions and activities of the living. If family herds were squandered, ancestors took note and punished. If drought threatened the family herds, old chiefs in the spirit world might take pity and send rain. The power of ancestral spirits was commonly recognized.[19]

Belief in ancestoral spirits, in life after death, and in the significance of that future life gave funeral and burial rites a central place in African existence. Sick-bed attendance and a fitting send-off were essential observations of this rite of passage. Death halted routine activities when marriage or other rites did not. Failure to properly observe the death ritual could either implicate one in that death, or bring ill will to the erring clan member. The curse of the dying was much dreaded. In the American South, as noted by Herskovits, Bastide, Thompson, and others, black cemeteries represent a special historical relic. For here one finds the clearest, strongest visible examples of memories of African-inspired customs. African reverence for departed members of the family and group remained a factor in Gullah religious life even after they accepted Christianity. Gullah regard for deceased family members could not have equalled the homage paid to these spirits by Old World or "New" Africans. Still, spirits of the dead had to be reckoned with, and slaves believed they took the form of either good or evil supernatural forces. Vengeful spirits of the dead were those wronged during their lifetime, or "on easy" spirits perhaps indicating bewitchment, or they were the ancestors of outside families or groups. Hence in keeping with their traditional African heritage, Gullahs employed various means of pacification of the living dead, seemingly more derived from Bantu influence.[20]

Supernatural causation of suffering, disease, accidents, death under obscure circumstances, and other misfortunes was a core of African thought. Magic and medicine were employed for protection and healing. The use of sacred medicines called *minkisi* (singl. *nkisi*) was, along with ancestor reverence, fundamental to religion among Bantu peoples who lacked a complex system of lesser deities possessed for instance by the Yoruba peoples. Although *Nzambi* allowed death to come to humankind, the Deity also armed the people with *minkisi*. Minkisi power derived from two classes of medicine. They contained "spirit-embodying" (earth from a grave site for instance) and "spirit-admonishing" objects (seeds, claws, miniature knives, stones). Hence the basis of *nkisi* life source was a "captured soul," "spirit controlled by a man," and the charm's owner directed the spirit of the object to accomplish certain things.[21]

Medicine specialists, priests, and priestesses were, like ancestors, significant spiritual intermediaries. They were the great healers, or practitioners of "white magic" often symbolized by adornment with white chalk. Medicine specialists, called *nganga* by the BaKongo, discerned the cause of illness, holocaust, or unhappiness, discovered the culprit, and prescribed treatment and a means of preventing recurrence of the calamity. Since afflictions and misfortune were the workings of "black magic," called *kindoki* in KiKongo, diviners employed miraculous as well as herbal healing elements in their profession. As combatants of evil and antisocial behavior, they interceded spiritually with the supernatural and in some societies instructed patients regarding which ancestors or minor deities to approach for defensive and preventive measures. John Mbiti, an East African theologian and scholar, has offered a general synthesis of the African specialists' practice:

The medicine man is in effect both doctor and pastor to the sick person. His medicines are made from plants, herbs, powders, bones, seeds, roots, juices, leaves, liquids, minerals, charcoal and the like; and in dealing with a patient, he may apply massages, needles or thorns, and he may bleed the patient; he may jump over the patient, he may use incantations and ventriloquism, and he may ask the patient to perform various things like sacrificing a chick or goat, observing some taboos or avoiding certain foods and persons—all these are in addition to giving the patient physical medicines.[22]

Thus, diviners combined physical, religious, and psychological approaches in their treatments. Perhaps in instances where a physical cure was warranted herbal medicines sufficed. But when a patient was convinced that superhuman agencies were at the root of the problem, a diviner resorted to similar countermeasures of supernatural proportions, and it was a case of spirit acting upon spirit. Patients with faith enough in their specialists, priests, or priestesses might be relieved of a spell they felt in the grip of, "cured" of a psychosomatic complaint, or the healer might even employ an effective herbal remedy while prescribing an amulet, in which case the two powers working together were credited with effecting a cure.[23]

African diviners were specialists who usually considered themselves "called" to their positions, either as youths or later in life. The profession was also passed on within the family. The nature of the "calling" was generally through dreams in which deities or ancestors summoned a would-be diviner to the work. The training process was extensive and candidates were schooled in medicinal knowledge, magic, and witchcraft countermeasures. In the Upper and Lower Guinea regions, mandatory secret societies assumed the task of training religious specialists and the process took place over a number of years in which candidates were isolated from everyone except other initiates and teachers. Among ethnic groups of the Kongo, medicine specialists were sometimes trained in special secret societies. The class of diviners was elaborate (with over fifty orders), since BaKongo religion was solidly based on magico-healing (minkisi). Yet a "proper specialist" or nganga need not necessarily belong to any society.[24]

Functions of spiritual leaders and diviners were of paramount significance in the New World setting. In the colonial era these leaders most likely provided a direct link with and representation of the past. Later they demonstrated the African-American adaptive capacity as they incorporated their influence into the Christian religion as well as sometimes operating completely outside of it. In the early days, when memories and reminiscences of Africa were fresh, African diviners assumed religious leadership. From this group may have emerged the "spiritual parents"—men and women whose position was unauthorized by whites, but central to the slaves' spiritual and religious orientation. Their existence predated the coming of organized Christian instruction to the Sea Islands. Yet they became the Gullahs' plenipotentiaries, responsible for guiding potential Christian converts through the "seekin' " experience just as Poro and Sande leaders conducted the neophytes through the "bush" experience.[25]

A second group of leaders worked on the periphery of Christianity. These "doctors" or "conjurers" were highly regarded by Africans and by African-Americans tied to their past while also creating a present. Some resembled the African specialists, in Kikongo the *nganga*, practitioners of *minkisi*. Yet others practiced *kindoki*, and brought evil. For if *Nzambi* and the ancestors set the limits of human possibility, and gave humans countermeasures against catastrophic forces, this influence was not always successful. The sorcerer *ndoki* brought chaos, disorder, sterilization of nature, and even death. Hence we fine among the Gullahs the belief in conjuration and in witches of human form who brought evil via mystical actions, and in root "doctors" and healers who worked for the forces of good.

As Christianity crusaded through the slave quarters during the last generation bondage, another type of major leadership is identified as having a commanding influence upon the Gullahs. These plantation meeting house elders, chosen by whites, were the last group to develop. As spiritual parents, root doctors, and conjurers were a bridge between old and new traditions, with accentuation of the former, the "praise house watchmen" were the embodiment of creative forces that congealed past and present into something exceptional. But the new leadership, unlike the old, was probably more definitely in alignment with the new religion. Still black elders were pillars of strength in the slave quarters, and often above reproach among the members of the socioreligious communities.[26]

Association with African traditions obviously weakened, first in wake of new circumstances and later due to the power and appeal of the new religion. Yet while many elements of Africanity disappeared, other beliefs and customs took on new forms. Some features basic to traditional experience and thought outlived the capture, homeland enslavement, Middle Passage, and Protestant influence. African religious orientation was fundamental to early ethnic groups brought to the Sea Islands and coastal Lowcountry. Additionally, in the process of community-building, a cosmology significant in traditional African societies formed another basis of the Gullah world view and spirituality. A sacred concept of reality and of the universe not only explained natural and supernatural phenomena for Africans, but fashioned notions about human relationships as well. The ontological[27] category of traditional African societies, and which also formed the basis of the Gullah world view, was the fusion of spirituality with human activity and the impact of a sacred presence in all areas of life. Spirituality was a main element of culture, integrating and coordinating other aspects of communal behavior. Such a pattern, so deterministic to group attitudes in West African society, was difficult to obliterate especially among a people so completely defined out of the new social and cultural structure into which they were thrust.

West African world view was consonant with the idea that in a cohesive and integrated community each member had a place. In colonial Kongo whites tended to assume that individualism was absent from black behavior, and attributed to Africans a "Bantu mentality," completely different from "European mentality." As one author noted, this was a rationalization for despotism over Africans. Wyatt MacGaffey maintains that a "purely dogmatic" assumption of some scholars led to insistence that the individual is not differentiated from the collective or clan. One solution, writes MacGaffey, is to distinguish between "true individualism," a commendable trait among the BaKongo, and "egocentrism" which was deplorable. Additionally, MacGaffey sees a difference between progressive "civilized collectivism" and primitive forms of collectivity, the latter stagnating a society. These insights explain much about traditional African society. Certainly Africans had civil, structured communities in which individual activity was forged with collective necessity. Traditional African spiritualism was an individual as well as collective experience. It encompassed the total well-being of the community, but each person had a role in society, guided by spiritual forces. In this sense, religion for Africans and Gullahs, whether essentially traditional or Christian, was a total immersion phenomenon. The sacred was not set apart from temporal, individual, communal, material, or even political concerns, and religion assumed a meaning outside of a "holy" building, a "sacred" day of the week, or a set of dogmas and creeds to be accepted at face value. In traditional African philosophy, spiritual elan affected one's whole system of being, embracing feelings, social interactions, values, fears, and the disposition of the community at large. John Mbiti succinctly expresses this consciousness:

. . . in traditional society there are no irreligious people. To be human is to belong to the whole community, and to do so involves participating in the beliefs, ceremonies, rituals and festivals of that community. A person cannot detach himself from the religion of his group, to do so is to be severed from his

roots, his foundation, his context of security, his kinships and the entire group
of those who make him aware of his existence. To be without one of these corporate elements of life is to be out of the whole picture. Therefore, to be without
religion amounts to a self-excommunication from the entire life of society.[28]

Viewed in this light, the power of Poro-Sande, of the ancestors, and
of *minkisi* were key unifying socioreligious forces. Each was effective because of divine supernatural intervention which demanded individual and
group propriety. God gave Upper Guinea peoples Poro-Sande, gave *minkisi*
to the BaKongo, and transformed the ancestors into spiritual guardians.
Hence God was not only a Supreme Spirit but a lawgiver as well. The
supernatural existence of Poro-Sande was thus ordained and the pantheon of Poro-Sande spirits, through association with God, decreed laws,
set standards, modes of behavior, worship, and customs. The "captured
spirit" in each *nkisi* was incarnated power sent directly from *Nzambi* (similar perhaps to the Christian Holy Ghost). Ancestors were the emissaries
of the withdrawn Supreme Deity. This idea of the remoteness of God,
noted by writers and observers, is disputed by some recent African
scholars. Still both sides of the debate acknowledge the presence of a
Supreme Deity in African spiritual concepts, and that God had agents
through which divine will was dispensed. This provided a linkage of
spiritual virtue with communal responsibility. The attributes of God
(discussed earlier), corresponded with characteristics of harmony and social order, the antithesis of bush living which was a wild, antisocial state
of consciousness. Similarly, Gullahs who accepted Christianity associated community socialization with religious piety. The laws of God were
synonomous with correct conduct toward other members of the slave
quarters. In maintaining this African socioreligious connection in the
American ambiance, bondspeople operated on an internal logic that excluded planters, overseers, and even white Christian ministers. There
was a parallel between the structural configuration of what became Gullah folk religion and composition of social order in the quarters. Thus in
Gullah antebellum communities their interpretations of spirituality played
a major role in attitudes toward collective accountability.[29]

African codes of ethics stemmed from spiritual orientation. Moral de-
fects were considered spiritual flaws in traditional society and a blight
on one's character. Individuals were expected to be guided by ethics
characteristic of God, the ultimate source of moral order. Patriarchs,
diviners, ancestors, and other spirits that one met in the sacred grove

and through communion, were daily guardians of human behavior. Punishments and restitution for breaches in morals and ethics were not the province of a future world judge but dealt on earth.[30] Thus, although West African peoples were not generally adherents to the concept of a future tribunal, they did believe that evil activities and failure to obey social regulations warranted earthly censure and punishment according to the degree of depravity involved. And they developed institutions to carry out regulatory functions. This was obviously a more effective method of controlling deviant social behavior. In communities so heavily based on interdependency, assurances of immediate repercussions and ostracization were a more direct and real threat than fear of a remote world beyond.

Inherent in the traditional African world view that places sacredness foremost as a sociocultural component was an anthropocentric philosophy. Although employing a different purpose from what is being suggested here, John Mbiti, one of the adherents of this approach, divides the categories of African ontology thusly:

1. *God* as the ultimate explanation of the genesis and sustenance of both man and all things
2. *Spirits* being made up of superhuman beings and the spirits of men who died a long time ago
3. *Man* including human beings who are alive and those about to be born
4. *Animals and plants* or the remainder of biological life
5. *Phenomena and objects without biological life*.[31]

Reverend Mbiti would perhaps disagree, but sociologically speaking African ontology appears to place more emphasis on humankind than on God and the spirits. While God is the apex of the African theory of being, humankind is the center since everything is viewed in relation to human existence.[32] This expresses affirmation of human and earthly life. Ontological categories are significant mainly within the context of human essence, experience, and environments, from the highest to the lowest form of being. Human spiritual activity is directed toward justification, preservation, protection, and enrichment of life. God explains creation of life and is a model of virtue that all should strive toward. Spirits are intermediaries representing assurance of perpetuity beyond the grave. The thrust of spiritual behavior confirms that mortal life is the nucleus of being, though not the end of the cycle. Recognition of ancestors, the power of Poro-Sande, sacred medicine, and the Supreme God, represent

endeavors to contribute to the natural and supernatural processes believed to govern life. The relationship between the pivotal position of
humanity and religion in African ontology is seen in general concepts
regarding life in an African village on the individual as well as the communal level.

While communal concerns are paramount, individual experience also
represents group totality. Hence a sense of the sacred accompanied one
from conception, through physical death and beyond. Life activity was
fashioned by beliefs and rites with strong religious connotations. For
example, African women participated in numerous rites and ceremonies
to insure bringing a healthy child into the world. The fate of the unborn
was placed in the care of spiritual beings and forces. A newborn's survival past three to seven days was a sign that it had been blessed by the
spirits and a sacred naming ceremony was held where the infant was set
apart for a certain occupation and a life of good habits and industry. At
childhood's end, the spirits were celebrated and appreciation shown cer-
emoniously for watch and care during those formative years. Upon entrance into puberty a religious rite customarily prepared the youth for
the initiation process. After initial training in the bush, the neophyte reentered society through a lavish sacred confirmation, recognizing that the
individual was no longer a lost soul but a member of the village. Marriage rites also had consecrational connotations, a commemoration of
continued procreation of the human species, longevity of the community, and individual self-fulfillment. Hence, introduction into various stages
of life was accompanied by sacred observations, ceremonies, and festivals. Additionally, during the periods of crisis and stress of normal adult
life, one naturally looked to an depended upon supernatural succor (via
sacred medicine ancestral intervention) for guidance and assistance. Of
course, death was epitomized by a religious send-off to the spirit world,
with which the living had maintained such close contact. Death, then,
was but the climax of one existence and the beginning of another. And
afterlife concepts were perhaps the fullest embodiment of spiritualism as
well as convictions of human perpetuity.[33]

Thus African religion can be viewed as primarily a celebration of collective human life through individual experience. To live fully and ro-
bustly was a basis in African thinking and a reasoning behind their particular cosmology. That which threatened this will to live, or "vital force"
was considered dangerous to the individual and to society. Inhabitants

of the spirit world were guardians of life. They were appealed to when illness, environmental disaster, or the malice of wrongdoers jeopardized the life force. Often they were placated in the interim as a precautionary measure, always with the end being the perserverance of the individual, the clan and village, and the group. The underlying and perhaps most dynamic force operative in the development of a religion among the Gullahs was rooted in these processes. In some respects, African traditional religion was complimented by certain Christian beliefs. But it was mainly a pristine element of sacred thought that remained with the slaves and accounted for the vitality of African-American culture and creation of an African-American ethos. It was a spirituality which represented a zealous affirmation and celebration of life, that did not separate sacred from secular responsibility, and that placed community above individual interests without completely sacrificing personhood. The effects of this broader guiding African influence on Gullah religion explain their striving and motivation in maintaining, within the realm of bondage, a reason for being. Spiritual causation was one of the few means available in their attempts to fulfill needs, interpret experience, and articulate the expectations of an emerging people. This, along with practical and applied examples of Christianity, formed the basis of Gullah folk religion. Yet the process of socioreligious community formation was slow, traumatic, and filled with pitfalls. In the early years there were problems of cultural alienation on both sides. Even later, whites were not generally anxious to include the masses of African-Americans into the Protestant spiritual ethos. Nor were Gullahs exactly bursting with enthusiasm for a religion whose doctrines supposedly ordained their foreign bondage. This polarization lessened, for whites realized benefits in adopting an *unequal* spiritual coexistence, and Gullahs decided the new religion could be interpreted on a number of levels.

PART II

Early Carolina's Religious Environment, 1670-1775

CHAPTER 3

Missionaries and Masters

The ignorance therefore of these poor slaves in the principles of Christianity in a Christian country and under a Christian government is not so much their fault as their unhappiness in falling into the hands of such ill masters who not only neglect to instruct them but scoff at those that attempt it, and give them likewise strange ideas of Christianity from the scandalous lives they lead.*

We apprehend the Master, acting according to the law of your Province, in gelding his slave hath not committed any crime, to give any offence to any member to break communion with him in the Church.**

Anglicans

In 1701, about thirty years after the founding of Carolina, the Society for the Propagation of the Gospel in Foreign Parts was established in order to bring the Anglican church to the British colonies. The SPG was also chartered to Christianize so-called heathen blacks and Indians. In South Carolina the two missions were at variance throughout the Society's presence there.[1]

South Carolinians first came into contact with Indians through trade and war. The practice was to enslave Indian prisoners of war, and early eighteenth-century letters of Society missionaries mention Indian slaves often enough to indicate their sizable presence among the bondspeople. The Society hoped to address the spiritual needs of both slave and free

*South Carolina Clergy to Gideon Johnston, March 4, 1712, SPGLL, BV6, reel 6, series A, vol. 8.

**Baptist Church in Devon, England to Baptist Church at Charles Town 1710, from William G. McLoughlin and Winthrop D. Jordan, eds., "Baptists Face Barbarities of Slavery in 1710," *Journal of Southern History* 29 (November, 1963): 501.

Indians, and of black slaves. Ministers met resistance from every quarter, especially in regard to blacks. Indians were considered more "civilized" by both Society missionaries and planters. Also, African slavery increased while Indian slavery waned, with the latter group becoming less of a threat to planters and less of an insurmountable challenge to Society missionaries. Some white adventurers on the frontier were deeply involved in trading with Indians and welcomed the presence of a missionary for their own personal reasons. From St. Helena, Thomas Nairne, Anglican missionary and Indian trader, wrote to the Society in 1705 that their "good faith and charitable intention" toward the Indians was being "perverted" under the notion that converting Negroes was "a work good and necessary." "You know as well as I," wrote Nairne, "that all Carolina laughs at that untruth."[2]

Early efforts to Christianize blacks were attempted only in more settled areas of Charleston and surrounding frontier plantations. Nevertheless, hostility to the enterprise continued as the colony developed and the slave population increased. Society missionaries listed numerous "rubs and impediments," mostly under the rubric of desire for profit on the part of planters, the master's own impiety, or fear of insurrection. Planters of all denominations struggled financially in the early eighteenth century and considered slave conversion inimical and inconsistent with their pecuniary interests. They were unwilling to give slaves time for instruction on workdays, and even Sunday teaching was not generally permitted. Sunday was the day slaves worked for themselves. "There are many Planters who to free themselves from the trouble of feeding and clothing their slaves allow them one day in the week to clear ground and plant for themselves as much as will clothe and subsist them and their families," complained a Society clergyman in 1712 to the British Commissary. But, added the clergy, Sunday was already their ministers' busiest day for it was set aside to administer to whites. "I shall not mention any conversion of heathen servants," wrote William Taylor from "St Martin in the field," owing to the "backwardness of masters." From Christ Church, a frontier area just south of Charleston, Gilbert Jones insisted in 1716 that his work was hindered by the "pursuit of wealth." He wrote that "the least apprehension of entrenching upon their darling interest overbalances the most urgent argument we can use to persuade them to their duty. . . ."[3]

What was needed, according to the frustrated South Carolina clergy, was the force of local government which could pass binding legislation on the colonists, and itinerant catechists sent by the Society who could devote full time to missionary work. The choice of whether or not slaves were exposed to Christianity had to be taken out of the hands of masters:

> They know that if they would encourage their [slaves] conversion they must allow them some reasonable time for their instruction; and this would consequently be a hindrance to their work and an abatement of the Master's. And this is not openly owned and avowed to be the cause of that . . . unwillingness they express on this occasion, yet I may venture to say 'tis so at the bottom. Nor can some of them forbear to speak out their minds, though they endeavor to justify and excuse themselves by pretending that the slaves (the Negroes especially) are a wicked stubborn race of men and can never be converted, tho to gull and deceive their Masters they may put on the air and appearance of religion.[4]

Society representatives were in an unenviable position. Depending upon white colonists for salary and substance, ministers rarely took planters seriously to task for hostility to slave instruction. Letters received by the Home Office sometimes reveal a life of sacrifice and futile struggle on behalf of the enslaved. But correspondence also presents the uneven character of clergy and planters alike. Not all Society clergymen used their office prudently or even spiritually. Sometimes, those who did found the vestry rallied against them. The planters were known as a loud, boisterous, impious group. One distraught clergyman wrote from Goosecreek that conversion of slaves would be greatly facilitated if masters themselves could "be persuaded to lead truly Christian lives." He continued:

> It is a melancholy reflection to consider how very much the wicked lives and scandalous behaviour of many professing Christianity have hitherto retarded in these parts of the world, for not a few of these . . . have sometimes been guilty . . . of such gross enormities as even the more modest heathens . . . have been ashamed of. . . .[5]

Ministers related that among the planters, "Religion was the thing they troubled themselves with the least." From St. George's Parish Francis Varnod wrote that "Sunday was only distinguished from other days because it was a day of rest and pleasure." Some ministers admonished too consistently and as a result suffered ridicule, harassment, and removal. At St. Phillips Church in Charleston the Reverend Marston was turned out "without salary due him," though many considered him a "good, moral, hospitable" man who noted "vice and virtue with no respect of person." For some time there was no one in the province to preach or administer sacraments until one more to the liking of certain communicants was substituted. The new rector was reportedly of "evil fame" and on one occasion, "in his cups baptised a bear."[6]

Some Carolina clergymen had harsh words for the planters who made their lives and work difficult. The most dedicated minister, Francis Le Jau of Goose Creek, wrote that "revenge, self-interest, engrossing of trade, peaces of profit" in anything whatsoever were the only concern of planters. Le Jau was convinced that the "topping men" of the colony "were satisfied with a church which they could largely control and which made no pietistical demand on their way of life." And in a voice of unity the clergy wrote to the Society in London that the worse "generation of infidels" they had to deal with were not "those poor heathen slaves," but their masters. Speaking with "equal grief and truth" the clergy considered the planters' actions and attitudes to "have made themselves worse than dogs."[7]

The problem of Christian instruction was even more dire in the Sea Island Parish of St. Helena. Until 1733 when Georgia was settled, this was South Carolina's southernmost frontier, embracing the township of Beaufort and surrounding islands. While more settled parishes were populated with whites and Africans, St. Helena was primarily still part of the Indian lands. The major occupation of the handful of settlers was Indian trade. Yemassee Indians inhabiting the region tried to maintain friendly relations with white settlers. But avaricious land grabbing and broken trade agreements caused conflicts that endangered the parish's existence. In 1715 the Yemassee waged all-out war, and the entire province faced extinction. Many settlers took refuge in Charleston. St. Helena was completely uprooted while an army of 600 whites and 400 slaves was obliged to engage the Indians throughout the southern regions of Carolina. Not until 1716 did white families return to St. Helena and rebuild their dwellings. But frequent alarms occasioned by Spaniards as well as Indians forced homeseekers to flee at a moment's notice to more densely occupied and better protected parishes.[8]

Although missionaries were sent among Indians around St. Helena as early as 1704, twenty more years passed before a church building for whites was erected. Prior to 1725 the nearest parish church was forty miles away from St. Helena by water travel. Six pews accommodated the Anglican communicants which consisted of around thirty-nine families in 1728. The first rector was Lewis Jones who served in that capacity until 1745. Jones painted a bleak picture of life on the frontier. "The inhabitants are mostly poor planters of corn, pease, rice and a good many of them living at a great distance from each other," he wrote in 1728. There were at that time sixty-two families in the parish, thirty-nine of whom were Anglican, twenty-one Presbyterian, one Independent, and one Anabaptist. At that time only 170 slaves lived in the entire parish, and hence they were a minority, an atypical situation for early Carolina.[9]

The parish had no school although a few families had private teachers. As for the Negro slaves, Jones admitted in 1728 that "no care" was taken in Christianizing them. The reason, he cited, was due to their frequent removal to other areas, since Spaniards and Indians plagued the frontier, carrying away slaves. As a result, the number of St. Helena slaves decreased rather than increased from 224 in 1727 to 170 in 1728, while the entire colony's black population was over 20,000 in 1727.[10] Several possibilities may explain the disappearance of slaves. Spaniards provided a safety valve and chance for freedom. Indians may have done the same or may have simply attempted to decimate the white people's black labor force. Proximity to freedom and the paucity of whites must have intensified slaves' expectation of obtaining liberty. If later developments are any indication, slaves took advantage of these opportunities and the removal of slaves from the area represented white efforts to prevent this. The pattern continued until the Spanish and Indians were pushed back by the settlement of Georgia.

But the Sea Island region received early missionary attention for the slaves from another Anglican source. Thomas Bray (1658–1729/30) was the chief organizer of the three Anglican missionary efforts—the Society for the Promotion of Christian Knowledge (SPCK), established in 1699, the Society for the Propagation of the Gospel in Foreign Parts (SPG), formed in 1701, and the Associates for Dr. Bray, established in 1723/24 and reorganized in 1729–30. Bray's first concern was Christianizing blacks and Indians. But he also shared, with Georgia founder James Oglethorpe, an interest in improving the lot of prisoners in England. With encouragement and financial support from high places, Bray and a group of sympathizers attempted to put a missionary plan into operation, hence the founding of Bray's Associates. Because Thomas Bray and a number of Associates became involved in plans to found Georgia, it was determined that the southern missionary movement should begin near Savannah (since the Trustees did not initially intend to have slaves in Georgia). One Associate and Georgia Trustee wrote to John Wesley prior to the latter's departure for Georgia as a missionary to whites:

> One end for which we were associated was the conversion of Negro slaves. As yet nothing has been attempted in this way; but a door is opened, not far from home [i.e. Georgia]. The Purryburgers have purchased slaves; they act under our influence; and Mr. Oglethorpe will think it advisable to begin there.[11]

Thomas Bray did not live to see Oglethorpe settle Georgia or to witness the missionary attempt among South Carolina slaves. But he and his Associates were instrumental in bringing about one endeavor to Christianize slaves in South Carolina.[12]

A colony of Swiss Protestant refugees, led by Jean Pierre Purry, settled on the southern frontier on the north bank of the Savannah River in 1731. This was about 20 miles from where Savannah, Georgia, would be located in 1733. Two Moravian missionaries, commissioned by the Associates to instruct slaves in Purrysburg, arrived there in 1739. The missionary venture failed. Few blacks were in the area, and one missionary became ill and died within six months. The other sailed for Philadelphia the following year. But an even more significant note on the ill-fated nature of the plan was the fact that these missionaries apparently could not even speak English. Yet this early activity and interest in slave conversion in the South Carolina and Georgia Sea Island region set the stage for future developments. The Georgia Trustees' alteration of their brief policy of slavery exclusion in the colony, the proximity of the two colonies, and the Trustees' early concern for religious instruction made the Sea Island region fruitful territory for the evangelism of George Whitefield during the Great Awakening. These early associations also perhaps laid the foundation for later acceptance of black independent churches at a time when such institutions were forbidden elsewhere. Georgia's evangelistic fervor and liberalism spilled over into the South Carolina slave population in the Sea Island region.[13]

Lewis Jones remained at St. Helena until his death in 1745 and his main concern as rector was with white communicants. In 1736 he complained to the Society that despite his endeavors he had only been allowed to baptize one black and one mulatto slave. Bringing Christianity to slaves in St. Helena was discouraging work. Writing to the Secretary in England he stated that "the pious zeal of the venerable Society, and of its worthy Diocesan for promoting Christian knowledge among the Negroes meets with but a cold reception." This attitude was further strengthened by the 1739 Stono Rebellion. From St. Helena Lewis Jones lamented the fact that twenty-three "much indulged" slaves from his parish had joined the rebellion.[14]

But St. Helena witnessed some spiritual awakening. Whitefield preached there in 1739 and convinced a few whites to instruct slaves in Christianity. Whitefield however was not popular with the Anglican hierarchy. Unbeknownst to Lewis Jones, Whitefield had been censored by Commissary Alexander Garden in Charleston, and the latter was outraged upon learning that the outspoken evangelist was preaching in the Anglican Church at St. Helena. Further problems were created for Jones by one of Whitefield's St. Helena disciples, a planter named Hugh Bryan. Bryan, considered a mystic and an eccentric, preached to his slaves and reportedly openly predicted they would rebel and obtain their freedom.[15]

Like sister parishes, St. Helena suffered from problems of white communicants with only marginal interest in spiritual matters. Jones complained that duly elected vestrymen refused to serve even after accepting appointments. Church attendance was also poor. Jones suggested Sunday worship be held only once in five weeks. But even these infrequent services were poorly attended with the total numbers of communicants usually not exceeding twenty. Still, the long tenure of Lewis Jones brought an added stability and consistency for the Church of England on the frontier and it remained the dominant denomination throughout the colonial era. After Jones' death, ministers came and went in rapid succession. As the parish grew in economic enterprise through cultivation of indigo, a demand for slaves gave St. Helena a new significance. Yet, except for short-term effects of the Great Awakening, Anglicans in the Sea Island region remained aloof toward spiritual enthusiasm for themselves and their burgeoning African-born black population.[16]

Pecuniary interest and spiritual indifference were not the only factors that generated hostility and a "cold reception" from planters. The element of sheer physical self-preservation cannot be discounted as a reason for planter resistance. They were spread out on the frontier, surrounded by a predominantly hostile population—namely West Africans and Indians—and were in the process of exploiting both through bondage and unfair trade practices. Whites had every reason to fear of slave insurrection and Indian attacks. They wanted and needed docile, obedient servants, not "Christians" with a sense of spiritual freedom and "leisure" for worship. They were convinced Christianity would make laborers unfit for slavery and induce feelings of equality with whites. Geographical dispersement of white settlers was an added anxiety. Plantations were "remote and distant from one another," so that if the majority of slaves were frequently assembled their numbers would be known to them. This would provide "an opportunity of knowing their own strength and superiority in point of number," and possibly tempt them "to recover their liberty, tho' it were the slaughter and destruction of the whole colony." [17]

Some missionaries were convinced that planters used fear of insurrection as an excuse to prevent slaves from being instructed. The Reverend Varnod wrote that masters pretend "that the slaves would use the Lord's Day to make insurrection." If this was the real reason for non-cooperation, he queried, why was it that ministers were also prohibited by civil authorities from going into the slave cabins and instructing them? Yet other missionaries insisted that the fear was real. The frontier parishes provided opportunities for flight and resistance because of minimal fortifications, a small white population, and the presence of free Indians on the one side and anti-British Spaniards on the other. Whites were cognizant of their vulnerability and impatient with an Anglican clergy who saw Christianizing black slaves as an issue of consequence. Rather, it was the planters' policy to have red and black slaves "put check upon each other lest by their vastly superior numbers," whites would be "crushed by one or the other." [18]

The method of Christian instruction employed by South Carolina Anglicans added to the planters' uneasiness. Anglicans believed literacy was essential for communicants and their work consisted of compelling slaves to memorize the Lord's Prayer, the Apostle's Creed, a short catechism, and in explaining to slaves the life and death of Christ in brief discourse. But the major emphasis was on literacy, which most clergymen considered a prerequisite for baptism. Bibles and common prayer books were sent from England. Yet the amount of time needed to teach reading properly was not provided. Many whites were openly hostile to the idea of slave literacy. While Society representatives might persuade a "pious" planter to allow a "favorite" country-born slave the benefits of literacy, such an opportunity was unusual. Dissemination of knowledge among slaves served no useful purpose from the planters' point of view. [19]

In 1734, as a direct attack on SPG activity among the slaves, the planter-controlled South Carolina Assembly passed a law prohibiting slaves from leaving plantations on "Sundays, fast days, and holy days" without a ticket. Since few bondspeople were given passes to attend worship, and clergymen were not normally allowed in slave cabins, the law was a serious setback for the already languishing missionary movement. Peter Wood has discussed "mounting anxiety and patterns of control" on the part of whites in the 1730s, as the black, foreign-born slave population around Charleston expanded dramatically through importations. This apprehension was increased as planters also associated religious instruction with rebelliousness. An insurrection plot uncovered in Antigua in 1736 fed Carolina planters' fears and their belief in the ill effects of the Society's endeavors. The conspiracy was widespread and accounts stated that many of the leaders were literate, having been taught by Anglican clergy.[20]

But it was the Stono Rebellion of 1739 and two subsequent abortive uprisings that brought home the issue for white Carolinians. The Stono uprising began in St. Paul's Parish, twenty miles from Charleston. It gained momentum as the rebels headed farther south for Spanish St. Augustine, gathering recruits as they went. White Carolinians were especially enraged by the fact that notices posted by Spaniards offering freedom to runaways could be read by slaves who had received instruction from Society missionaries. The New Negro Act passed in 1740 curtailed the Society's freedom to teach slaves to read and write English. It was the biggest setback for the Society's program thus far.[21]

Still the Society persisted in more settled regions, though not with unified enthusiasm. While most legislation following the Stono Rebellion was repressive, it was also intended to reduce the incentive for revolt. In 1740 Alexander Garden, South Carolina Commissary for the Bishop of London, made a proposal. He suggested placing young, Carolina-born slave boys, ten or twelve years of age, under full Society tutelage for two years. Once trained, these youths would return to the plantations as religious school masters, adequately prepared to instruct slave children and adults in the neighborhood. Garden insisted that the most effective method was to have a teacher come from the slaves' own numbers. "As among us religious instruction usually descends from parents to children, so among them it must at first ascend from children, or from young to old." Garden confidently asserted that in twenty years, "knowledge of the gospel among the slaves . . . in general (excepting those newly imported) would not be much inferior to that of the lower sort of White People, servants and Day Labourers . . . either in England or elsewhere."[22]

In 1743 the "Charleston Negro School," was opened by Commissary Garden where a few slave children were taught catechism and elementary education. The school functioned after Garden's design, and the Society convinced the colonial government to support it. Society missionaries had always maintained that the key to obedient servitude was promulgated on the "principle of conscience" generated by instruction in Christian doctrine. They argued that while slaves continued in "darkness," planters could "expect at best an eye service from them and such obedience as proceeds through fear." Garden also had insight into the power and appeal of a *black-to-black* effort in Christian instruction and the pliability of young minds.

The school operated for about twenty years, but was finally closed when no suitable teacher was found upon the death of the old one. It did not have a lasting impact on the black population of Charleston. But the school is part of the religious revitalization movement called the Great Awakening and is discussed in the next chapter. Furthermore, establishment of the Negro School perhaps represents the SPG's most significant though unsuccessful effort to bring Christianity to the slaves.[23]

Baptists and Other "Dissenters"

The Fundamental Constitution of Carolina identified the colony with principles of religious toleration, although the proprietors quickly added a clause proclaiming the Church of England as the "National Religion," and empowering the governing body with a right to levy taxes to support it. Still, early Carolina offered more religious freedom than England or any other American colony except Rhode Island. One of the Carolina proprietors, John Archdale, was a Quaker and served as governor of the colony between 1694 and 1696. Although the Society of Friends was never a large denomination in South Carolina, Quakers were an important part of over 2,000 Dissenters by 1700, out of a white population of about 4,200 people. George Fox, founder of the Society of Friends, never reached South Carolina when he journeyed to America, but did travel to North Carolina in 1672. Although not against slavery, Fox encouraged benevolence toward slaves and encouraged Quakers to instruct their slaves in Christianity. Yet most Quakers followed a policy of excluding blacks from meetings even though they may have provided religious instruction.[24]

Presbyterians and Baptists immigrated to South Carolina in the 1680s, settling in Charleston and nearby areas. Encouraged by the promotional campaign which the colony's proprietors initiated, two wealthy groups of English and Scottish Presbyterians settled in Carolina. The first Presbyterian church, the Circular Church, was organized in Charleston by 1690. Like early Baptists who settled in Carolina, Presbyterians were Calvinists who practiced the doctrine of election and restricted church membership. Hence, they did not actively engage in programs of slave conversion.[25] Yet despite their Calvinism, early Baptists had divergent view about doctrine which separated them from other independent denominations and which later led to adoption of evangelism that included their slave population.

The name "Baptists" or "Anabaptists," given to the adherents of this particular denomination, has deceptive connotations. It was not a self-chosen name but one attached to the denomination by enemies during the Reformation. Baptists asserted that infant "sprinkling" was not warranted in the scriptures, and was thus contrary to the principle of voluntary action in religion, hence inviting corruption. These Christians made baptism on a profession of faith a condition of church fellowship. This, along with their denial of the validity of infant baptism and adherence to total immersion, did more than anything else to place Baptists at variance with other denominations. Yet rejection of infant baptism did not occupy as prominent a position in Baptist belief as opponents gave it. Baptists' most uncompromising religious position was their belief in the absolute authority and sufficiency of scripture and a regenerate church membership (principles which all evangelical sects ultimately embraced). This meant applying scripture to details of doctrine, practice, and daily life. Those Baptists who owed their origin to English Puritanism, and who rejected the medieval evangelism in the Augustinian tradition, strongly believed in Calvinism, especially predestination. (They were called Particular Baptists.) Puritan-oriented Baptists, led by William Screven, moved from Maine in 1683 and settled in Charleston at the same time that another group of similar persuasion arrived from England. By 1699 the two groups had emerged and formed one church. Quarrels and infighting over leadership and doctrine caused a schism in the 1720s that led to the Old England group moving out of the building. Ultimately the Old England branch settled at Stono. It was the Screven-influenced groups that spread the tenets of the Baptist faith throughout the coastal regions. They broadened and tempered their Calvinism and, under the preaching of Whitefield, adopted for a short time a modified evangelism.[26]

Thus Baptist presence in Carolina predated that of official Anglican representation. Of all the dissenting sects, SPG ministers found Baptists the most troublesome. Society ministers found Church of England adherents attending Baptist meetings, choosing "rather to hear them . . . than none." This provided an added dilemma for Anglican ministers trying to establish the Church of England. They had to compete with believers whose practices were radically opposed to Anglicanism. Anabaptists presented their views in a heavy-handed manner according to Society ministers. Le Jau wrote that on one occasion an Anabaptist teacher espoused the doctrine of predestination in "so terrifying a manner that the next day after his preaching . . . a good man of my acquaintance hanged himself." It was a direct result of Anabaptist fatalistic preaching which threw the man into melancholy. And although the death "mortified" the sect, they continued their style of preaching, causing Le Jau to define Anabaptist character as consisting of "much obstinacy and little sense."[27]

Most early Baptists came to Carolina in search of religious freedom and economic opportunity. Some were well-to-do, but most were poor or "middling" people engaged in planting, trading, and the skilled crafts. In addition to fervor for their faith, Baptists were as eager as others to acquire obvious forms of individious distinction—land and slaves. In proportion to their numbers, which remained comparatively small as the colony grew, Baptists expanded their economic interests and spiritual influence throughout the Lowcountry. Every parish had its share of Dissenters and Baptists were the most aggressive. Usually Baptists spread out as families rather than as a sect. If conditions were favorable, established Baptists encouraged others to settle. In 1728 the most remote parish, St. Helena, had only one Anabaptist family out of a total of sixty-two. Christ Church Parish, closer in but still a frontier settlement, had twenty Baptist families out of fifty-three in all.[28] But the opening up of land taken away from Indians, the revocation of the Edict of Nantes in France, and later the demand for indigo, led to increased Baptist presence and influence in the coastal and Sea Island regions.

As slaveholders, Carolina Baptists contributed to developing attitudes about slavery and blacks. They were, for the most part, Calvinist (or Particular) Baptists. Early Baptists did not attempt to bring Christianity to slaves and would not allow other sect's missionaries among their bondspeople. Nevertheless, at least one aspect of slavery caused anxiety among early Baptist slaveholders as it did among the Anglican ministers who spoke out in protest. By law, South Carolina masters were *required* to castrate a slave who ran away four times, or the master faced forfeiture of ownership to the white informer. Perhaps because of the strong protest raised by Society minister Francis Le Jau, perhaps because of the dissension it caused within their own sect, Baptist planters questioned the validity of this particular law. Charleston Baptists wrote the Baptist Church in Devon, England, for an opinion. Was this form of punishment a sin and a travesty against religious conscience? The Devon congregation replied in the negative by way of a lengthy expository. Intentions of the law were corrective not malicious wrote the Devon minister. Also, the law was passed for the "common good" and preservation of order. ". . . are not those Negroes a sort of rude, unpolished people whose nature requireth a stricter hand over 'em?" queried the English minister. Furthermore, not to punish a slave severely would be "a means of encouraging him in rebellion for the future." The Devon Church also put the matter to the Baptist Association for a verdict. The several churches agreed with the Devon congregation:

We apprehend, the Master Acting according to the Law of your Province, in gelding his slave, hath not committed any crime, to give any member to break communion with him in the church; because we see by Scripture, that 'tis lawful to buy them. (Gen. 17: 13, 23, 27). And if lawful to buy them 'tis lawful to keep them in order, and under government; and for self-preservation, punish them to prevent farther mischief that may ensue by their running away and [?] rebelling against their masters, Exodus 21: 20, 21.[29]

Like fellow Anglican settlers, Baptist planters viewed slaves as a labor force, not generally as potential Christian converts. What troubled Baptists about the castration law, as pointed out, was concern for their own souls. Also, Calvinist-oriented Baptists followed the tradition of civil law being in agreement with God's law. Hence they sought justification, not to say rationalization, for the sake of their sense of piety and not out of concern for black humanity. Additionally, the law applied to black slaves, not apparently to Indians or white, indentured servants. Clearly, a double standard operated even in terms of blacks and Indians, both of whom were enslaved, but not considered by some on the same level in the chain of being. Once again scripture was used to rationalize specialized cruelty and racism. The law of Moses distinguished between "Jewish and hea- thenish servant(s)," with the former receiving "greater mercy" according to the Devon congregation. Was not the case "somewhat the same" since the "nature" of Negroes required more severity? It was a new low for Carolina slavery, already filled with atrocities. For the gelding law had no Southern colonial precedent. Barbados, from where the colony bor- rowed its code, had no such law, although New Jersey passed a gelding law in 1706.[30]

Early Baptists' questioning of the gelding law had little or nothing to do with concern for slaves, but was primarily to purge and "save" their own souls. As William McLoughlin and Winthrop Jordan point out, let- ters such as those sent to the English Baptists by Carolina Baptists, which compile an entire collection, indicate some opposition to cruelties im- posed upon slaves, but are even more telling for other reasons. The cor- respondence demonstrates how religious values were malleated to con- form with civil institutions in South Carolina, and illustrate a belief that civil authority and God's law must be obeyed equally. Furthermore, these letters centering on problems of conscience and conduct reveal the use of biblical sanction of slavery and the slave code to maintain the social order.[31] These uses of religion by a later generation of South Carolina Baptists is explored in Chapter Seven.

A favorite slave might be allowed into the denomination fold. But for the most part, early Baptist interests as slaveholders and their doctrinal beliefs precluded accepting masses of slaves into the sect of a "chosen few." Hence Baptists were not troubled about the fate of black souls. Nevertheless, as the black population increased in Charleston, some were allowed the "privilege" of attending Baptist worship. Slaves whose Bap- tist masters embraced the evangelism of Whitefield were probably ex- posed to Christian instruction. Yet Whitefield's impact on Baptists was not totally positive from a spiritual perspective. General Baptists, es- pousing essentially Arminian views, were opposed to Whitefield. But many Particular Baptists of Calvinist-Puritan orientation accepted Whitefield. The latter group spread to the Lowcountry and were respon- sible for the missionary activity of their sect during the Great Awak- ening.[32]

CHAPTER 4

Christianity, Bondage, and the Great Awakening

Just as Mr. Whitefield was naming his text and looking round . . . as I thought directly upon me, and pointing his finger, he uttered . . . "Prepare to meet thy God O'Israel." . . . I was struck to the ground and lay both speechless and senseless. . . . When the people were dismissed, Mr. Whitefield came in to the vestry, and being told of my condition he came immediately, and he said, "Jesus Christ has got thee at last."*

As among us religious instruction usually descends from parents to children, so among them it must at first ascend from children to parents, or from young to old.—They are as 'twere a Nation within a Nation. In all country settlements, they live in contiguous houses, often 2, 3, or 4 families in one house, slightly partitioned into so many apartments, so they labor together, and converse almost wholly among themselves, . . .**

The Coming of George Whitefield

The late 1730s were trying times for South Carolina as one calamity after another befell the province. In 1737, widespread fear and alarm occurred over a pending Spanish attack which never came. In 1738 and 1739 smallpox and yellow fever ravaged the colony. In 1739 the Low-country was shaken by a slave uprising that left more than sixty people dead. It was no wonder that many residents of pleasure-loving Charleston were psychologically prepared for the coming of George Whitefield

---

*William Aldridge, ed., *A Narrative of the Lord's Wonderful Dealings with John Marrant, A Black*, 4th ed. (London: Gilbert and Plummer, 1785), 13.

**Alexander Garden to London Office, May 6, 1740, Box 20 from Lambeth Palace Library, vol. 941, no. 72, Ms. of Archbishop of Canterbury.

in 1740. Indeed, the inhabitants seemed to anticipate that on the heels of disaster would come one preaching penitence and redemption.[1]

Before his first journey to America in 1738, George Whitefield was a rising, controversial Anglican cleric, known for his enthusiasm and capacity to draw masses of people from many walks of life, but especially the lower ranks of society. In the colonies, he established headquarters in Savannah, Georgia, where at twenty-three he served as Anglican missionary and founded Bethesda, an orphanage for white children. At twenty-five in 1740, Whitefield's reputation in the colonies was well known and he moved thousands, particularly in the middle colonies, through the spiritual force of his sermons. Whitefield was of humble birth, and a friend as well as former Oxford mate of the more erudite Wesleys, John and Charles, although in 1741 the brothers broke with Whitefield for doctrinal and personal reasons. (This breach lasted for a number of years.) Still, both the Wesleys and Whitefield were part of the "despised" Methodist group which John Wesley later stabilized, organized, and shaped into a massive denomination. Yet Whitefield and the Great Awakening laid the groundwork for Wesleyan Methodism in America some thirty years before the first itinerant was sent. Young Whitefield's appeal, his introduction of open-air and extempore evangelical preaching, captured the spiritual pulse of England and America.[2]

Whitefield's first visit to Charleston was in late August, 1738:

Arrived last night here, and preached twice to-day, I hope with some good effect. The Bishop of London's Commissary, the Rev. Mr. Garden, a good soldier of Christ, received me in a most Christian manner. . . . How does God raise me up friends whereever I go.[3]

This initial positive impression of Charleston and Commissary Garden was short-lived. Upon his return to England, Whitefield was under increasing attack and criticism. He and Wesley were shut out of many Anglican pulpits because of their doctrinal views and method of preaching. Whitefield also introduced into religious revival open-air worship, because, in the words of Charles Wesley, "The Churches will not contain the multitudes that throng to hear him."[4]

Yet popularity with the people caused problems with the clergy in England and in the colonies. Although a minister of the Church of England, Whitefield openly attacked Anglican preachers and warmly fellowshipped with dissenting congregations. Colonialists, already involved in a religious awakening, welcomed Whitefield. In 1739, on his second visit, his evangelical tour attracted thousands. Whitefield's controversy with the Anglican clergy centered on his belief in regeneration and the necessity of rebirth for salvation. Additionally, the young evangelist preached that the doctrine of "works" should be replaced with "justification by faith," and he took this controversy into his public ministry. Thus Whitefield aligned himself with many Dissenters and soon gained general opposition from almost all of the Anglican clergy.[5]

Following his tour of the middle colonies, Whitefield journeyed South overland, preaching along the way and freely espousing his theological views among all who listened. Upon reaching Charleston he was denied use of the Anglican Church, St. Phillips, because "the curate had not a commission to lend the pulpit," without the consent of the Commissary, who was out of town. This did not silence Whitefield. He preached at a meetinghouse to a large but lukewarm audience. Whitefield noted the affectation of dress and gaiety which he thought ill-becoming an audience receiving the Word, and he made this the subject of his sermon. Next day, many more came to hear the evangelist and he felt rewarded for the previous day's efforts:

. . . Many were melted to tears. One of the town, most remarkably gay, was observed to weep. Instead of the people going out (as they did yesterday) in a light, unthinking manner, a visible concern was in most of their faces.[6]

Whitefield was moved by this sentiment and agreed to stay another day, preaching in the largest meetinghouse in town. He left Charleston, "full of joy at the prospect of a good work having begun in that place."[7]

This optimistic attitude, however, was not completely reflected in Whitefield's journal, as he penned his impressions of the American colonies. Pennsylvania he believed was the "garden of America." He found the people sociable, sober, and hardworking. More significantly for Whitefield, "they have the Lord for their God." He had not yet seen New England. The Southern colonies had little esteem for religion according to the evangelist. Maryland was worse than Virginia, not because of Catholicism but because of the Church of England. Yet neither colony was exemplary because of slavery, indentured servitude, an Anglican clergy spoiled by "too much tobacco," and because people lived great distances from each other and used this excuse to forego public worship. North Carolina scarcely had even "the form of religion" with no church house yet completed. His most biting criticism was for South Carolina where there were abundant ministers of many persuasions and where Commissary Garden was "strict in the outward discipline of the Church." Yet despite the prevalence of ministers, meetinghouses and outward spiritual form, Whitefield surmised of South Carolina, "I hear of no stirring among the dry bones."[8]

An open controversy between Whitefield and Commissary Garden erupted in full force when the former returned to Charleston for his mail from England, in the spring of 1740. Whitefield called upon Garden and was surprised with a "cool reception." His attacks on the Anglican clergy, his unorthodox preaching, and his decision to commune with dissenting churches had angered the Commissary. Garden accused the evangelist of "enthusiasm" and "pride" for speaking against the clergy. Wherein, asked the Commissary, was the clergy to blame? Whitefield replied, "they do not preach justification by faith alone." After discussing the matter, the evangelist, known for his self-righteousness in spiritual concerns, determined that Garden "was as ignorant as the rest." Garden raged at the young cleric, accusing him of breaking his "Cannons and Ordination vow." Whitefield reminded Garden that he was an ordained minister with letters from the Bishop of London. The conversation grew more heated before it concluded. Garden warned Whitefield that if he preached at any public church again in Carolina, he would suspend him. Whitefield wrote in his journal:

I replied, I should regard that as much as I would a Pope's bull. "But, Sir," I said, "why should you be offended at my speaking against the generality of the clergy; for I always spoke well of you?" "I might as well be offended . . . at you saying 'the generality of the people are notorious sinners' . . . because I am one of the people." I further added, "you did not behave thus, when I was with you last." "No," he said, "but you did not speak against the clergy then." Then I said to him, "If you will make an application to yourself . . . let me ask . . . . Have you delivered your soul by exclaiming against the assemblies and balls here?"

"What," said he, "must you come to catecize me? No. I have not . . . there is no harm in them." "Then," I replied, "I shall think it my duty to exclaim against you." "Then, Sir," he said in a very great rage, "Get you out of my house."[9]

The enmity continued, with Whitefield preaching to Charleston and experiencing unprecedented popularity as he bewailed the hand of God in the problems that befell the province. Garden sometimes attacked

Whitefield from the pulpit of St. Philips when the young minister came for worship, and he refused to give Whitefield the Sacraments. Nevertheless, Dissenters and probably more than a few Anglicans came under the spell of Whitefield's doctrines of regeneration and rebirth. The enmity was taken up in the newspapers and through letter writing campaigns.[10] Thus the two most significant men to address the issue of the religious instruction of slaves were bitter antagonists. And within the conflict the subject of slavery as well as doctrinal differences had a place.

Alexander Garden began the Charleston Negro School in 1743 with the approbation of the Society and a few slaveholders. He was familiar with the Carolina scene, having arrived there in 1719. Through his efforts the school lasted for over twenty years, although its success was very limited. Two young boys were purchased, taught to read and write, and then instructed in elementary Christianity. Reaction toward the school was positive in some quarters. As soon as Garden's two protégés, Harry and Andrew, were trained, students were admitted. Spelling books, Testaments, and common prayer books were contributed by the Society, the Bray Associates, and a few concerned residents. Thirty students were enrolled at first, and by 1747 the school had forty "scholars" who were "graduated" with a basic, elementary knowledge of Christianity and literacy. The school appeared to be thriving and in 1748, Garden wrote that ". . . the Society's negro school at Charles Town continued to go on with all desirable success and last year discharged about 17 scholars discharged as proposed."[11]

Thus while Garden was engaged in a bitter debate with George Whitefield, partly over slavery as we shall see, the Commissary was also using his efforts to bring Christianity and literacy to some slaves. The Charleston Negro School was extremely limited in outreach capacity, but important community leaders (such as the Pinckneys, Pringles, and Wraggs) believed in it. When the school was blown down by a tempest in 1752, it was built within a month and the supplies replaced. The year 1755 was a peak one for the school, with seventy children enrolled. But Garden resigned his position that year and his successor, Richard Clarke, was not as influential a rector. Slaves certainly seemed willing and eager to attend, probably for an opportunity at literacy rather than religious instruction. Hence while there was no lack of pupils, white support was a problem. Though they had to "pinch it off their own backs and out of their own bellies, Blacks sought education for their children."[12]

There was also a problem with one of the teachers, Andrew, who was subsequently dismissed and efforts made to sell him to the West Indies. First reports were that Andrew was simply a slow learner. Later, it was determined that the boy was "profligate." Efforts to sell him out of the province were halted out of sympathy for his parents who were Carolina slaves.[13] Beyond this we know nothing of Andrew. Obviously he did not go along with the Anglican program. The desire to sell him out of the province indicates he may have been sabotaging the school's efforts. Andrew learned to read and write but apparently did not accept Christianity, and may have passed on his doubts or disdain to his "pupils." Yet Harry continued as the only teacher until his death in 1764. Not finding another "suitable" teacher, and unable to maintain community support, the school closed. Yet even before 1764, the Charleston Negro School was languishing, as judged from Clarke's report:

The Rev. Mr. Clarke . . . writes that the Negro School there is full of children and well attended; but he laments the great negligence of the white people in general regard to the Blacks, there not being so much as one civil establishment in the colony for the Christian instruction of fifty thousand Negro slaves.[14]

The ministry of George Whitefield attracted blacks and the evangelist was sensitive to the lack of Christian instruction among them. In his travels, he took extra care to discuss the doctrines of "free grace" and salvation, and explain to free blacks and slaves that they also could attain this "new birth." He was not long in the colonies before concerning himself with religious instruction among blacks. In 1739 he wrote from North Carolina:

. . . I went, as my usual custom is, among the Negroes belonging to the house. One man was sick in bed, and two of his children said their prayers after me very well. This more and more convinces me that Negro children, if early brought up in the nurture and admonition of the Lord, would make as great proficiency as many white children's people. I do not dispair, if God spares my life, of seeing a school of young Negroes singing the praises of Him Who made them in a psalm of thanksgiving. Lord, Thou hast put into my heart a good design to educate them.[15]

Garden and Whitefield had the same idea: to bring Christianity to the slaves through the young, and to establish a school. Besides his persistent evangelizing, Whitefield is significant here for two other reasons: his early position on the treatment of slaves and his influence on the Bryan family, who attempted some of the things the evangelist hoped for.

The occasion of Whitefield's overland journey from Philadelphia to Savannah brought him face to face with the institution of slavery. Slavery was ingrained in the fabric of American life and Whitefield viewed it firsthand, lodging on large and small plantations, observing the slaves in their arduous labor. He was struck by their treatment of their foreignness. Whitefield generally insisted that his hosts allow him access to their slaves, among whom he talked and prayed. As a result of this journey and subsequent observations, he composed his famous letter to the slave owners. Never one to mince words, Whitefield was clear and forthright in his attack. At the time he prepared his letter to the slaveholders, he also wrote an equally controversial piece attacking the late Archbishop Tillotson. Tillotson's memory was revered in England and America by Anglicans as well as Dissenters who adhered to a doctrine of works. Yet Whitefield took issue with the cleric's position, declaring that in terms of scriptural and Anglican doctrine of justification by faith, the late archbishop "was certainly as ignorant thereof as Mahamet himself." Thus both letters, published simultaneously, created a howl of protest.[16]

Just as Whitefield eschewed any sense of obedience to ecclesiastical superiors, so he took on the slaveholding class. When the confrontation with Commissary Garden occurred, both letters were already written. And when he arrived in Philadelphia, less than a month after the angry session in Charleston (April 1740), he gave the letters to Benjamin Franklin to publish, and then submitted copies to newspapers throughout the colonies. "A Letter to the Inhabitants of Maryland, Virginia, North and South Carolina, Concerning their Negroes," was a bold attempt to expose the conditions of slavery to America and to chastise slaveholders for withholding Christianity from slaves. Avoiding condemnation of the institution of slavery, Whitefield abhorred the "miseries of the poor Negroes":

. . . I think that God has a quarrel with you for your abuse of and cruelty to the poor Negroes. Whether it be lawful for Christians to buy slaves, and thereby encourage the Nations from whom they are bought, to be at perpetual war with each other, I shall not take it upon me to determine; sure I am, it is sinful, when bought, to use them as bad, nay worse, than brutes; and whatever particular exceptions there may be . . . I fear, the generality of you . . . are liable to such a charge; for your slaves, I believe, work as hard if not harder than the horses whereon you ride.[17]

Horses, went on Whitefield, were at least fed after their labor, while slaves were forced to grind their own corn after a day of hard labor. He added that while dogs were "caressed and fondled" at tables, slaves were "scarce permitted to pick up crumbs which fall. . . ." Whitefield discussed accounts of punishments, of slaves having forks thrust into their flesh at the slightest provocation, and of inhuman usage by "cruel taskmasters," which at length brought death. He condemned the fact that slaves enjoyed none of the fruits of their labor while owners claimed cleared, cultivated plantations, spacious homes, and sumptuous fares.[18]

Yet worst of all, added the evangelist, "I have great reason to believe, that most of you, on purpose keep your Negroes ignorant of Christianity." Slaves were allowed to "profane the Lord's Day by their dancing, piping and such . . ." wrote Whitefield, and he added that he was familiar with the slaveholders' rationale. Many felt that Christianity would render slaves less submissive. He chided slave owners for not knowing their Bible. "Do you not read that servants, and as many as are under the yoke of bondage are required to be subject, in all lawful things to their master." One need only observe the blacks of the North to realize that Christianity would not undermine slavery.[19]

Whitefield issued a shrill warning to the slaveholders, reminding them that God would not reject the prayers of the "poor Negroes." Considering their treatment, Whitefield wondered why there had not been more instances of self-murder among them, or why uprisings were not more frequent. But the day might come:

'Go now, ye rich men, weep and howl for your miseries shall come upon you!' Behold the provision of the poor Negroes, which have reaped down your fields, which is by you denied them. 'crieth the cries of them which have come into the ears of the Lord of Sabaoth.'[20]

Slave masters' ill-use of bondspeople had long been documented by Anglican ministers in private correspondence, though never broached publically as Whitefield did. Francis Le Jau was horrified at the "unjust, profane and inhumane practices" of the planters. In 1709 he witnessed the death of a slave woman who was "barbously burned alive near my door without positive proof of the crime she was accused of." The woman professed her innocence to Le Jau "to the last." In 1712 Le Jau opposed the law that punished slaves with castration for running away. He also noted other barbarous methods of punishment. Planters put slaves in a coffin "to punish small faults" where they were almost crushed to death. For twenty-four hours slaves were chained thusly with lead "pressing upon their stomach." Le Jau commented that the "sickness and mortality" which was so high among whites at that time, was the "wrath of God" seeking retribution for the inhuman treatment of slaves. "When I look upon the ordinary cause that makes those poor souls run away, and almost despair," wrote Le Jau, "I find it immoderate labor and want of victuals and rest."[21]

One minister at Christ Church Parish, John Fulton, was continuously "harassed" by white parishoners who resented his efforts to protect the slaves. On one occasion some of Fulton's church members invaded his home with pistols, sat up all night drinking, and slept off the effects in the minister's "best beds." On another evening whites entered Fulton's home, "fired one pistol in my bed, another . . . at my Negro boy because he would not supply them with drink. . . ." Fulton had purchased a slave boy from a parishioner on a night when the man "supt" at his house, "merely to deliver him from the severe usage of his master . . . ." The minister deplored the treatment the slaves received. Some he said were whipped to death, others were branded "in sundry places with hot irons." Planters, according to Fulton, made a practice of "cutting off their ears and scarifying their faces." Fulton was accused of secretly instructing slaves at night and his church members met repeatedly to "contrive and plot" his removal, which they ultimately succeeded in accomplishing.[22]

Such were the conditions that moved George Whitefield to speak out, that led to acts of insurrection so feared by planters, and that generated instances of escape so common in the colonial era. Some parishioners were "forced to come to church with loaded guns." According to Fulton, "a great many slaves" engaged in insurrection in that parish. In the early days of the Society's presence Le Jau noted that masters could not be persuaded "that Negroes and Indians were otherwise than beasts, and use them like such." One of his female communicants inquired of him if it was really possible that any of her slaves could ever get to heaven and she have to see them there. Another young man stated that "he was resolved never to come to the holy table while slaves are received there." These attitudes were reinforced later as other Society ministers continued to privately comment on problems they faced.[23]

Whitefield's public rebuke caused bitterness between himself and many slaveholders. Response against him was vehement, although it apparently did not hurt his cause among Dissenters in Charleston, and may have convinced some Anglicans to do more toward Christianizing slaves. The summer of 1740 was a high point for the young evangelist, despite Garden's accusations that he was inciting insurrection. No matter how much the established church grumbled against him, Charleston residents thronged to hear Whitefield in August of 1740. This is all the more interesting, because he directly referred to Charleston in his "Letter" and preached that their misfortunes were visitations of retribution from God:

. . . God has already begun to visit for this as well as other wicked things. For near this two years last past, he has been in a remarkable manner, contending with the people of South Carolina. Their houses have been depopulated with the small-pox and fever, and their own slaves have rose up in arms against them.
These judgments are undoubtedly sent abroad. . . . And unless you repent, you must in all like manner expect to perish.[24]

Clearly the evangelist had hit the mark with some Carolinians, judging from his popularity after publication of his "Letter." Most of these several thousands were Dissenters but they were also slaveholders. Whitefield's message may have struck a respondent chord. Some in the Charleston community, for a time at least, attempted to rectify the spiritual distance between master and slave through support for the Negro School. Thus it must be assumed that George Whitefield had a temporary reforming effect on some slaveholders. On the other hand, there is an additional explanation.

George Whitefield was far from a prototype abolitionist. True, he attacked the abuse of slaves, he willingly preached to blacks, and he admonished slave owners for not providing religious instruction. But one year after writing his grave accusation regarding excesses of the institution of slavery, Whitefield used his influence to persuade the Georgia Trustees to permit slavery in the new colony. He insisted that Bethesda Orphanage could not function without slave labor, that Georgia would never flourish without it, and that only blacks could work in the hot, mosquito-infested regions. Furthermore, according to Whitefield, enslaving Africans was missionary work, since they would be instructed in Christianity. Moreover, ever mindful of a need to justify actions through holy writ, Whitefield maintained that slavery was consistent with the Bible, citing Abraham as a slaveholder. He had made it clear in his "Letter . . . Concerning . . . Negroes" that scriptural arguments were on the side of the masters as far as ownership of slaves was concerned, though not in the denial of Christian instruction. Surely those who listened and read carefully could find little to quarrel with as far as White-field's stand on slavery. His plea for better treatment was only "Christian duty." And, despite the flowery eloquence of 1740, Whitefield himself soon became a slaveholder, and an absentee one. By 1747, he was using profits from his South Carolina plantation, ironically called "Providence," to keep Bethesda afloat. In the accounts of Bethesda, an inventory in Whitefield's own hand thanks God for "the increase in Negroes," and further states, "I entirely approve of reducing the Orphan House as low as possible, and I am determined to take no more than the plantation will maintain until I can buy more negroes." At his death in 1770, Whitefield was a slaveholder and a buyer of slaves. He willed them, as he did his livestock, his land, and books, to Salina, the Countess of Huntingdon,[25] assumedly for the glory of God and the good of the orphanage.

It was a typical kind of clerical hypocrisy, this "straddle the fence" logic of George Whitefield's. He reasoned that importation of Africans was stamping out "heathenism":

though it is true, that they are brought in a wrong way from their country, and it is a trade not to be approved of, yet as it will be carried on whether we will or not; I should think myself highly favoured if I could purchase a good number of them, in order to make their lives comfortable, and lay a foundation for breeding up their posterity in the nurture and admonition of the Lord.[26]

No mention of the separation of kin, brutality of the trade, the unearned labor he spoke of so eloquently in his "Letter," or scriptural references that abhor slavery. It was a curious perpetuation of one kind of misery to alleviate another. It was also as logically "un-Christian" as any act committed by anyone Whitefield attacked. Planters admittedly used slaves for profit, but the sacrosanct dualism of Whitefield represents an even greater travesty because he attached to slavery the name of brotherhood and spiritual equality. One could simply explain Whitefield's activities as the workings of the eighteenth-century mind, were it not for the glaring difference between his position and that of John Wesley's. While Whitefield was justifying the institution, John Wesley spoke against its great evil. In 1743, in writing the General Rules, he prohibited "the buying or selling the bodies and souls of men, women and children, with an intention to enslave them." One Methodist went to his grave denouncing slavery. The other, equally renowned, died a slaveholder and justified the institution as a fomenter of spiritual beneficence. Viewed in light of his schizophrenic position on slavery, one can better understand the disciples of Whitefield in the Lowcountry, the Bryans and, secondarily, the Hutsons. Wealthy slaveholders and longtime residents of Beaufort with a branch later moving to Savannah, the Bryan family, under Whitefield's influence, attempted to bring Christianity to slaves in the Lowcountry when few others dared or cared to. They, along with Georgia merchant and slave trader James Habersham, also purchased Providence Plantation for Whitefield.[27]

Hugh Bryan was one of the earliest and most consistent followers of George Whitefield. His father, Joseph, migrated from England in 1680 and settled in the Sea Island region in the vicinity of Pocotaligo and Prince William Parish, where his children were born. Joseph Bryan was reportedly a successful and hospitable planter, particularly known for his long, close association with the Yemassee Indians. This fact saved the life of his son Hugh (1699–1753), who was captured by the Indians during the Yemassee War of 1715. Indeed, the entire family escaped massacre and plunder because of the elder Bryan's relationship with the Indians. Young Hugh was carried to Florida and, despite clamorings for his death, was kept safe by the king. Hugh found a Bible belonging to a massacred white family and it became his constant solace. Although he apparently suffered many hardships, Hugh was released at St. Augustine after about a year. But the experience—loneliness, fear, and suffering—undoubtedly deeply affected Bryan who was reunited with his family. Following his conversion by George Whitefield, Hugh Bryan sometimes exhibited rash, mystical, eccentric behavior which attracted the authorities and on one occasion led to his arrest and near-arrest of his spiritual mentor. Yet his conversion turned his mind toward the slaves' spiritual condition as well as his own.[28]

George Whitefield converted Hugh Bryan in 1740. Whitefield's Journal informs that in 1740 Bryan and his wife, at Whitefield's suggestion, "resolved to begin a negro school." A young actor whom Whitefield converted in New York and who went South, was to be the schoolmaster. This was apparently William Hutson. Whether Hutson was an instructor of slaves is unclear, and probably unlikely. But he did work as tutor for Bryan's children and later at Bethesda. By 1743, he was pastor of a new church, Stoney Creek, which the Bryans had joined, and he had also married a well-born slave-owning widow. The "school" Whitefield spoke of may have simply been the assembling of slaves which Bryan became known for and which got him in trouble with the authorities.[29]

Hugh Bryan, an Anglican, experienced a number of difficulties between 1740 and 1743. His close friendship with Whitefield led him to express ecclesiastical pronouncements against the Church of England and especially to undertake his work among the slaves in the Sea Island region. In a letter to the *Gazette* in 1741, Bryan predicted the doom of the province because of "the wickedness of the people and the sloth and indifference of the clergy." He went on to berate the Church for persecution of "the faithful minister [Whitefield] for not conforming exactly to their appendages of religion. . . ." Bryan was jailed for his calumnies and it was discovered that Whitefield had supervised and edited the letter. The "faithful minister" was about to sail for England but had to postpone departure, post bond, and meet court. Both Bryan and Whitefield apparently answered the charges satisfactorily and the proceedings were abandoned.[30]

Hugh Bryan, however, soon drew adverse attention of the worst kind. His work among the slaves created a stir because of charges that he prophesized the destruction of Charleston and gathered large groups of them under a pretext of religious instruction. Bryan did not admit to the charge of inciting rebellion but did confess his error in listening to a wicked voice, and asked for a pardon:

I find that I have presumed in my zeal for God's glory beyond his will, and that he has suffered me to fall into a delusion of Satan—. . . . This delusion I did not discover till three days past when, after many days' converse with an invisible spirit . . . I found my teacher to be a liar and the father of lies, which brought me to a sense of my error and has much abased my soul with bitter reflections on the dishonor I have done to God as well as the disquiet which I may have occasioned my country. . . .

Yet the "invisible spirit" was not done with Bryan. This supernatural force directed him, like Moses, to take a rod and smite the waters in order to divide them. Bryan tried this and assuming the waters would separate any time, he proceeded into the sea until he was up to his chin in water. He was rescued by his brother who had followed him and convinced him to go home.[31]

Such antics from Whitefield's most faithful Carolina disciple did little to encourage the cleric's cause among Anglicans. It did even less for religious instruction. Whatever efforts Bryan was attempting were apparently abandoned. In spite of his apology and his assurances that he was doing nothing to incite insurrection, the Assembly thought otherwise. The grand jury of the province condemned the gathering of "great bodies of Negroes . . . assembled together on pretence of religious worship." This they said was against the law and dangerous to the peace of the inhabitants. Hugh Bryan and his several associates were forbidden to assemble slaves for preaching purposes, or from "preaching to them at private houses without authority for so doing." Thus if there ever was a "school," it was quickly abandoned. Hugh Bryan apparently behaved himself following his indictment by the Assembly. For we hear nothing in the records of his attempting to disobey the ruling, although from his diary it is clear that he did not completely give up on his own slaves. Still, for the most part, Bryan seems to have settled back into the role of a comfortable, although guilt-ridden, patriarch.[32]

The Bryans soon left the Anglican fold, helping William Hutson organize the Stoney Creek Independent Church in Beaufort. The church register indicates that between 1743 and 1756 twenty-seven slaves and eight children were baptized. This is an unimpressive record and demonstrates how little progress was taking place. Yet more slaves were probably being instructed than the register suggests, and nearly all those baptized were slaves of the Bryans or Hutsons. Nevertheless, results were meager compared to the burgeoning black population in the Lowcountry. And Lewis Jones, rector of St. Helena, in Beaufort, reported to Commissary Garden that whatever objections the Church had to Whitefield, it was only through his influence that "two or three families in this Parish . . . have been lately prevailed upon to have their negroes intructed in the . . . Christian faith."[33]

Jonathan Bryan's story (1708–1788) is one of a more solid and seemingly more stable commitment to Christianizing slaves than Hugh's, at least his efforts bore more results. British-educated Jonathan was brought under Whitefield's influence around the same time as his brother. He evinced similar religious zeal but a more controlled enthusiasm. The proximity of the Bryan plantations to Georgia facilitated frequent visits to the new colony. Jonathan was active as an adviser in Georgia, was selected by founder Oglethorpe to survey roads there, and frequently went into that territory for runaway slaves. Hence Jonathan was familiar with the affairs of the new colony and joined Whitefield in advocating slavery. In fact, Jonathan loaned slaves to Georgia to help with their labor shortage. Obviously, religious enthusiasm did not interfere with a proslavery attitude. As a substantial Carolina planter, Jonathan hoped to continue increasing his holdings. But the price of land was high and for Jonathan "avenues of mobility in the Carolina social order were clogged." Thus when Georgia legalized slavery in 1751, Jonathan Bryan settled there that same year.[34]

Georgia's founding was closely tied to creating a place for the unfortunate. This, along with the religiosity expressed by the Trustees, Bray Associates, and others involved (like the Wesleys and Whitefield) in the colony, may explain the first slave code. Once slavery was established, a clause supporting religious instruction of slaves was part of the code. Masters were required to address their slaves' spiritual welfare. Slave labor on Sundays was forbidden, and owners were obliged to see that slaves be gathered "at some time on the Lord's Day for Instruction in the Christian Religion." Thus the slave code emphasized the master's Christian duty toward bondspeople. It was a policy most owners ignored on the one hand, and within five years the code was rewritten along the South Carolina model (not surprisingly, since many Carolinians and West Indians settled there), and the religious instruction provision was deleted. On the other hand, this early legal support for Christian instruction, supported by Bryan and others, probably contributed to a more liberal attitude regarding this issue in Georgia. This is most evident in events which led to the establishment of the African Baptist Church at Savannah, which was formed under the leadership and pastorship of Jonathan Bryan's slave Andrew. In South Carolina, a black man named David George probably set up the first black Baptist organization in the South, at Silver Bluff near the Savannah River, between 1773 and 1775. Yet following the disruption caused by the War for Independence and George's removal to Nova Scotia, the Silver Bluff Church found a more hospitable environment in Georgia, becoming the First African Baptist Church at Augusta (just twelve miles away).[35]

Thus by the time of the War for Independence, there were several black preachers in the Lowcountry. Their movements were proscribed, they were frequently persecuted, and their contact with slave masses was negligable. Often they preached to whites or to mixed audiences. Still, they represent the beginnings of an emerging African-Christianity. Most of them either came under the influence of George Whitefield's preaching or were converted to Christianity by those preaching a message similar to that of the enthusiastic evangelist.[36] Hence it was primarily a small acculturated group of blacks who took in the Great Awakening, while the countryside swelled with new Africans. Within this sociocultural tug-of-war, Africans and American slaves formed their communal outlook and clung to those features of life which provided a sense of identity, personhood, and autonomy.

Old Ways Die Slowly

The steady stream of Africans pouring into the Carolina Lowcountry, and the lack of a meaningful imparting of the Christian religion could not help but reinforce an African cultural and spiritual presence. In the country and island parishes especially, whites lived among a foreign-born servile labor force. Ministers were not only exasperated by the resistance of planters to having their slaves converted, but even more frustrated by the problem of communicating with Africans. First was the challenge of language. "Those brought up among us," wrote one early Society missionary, "are both civilized and speak good English . . . whereas those that are brought hither from their own country, except a few that come very young, seldom or never speak good English."[37]

African slaves lived, worked, and socialized among each other. Their lack of exposure to English and concentration on developing a mode of communication among themselves undoubtedly slowed the process of learning a totally foreign tongue. Gullah language was being created during the colonial decades and the lengthy period of African slave trading. This was also happening elsewhere, such as in the Savannah region, where Africans imported mainly through Charleston were laboring in the country and island reaches of Georgia. As long as Africans remained isolated and their numbers greatly reinforced, language was a problem. Bray Associate missionary Joseph Ottolenghe (an Italian Jew converted to Christianity), provides some insight into the problems and difficulties encountered in the seacoast region. In a letter to the Associates, he reminded them of the impediments faced by "primitive Christians" in olden times, but added that they faced no "Hindrancies, & great Difficulties" which compared to the instruction of African slaves:

The formers understood ye language of ye instructos, & if not persons were appointed skill'd in ye language of ye novices, whereas our Negroes are so ignorant of ye English Language, and none can be found to talk in their own, yt it is a great while before you can get them to understand what ye meaning of words is & yt without such knowledge instruction's would prove vain & ye ends pr[o]posed abortive, for how can a proposition be believed, without first being understood? & how can it be understood if ye person whom it is offered has no idea even of ye sound of those words which expresses ye proposition? [38]

Ottolenghe, himself a slaveholder, cited as an example a young couple he had purchased four years previously. According to the missionary, he had instructed the pair diligently and forbade their association with any slaves except those at his "Negro school." Despite his "pains in their education," they were in his words, "in point of learning very slow and difficient." He could never send them on an errand successfully unless his wishes were put in writing. [39]

The creation of a medium of communication within the black community undoubtedly engaged older as well as newer inhabitants. As a result, elements of several ethnic language families seem evident. Additionally, similarities of Gullah to Jamaican dialect and the dialect spoken by Bush African-Americans in Suriname imply a certain commonality in black pidgin languages formed by isolated societies from similar African roots. No one can say for sure when Gullah began to crystallize into a common method of communication among the majority of slaves. Nor can it be denied that influence from non-African sources helped create Gullah. Yet formulation of the dialect itself was a unique communical experience. Shaping a language reinforced social cohesion and community. With the large influx of Africans coming in during the middle period of the slave trade, quite possibly the dialect took permanent root during that time, drawing, of course from groups of blacks already in the region and already adapting to white culture. The following is an example of Gullah-Jamaican dialect, taken down in the late eighteenth or early nineteenth century, and perhaps one of the earliest efforts to formulate the pidgin into a literal, written form of communication:

BUDDY QUOW	A Key to Buddy Quow
Was matter Buddy Quow?	What is the matter Brother Quow?
I ble Obesha bang you,	I believe the overseer has beaten you,
You tan no sabby how,	You look I don't know how,
Dah Backrow Man go wrong you,	That White Man has wronged you,
Buddy Quow,	Brother Quow,
Dah Backrow &	That White Man &

2

No hawte bun morrowgo,

Nusso grandy hungry do you,
I hab some Barbaracco,
I bring dem all for you morrowgo

I bring dem all &

Don't let your heart be troubled
Country Man,
Nor great hunger distress you,
I have some Barbaracco's*
I will bring them all for you Country
Man.

I will bring &

*Horse Beans

3

No hungry nor so dry
For true now no me yerry
Make vawter for me yie
I cry so, tell me vary vipe me yie

I cry so tell &

I am not hungry nor dry,
Indeed now only hear me,
It makes my eyes water,
I have cried so, until I am tired wiping my eyes.

I have cried so &

. . .

. . .

5

Dah time Quasheba tell,
De Pickney he bin coming
I gow go for to sell

De hog me mommo gibe me, berry well

Dah hog &

When Quasheba said,
She was with child,
I went immediately and sold very well,
The hog my mother gave me.

The hog &

6

Von coat I buy um new,
Von ropper I bin bring come
Von new hankisha too
I nebo bin go tink um nusso true.

I nebo bin &

I bought a new coat,
A wrapper I bought also,
And a new handkerchief too,
I thought of nothing but that it was true.

I thought &

7

When Unco Quaco say,
De Pickney he was come now,
I no go morrow stay
My harete bin knock pum pum on true grangie

My harete &

When Uncle Quaco said,
The child was just born,
I did not stay till the morrow,
My heart beat pum, pum for great joy.

My heart &

8

Gor Mighty da nah Buf
See how Quasheba do me
Dah Backrow Man he luf
He bring molatto for me Gor nah Buf

He bring &

God Almighty above!
See how Quasheba has used me!
She loved the White Man,
And has brought a Mulatto for me,
God above!

And has brought &

9

He yie, he nose, he mout,	Its eyes, its nose, its mouth,
(I bin good mine for hit um)	(I had a great inclination to strike it.)
Tun ebery mossel bout	Take every part of it together,
Lak Obesha bin pit um out he mout.	'Tis as if the overseer had spit it out
	of his mouth.

Lak Obesha &   'Tis as if &

The poem, "Buddy Quow," is a fascinating example of Gullah-Jamaican dialect and demonstrates the contribution of various ethnic groups in the formation of pidgin. The names Quow, Quasheba, and Quaco are derived from the Tshi language (Ashanti and Fanti), Africans of the Gold Coast region. Gold Coast Africans, as noted previously, were the first black Carolinians. They were not imported in as large numbers as other groups, but were preferred by South Carolinians, and represent a continuous contribution throughout much of the slave-trade era. Hence their early presence and reinforcement made a strong base. The word "pickney" is derived from the Portuguese and Spanish "pequeno nino" (small child), and barbaracco means horse bean in both languages. This may be a Kongo-Angolan influence since Portuguese ports were in Kongo-Angola and many Africans from that region were imported to South Carolina. The masculine pronoun used to refer to both genders may indicate Upper Guinea influence, where such usage was common among Africans learning English on their native coasts from Methodist missionaries or traders, as previously discussed. Since Gullah is a spoken rather than written dialect, the interpreter of the poem may have lost some of the meaning. Yet most of the interpretations correspond to what is known of Gullah dialect and offer a sense of what Gullah was like when it was a true dialect. Writers who believe that there is no sharp break between Gullah and general black vernacular may not fully consider the historical Gullahs and their creative means of communication in an isolated setting. While there are obvious similarities between twentieth-century black vernacular and Gullah as recorded in the twentieth century, the geographical isolation in which Gullah was originally created points to a dialect peculiar to the Sea Island region, where Africans made their own language adjustments with minimal acculturative influences.[40] In any case, the adoption of a means of communication common to all the slaves in the area was a significant community-building mechanism, and previous African language orientations played an important role.

In addition to a language barrier, ministers realized that the black population had their own spiritual and religious orientation, and clergymen were cognizant of the conditions that kept Africanity from being challenged by white culture. Adaptations being made in the slave quarters during the colonial era were different from those of the antebellum period. Early adjustments and acculturation were taking place more from within than without. African ethnic groups were adapting to each other's manners, mores, and beliefs, in a sense creating several dominant cultural groupings out of many, and retaining the most useful, modifiable, and tenacious elements of Old World tradition. As far as religion was concerned, some of the oldest and most common traditions, as previously discussed, can probably be termed universal among human cultures. Others seem peculiar to societies where interdependency is more directly related to collective survival.[41] Those engaged in religious instruction knew how deeply embedded the seeds of traditionalism were among African slaves. Missionaries maintained that the slaves' old habits and customs died slowly. But white disdain for African religion prevented missionaries from making pointed references to actual practices unless these were reminiscent of Christianity. All that was not Christian was "heathen." A Christ Church minister in 1723 found all parish slaves "still confined to heathenism." In 1740, Alexander Garden lamented the same state of affairs in his plea for more tolerance from the planters, and more effort toward educating the young rather than reeducating adults. But growth and maturation of the colonial economy further cloistered the slaves, leaving them to their own spiritual devices and allowing them to continue to be "nursed in extravagant idolatry." Nevertheless, beliefs and practices that remained past the Christian indoctrination of the antebellum period provide clues of what transpired earlier in the religious consciousness of New Africans. From neighboring Savannah, Ottolenghe succinctly expressed the missionary attitude, leaving an impression of ineffectiveness when Christianity competed with Africanity:

. . . slavery is certainly a great depression of the mind which retards some of their learning a new religion, proposed to them in a new and unknown language, besides the old superstitions of a false religion to be combatted . . . and nothing is harder to be removed (you know) than prejudices of education, riveted by time and entrenched in deep ignorance, which must be overcome by slow advances with all the patience and engaging means . . . to make them fall in love with the very best of religions and so to captivate their minds as to give all their very little leisure to the study of it.[42]

Ottolenghe's statement probably represents more wishful thinking than reality. Most Africans no more welcomed the colonial missionary than they did their masters, albeit for different reasons. There were few immediate redeeming qualities in the new religion that warranted acceptance. Ministers actually offered further bondage of a different type. While there was apprehension among planters about baptism conferring freedom, clergymen were quick to disclaim such intent. In 1710 Robert Maule wrote from Goose Creek that he "frequently made it my business . . . to represent the groundlessness of such an opinion." As far as the Society was concerned "baptism makes no great alteration as to outward circumstances of . . . slaves in this world." For people still close to traditions that espoused the significance of the "here and now," the ministers' reasoning must have sounded strange and shallow. Francis Le Jau made slaves swear to a declaration before being baptized:

"You declare in the presence of God and before this congregation that you do not ask for the holy baptism out of design to free yourself from the duty and obedience you owe to your master while you live, but meekly for the good of our soul. . . ."[43]

Thus most slaves saw Christianity as representing obedience, duty to slavemasters, and a further tightening of the screws of the bondage system. If this were not enough to discourage interest in Christianity, ministers also insisted that slaves give up Sunday afternoon merrymaking in exchange for religious instruction. "It has been customary among them to have their feasts, dances and merry meetings upon the Lord's Day," wrote Le Jau from Goose Creek.[44]

Such feasts and forms of merriment probably had as much spiritual content as the ministers' Sunday sermons. Festivals, feasts, and ceremonies were generally associated with some sacred or spiritual observances among Africans. What missionaries deemed mere merrymaking was probably naming celebrations, forms of fellowship with ancestors and spirits, or even semblances of initiation commemoration. George Whitefield may have recognized something outside of his own spiritual cognizance when he secretly observed South Carolina slaves on his overland journey. It was a totally foreign and frightening situation for the young evangelist, never known for his physical courage. His experiences may have inspired his letter to slaveholders in which he spoke of the slaves' "paganism" and appealed for religious instruction.

The occasion was January 1740, on a night of the moon eclipse. Whitefield and his small group missed their path along the seacoast road. The weary travelers saw a light in the forest. Two from the party went to investigate and "found a hut full of Negroes," who appeared surprised at the sight of the whites. The visitors inquired after the planter whose home they sought but the blacks were no help, insisting they were "newcomers." The travelers became fearful and inferred that the blacks "were some of those who lately made an insurrection . . . and had runaway from their masters." Whitefield and his friends "thought it best to mend our pace." But apprehensions had no sooner subsided when the galloping group encountered another eery scene:

We saw another great fire near the roadside, and imagining there was another nest of such Negroes, we made a circuit into the woods, and one of my friends at a distance observed them dancing round the fire. The moon shining brightly, we soon found our way into the great road again; and after we had gone about a dozen miles (expecting to find Negroes in every place), we came to a great plantation, the master of which gave us lodging, and our beasts provender. Upon our relating the circumstances of our travels, he . . . informed us whose they were, and upon what occasion they were in those places. . . . This afforded us much comfort, after we had ridden nearly threescore miles, and, as we thought, in great peril of our lives. Blessed be Thy Name, O Lord, for this, and all other Thy mercies, through Jesus Christ![45]

The event affected Whitefield deeply, seeing the primitive scene of blacks dancing around a huge fire. It undoubtedly conjured up all sorts of images in the mind of the evangelist—images of black rebellion, "black paganism" and even white oppression. That same month he wrote his letter to slaveholders, and his observances on that moon-eclipsed night represented only a small portion of what he witnessed about slavery.

But it was difficult to convince slaves to relinquish their festive observances, practiced only on Sundays or when away from the immediate auspices of white power. Sunday was the only day slaves could engage in activities unrelated to laboring for whites. Attempts to strip them of this small means of cultural independence must have appeared to be the height of folly. Six days a week slaves labored in the white man's fields, on his wharves, in his home, in his forests, and in his businesses. And on the seventh day, for some if not all slaves, a day of "rest," they were implored to worship the white man's god, the same God whom Africans were told decreed their foreign bondage. Furthermore, even planters used

Sunday as a day of pleasure. Certainly, it was difficult to convince slaves that they should be more exemplary than their masters. These early Carolinians were described as a boisterous lot, frequently engaging in "cursing, swearing, drinking and gaming and barbarous misuse of their Negroes." For ministers and missionaries then, there was the double obstacle of combatting "the strong prejudices" of Africans "grown in years," and "the backwardness of masters."[46]

Not all masters were "backward." Some, such as Hugh Bryan, were atypical in that instead of depriving slaves of Christianity, it was sometimes forced upon them. Bryan was accused of inciting the St. Helena slaves to revolt in 1741, when he was probably just attempting to provide religious instruction. His utterances may have generated some discontent among the slaves since he counseled in words similar to those used by Whitefield in his letter to slaveholders. But Whitefield was speaking to masters not to slaves. As ill-advised and eccentric as Hugh Bryan's statements may have been, he was a planter, and as his letter of apology reaffirmed, was in sympathy with the planter cause. He soon settled down to a less public life. But his diary and letters indicate that the spiritual welfare of his slaves was a continual concern. Still, he seems to have been no more successful in creating a change of heart among his bondspeople than he was in mastering his own sense of sin and guilt. Some slaves were baptized and admitted into the Stoney Creek Church, as demonstrated by the church register. Their numbers were small, probably household servants. And, slaves were listed only for baptism, while the baptism, marriage, and burial of whites was recorded.[47]

Of course, church lists do not tell the whole story. And while few slaves cared to convince the Stoney Creek white membership that they had a "true experience," some probably had to listen to sermons and instruction in their "duty." Certainly Bryan's slaves were rarely deleted from his fervent prayers. He found them inattentive and continued to pray for them. "My servants were called to prayers, but none came," he wrote on one occasion. On another he wrote of it being "a time of trial and uneasiness from the disobedience of servants. . . ." Thus the slaves heard but did not listen and Bryan's frustrations for his soul and theirs seemed to weigh heavy on his heart.[48]

It was a strange relationship between master and slaves. Bryan seemed sincere although his own spiritual enthusiasm was often mixed with periods of gay indulgence and the conviviality so common among individuals of his stature. This inconsistency may have been noticed by his slaves. But more significantly, his dualism was evident in the fact that he believed in bondage and protected the institution. He was prominent in the Sea Island community and had an economic stake in slavery. While he preached to his slaves he apprehended runaways. Thus Bryan, while he prevailed upon the Lord, "for my poor servants, that they might be delivered from the power of the devil," he also hired people to help him search for slaves who deserted his plantations for freedom in St. Augustine, and was reimbursed by the authorities for his expenses. Regardless of his individual sincerity, Bryan's bondspeople might have believed a contradiction existed between what was preached and what was practiced.[49]

Certainly George Whitefield's attempt to reach blacks had some effect. His influence not only disseminated Christianity to slaves via white emissaries such as the Bryans and Hutsons, but was carried by some black believers as well. Whitefield's impassioned sermons moved many blacks in the Northern cities and he cites cases of the "poor Negroes" in the Southern districts being moved to tears. What these tears represent is entirely open to question as far as most slaves' understanding is concerned. But in some instances of conversion, the evangelist definitely made a mark. Such was the experience of John Marrant, who left a vivid account of his meeting with Whitefield.[50]

John Marrant was apparently born free, in New York in 1755. He moved to Georgia with his mother, brother, and sisters (his father having died when Marrant was four) and in the South his mother sought an apprenticeship for him. Marrant loved music and persuaded his mother to apprentice him to a music school in Charleston. By the age of thirteen, he had quickly mastered the violin and French horn. Such talents in the gay city made Marrant "much respected by the gentlemen and ladies whose children attended the school, and also my master." As a musician young Marrant was exposed to all the "vanity and vice of the city." He frequented balls and parties, meeting with "general applause" wherever he went. He grew accustomed to staying up all night, was "a stranger to want," and was "devoted to pleasure and drinking in iniquity like water."[51]

This life of debauchery continued as Marrant's year-and-a-half apprenticeship drew to a close. But before his service was complete, Marrant experienced his "awakening." On his way to play for an occasion, he and a companion passed a meetinghouse. His companion explained that "a crazy man was hallooing there." His curiosity aroused, Marrant went in to hear what the man was "hallooing about." His companion, apparently white, suggested that Marrant "Blow the French horn among them," and vowed to defend him if the crowd tried to beat him for disturbing the meeting. Marrant pushed through the crowded room, took his French horn from his shoulder, and prepared to blow:

just as Mr. Whitefield was naming his text, and looking round, and as I thought, directly upon me, and pointing his finger, he uttered these words, "Prepare to meet thy God, O' Israel." The Lord accompanied the word with such power that I was struck to the ground, and lay both speechless and senseless near half-an hour.[52]

Marrant awoke to find himself attended by two men throwing water on his face and a woman applying salt to his nose. As he recovered and recalled the nature of his condition he was once again thrust into a sense of affliction. "I thought I saw the devil on every side of me," he wrote, and he began to "halloo" in the midst of the congregation. His disturbances caused him to be carried away for he "could neither walk nor stand."[53]

Upon completion of his sermon, Whitefield went to the boy, and "being told of my condition, . . . the first word he said to me was. 'JESUS CHRIST HAS GOT THEE AT LAST.' " Whitefield talked with him, put him under the care of the Baptist minister, the Reverend Hall, and took his leave. Still unable to walk Marrant was carried home where his "distressed" sister got medical help. But to no avail. According to Marrant, his "wounded spirit," not his body, was in need of help. Marrant could neither eat, drink (except sips of water), walk, or stand for three days. The Baptist minister called on him and prayed with Marrant until finally he was made "happy" in conversion and lost his physical impediments.[54]

It was a deeply moving experience for the boy of fourteen, and throughout his many trials and "backslidings," Marrant's conversion always returned him to the fold of Christianity. His change of heart prompted a piety which caused him to leave the service of the music master and to begin reading the scriptures. This made him a laughing stock in his sister's home and in the neighborhood. He was considered "crazy and mad." Under such persecution, he resolved to return to his mother in Georgia.[55]

Marrant was at first well received at his mother's home. But soon persecutions began anew. The youth was pained because no one in his family cared the slightest for religion, and did not even wish to say grace at mealtime. When his mother also grew impatient with him, the disheartened boy left home and headed into the Georgia wilderness. His trials with the Indians are another story. But his life was spared, for he successfully converted his "executioner," converted the king's daughter and "cured" her of an illness. Marrant remained with the Indians for nearly two years, eventually returning to his family. He served with the British navy during the War for Independence and even saw his old Cherokee benefactor, who marched along with General Clinton in the seige of Charleston. The two friends greeted each other warmly and conversed, but Marrant was shipped out the next day. John Marrant eventually went to England, became a minister, was patronized by another Whitefield convert, the Countess of Huntingdon, and eventually went to Sierra Leone as a colonist.[56]

Marrant represents one type of black convert who came under the suasion of Whitefield's evangelical preaching. He was literate, urbane, free-born and far removed from the rural, isolated experiences of the majority of African-Americans. He was also "awakened" at a young, impressionable age. Marrant's high living and Dionysian activities may have created an unconscious sense of guilt which the magnetic presence of Whitefield brought to the surface. Marrant's belief that Whitefield was looking directly at him as he announced his text was perhaps also a function of the boy's feelings of guilt. But the evangelist reportedly possessed an enrapturing sense of presence, thundering voice, and extemporaneous preaching style that swayed audiences. He also had a manner of looking around the crowd with his intense blue eyes. Add to all of this the fact that one of Whitefield's eyes was permanently misfocused (or crossed actually), and it presents a rather formidable picture. Eyewitnesses stated that instead of a distraction the misfocused "squinting" eye was an attraction.[57] It is possible then, that Whitefield was looking elsewhere when he appeared to have fastened his eyes on young Marrant. But of course, a black youth at the meetinghouse with a French horn, preparing to "blow," was not exactly an inconspicuous sight. The seasoned evangelist had had enough disruptions of sermons to spot troublemakers, and knew how to unnerve them, expecially one so young and vulnerable.

John Marrant apparently did not hear Whitefield's sermon, and after that 1769 encounter they never met again. Yet it was the Methodist's message which won over black converts like Marrant. Whitefield was not a theologian in a strict sense—although he did produce a theology of sorts. Indeed he spoke against the clergy's erudite learnedness. Rather than a teacher, he was a preacher, and saw his role in a prophetic sense. He shunned speculative theology and organized religion. His authority was the Bible, at least certain doctrines from it. But he rarely preached from the Bible. His message was simple: all humankind is guilty of sin and must ask forgiveness, immortality comes through regeneration and rebirth through Jesus Christ. Inherent in his sermons, which probably appealed to blacks, was his stress on the mercy and love of Jesus Christ and his emphatic renditions of the benefits of divine grace. His insistence that God "was no respector of persons" found attentive ears. Whitefield's traveling companion, William Seward, noted the numerous occasions in the North when blacks became "greatly affected" by the evangelist's sermons, "especially when our brother invited the poor Negroes to touch Christ by faith, whereby they would gain freedom from the slavery of sin and satan." Whitefield's insistence that "God intends salvation for Negroes" probably struck a responsive chord for some acculturated blacks, both slave and free.[58] His message was one of offering blacks incorporation into the Christian spiritual family, of providing them with a spiritual identity. For a group defined out of American social institutions and laboring under restrictions of racism, it was a comforting, appealing overture.

The directness of Whitefield's vision of rebirth and his invitation for blacks to expunge the "devil" from within was one manner of appeal. He often began his sermons with a rendition of his own conversion. Additionally, his sense of caring, his abortive efforts to begin a "Negro school" in the North, and his attack on the treatment of slaves also indicated that the evangelist was at least an ally. While cultural and spiritual differences prevented others from addressing blacks, Whitefield's people's religion emphasized commonality. His capacity to simplify "divine truth" and present biblical narratives and the Gospel message in clear, vivid fashions gained him a black audience. The following excerpt summarizes his message and method when addressing black people. In this case it is the slaves of the Jonathan Bryan household:

Welcome to Christ's fold . . . This is a mystery . . . for unsearchable grace . . . would Jesus Christ take you . . . even you dispised Negroes and join you in one fold with is people? Oh what manner of grace is this? Would he lift you . . . from the dust, you beggars from the Dunghill, from the depths of vile slavery . . . to set you among princes, the princes of his people and to make you inherit the Throne of Glory?[59]

His words are full of condescension to be sure. Yet it is also an exalted message indicating equality in spirituality. Many blacks, especially slaves, probably understood little of what Whitefield said but *felt* what they thought he meant deeply. Some, as evidenced by the Marrant family, heard him and ignored him. The majority never saw or heard Whitefield at all. But those who did and believed took the message, in their own way, back to the slaves, altered it, and even practiced it under another denomination. Additionally, the disciples of the evangelist kept his message alive among a few favored slaves. Hence arose the early religious slave gatherings at Silver Bluff, South Carolina, around 1773, and the beginnings of a black church at Savannah under British occupation during the War of Independence. Additionally, John Wesley sent his first two itinerants to the American Colonies in 1764 with a doctrine not only of spiritual egalitarianism (minus the Calvinist predestination of Whitefield), but of antislavery convictions as well. Yet in the slaveholding Lowcountry, as probably elsewhere, planters who allowed religious instruction distorted Christianity. Slaves who accepted the religion as taught by slaveholders ostensibly accepted a servile position in the spiritual world as they were forced to in the temporal realm. The "very short summary of religion" which the "best" slaveholders espoused emphasized obedience. Slaves were instructed that:

There is one God in heaven who never dies, and who sees and knows everything. That he punishes all roguery, mischief, lying, either before death or after it. That he punishes them for it before they die, by putting it into their masters' hearts to correct them, and after dying by giving them to the devil to burn in his own place. That he will put it into their masters' hearts to be kind to those who do their work without knavery or murmuring. To take care of them in old age and sickness, and not to plague them with too much work, or to chastise them if they are not able to do it. That in the after world, after they die, he will give all good Negroes, rest from all labour, and plenty of all good things.[60]

Thus the period of the Great Awakening can be viewed as seedtime for planting Christianity in the Lowcountry. Whitefield's journeys there continued until his death, and left an impact on the spiritual consciousness of some acculturated slaves. Also, Commissary Garden's Charleston Negro School may have had some influence, although it seems negligible. Finally, the Bray Associates made yet another early attempt at

Christian instruction, leaving a record of trying experiences and impediments. The germination process was slow and uneven. Black acceptance and understanding, the hostility of the master class, and the paucity of missionaries devoted to the enterprise were the major reasons for hindrance. Also, the Great Awakening came on the heels of economic possibilities that could only be realized through exploitation of a massive labor force. Immediately after the 1739 Stono uprising, few Africans came into Charleston because of a prohibitive import duty. Between 1740 and 1750 less than 1,900 slaves arrived. However, after this ten-year moratorium the trade was on an upswing, halted only (temporarily) by the War for Independence. Furthermore black population in the Lowcountry south of Charleston increased most rapidly, a trend which continued through the period of the slave trade.[61]

Georgia's slave population was at first bought in small groups. By 1760, ten years after the trade was legalized, Georgia merchants began importing directly from Africa while continuing to purchase from Charleston. It is ironic that the major supporters of religious instruction in the seacoast region of Georgia were not only large planters but slave merchants.[62] Yet the fact remains that many owners offered no version of Christianity. Many slaves concerned themselves with creating a communal environment within bondage, seeking ways to assert their autonomy. Others sought autonomy by fleeing bondage altogether. For a number of slaves, the agitation among white colonials for independence, the resulting war, and subsequent period of adjustment provided opportunities for liberation.

PART III

Christianity and Autonomy: A Struggle in Black and White

CHAPTER 5

An Almost Chosen People

"How is it," asked Samuel Johnson, "that we hear the loudest *yelps* for liberty among the drivers of negroes?"*

Mingo said *that all those belonging to the African Church are engaged in the insurrection, from the country to the town—that there is a little man among them who can't be shot, killed, or caught, who was to be their general, and who would provide them with arms—that some arms were provided but he did not tell me where they were.***

Rebels and Outlaws: White Independence, Black Liberation

On November 9, 1861, a Massachusetts man, S. M. Weld, was going through "old pamphlets and newspapers" in the garrett of Baptist planter William Pope's deserted house at Hilton Head Island. It was two days after the battle of Port Royal. The papers Weld found had apparently been "thrown out and forgotten by the owner," who like every other white Sea Islander, had fled to the mainland at the thundering sound of Yankee gunboats. Among the pamphlets found was one entitled "Official Report of the Trials of Sundry Negroes Charged with an Attempt to Raise An Insurrection in the State of South Carolina." Weld observed that the pamphlet was rare, since every effort was made to destroy all

---

*Quoted from Ira Berlin, "The Revolution in Black Life," in Alfred F. Young, ed., *The American Revolution: Explorations in the History of American Radicalism* (DeKalb: Northern Illinois University Press, 1976), 35.

**Testimony of slave informant Willian, in Lionel Kennedy and Thomas Parker, *The Trial Record of Denmark Vesey*, Intro. by John Oliver Killens (Boston: Beacon Press, 1970; repr. from 1822 ed., and published under title: *An official report of the trials of sundry Negroes*), 85–86.

copies soon after they were published because the contents were thought "dangerous for the slaves to see."[1]

Yet William Pope saw fit to keep the document and no doubt spent many hours pondering the intended rebellion. The title of the pamphlet reveals the prevailing attitude about the magnitude of the insurrection. Many believed it extended as far north as Georgetown and the Santee, and as far south as the Euhaws and Sea Islands. Some testimony indicated that the insurrection was even known of in Columbia. Certainly Pope, like the majority of slaveholders, had total confidence in the trial procedure, the validity of the document, and in the verdict that a large-scale, well-planned insurrection was barely averted. At the time Pope also shared the planters' conviction that teaching Christianity to the masses of slaves was tantamount to breeding insurrectionists. The slave insurrection which centered in Charleston in 1822 was spawned in the all-black class meetings of the African Methodist Episcopal Church. On a national level the incident, known as the "Denmark Vesey Conspiracy," gripped the religious sector, antislavery advocates, and proslavery elements, each group believing that events supported their respective philosophy of right. In South Carolina however, and especially in the Low-country, the attempted insurrection was viewed in more immediate terms. The safety of the white population, outnumbered eight to one by the black laboring class, was considered to be in great jeopardy. An examination and analysis of the intended insurrection provides significant evidence about the way in which some slaves put Christianity to use, about the African religious influence in the Christian church, and the effort of whites to permanently trample the seeds of nationalism, unity, and resistance in black South Carolina.[2]

No one who carefully examines existing sources can maintain that a spirit of rebellion and strong will to freedom was not prevalent among South Carolina slaves. As far back as the record goes evidence reflects this resistance on a number of levels. In 1720 a group of slaves in Charleston rose up and attacked whites in their homes and in the streets, killing a white man, a white woman, and, inadvertently, a small black child. Of those apprehended, six were convicted but three of them escaped. In 1730 South Carolina slaves again attempted an insurrection and were reportedly well armed. Each slave was to murder his master during the night and, after assembling for a victory dance, rush into Charleston and kill every white they met. The year 1739 was especially momentous. The uprising at Stono, discussed by Peter Wood and Vincent Harding, epitomized the spirit of rebellion among African-born slaves. For eighteenth-century bondspeople the price of freedom and rebellion was frequently death, and invariably repression and terrorism. In 1740 the Negro Act, a direct result of the Stono uprising, restricted activity and mobility in various ways. Additionally, indiscriminate, sporadic, knee-jerk acts of violence against the general black population were designed to instill fear and cowering among those bold enough even to contemplate a means of freedom. Moreover, an internal check on the slaves was devised by instituting a bounty system among their own race. Those who divulged any insurrection plot were amply rewarded with a full purse and freedom papers. These measures periodically kept the lid on collective resistance until the time around the American War for Independence. Still, individual and small group acts of freedom continued throughout. A major manifestation of this was flight, and Carolina newspapers are replete with examples. More often than not, individual fleeing slaves were African-born. Philip Morgan writes that while South Carolina's eighteenth-century slave population was less than half that of Virginia's, the most populous American colony, the former's runaway population was four times as large, if newspaper advertisements alone are measured. Morgan maintains that not all runaways are rebels. Still, flight is an act of resistance, and even newspaper notices, according to Morgan, represent "only the most visible tip of an otherwise indeterminate iceberg."[3]

Runaway activity increased after the reopening of the trade in 1750 as Africans poured into the colony. Advertisements reveal a slave society as tumultuous as it was economically prosperous. Slaves fled individually and together. While recently imported Africans may have had little if any idea of where they were headed geographically, other more seasoned slaves did. Many from both groups managed to remain undetected for months. In April 1759, an African woman called "Statira" had "lost herself." She could not speak "one word of English," nor "even tell her own name." Yet she was still at large in September. She was of the "Gola Coast Country" and had tribal markings upon her temples. A Gambia slave who fled his master in July 1751 was still at large in October. Sometimes masters did not even get slaves broken in before they absconded. One slave brought to the work house at Charleston, spoke "bad English," and could not say who his master was. Yet he was able to convey to the other incarcerated slaves that he was among nine "new negro men and 1 woman," whom a white had purchased, "most of which ran away."[4]

No clear line of demarcation existed between American and African-born slaves when it came to acts of escape on a group level. While more native Africans fled than African-Americans, in collective situations they frequently ran together, as the following advertisement from a September issue of the *Gazette* illustrates:

> Run Away from the subscriber on St. Helena Island on the 11th of July last a negro fellow named Mingo, about 40 years old, and his wife Quante, a sensible wench about 20 with her child a boy about 3 years old, all this country born: Also Cudjo a sensible Coromantee Negro fellow about 45 years old, stutters and his wife Dinah, an Ebo wench that speaks very good English with her two-children a boy about 8 years and a girl about 18 months. Whoever takes up and delivers them to me or to the work house in Charles Town, shall have £10 Reward. Besides reasonable charges.

This group of slaves had also remained undetected for several months. By the time the advertisement was placed they could have been well out of the colony, given St. Helena's proximity to Spanish and Seminole Indian territory, or have joined one of the runaway camps that dotted the South Carolina frontier. Indeed, maroon settlements were one safety valve that provided an alternative to insurrection. The existence of these settlements represents an example of organized rebellious activity in the generation between the Stono uprising and the War for Independence.[5] The first two runaways mentioned, though American-born, had African given names. Forebears with strong ties to Africa had left a legacy of resistance along with the Old World naming. The fact that this was a mixed group of African and country-born slaves expresses the camaraderie that could be forged by oppression and kinship.

Another apparently country-born group of accultured slaves made their escape from Purrysburg in the Sea Island region. Two men and a woman with two small children escaped in "a boat with four oars" from their master's plantation. He offered £5 sterling as reward for their return and informed the public that they not only spoke good English but also French and German. These slaves probably made their way to the Savannah River and into Spanish and Indian territory. That was certainly the avowed intention in another case in which a Beaufort slave was "gibbetted" for the murder of one Charles Purry. In his death agony the slave confessed to the murder and disclosed that he and eight others had planned to murder two more whites as well but were prevented by the immediate discovery of Purry's body. The slaves intended to steal a boat and make their way to St. Augustine. The proximity of the Sea Islands to St. Augustine caused planters much anguish. Various methods were used to deter slaves from fleeing to this Spanish settlement. Hugh Bryan spent much time and energy in efforts to locate runaways heading south. Entries in the *Commons Journal* reveal that in some instances white servants joined black slaves in flight and in taking even more aggressive measures. The Bryans, other planters, and hired individuals pursued, apparently unsuccessfully, a white servant and several slaves who, prior to making their escape, killed one white.[6] Thus the common oppression experienced by blacks and whites (probably Indians also) sometimes led to unified acts of resistance.

Slaves who ran away in groups of various sorts, as Michael Johnson has noted, typified the collective resistance spirit and kinship attachment present among rural and urban Africans and African-Americans. But at times the spirit of disenchantment assumed more dramatic and telling proportions. The Sea Island bondspeople, black and white, who engaged in the above plots were not satisfied with absconding which they might have accomplished undetected. Instead, they chose to strike out in a far more violent manner. Nor was the slaves' sense of wrong always eased by mere absence from the masters' plantations. At times a more exacting retribution was resorted to. Some slaves became highwaymen, robbing and plundering the white countryside until they were apprehended or killed. In 1759 an escaped slave thusly engaged was finally captured. During the night he managed to free himself, and with an axe the slave killed the white who had apprehended him, the man's wife, and one of his children. The slave remained free for a month, and on his continued rampage through the countryside killed another white man and his two children. The fugitive was finally caught in Charleston, convicted, and "hung in chains" at the city dividing path for all the population to view.[7] Thus eighteenth-century slave society was far from tranquil. What has often been represented as "planter paranoia" was actually recognition that the black population was unsubmissive, resistant, and, in many cases, very much on the move. Most of the rebelliousness was not collectively organized or planned, yet that is not surprising. Africans and African-Americans were not yet a homogeneous group, often did not speak the same language, and sometimes could not even trust each other. Additionally, in a foreign country it was difficult at best to organize movements that would lead to specific goals other than immediate freedom. Still, liberty itself was a determined end.

Yet the absence of notable collective resistance activity seemed to precipitate laxness in law enforcement in small quarters. Repression, severity, high mortality, and overwork was the fate of slaves inhabiting the rice and indigo regions in the last half of the century. But the continued importation of foreign-born Africans engaged in the drudgery of plantation work helped to create mobility for acculturated, urban slaves on whom masters depended for their personal and leisurely inclinations. In the urban ambiance, the slave code of 1740 sometimes faded in memory along with the rebellion that precipitated it. This was especially the case as turmoil leading to rebellion against England increased. White South Carolinians, concerned with the jeopardy of their own political independence and becoming more at ease with an urban acculturated black population, allowed some practices to exist unmolested that were illegal by statute. Slaves in and near Charleston were known to gather in large numbers without white supervision for festivity, frolic, and perhaps more sober business. In 1772 a "stranger" to South Carolina engaged in a series of editorials printed in the *Gazette* regarding the "deluge of enormous vices" that prevailed among the slaves. According to the stranger, laws passed by the colony were "treated with contempt." One of the most important features of the 1740 Act was the provision that no slave be outside plantation or town limits without a ticket on pain of twenty lashes. Yet the writer maintained that fugitive slaves freely walked the roads, engaged in "theft and robbery," and were harbored in the city. Additionally, the stranger observed that on any given weekend, before sunset on Saturday until two hours before sunrise on Sundays, the numbers of slaves passing on the main road was "never less than four hundred but often exceeds seven." Yet, insisted the alarmed citizen, "one rarely met with more than 40 or 50 tickets or letters in the hands of the country Negroes and never more than four or five such licenses amongst those that belong to the Town." Any white man who questioned one of these slaves was either ignored or answered with an impudent, "I belong to my master!" which ended the conversation. Furthermore, it was noted that the slaves carried heavy hickory sticks or clubs which, thus serving as hangers for provision and "plunder," could easily double as weapons.

Through the graces of an "old grey-headed Negro" the stranger claimed to have witnessed much. On one occasion he watched a "country dance, rout or cabal," from a concealed position:

Every one carried something . . . liquors of all sorts; rum, tongues, hams, beefs, geese, turkies, fowls, both dressed and raw, with many luxuries of the table, as sweatmeats, pickles, etc., (which some did not scruple to acknowledge they obtained by means of false keys procured form a Negro in town who could make any key, whenever the impression of the true one was brought to him in wax). . . . The entertainment was opened by the men. . . .[8]

The informant pressed on, describing a graphic picture of social activity among urban and country slaves in an unscrutinized setting. The blacks exerted surlines, insolence, and a readiness to protect themselves against an offending white party with no immediate legal jurisdiction over them. The stranger reminded the public that such gatherings as these were prohibited by the 1740 slave code, because they allowed slaves to take note of their own strength and to measure opportunities for rebellion. In addition to obvious conviviality, the assembly was not without its serious elements. From his hiding place, the informant observed "private committees" whose deliberations were conducted in low, cautious voices so that even other slaves could not overhear. Perhaps these men were discussing means to remedy their own plight or ways of aiding others in hiding. That was the implicit impression the stranger conveyed as he commented on the scene:

The members of this *secret council* had much the appearance of doctors, in deep and solemn consultation upon life or death; which indeed might have been the scope of their meditations at that time. No less than 12 fugitive slaves joined this respectable company before midnight, 3 of whom were mounted on good horses, these after delivering good quantity of mutton, lamb and veal, which they brought with them, directly associated with one or other of the private consultators; and went off about an hour before day.

Where was the patrol duty intended to prevent such "irregularities and the manifest ill-consequences there of"? demanded the stranger. Why, he wondered, as this negligence so grossly overlooked instead of being promptly punished?[9]

Exaggeration perhaps. Yet secret goings on, solidarity, and kinship between slaves and fugitive slaves were not uncommon. The small white population was engaged in economic pursuits and in maintaining political liberty in the face of perceived British "oppression." Hence it was hardly possible to keep constant vigilance on the large servile labor force. Most slaves were isolated on plantations and could not gather for large nocturnal frolics and surreptitious planning sessions, or conspire with runaways. Nevertheless, this generation of slaves refused to accept the jurisdiction outlined in the strict legal codes of the colony. The frequency of runaways, evidence of crimes against whites, and other black assertions of free will characterized their response to the institution of slavery. James Oakes has suggested that the only period with claims to parternalistic elements in the history of North American bondage was the colonial era. To some extent in the latter stages of colonial South Carolina, this may have been the case, and here only in a limited sense. One cannot imagine how a padrone or signeurial attitude could prevail among market-oriented rice and indigo planters. And there is little evidence to support a paternalistic argument for that experience among the slaves. But the ideology could have taken root in urban centers like Charleston and perhaps Beaufort, or within planter households where master-slave interaction was not guided by their relationship to a staple crop which depended on a driven labor force for profit.[10]

In the 1770s agitation about human rights, liberty, and equality pervaded the country and was not lost on the slaves. Such discussion increased their sense of momentousness and enhanced an already present desire for freedom. The spirit of the age fostered insurrection activity in the Southern colonies. Many feared that rupture with Great Britain would bring rebellion among slaves. In Charleston a supposed conspiracy was uncovered in the summer of 1775, and in Virginia a planter cautioned that prudence dictated that "such attempts should be concealed as well as suppressed."[11] This logic was not only designed to prevent general fear among whites but also to preclude slaves from taking advantage of white vulnerability and making connections between the two struggles.

When the War for Independence moved south, many slaves made every effort to take advantage of freedom proclamations issued by the British. Under Virginia Governor Dunmore's Proclamation of 1775 and General Clinton's promises of freedom for defecting slaves in 1779, thousands fled plantations in hope of liberty. It did not require urging from Britons to inspire slaves toward liberty. The black population in some regions was already on the move and not necessarily fleeing to English forces. But for many, the British seemed to offer the quickest, and sometimes only route to possible freedom. How well slaves understood the offer of freedom is demonstrated in a letter written by Stephen Bull to Henry Laurens in March, 1776. "It is better," he wrote, "for the public and the owners, if . . . deserted Negroes . . . be shot, if they cannot be taken." This measure would, Bull hoped, "deter other Negroes from deserting." Such was not the case. In the Southern region, prospects of liberty took on new meaning for some Lowcountry slaves. British occupation of coastal Georgia began in December 1778 after an aged slave guided the British in a surprise attack, and continued until July 1782. Charleston was literally battered into submission in May 1780. The British kept lists of blacks given certificates of freedom signed by General Samuel Birch, British commander of New York, and allowed to leave America in 1783. These inspection rolls are useful evidences of social history. They contain names of blacks, ages, a brief description, former owners, and length of time away from owners. While the majority of the South Carolina slaves on these lists are from Charleston, most of whom left during the seige, there are also listings of slaves from the region south of that city:

Brass Watson (30), scar on forehead, slave of John Day, Charleston.
Nancy (his wife) (30), 2 small children, slaves of Mr. Quince, Wilmington, N. C., left 7 years ago.
MaryAnn (23), very small, formerly owned by Thomas Cooper, Santee, left at seige of Charleston.
Mellia Marrant (30), squat wench, property of John Marrant, near Santee, left at seige of Charleston.
Amelia (6), child of above.
Ben (4), child of above.
Michael Thomas (18), of Richard Garret, Beaufort, S. C., left 7 years ago.
James Brown (21), belonging to William Williamson, Black Swamp, left 4 years ago.
Sally Beauman (25), fine wench, of Thomas Beauman of Beaufort, left 4 years ago.
Lampson Miles (12), fine boy of John Miles, Indian Lands, left 5 years ago.
Sam Hutchins (26), property of Wm. Harden, Indian Lands.
Sara Jones (33), stout wench of Richard Stevens, Port Royal, S. C.[12]

So reads the "Book of Negroes," as the British army approved passage from America for those slaves with their certificates of freedom signed by General Birch. The lists indicate that a number of the "elderly" and "worn out" former bondspeople had nevertheless somehow gotten to New York in anticipation of freedom. Black women figure prominently in the lists, some of whom had been behind British lines, or away from owners, for a number of years. Many either brought their children with them or formed partnerships after flights, giving birth to children behind British lines, that is, born free. The existence of this "Book of Negroes," with large numbers of South Carolina slaves on the lists, refutes claims that the War for Independence little affected the black population in the Lowcountry. Also, the lists demonstrate bondspeople's sense of autonomy in familial matters, and what E. P. Thompson, in another context, characterizes as representing "symbolic authority." Many did not give the surname of their masters as their own, making their detachments from previous status as complete as possible.[13] Furthermore, we find few African names on the inspection lists. Except for an occasional Cudjo or Mingo, most slaves have English names. Perhaps this represents a demarcation line between those slaves who decided to cast their lot with the British and less assimilated, African-born slaves, who remained in the swamps and woods of coastal Carolina and Georgia, becoming part of the groups that plagued the region after the War for Independence.

Among those who took refuge with the British in New York was Boston King. Although King was the son of favored slaves on the Waring plantations in the Sea Island region, this was not a mitigating factor in his bondage. He was apprenticed to a carpenter at sixteen who was a cruel man, and King "suffered many hardships." On one occasion he was falsely accused of stealing nails. "For this offense," wrote King, "I was beat and tortured most cruelly, and was laid up three weeks before I was able to do any work." King's owner's objections and his threats to break the apprentice agreement led to fairer treatment for a time. But another incident occurred for which the young man anticipated "severest punishment." It was 1780, and the war between Britain and the colonies provided the safety valve King needed. Though "much grieved at first," to reside among strangers, King nevertheless "determined to go to Charles-Town and throw myself into the hands of the English," who received him "readily."[14]

For the first time Boston King "began to feel the happiness of liberty." Despite many dangerous exploits that year, as well as a bout with smallpox, King managed to stay in British service and joined the crew of a man-of-war bound for New York in 1781. His adventures and hardships continued, culminating in capture by Americans while serving on a British pilot boat. King was taken to New Brunswick, and though well-treated, he longed for the freedom he had briefly known with the British. The resourceful young man managed his escape to British-occupied New York, and was one of those who "received a certificate from the commanding officer," General Birch, setting sail for Nova Scotia in 1783.[15]

Boston King and the loyal blacks left New York with great expectations, most of which went unrealized. But that first winter, "the work of religion began to revive" among the black colonists, thankful for their deliverance from bondage. Throughout his war exploits, King had prayed fervently for deliverance. In his many close encounters, King's most earnest supplications were expressed when he was back in bondage in New Brunswick. He thought of nothing but freedom: "I called to remembrance the many great deliverances the Lord had wrought for me and besought him to save me this once and I would serve him all the days of my life." It was a promise not immediately fulfilled, for King was occupied by more practical concerns. Yet the Nova Scotia experiences, the hardships the black colonists endured, and the racism at the hands of white loyalists drew the little black band together and King soon became their spiritual leader. For both Boston King and John Marrant, early exposure to missionary activity, early visionary spiritual experiences, positions of acculturation, together with their unusually eventful lives and deliverances all contributed to lasting commitments to Christianity and subsequent call to the ministry.[16]

To alleviate anxiety over absconding property and fear of uprising, some whites advocated that slaves be armed in the South with a promise of freedom as was occurring in the North. In South Carolina, bondspeople were used in many ways during the war, but they were never armed. David Ramsey, a Philadelphian who moved South after marrying the daughter of Henry Laurens, at first considered slaves "too dastardly" to fight. Defections to the British army notwithstanding, Ramsey believed that "abject submission had destroyed every spark of courage in their breasts." Others disagreed, and thought slaves quite capable as soldiers, as indeed they had proven on previous occasions in South Carolina. General Moultrie, a South Carolina planter, continuously urged from the battlefields that slaves be employed as soldiers by his state, especially since they were already fighting in the British army. John Laurens also argued for use of black troops, but his minority proposal was quickly defeated. But even Ramsey changed his mind as British forces prepared to blockade Charleston. Arming slaves probably would not have saved the city from the long-costly seige, because blacks thought it safer to trust "the devil you did not know." But such actions would have destroyed slavery. South Carolinians had no such intention. And even though blacks felt their best opportunities lay with the British, tragedy took a heavy toll. Unlike the resourceful Boston King, other slaves were trapped in the South when American victory became imminent. Although an estimated 5,000 to 6,000 Georgia and South Carolina blacks were evacuated from Charleston in 1782 under British protection, thousands more were transported back into slavery in the West Indies and East Florida by British "liberators" during the course of the war. And apparently many of those left behind made every effort to leave, as David Ramsey's contemporary account reveals:

They had been so impressed by the British with the expectations of severest treatment . . . that in order to get off with the retreating army, they would sometimes fasten themselves to the sides of boats. To prevent this dangerous practice the fingers of some were chopped off, and soldiers were posted with cutlasses and bayonets to oblige them to keep at proper distance. Many of them, labouring under diseases, forsaken by their new masters, and destitute of the necessaries of life, perished in the woods. Some who got off with the army were collected on Otter island, where the camp-fever continued to rage . . . some hundreds of them expired. Their dead bodies . . . were devoured by beasts and birds, and to this day (1785) the island is strewed with their bones.[17]

The American War for Independence did not bring freedom to South Carolina slaves, even though the British presence had shaken the institution more than whites cared to admit. Blacks were largely unarmed, still consisting of many foreign-born Africans and actually caught between two enemies. The condition of the majority of slaves was not greatly altered. Yet their expectations had risen. Espousals of republican and human rights philosophies, the sense of independence some slaves experienced through wartime displacement, as well as white Carolina's renewed strengthening and commitment to bondage, created postwar spurts of active collective resistance. Postwar living conditions also contributed much to unrest, as slaves bore the brunt of the depressing aftereffects. In the city slaves resumed performance of the essential tasks of market merchandising, butchering, fishing, carting, skilled labor, public works, and myriad domestic tasks. Many slaves were hired out to perform various jobs and provide revenue for masters. On coastal plantations rice productivity was soon on the upswing again, and in the up-country short staple cotton was not long in benefiting from the invention of the cotton gin. On the Sea Islands indigo planters marked time and clung to their slaves, although their new relationship with Great Britain cut off their monopoly of indigo profits. Shortly, a new commodity, sea island cotton, proved to be a vastly profitable substitute for indigo. There was never a question as to whether or not slavery would survive in South Carolina and Georgia.[18]

Postwar South Carolina settled back into a system of slavery which was unbending in its oppression. Signs of brutality and harshness were clearly visible. One 1785 traveler was awestruck by the natural beauty of the state, but also mused on how quickly "heaven's best gifts" were forgotten, "as well as the bountiful giver." Upon visiting a structure jocosely referred to as the "sugar house," the observer was repulsed by what he saw. Here Charleston slaves were punished. The place contained "dreadful machinery" on which slaves were confined and suspended. "I marked the scourge which was tinged with human blood and other apparatus of more than savage barbarity." More revolting than the "machinery" said the observer, was the "viewing bench" designed for "such spectators as chose to regale themselves with a view of the agony of suffering humanity." How was it possible, wondered the traveler, that "a people who have just risen up from the struggles of virtue and liberty should be so insensible of their inestimable blessings . . . as to consign to sining and dispair creatures like themselves and to triumph in their destress." Another example comes from Georgia. Philadelphia physician Benjamin Rush noted that on the Sea Island plantations of Pierce Butler, the overseer, Mr. Mitchell, whipped slaves "til they laughed."—"Pain," said Rush, "changed to pleasure."[19]

Whatever mechanisms of escapism prompted this "hysterical" reaction to whipping, it is doubtful that pain was turning to pleasure as the usually sensitive Dr. Rush believed. But the statement represents more than an ignorant comment about an oppressive system, since the incident took place on a Butler plantation. This latter fact demonstrates the limitations inherent in viewing bondage from what may seem to be a redeeming ideology—paternalism. While Butler himself can probably be considered as close to any planter in representing "paternalism," this only reveals the inadequacy of the term in describing master-slave relationships. He was known for buying slaves in family units and for trying to keep them together on his plantations. He was also remembered by his old house slaves for having been a caring master. But Butler was often absent, and with an eye toward profit to support his elegant Philadelphia life-style, he hired hard-driving overseers and gave them free reign in his absence. His heirs continued to manage the estates in this way, and just before the Civil War, many "faithful" Butler slaves were sold to maintain that life-style.[20]

The postwar runaway situation among the slaves in the country and cities created alarm. In rural areas maroon groups were strengthened by the war with Britain. Slaves who aided the British in the siege of Savannah fled after their allies lost the war and maroons lost their hope of freedom. After the war, campaigns against maroons were conducted by the South Carolina and Georgia militias. The situation was discussed in both states' legislative bodies. Major Pierce Butler frequently expressed anxiety over maroon groups, and in 1789 noted that his island plantations were threatened from two sources—Indians and groups of runaway slaves, both of which were aided by the Spanish. It was, he wrote, "such an alarming and serious a nature as to threaten . . . ruin and depopulation unless timely protected by Congress." He proposed making war on the Creeks, taking Florida from the Spanish, and sending federal troops to combat slave maroon problems. He and other elected officials from his region "sounded" the new national Congress on the issue. But the new government was too engaged in more "pressing" business. These groups of fugitives, sometimes aided by the Spanish, remained part of the Lowcountry landscape even in the vicinity of Charleston. Some could be linked to the wartime period. In one 1786 account a militia expedition attacked a band of about one hundred fugitives who had sheltered on "Belleisle Island, about 17 or 18 miles up Savannah River." The band had boldly committed robberies on neighboring plantations. The first attempt to dislodge the group failed although several fugitives were killed, and four whites wounded. That same evening the whites were reinforced and continued their assault, "but the Negroes came down in such numbers" that it was decided to return to the boats. The fugitives attempted to cut off this route, "but were prevented by Lieutenant Elfe of the artillery," whose company discharged grape shot, killing or wounding several as evidenced by the amount of blood seen afterwards in the place where the shot was aimed. Several days later, after the fugitives had abandoned the scene, "General Jackson" went to the Island and destroyed the provisions, canoes, and boats. He also burned their homes and fields where rice was being cultivated. It was generally expected that deprivation of food and shelter would "occasion them to disperse about the country, and it is hoped will be the means of most of them being soon taken up."[21]

Discontented slaves engaged in various forms of violence against the white community in the late eighteenth and early nineteenth century. In the city the most common act of resistance was setting fires. Numerous cases of arson were reported, and in 1797 three slaves were executed and two banished for attempting to burn Charleston. As historians who recognize the character of the African-American struggle have noted, the year 1800 was momentous. Gabriel's aborted uprising in Richmond, Virginia corresponded in time with the date of Denmark Vesey's purchase of freedom and Nat Turner's birth. Gabriel's attempt in 1800 may have inspired two failed South Carolina efforts later that same year. In September plantation slaves rebelled, killing several whites. Troops were ordered out but the insurgents held their ground for some time in the swamp regions before capture. Later in the year another outbreak began but was quickly dispersed. In 1804 in the Sea Island region south of Charleston, there was "a rumor afloat" that all slaves in the area were planning a revolt. Whites began taking guns to bed. The rumor was reportedly true and whites were saved by a slave informant just before the outbreak. The leaders were seized, quickly tried, and "ten or a dozen" condemned to death. Following execution, the slaves' "heads were cut off, stuck on poles, and set up along the highway, from Purrysburg, the place of the trial, to Coosawhatchie," the old Beaufort judicial seat. In 1805 news of a conspiracy in the up-country created panic and led to the death of at least one slave.[22]

Unrest in the Lowcountry continued, and was evident during the War of 1812 as well as afterwards. In this war between Britain and the fledgling nation, another overture to desert was made to the slaves of the southeast coast. Many responded and left with the British, 3,000 going to Nova Scotia. On one of the islands near Charleston, slaves in 1813 readied themselves for an anticipated British attack which would ignite a black insurrection. The gathering, in anticipation of the British and prospects of freedom, gave rise to a "freedom hymn." According to an informant, the hymn and account of its creation was given to him in 1835 by an English abolitionist-missionary, and was compiled by one of the leaders of the intended insurrection. The slaves held secret meetings on one of the islands near Charleston and the "proceedings were opened and closed by the singing of this "Hymn of Freedom":

Hail! all hail! ye Afric clan
Hail! ye oppressed, ye Afric band,
Who toil and sweat in Slavery bound;
(Repeated)

And when your health & strength are gone
Are left to hunger & to mourn.
Let *Independence* be your aim,
Ever mindful what 'tis worth.
Pledge your bodies for the prize
Pile them even to the skies!
   Chorus
Firm, united let us be,
Resolved on death or liberty
As a band of Patriots joined
Peace & Plenty we shall find.

Look to Heaven with manly trust
And swear by Him that's always just
That no white foe with impious hand
(Repeated)

Shall slave your wives & daughters more
Or rob them of their virtue dear.
Be armed with valor firm & true,
Their hopes are fixed on Heaven & you
That truth & justice will prevail
And every scheme of bondage fail.
   Chorus

Arise! Arise! shake off your chains
Your cause is just, so Heaven ordains
To you shall Freedom be proclaimed.
(Repeated)

Raise your arms & bare your breasts,
Almighty God will do the rest.
Blow the clarion! a warlike blast!
Call every Negro from his task!
Wrest the scourge from Buckra's hand,
And drive each tryant from the land.
   Chorus

The British fleet that was "anxiously looked for" never came. And while "the rising of the slaves was abandoned," many took advantage of white preoccupation with the war and absconded from plantation and city.[23]

The last two known incidents of collective rebelliousness prior to 1822 occurred in 1816. In Camden, South Carolina, slaves planned a move for freedom that was ironically set for July 4. At the time, Rachel Blanding was a Camden resident, although originally from New England. She wrote a Philadelphia cousin that the "whole village and neighborhood" was in "confusion" over the fear of insurrection, and that "nothing but the interposition of that Being to whom we are indebted for all our mercies has saved us from destruction." The plan had been "in agitation" since the previous Christmas. The slaves intended to set fire to a wealthy part of town and while whites were thusly engaged, the would-be rebels "meant to have possession of the arsenal . . . and proceed to murder the men," while the women would reportedly be reserved for other "purposes." The jail was filled with slaves, "stretched out on their backs on the base of the floor and scarcely move their heads, but have a strong guard placed over them." For Rachel Blanding, it was "a dreadful situation to be in," believing she could not "go to bed in safety." She shuddered especially at the slaves' "thirst for revenge." They would not hear of sparing even an "old gentleman who is a preacher," never owned slaves, and "devoted his time to preaching to them on the plantations."[24]

As the trials commenced, it was feared that sentencing and executions of those in custody would "exasperate the others to do a great mischief." Camden remained on the alert during most of July. Able-bodied men took turns at nightly guard duty until the sentencing was carried out. Of the nine ring leaders discovered, six were found guilty and hanged and two others imprisoned in "solitary confinement." The ninth conspirator, Stephen, was undoubtedly the divine "interposition" of whom Rachel Blanding spoke, better known as informer. The slaves never knew who the informer was. Orders pertaining to Stephen were that he was guilty and to have the "sentence of death passed at the same time as his fellows, but he is to be pardoned." Even whites were not privy to the identity of the insider, who requested that his master send him out of the country because the conspirators "had engaged all for a great distance, . . . and he knew the Negroes would not let him live here."[25]

According to the *Camden Gazette*, those "most active in the insurrection attempt occupied a respectable stand in one of the churches, several were professors and one a class leader." Apparently the church was Methodist—a portent of plans to come on a larger scale. All leaders entered pleas of "not guilty" to the charges, although Rachel Blanding wrote, "two or three" finally confessed "and died like heroes," stating they were dying "in a good cause." The rebels obviously saw no contradiction between religious beliefs and raising an insurrection for their freedom. On the contrary, as was the case with the Charleston rebels in 1822, the Camden conspirators' reading of the scriptures probably justified rebellion. According to Blanding, one of the leaders, "a professor of religion said he had only one sin to answer for, and that was he sat down to the communion table with white people when he knew he was going to cut their throats as soon as convenient."[26]

Although the town of Camden regained its composure following revelation of the insurrection plot and subsequent punishments, the Blandings did not. Even before the conspiracy, Rachel Blanding considered living in the South "a sacrifice." Despite gala social occasions, weddings, balls, and "great parties," she wrote in 1808, "I can assure you I am not well pleased with South Carolina," and hoped her physician-husband would prosper enough to enable them to exchange the "land of slavery" for the "land of liberty." She was weary of "a land of luxury acquired by the hearts' blood of the poor ignorant Africans." Following the Camden conspiracy, the Blandings determined to move to the North the next spring even though it was against their "interests." "We have taken such a disgust of slavery," Rachel Blanding wrote, "that we cannot feel satisfied here."[27]

Later in the year, white troops battled a community of runaways in the seacoast region near the Ashepoo River. The maroons were a menacing presence as their numbers had increased and their depredations became more bold. They were finally captured and their stronghold destroyed. Thus did superior arms and numbers gradually doom maroonage in South Carolina. But even as late as 1821 an outlaw community clashed with whites near Georgetown. One slaveholder was killed in the attack and several fugitives captured.[28]

This unsettling activity was intensified by the frequency of flight in the coastal and island regions. But most strivings for freedom were largely sporadic and did not reflect long-range planning as did the efforts of Gabriel and his lieutenants or the Camden group. Yet conditions seemed as ripe in South Carolina as in Virginia for an organized movement for freedom. It came in Charleston. As John Lofton points out, Santo Domingo provided a practical example of a successful black revolt, the age offered a philosophy, while natural inclinations and oppression supplied a rationale.[29] By 1822 ideology and leadership were present. The record shows that legions of slaves in the Lowcountry, hoping to spur a statewide insurrection under the contagion of freedom, prepared to take by force what was rightfully theirs. The rebellion strategy was formulated and formented under the guise of an African-Christian association in Charleston known as the African Methodist Episcopal Church. This strategy and the rebellion's leadership reflected the composition of slave society in coastal South Carolina and the spiritual orientation of the insurrectionists. Indeed, the attempted rebellion embodied militant aspects of two religious traditions. It was closely linked with the Methodist Church but was to be carried out under a mystique of African supernatural forces. Moreover, the relationship with African religious tradition may have been the strongest bond among the insurrectionists in their designs. In the Lowcountry, the real language of egalitarianism came from Christian ideology. This did not always translate into support for emancipation, although some whites, for a time, broached the issue. More significantly, the liberal trend led to black exposure to Christianity on a level not previously experienced. Although some slaves may have accepted Christianity just as it flowed out of the white man's mouth, many did not. This latter group used the Christian religion to help provide the genius of their liberation struggle.

Slave Religion in the Postwar Lowcountry

In the Lowcountry, early black exposure to Christianity was largely the work of those previously influenced by George Whitefield, and of postwar Methodists. Although a member of the Anglican clergy, Whitefield, as previously discussed, was not popular with the established church in South Carolina. His staunchest followers were within dissenting congregations. The English evangelist was particularly effective among Puritan-Baptists because of his Calvinist stand on scriptural authority, regenerate membership, and justification by faith. The first Lowcountry extension of the Old England Baptists was the establishment of a church at Euhaw in 1746, for the benefit of communicants who moved their habitations south to these Indian lands and to Edisto Island. Other churches were organized and preceded by missionaries who set up preaching places in the Beaufort district and in the Savannah River area. The novelty of Baptist views on baptism and church membership were so different from other traditions that they attracted much attention and at first ensured ostracism in the Sea Island region. The Baptist mission at Beaufort was organized into a church in 1800. But upwardly mobile Baptists did not immediately gain respectability from the Episcopalian community. The Reverend Henry Holcomb lived in Beaufort and served the Baptist Church there for a number of years before and after the War for Independence. In a letter he discussed early attitudes toward the Baptists:

The principal inhabitants of Beaufort though possessed of learning, wealth and talents, were with a few honorable exceptions, strangers to true religion, and strongly prejudiced against the Baptists. The doctrine of regeneration they treated with contempt; and baptism, if we understand the meaning of the word, had never been administered in their vicinity. If ever I felt the ensnaring fear of men, it was then, but . . . God and truth were on my side. . . . Several "fellows of the better sort" made attempts to turn ministerial exercises into ridicule . . . stealing my Bible . . . while I was administering the Lord's Supper.[30]

Yet Sea Island Baptists overcame initial prejudice, and Episcopalians (postwar Anglicans) grew accustomed to witnessing baptizings in the Beaufort River. Contrary to Episcopalian apprehensions, baptismal rites were administered with the greatest solemnity, and even Baptist church services contained none of the evangelical enthusiasm that characterized Methodists at that time. Leading citizens eventually converted to the Baptist faith. Episcopalian acceptance was probably influenced by Baptist economic success. Before the War for Independence, Baptists were already on the list of Sea Island "aristocracy", rivaling Episcopalians in wealth consisting of land and slaves. This occasioned intermarriage between the once rivaling denominations. One of the most illustrious Baptist ministers of South Carolina, Richard Fuller of Beaufort, came from an Episcopalian lineage which included colonial Indian fighters, legislators, and signers of the Declaration of Independence. The Fuller family owned several Sea Islands and hundreds of slaves. The Lawton-Robert family, Baptist converts from the Huguenot sect, migrated to South Carolina from France. They organized the little Black Swamp Church upon acquiring properties at Robertville (between Beaufort and Savannah). Robertville became one of the wealthiest areas in South Carolina and the Lawton-Roberts were among the most prominent families in the Lowcountry. Other affluent Baptist-Episcopalian members of the slavocracy in the Sea Island region included the Bosticks, the Elliotts, the Popes, and the Fripps. Thus the stigma attached to Baptists subsided. By 1812 the once dissenting faith was a respectable form of worship in the Sea Islands. Lowcountry Baptists had always identified with planter interests and with slaveholding. The Reverend Holcomb lived long enough to see "the flower of Beaufort filling their seats at the Lord's table" for communion at the Baptist Church.[31]

When George Whitefield appealed to planters for religious instruction of slaves, Baptist compliance may have been more forthcoming, in some cases, than among other denominations. His remonstrances did not seem to diminish Puritan-Baptist attraction to his preaching. Whitefield, after all, was a slaveholder himself. Thus in isolated pockets of coastal Carolina and Georgia, preaching to blacks did occur and had obvious results around the time of the War for Independence and afterwards.

As previously discussed, the first organized black religious gathering under Christian auspices in the South was at Silver Bluff, South Carolina, between 1773 and 1775. That occurred on the estate of planter and Indian agent George Galphin, through the efforts of a Connecticut Baptist named Wait Palmer. David George, one of Galphin's slaves, was a convert of Palmer's, and was appointed elder over the little band of eight after being instructed in that office. David George was greatly influenced and encouraged by a black Baptist preacher named George Liele (also called George Sharp). Liele, under the guidance of Georgia white Baptists, had become a practicing exhorter. His master, Henry Sharp, a deacon of the Burke County church where Liele was "called," freed his slave, although Liele continued on with the white family. In his capacity as a preacher George Liele ministered to various plantations as well as to whites and blacks in his own church near Savannah. Liele's master, a loyalist, fought with the British and was killed. Liele remained with the British during the Savannah occupation.[32]

When the War for Independence began, slave owners prohibited ministers from visiting the plantations, fearing that information about the war, especially Dunmore's and Clinton's freedom offers, would cause black defection. With ministers no longer visiting, David George, who had experienced a call to preach under the ministrations of Liele, took over the little church, then numbering about forty. When the British overran the seacoast region, American patriots, Galphin among them, fled for their lives. David George, along with fifty other slaves, sought freedom and refuge under the British flag in Savannah. There they were reunited with George Liele, and the little community of Baptists thrived in wartime Savannah. Although the core of the membership was probably from Silver Bluff, it was George Liele's influence as a servant to a British officer that gave the black church its recognition in the military government.[33]

Included in the wartime black church membership were two men who did not take advantage of their opportunity to remain free through British service, but elected to remain slaves, becoming founders of black churches in Georgia. One was Andrew, favorite slave of Jonathan Bryan. Bryan, like other American patriots had fled Savannah. Andrew was baptized by George Liele just before the latter evacuated for Jamaica with the British in 1782. Andrew began preaching in the neighborhood and was brutally whipped and imprisoned on more than one occasion. Those who endeavored to hear him were also punished. Finally, prominent citizens interceded, among them Andrew's master. It was determined that the slaves were "sincere." Jonathan Bryan provided them with a barn for worship, the white Baptist divine, Abraham Marshall, ordained Andrew, and by 1788 the African Baptist Church of Savannah was flourishing. They claimed 570 converts, "many of whom have not permission" from their owners "to be baptized." Andrew, already in his fifties, was given his freedom and the church continued to grow.[34]

Jesse Peter (called Jesse Galphin) was another one of those who obtained freedom by going to the British, but who returned to his master's estate and to slavery after the war. Peter was ordained along with Andrew and became pastor of the reconstituted Silver Bluff Church. In 1793 the church had sixty members, but after that date it apparently no longer existed. This occurred at the time the Springfield (First African) Baptist Church at Augusta was formed with Jesse Peter as pastor. Thus no black church existed in South Carolina after 1793 until the African Methodist Church of Charleston was organized. Why the Silver Bluff Church disappeared cannot be explained merely by the removal of Jesse Peter, although Augusta was but twelve miles from Silver Bluff. Most likely South Carolina planters were hostile to the presence of a black church. George Galphin, an Irish-born man, known for his kindness to both blacks and Indians, was exceptional. But Galphin died before the war ended. Jesse Peter undoubtedly felt his work was more secure in

Georgia. He remained a slave, but was given "uncommon liberty." He preached at several places in addition to his church, and "a number of white people admired him." In any case Savannah and Augusta are atypical examples of black early participation in the Christian religion. These churches were closely controlled and carefully watched. They essentially were under receivership of prominent white Baptists such as Abraham Marshall. While the "regulating touches" of white authority reportedly gave the black churches "standing and influence,"[35] this scrutiny probably gave them little autonomy.

David George did not feel the attachment to familiar places and people that Andrew Bryan and Jesse Peter felt, perhaps because he was not born and raised on the seacoast. David George was a Virginia slave whose life had been hard before coming to the Galphins. His African-born parents had nine children. All were brutally treated. George had witnessed the whipping of his sisters, brothers, and mother. At times George was flogged "till the blood . . . ran down over my waistband." This caused George to flee, finding odd jobs, living with Indians, and finally ending up in South Carolina where Galphin purchased him from the Virginia master who was ever on his trail. Although George remembered Galphin as a kind man, he had no intention of returning to bondage. In Savannah, George and his half-Indian wife fared well. She worked as a laundress, at one time taking in General Clinton's wash. George operated a butcher's stall, and rented a house with a garden and field. His trade took him into the country (where his brother-in-law supplied him with meat). George was given a pass certifying that he was "a good Subject to King George," as well as a "Free Negro Man." When the Savannah evacuation began, George took his family to Charleston where he attached himself to Major General James Paterson. When Paterson was ordered to sail for Halifax, Nova Scotia, George and his family went with him.[36]

Despite this flurry of religious activity in a few areas of the Lowcountry for a short period of time, and although several black churches were established in coastal Georgia by the turn of the century, religious instruction was not widespread. If Georgia was exemplary as an area where religious activity was taking place, it also demonstrates how little was actually done. Jonathan Bryan wrote to a London Methodist in 1785 of his concern for the "unhappy condition of our Negroes, who are kept in worse than Egyptian bondage." Worst of all, wrote Bryan, was their spiritual state. While slave labor produced "the clothes we wear, the food we eat, and all the superfluities we possess," they received "nothing equivalent." On the contrary, wrote Bryan, "we keep from them the key of knowledge, so that their bodies and souls perish together in our service."[37]

If Christian instruction among slaves languished in supposedly liberal coastal Georgia, in coastal South Carolina it was deplorable among many Baptists whose attachment to the former preachings of George Whitefield stopped short of missionary work among the slave masses. Baptists were interested in extending the faith, as evidenced by how quickly they spread to the coastal and upcountry frontier. But this evangelical zeal did not extend to the general slave population. Early Sea Island Baptists were involved in protecting slavery, consolidating property, and maintaining a money crop. Like Episcopalians, they viewed efforts of spiritual uplift among masses of slaves as dangerous and antagonistic to economic interests.

The War for Independence did much to unsettle growth in the Sea Island region. Once the war ended the people engaged in reconstructing their society and reconstituting their economic priorities. Little time was spent on contemplation of their souls. In 1792, Matthew Tate, a friend of Benjamin Rush and an Episcopalian minister, became rector at St. Helena Church in Beaufort. The spiritual life was low according to Tate, who was himself primarily interested in economic advantage. Since there was no other Episcopal clergyman for 40 miles, Tate boasted of the money to be made from conducting marriages and funerals. Also the availability of single, preferably wealthy widows was a notable concern of the rector's.[38] Given such pecuniary preoccupations on the part of ministers it is understandable that the state of Christianity suffered.

Religion did not assume a prominent role in the lives of either Baptists or Episcopalians in the coastal and Sea Islands region. Indigo, cotton, rice, slaves, and a well-planned social calendar received highest consideration. In 1766 a Philadelphian, John Bartram, visited the coastal and Sea Island regions of South Carolina and Georgia. Even at this early stage of development a certain affluence was observed. Bartram wrote in his diary that the "best inhabitants" had great farms distanced from the seacoast towns. On the farms "they keep numerous Negro slaves, who are closely employed in cultivating the ground, or sowing plank, or looking after their stock for maintenance of their masters." The farms were maintained by slaves' industry while the masters "live in the towns in opulency and ease" riding out to the "farms" once in a fortnight "as any urgent occasion requires, sometimes taking their ladies with them and children in chairs so that there is not the appearance of . . . business."[39]

The first census return for the new nation reported a population of 18,753 in Beaufort District (St. Helena, St. Luke, and Prince William Parishes). Of this number, 14,236 were slaves and 153 were free blacks. The resort town of Beaufort contained about thirty houses, and the majority of the population was scattered over the islands and on remote mainland plantations. Timothy Ford, a Northerner whose sister married into the DeSaussure family of South Carolina visited the region during that time. He commented on the absenteeism, the superfluity of servants, and the idleness of Southerners who called themselves planters, "yet know little about the process and art of planting . . . all is committed to overseers and drivers." Of religious life, Ford noted that the Episcopalian Church was the "preeminent and fashionable mode of worship," but also observed that:

. . . the spirit had not lately visited this parish; the shattered and forlorn condition of this church gave but too much room to question their zeal; and the few that attended it (about fifty whites) to doubt the ardor of their devotion.[40]

A St. Helena planter's wife, Abigail Capers, wrote a friend in 1791 that there were about seventy families on the Island, forty of whom were eminent planters "with strong attachments to each other." The only church, she wrote, was a tiny Episcopal chapel of ease. Sundays were for the most part not spent in church but among "genteel company" on various plantations and engaged in a variety of "amusements." It was a simple but elegant life where "nothing is so much coveted as the pleasure of possessing many slaves . . . happiness is confined within the narrow limits of a plantation with a great many slaves."[41]

In the early nineteenth century Baptist churches were still tiny unpretentious houses of worship with no slave galleries, although personal servants did attend services. White memberships were so small that no specific seating arrangements were needed—blacks occupied the back of the churches and whites sat in the front. Furthermore, even though revivals were conducted in the Beaufort area in the early 1800s, church rolls indicate no significant gain in black membership. Not until 1817 did the Beaufort Baptist Church have its first extension to admit galleries and a tower, a first indication of a notable black membership at this Island church. In 1819, the Euhaw Church reported a membership of "18 Whites and 4 Colored," and the church at Black Swamp had thirty white and one hundred black members.[42]

Some slaves, during the "Second Great Awakening," beginning around 1800, were exposed to Christianity in Baptist churches. Often blacks were "converted" when no whites came forth. In 1800, Richard Furman of Charleston wrote to a Philadelphia Baptist minister of the success the new minister at Euhaw Church was experiencing. In nine months, "Mr Cook" had "baptized about twenty persons." Most of them "are Negroes."[43] This is a very small number, but nonetheless demonstrates that actual black membership does not tell the whole story. Obviously blacks were baptized in many instances without being given church membership. While this demonstrates black exposure to Christianity, it also illustrates the paucity of "Christian" instruction.

Even the religious revitalization that began in the North after the War of 1812 and spread to some parts of the South, was not greatly effective in the Carolina Lowcountry. In 1821, a long-term visitor from Connecticut living in Robertville wrote:

> The Religious state of things here it is hoped is improving. A few are enquiring "What they Shall do to be saved" . . . we who have been accustomed to having ministers settled in every village must feel the dearth of ministers in this part of our country where the toilers are ripe for the harvest and seem only to want Faithful Laborers in the vineyard. . . . The inhabitants of this place are all connected by inter-marriages, and I am afraid are very wordly minded and even the Professors appear to think more of the rise and fall of cotton than the rise and progress of religion.[44]

Although Baptists had no national association, local organizations exemplify how negligible black membership was in white churches. By 1806 there were 130 Baptist churches in South Carolina, most of which were in the upcountry. Communicants totaled 10,560, 3,500 of whom were reportedly black. Sixteen years later, according to the 1822 South Carolina Baptist Convention, the number of black Baptists had not greatly increased. The Baptist Church at Charleston had a black membership large enough to allow for separate meetings with "proper" regulations by 1819. It is questionable how many of the total black church membership was made up of slaves. In the case of the Charleston Baptist Church's black membership, the majority of the congregations were free. Yet an interesting example of possible autonomy is that Charleston black Baptists, slave and free, were allowed to meet together apart from the white church and to discipline their own members. This practice was probably discontinued after the Vesey Conspiracy of 1822.[45]

The first two emissaries of Wesleyan Methodism arrived in the colonies in 1769. One of them, Joseph Philmoore, went to Charleston in 1773. Philmoore, who had "traveled many thousands of miles in England and Wales," and had seen "much of North America," considered his journey over the sandy, boggy roads "the most distressing of all ever met with before." Philmoore's opinion of religion in the Lowcountry was no less negative. The unpopularity of Methodist preaching forced him to limit himself to daytime sermons. Thirty-three years had passed since George Whitefield made his final appearance in Charleston. Long before his last visits, Whitefield's popularity had waned. Methodism was unpopular within the established church. The Methodism of Wesley was even more abhorrent, because it rejected the doctrine of election and was against slavery. Philmoore found an inhospitable people in Charleston who, under nighttime cover, resorted to overt acts of aggression against Methodist preaching. On one occasion, he preached in a theater and was forced to flee "through a trapdoor—used for the ghost in *Hamlet*." Philmoore's short stay had little permanent effect for Methodism.[46]

It was 1785 before the Methodists made another trip to Charleston. Francis Asbury, the man responsible for organization of the Methodist Episcopal church in America the previous year, arrived in Charleston to organize a church. At that time the Methodists were a small, weak group nationally. American Methodists had been pacifists during the late war and their British leader was a Tory. These facts, along with their doctrines and moral stand on slavery, made them distrusted, especially in the South, where the majority of American Wesleyans resided. Asbury and his coadjutors, Henry Willis and Jesse Lee, found that while they had some "friends" in the upcountry, the people of Charleston would "receive nothing." The only group with any appearance of religion he wrote were the Calvinists. Asbury was alarmed and "dejected in spirit" because of the small congregations. Nevertheless, through the efforts of his two associates who remained in the city, by the end of the year a church was established consisting of "thirty-five whites and twenty-three colored." Having no church of their own, Methodists first met in a deserted Baptist meetinghouse. One Sunday they found the pews flung out in the streets and the entrances and windows of the church barred. The group met in each others' homes and even attempted to purchase an unused "French Church." Their unpopularity was such that negotiations were terminated. But by 1787, the determined group had erected their own edifice, the Cumberland Street Church.[47]

Belief in extempore preaching and evangelism inspired Methodists to gather in the public market, the streets, and in private homes for worship, even after their church was built. These assemblies were frequently broken up by the Charleston intendant and city guard. Threats, harangues, and arrests were common occurrences. Services held in homes were bombarded with missiles thrown by youths from families of "standing." Methodists who preached and exhorted in public were arrested for "disturbing the peace." Bishop Francis Asbury noted in his journal in 1788 that Methodist preaching occasioned riots in Charleston, even within the confines of the church building. One such commotion which began outside the church door so alarmed the congregation that "ladies leaped out at the windows of the church and a dreadful confusion ensued." That same night, while Asbury himself was preaching, "a stone was thrown against the north side of the church; then another on the south; a third came through the pulpit window, and struck near me inside the pulpit." Undaunted, Asbury continued with his preaching and insisted that he had "more liberty to speak in Charleston this visit" than ever before.[48]

The early Methodist church was not antislavery in terms of membership, although its proclamations, reputation, and some individual action imply otherwise. Few Southern-born lay preachers favored emancipation even though British-born Methodist leaders like Coke, Asbury, and Whatcoat did. From the Charleston region Asbury wrote in 1795:

Here are the rich, the rice and the slaves; the last is awful to me. Wealthy people settle on the rice lands of Cooper River hold from fifty to two hundred slaves on a plantation in chains and bondage: yet God is able of these stones, yea of these slave-holders to raise up children unto Abraham.[49]

Yet the American Methodist ministry was divided. Thomas Coke, sent by Wesley to help organize the denomination, was strongly antislavery. He and Asbury organized the new church under a discipline that required Methodists to free their slaves or be denied the Lord's Supper and expelled. Although antislavery rules were adopted at the first American Methodist General Conference at Christmas 1784, negative reaction was so strong that the rules were suspended at a June conference in Baltimore in 1785 on behalf of the entire church. Nevertheless, some emancipationist sentiment continued. In 1795 ministers meeting in Charleston signed an agreement which recognized slavery as "evil" and condemned "patrons of slavery as well as holders of slaves." Chastizing each other for "strengthening the hands of oppression," the signatories agreed that those of them who owned slaves should emancipate them immediately if permitted to do so by law. Where legal strictures prevented manumission, it was decreed that slaves "ought to be compensated for their labor and willed free." They further resolved that those acting otherwise thereby forfeited both their seat in the Conference and their Letter of Ordination. This was the basis of the 1796 "Articles of Agreement Amongst the Preachers" signed by many conference members in both regions. However, no account of the agreement was published in the Minutes, and as the action was binding only on those who signed, it carried little weight. When the second meeting of the whole church occurred in 1796, General Conference's language regarding slaveholding was conciliatory. It affirmed that it was "more than ever" convinced of the "great evil" of slavery, but actually retreated from the previous stand. Rather than deny membership to slaveholders as previously mandated, the new "anti-slavery" stand accepted them into the church after a preacher had spoken to them "freely and faithfully on the subject of slavery."[50]

Thus the Methodist church, though attempting to engage in Christian instruction of the slaves in some areas, took a compromise position on slavery. Many Southern Methodists bought and sold slaves. They were not proscribed for it by the episcopacy, and most were not troubled by conscience. Yet quarrels did develop over slaveholding, even in Charleston. In 1794 William Hammett, in charge of the Charleston Methodist Church, was himself a slaveholder. Yet he was still harassed and accused of negligently giving passes to blacks so they could "traverse the town at any hour of the night," and "turned out of the pulpit" as a consequence. The minister was able to overcome the incident and continued serving local Methodists. Yet he found that opposition came from another quarter as well. Hammett faced criticism and abuse from his own denomination for being a slaveholder. In 1795 the issue created tension and anger although the church majority stood with Hammett. Still some members, disgusted with the bickering, united with the Episcopal church. The controversy motivated Hammett to pen his private thoughts on slavery in his journal:

I cannot think the trade justifiable on general principles, but in a country where the custom has been handed down from generation to generation, and where free people cannot be hired as servants, and servants are necessary, it is as innocent to hold as to hire slaves.[51]

Hammett's further contemplation centered around a position that in the future would provide a major New Testament theme for slave sermons and a rationalization for slavery:

. . . we see then St. Paul, did not enjoin on Philemon to emancipate Onesimus who was at the time of his conversion a runaway slave, and this appears evident from the original *Doulos* signifying vassalage or slavery, tho' it is sometimes applied to service in general. St. P. sent him back to his Master to remain, or that the Master should receive him for *ever*. . . . If slavery under every circumstance was an evil, or a sin, Paul would have enjoined on Philemon to emancipate but all he recommends is treatment of a lenient kind, to treat him "as a brother," converted and received.[52]

Both the Old and New Testaments spoke to the actual practice of slaveholding. Pauline justification used by Hammett was in keeping with the thrust of the latter and passages from St. Paul were frequently read to slaves. The biblical example fitted conveniently into the schema of submission so much a part of the Christianity taught to plantation slaves in the antebellum period. Hammett's position also represents the dualism which characterized those who supported slavery yet claimed slaves were spiritually equal. Paul enjoined Philemon to treat Onesimus as he would his closest kin, and one does not normally enslave "a brother." Jesus was silent on the subject of slavery, except for using the master-slave relationship in a pedagogical sense. It was the letters of Paul which contain specific instructions on master-slave duties. Proslavery advocates also upheld bondage by noting that God's "chosen people" were slave owners.[53] Early slaveholding Methodists such as Hammett found ample scriptural justification for their practices.

Yet other Methodist ministers preaching in the South took a different position on slavery. An incendiary document written in the form of an appeal to the inhabitants of Charleston was the handiwork of a resident Methodist preacher named John Phillips. Phillips had been Hammett's leading accuser in the 1795 quarrel in the Charleston Church over slavery. The "appeal" was written in Charleston in 1796 while Phillips was still in the city. It was published in New York where the author had removed himself from harm's way. Phillips had been arrested and physically abused by Charleston authorities and citizens for public preaching, for teaching Christianity to slaves and free blacks, and for his antislavery views. The pamphlet denounced the "injustices" perpetrated by slaveholders and prophesied their doom. The author of the tract labeled Charleston masters "thieves" and "men stealers" who ranked with the "vilest characters" in scripture, the Sodomites. He attacked Charleston slaveholders for varied reasons, but especially on the slave trade and the lack of religious instruction. Phillips insisted in his preface that he had such "an entire aversion to war, that if the slaves could obtain their liberty by it, I would, *if possible*, dissuade them from it." Yet his unequivocal position came close to predicting violence:

And you say, you did not bring them to this country, and . . . blame and condemn those who did; but inasmuch as you perpetuate their crime in keeping them in ignorance and in perpetual slavery, . . . fitting out vessels in this port for the slave trade . . . soliciting that the trade may be opened again, prove, that you are men of like evil dispositions with those who first put this villainous and unnatural practice into execution . . . why do you insist on their being kept ignorant that they may be obedient? . . . Is this Republicanism? Is there not some fraud here? . . . If you have divine authority for what you are doing, whom or what do you fear? . . . Why do you introduce club law instead of equity? . . . Is it not more than probably that the very slaves you are now training up in sin and ignorance, and securing as a portion for your children, will be the very instruments of their, if not your destruction? . . . Are not the owners become the servants of servants. . . . Thus the head is become the tail, according to the saying of Moses in Deuteronomy.

The Phillips pamphlet was sent to Charleston, adding more fuel to an already volatile situation. Hostile white citizens were aware of the 1784 General Conference statement, the 1796 "Articles of Agreement," and the manumission activity in the Northeast and Upper South. Thus the association of early Lowcountry Methodism with antislavery attitudes was not without foundation, though such sentiment was not pervasive. Still, proclamations like Phillips' kept whites on the alert for Methodist depredations against "public safety."[54]

In 1802 a mob assembled in Charleston after news reached "leading citizens' that antislavery literature had arrived for the South Carolina

Conference from the Northeast and that a Methodist minister named Harper would distribute it. Asbury himself had approved distribution of the pamphlets. The situation "caused trembling" in the city. Nervous over the recent Gabriel plot in Virginia and remembering the Santo Domingo insurrection, Charleston residents had no intention of allowing Methodists to spread the antislavery tracts. The station preacher, Harper, received the papers and at first stored them. When the city intendant called upon Harper, he burned the papers in the official's presence. This satisfied the intendant but not the populace. An angry crowd determined that Harper should personally "atone for the injury he had inflicted on the peace and dignity of the state." Harper was cornered by the mob but with assistance managed to escape. The frustrated crowd turned their vehemence on the only other Methodist preacher in the city, George Daugherty, who was officiating for the evening at the meetinghouse. Daugherty was seized as he left the church and dragged through the streets. As an added indignity, the crowd decided to "pump him." They dragged him to a pump, placed his head under the spout, and continued pumping him for some time, a chilling experience in the dead of winter for a man already feeble in health. A "pious female" passing by halted the assault on Daugherty by boldly stuffing her shawl into the spout of the pump. Another citizen "stepped up with a drawn sword" and vowed to protect the minister at all hazards. Daugherty, though rescued, was nearly drowned and thoroughly chilled. He reportedly contracted a recurring pulmonary infection from the incident that proved fatal a few years afterward. At the 1804 meeting of the General Conference the slavery rules were mitigated by Asbury and two disciplines were published—one for Virginia and states to the North and one for those South of the Old Dominion. Privately the frustrated Asbury wrote, "I am called upon to suffer for *Christ's sake*, not for slavery."[55]

Despite the absence of a consensus among Methodists regarding slavery and religious instruction of bondspeople, in the Lowcountry the denomination attracted few white followers. Along the wealthier remote portions of the coast and even in the cities, from Cape Fear to the Savannah River, Methodist preachers were under a ban of suspicion as disorganizers who endangered "public peace." By 1800 there was only one Methodist church south of Charleston, on Edisto Island. Black participation, where Methodist churches existed, was generally discouraged even though slaves and free blacks responded to the personalism of the

Methodist denomination. Meetings were conducted exclusively on their behalf in Charleston, and blacks also attended white gatherings in churches, or went to the homes of white Methodists for worship, love feasts, and public prayers. But antislavery documents such as the one produced by John Phillips placed African-Americans in a precarious position. To attend Methodist meetings was to bring on wrath and physical abuse. The city guard arrested and whipped black Methodist followers for openly fraternizing with whites. Slaveholders opposed granting church membership in general to slaves, but to follow the Methodists was open defiance.[56]

But free blacks and slaves were attracted to the fervent Methodist preaching and their Armenian doctrines of universal salvation and individual free will. Like the preachings of Whitefield, Methodism must have been a welcome change for unlettered blacks from the stern, cold predestinarianism of other sects. And there was the ostensible egalitarianism. Black methodist exhorters addressed audiences of their own race and whites as well during this time, even in the South (although rarely during the antebellum period). Francis Asbury's traveling companion (who apparently also acted as his servant) was reportedly an impressive orator. Richard Allen and others less well known also went among integrated congregations. Asbury expressed pride in the Charleston "black" and "yellow" membership. "The Baptists have built an elegant church," he wrote, "they take the rich while the commonality and the slaves fall to us."[57]

Lowcountry black Methodists often paid a heavy price for their zeal, especially if they felt called to exhort. Such was the case with Sancho, an African-born Charleston slave formerly from an upper-class Moslem family, who was captured at age twelve en route to England for schooling. Sancho was converted to Methodism as a young man by Francis Asbury, which was when his "troubles began." Sancho's plight illustrates the slaveholders' attitude toward religious instruction for slaves as well as the dislike other denominations had of Methodism. His experiences are also comments on the limitations of Methodism as an egalitarian denomination. Furthermore, from Sancho we learn how strongly some slaves imbibed Christianity. Sancho's first master, a Catholic, was incensed over the slave's devotion to the Methodists. According to Sancho, he was beaten bloodily on many occasions because of his religious beliefs, and was repeatedly forced to pull his master in place of a horse.

The owner held "a double barrel gun in his hand to shoot me down if I should murmer or repine." When this master died, Sancho was sold to an Episcopalian master whose hatred of Methodism equalled that of the first. Sancho's religious enthusiasm was enhanced by previous experiences. The undaunted slave held prayers on his owner's plantations despite warnings and threats. Methodist emphasis on "suffering for Christ's sake" was carried to an extreme in the case of unfortunate Sancho:

He took me and tied me to an apple tree and one hundred and fifty lashes put upon me and told me to call upon Christ to take it off and also said he was Christ himself. He put me in the barn in stocks and a chain fixed upon my neck . . . I laid in that situation all night—covered with blood. . . . And O Paul I know the reason why you and your comrades sang praise to God in Midnight. . . . When I came out next morning . . . some of the people fainted at the sight of me. . . .

Sancho's seeming contempt for his personal survival perplexed his master who finally sold him to a man who reportedly would "break me of my religion." Ironically the slave breaker was himself a Methodist, and after he "tried" Sancho's faith, or perhaps his willingness to obey (or endure), he awarded him many privileges and allowed him to pray and hold meetings.[58]

Most slaves would not have endured such punishments for the sake of Methodism, or any other religion for that matter. However, some did. Certainly Andrew Bryan's example in Savannah was similar to Sancho's before whites finally believed that religion not rebellion occupied his thoughts. If some slaves took Christianity literally, many more viewed it symbolically. Of course slaveholders wanted bondspeople to imbibe subservient, not militant elements of Christianity. And proslavery advocates had difficulty believing that slaves accepted Christianity without questioning their temporal human condition. Apparently slaves, like Sancho and Bryan did. Although no one can say what these slaves were thinking when offering themselves as human sacrifices, it was not resistance or rebellion. Still, zealots such as Andrew Bryan and Sancho were exceptions. Many slaves, embraced Christianity without explicitly accepting their earthly station. Indeed, later events demonstrate that for blacks, among the attractions to Methodism in the early nineteenth-century was the church's temporary egalitarian posture.

Charleston African-Americans who accepted early Methodism only heightened suspicion and persecution on the part of whites. In 1800 the state restricted their right to practice Christian religion, as it soon restricted the right of masters to manumit them. Laws were passed in that year and also in 1803 forbidding black Methodists from holding meetings between sunset and sunrise, and decreeing that daytime meetings required the presence of a majority of whites, with the doors open. While the laws were only randomly enforced, they served to keep blacks away from meetings because of the city guard and patrols. Leagues of white citizens and "peace officers" broke down doors and dispersed "offenders." The Methodist leadership already preparing to retreat from its antislavery position for the sake of the denomination's survival in the South was disheartened and frustrated for they feared that access to the Charleston black population would be denied altogether. Asbury wrote that while "the rich among the people never thought us worthy to preach to them," they did sometimes give the slaves liberty to hear the Methodists and join their church. But now he noted, "it appears the poor Africans will no longer have this indulgence." Few slaves were allowed the liberty of attending daytime services, since they often worked until sunset. Thus to deprive them of the opportunity to attend worship in the evening was to prevent their church attendance altogether. The absence of black worshippers was keenly felt in Charleston. Night preaching at the Cumberland Church was not the same. "O, what a change for the worse," wrote itinerant James Jenkins in 1801. Customarily the galleries were "filled with the colored people," whose "most cheerful and delightful singing" rang throughout the church. Now Jenkins lamented, "there were not exceeding two or three to be seen, and they apparently afraid to show themselves."[59]

The message of white proslavery Carolinians did not fall on deaf ears. The Methodist church, like other denominations in the South, was already accommodating slavery. In 1800 Jenkins, on higher authority, ceased giving the sacraments to blacks. In order to prosper in the white community, the church needed to divest itself of antislavery attitudes and advocates. Also, rationalized the Methodists, to obtain access to the slaves, as the leadership desired, any teaching which even implicitly encouraged emancipation had to be silenced. In 1808 efforts to regulate conference members' proslavery activities were rescinded. The General Conference gave annual conferences jurisdiction over this issue. Asbury had already concluded that the church should work for the slaves' souls and amelioration of their condition rather than for their liberation.[60] In Charleston, as antislavery ardor waned, Methodists were gradually accepted. Blacks slowly returned to worship in large numbers. In 1793, the Charleston Church had 280 black and 65 whites as members. One year later the numbers had risen slightly for the entire state but not significantly in Charleston. This changed as Methodists moved away from a stand against slavery. Black membership rose to 3,128 in 1812 and in 1815 membership of the Charleston Methodist Church stood at 3,793 blacks and 282 whites. Methodists were the only denomination in Charleston that had such massive numbers of African-Americans on its membership rolls. Thus, in South Carolina close contact with Methodism was evident in Charleston among slaves and free blacks, and in regions farther north and west. For the rest of the Lowcountry slave population, not living in the midst of white society, large scale Christian instruction remained a movement of the future.[61] What slaves knew of Christianity in the country region they learned mainly from each other.

The Price of Freedom

Early liberalism within the Methodist church gave rise to a black leadership that helped foment seeds of organized insurrection among slaves in Charleston which may have spread through the coastal lowlands and surrounding Sea Islands. Soon after the church organized nationally, the General Conference took a significant step in gaining black converts by encouraging the development of a black ministry. Obviously this was more of a reality in the North than in the South. A ruling was passed, over strong opposition from Southern preachers, to ordain local black deacons where they had their own houses of worship. Desire for autonomy among blacks in the North led to establishment of independent churches before the turn of the nineteenth century. In 1794 Richard Allen of Philadelphia organized a separate black Methodist congregation. In 1799 Bishop Asbury ordained him deacon, and later elder of the Methodist Episcopal church. Allen's church was Bethel African Methodist Episcopal Church, fondly known as "Mother Bethel." But in Philadelphia the last vestige of ties with white Methodism were not truly broken until 1816. At that time, after a ten-year struggle with the General Conference, the blacks won, through a court order, the right to deny pulpit access to ministers of the white-controlled conference. It was a celebrated moment of independence and emergence of a black denomination. From this beginning sprang sister branches of African Methodist churches. That year five African churches had enough strength to bind together into one formal organization which embraced not only northern cities but congregations in Delaware and Maryland as well. With an eye toward joining this connection, African-American Methodists of Charleston created their own African Methodist Association.[62]

At a time when bondage in South Carolina was established more firmly than ever, the Methodist church was one area where urban slaves could experience a modicum of autonomy and freedom of spiritual expression. Black Methodists had enjoyed an independent quarterly conference in the early 1800s. They had control of their own collections from which they distributed to needy members of their community, and they maintained internal jurisdiction over the church trial of black members. Although many facets of black life contributed to seeds of discontent, the loss of this control over their religious life prompted visible action. White Methodists first moved against the black quarterly conference, abolishing it in 1815. Soon thereafter Charleston black Methodists contacted the Philadelphia AME Church, sending two representatives, Morris Brown and Henry Drayton, to be ordained for pastorates. Dispute over custody of a black burial ground gave the black secessionists their immediate pretext for withdrawal from the white organization. Led by Morris Brown, most of the black deacons, called class leaders, and over four-fifths of the 6,000 black worshipers removed their membership from the three white Methodist churches. This was clearly an illegal act and a move of group assertion, precipitating protests from white church leadership and repression from the authorities. In 1817 blacks organized the Charleston African Association, establishing several churches out of their massive numbers, one on Anson Street, one on Cow Alley, and one in Hampstead, the latter being most closely linked to the rebellion attempt. In December 1817, when blacks began holding worship, 469 were arrested for disorderly conduct. In 1818 the city guard arrested 140 blacks from the Hampstead Church including Morris Brown. The black Methodists were charged with instructing slaves without the presence of whites. "Bishop" Brown and four ministers were sentenced to serve either a month in jail or banishment from the state. Brown chose jail. Eight other black ministers were sentenced to floggings, fines, and banishments.[63]

The 1818 incident did more than any other to arouse the black community of Charleston. Abuse of their religious leaders brought home the fact that even spiritual liberty for bound and free African-Americans would be denied. Morris Brown was an exemplary figure in the black community. A prosperous shoemaker, Brown, unlike most well-to-do men of color, shunned false elitism and made every effort to bridge class-caste distinctions between slave and free or light and dark people of African origin. Brown's loyalty was with the lot of the slaves rather than free blacks. As head of the independent black Methodist Association, his congregations consisted primarily of slaves. A man of little education, Brown purchased members of his race specifically to manumit them before laws prohibited this. He hoped for legal sanction for the African Association even though harrassment, arrests, and physical abuse of black members continued. A group of freedmen petitioned the state legislature for permission to conduct separate religious worship. The petition was denied, yet the black Methodists continued their meetings.[64]

Finally, the closing of the black church in 1821 was apparently the final blow for most of the leading conspirators. A total account of the 1822 insurrection attempt is not within the purview of this study. Other scholars and observers have addressed events leading up to the attempted insurrection, its disclosure, and its effects on blacks and whites in South Carolina. At least one writer has maintained that there was actually no conspiracy at all.[65] However, the evidence supports the most widely held opinion that a plan of insurrection was in effect in Charleston. Uses of Christian ideology and African spirituality were essential in recruiting and in maintaining a large black following to carry out the insurrection. Within the leadership these two religious traditions nourished the rebels and were especially represented in Denmark Vesey and Gullah Jack. Vesey was a free "black" man and perhaps the first to contemplate the conspiracy. This has given rise to the notion that the insurrection was the work of free men more than slaves. Free men may have assented to the conspiracy as some evidence suggests. Yet the insurrectionists were, with the exception of Vesey, slaves from a variety of backgrounds— skilled artisans, rural people, African-born, and country-born.

Denmark Vesey, if not American-born, certainly represented black acculturation in other respects. Urbane, politicized, well-read, revolutionary, perhaps even a Christian, Vesey turned the black defection from the white Methodist Church into a dramatization of the plight of both slave and free African-Americans. Testimony indicates that the conspiracy was four years in the planning, corresponding to the period when slaves met in unsupervised assemblies for Methodist class meetings after their withdrawal from white churches. One black leader even stated that the African Church "met for this very purpose," but that in 1820, when a group from the Anson Street Church was "taken up," plans were temporarily shelved. Vesey and his closest associates, two of whom (Ned Bennet and Peter Poyas) were deacons, used weekly class meetings to discuss revolutionary passages in the Old Testament, as a forum for deploring the African-American condition and as a means to convey the political implications of the national debate over slavery. "He read to us from the Bible, how the Children of Israel were delivered out of Egypt from Bondage," confessed Rolla Bennett, one of Vesey's trusted who broke under pressure. Others proclaimed similar statements. The slaves' situation was compared with that of the Israelites. Favorite passages were from the book of Zachariah, especially the fourteenth chapter. Vesey and Poyas interpreted the chapter as predicting the doom of those who had enslaved or fought against God's chosen, and in this instance they substituted their own race for the Israelites. "My man," insisted Peter to one of the recruits, "God has a hand in it. We have been meeting for four years and are not betrayed."[66]

The harsh justice and strict moralistic tone of the Old Testament was also adopted by the slaves. None was to be spared. Vesey "read from the Bible where God commanded, that all should be cut off, both men, women and children," confessed one of the recruits. And the leaders insisted that "it was no sin for us to do so, for the Lord had commanded us to do it." Still some followers objected to the killing of women and children. The leaders would not hear, answering "what was the use of killing the louse and leaving the nit." Total destruction was not only prudent, but in keeping with the Word of God. Other recruits, similar to those in the 1816 Camden conspiracy, wondered about the ministers, believing that they at least should be spared. But white preachers were considered especially guilty. Vesey commanded:

Ministers were to be killed except a few who were to be saved and showed the different passages in the Bible from which Denmark preached (& the rest) and they were to be asked, Why they did not preach up this thing (meaning the passages on liberty & C) to them before. . . .[67]

One such passage was from Exodus. The first chapter deals with enslavement of Jews by the Egyptians, as undeserved a bondage as that of black servitude. Another favorite was Exodus 21:16:

And he that stealeth a man, and selleth him, or if he be found in his hand, he shall surely be put to death.

Slave religious leaders also had many questions to put to ministers about the nineteenth chapter of Isaiah, which seemed apocalyptic in the wake of Santo Domingo and the 1820 controversy over admission of Missouri as a slave state. The first two verses read:

The burden of Egypt. Behold, the Lord rideth upon a swift cloud, and shall come into Egypt: and the idols of Egypt shall be moved at his presence, and the heart of Egypt shall melt in the midst of it.
And I will set the Egyptians against Egyptians, and they shall fight every one against his brother and everyone against his neighbor; city against city and kingdom against kingdom.[68]

Some conspirators who became informants after the death of the leadership and capture of many stalwart followers, told the Court of the biblical analyses which Vesey and Poyas employed. Rebel leaders likened their struggle and compared their chances of success to the biblical narrative in which the Jews took the Canaanite city of Jericho. The poorly armed Israelites conquered the city with the help of a harlot and through divine intercession. The relationship between the seige of Jericho and the planned slave rebellion was more than coincidental as far as black Methodists were concerned. The assistance reportedly expected from certain "low life" undesirable white men in Charleston and the belief that God was working on their behalf emboldened the followers. Vesey's reading of the scriptures was well known. "He studied the Bible a great deal and tried to prove from it that slavery and bondage is against the Bible," said one witness. Another witness, a white youth who frequented Vesey's business, related that "all his religious remarks were mingled with slavery."[69]

Thus the fears and apprehensions of slaveholders were not without foundation. A literate, skilled, but oppressed black leadership, armed with the militant nationalism and spiritual example of Mosaic law, could easily transpose their situation and parallel it with that of the ancient Jews. But Denmark Vesey and his cohorts used more than scripture recitation to inspire rebellion. He reportedly told timid slaves the story of Hercules and the wagoner as a means of boosting their courage. Such a parable convinced Rolla Bennett to join:

I was one day on horseback going to market when I met him on foot; he asked me if I was satisfied in my present situation; if I remembered the fable of Hercules and the Waggoner whose waggon was stalled, and he began to pray, and Hercules said, you fool put your shoulder to the wheel, whip up the horses and your waggon will be pulled out; that if we did not put our hand to the work and deliver ourselves, we should never come out of slavery.[70]

Thus Vesey appealed to slaves through a kind of Greek rationalism as well as through his knowledge of the Bible. Biblical recounting of the struggle against bondage provided a major ideological weapon with which to reach the urban slaves who accepted Methodism. Yet even the most edifying features of the adopted religion would not be entirely acceptable or understood outside of the urban milieu. And even in the city the old ways died slowly. Many in the Methodist Church were African-born, nearly all of them slaves and not living in the "privileged" circumstances of the leadership. Hence, Vesey needed to draw partly on an African spiritual heritage. Vesey may have known of Boukman, the vodun high priest in the Santo Domingo revolt. Boukman used African religion as a conspiracy medium even before Toussaint joined the insurrection. Under a banner of the African god of revenge, he and his thousands of followers began the rebellion that brought terror to whites, freedom to slaves, and independence to the black island.[71] Similarly, in South Carolina the real spiritual force that bound the majority of known insurrectionists from Charleston to the country region, from the mainland to the islands, was the African priest Gullah Jack.

Jack, the slave of Paul Pritchard, and, like Vesey, a member of the Hampstead Church, reportedly advocated the rebellion when the black church members were first harassed and abused in 1818. Thus his association with the conspiracy was of the longest duration along with the original six first executed. If Denmark Vesey was the chief theoretician and Peter Poyas the arch plotter and organizer, then Gullah Jack was the religious embodiment of the movement. Jack's influence over the slaves did not derive from his role in the African Methodist Church but from his service as priest and doctor. He was African-born, a little man with "small feet and hands" whose trademark up to the time of his capture was a set of huge black whiskers. To avert capture after discovery of the first attempted revolt, Jack removed this symbol of his power. Jack headed the Gullah Society and his activities and recruiting efforts occurred in and outside of Charleston. As a force within the movement, he was well known among all the slaves. The arch-conspirators told recruits that they would be immune from death or injury at the hands of whites through Gullah Jack's potion and power. One follower related:

He gave me some dry food, consisting of parched corn and ground nuts, and said eat that and nothing else on the morning it breaks out, and when you join us as we pass put into your mouth this crab-claw and you can't then be wounded, and said he, I give the same to the rest of my troops—if you drop the large crab-claw out of your mouth, then put in the small one.[72]

Jack's charm, the crab-claw, and his dietary instructions are reminiscent of the BaKongo *nkisi*. The *nkisi* charm was a preserver, protector of life, and a healing agent. *Nkisi* derived its power from "spirit-embodying" materials which took on life, and from the user's confidence in its powers. Among the BaKongo, the "foot of a hen" and other claws suggest the captivating power of the spirit of the charm.[73]

Recruitment of slaves under the banner of Jack's mystical powers and invincibility may have been more effective than biblical rhetoric. Those who testified against him cowered in his presence. Jack apparently combined the positive powers of *nkisi* with the malevolent forces of *kindoki* to control the recruits. According to the Court, it was "not without considerable difficulty" that witnesses were convinced they need not fear Jack's "conjurations." While Jack was alive only one member of his Gullah Society spoke against him, at great fear for his life:

Gullah Jack is an enemy of white people. I attended a meeting at his house and he was the head man there. . . . Jack was my leader he is head of the Gullah Company. I heard that among them they had charms. Jack said if any man betrayed him, they would injure him, and I was afraid to inform. . . . If I am accepted as a witness and my life spared, I must beg the court to send me away from this place, as I consider my life in great danger from having given testimony. . . . I was afraid of Gullah Jack as a conjurer.

Only after the execution of Gullah Jack on July 12, 1822, did the extent of his participation in the rebellion and its massive organizational scope surface. His death released a wave of recriminations against him and his associates that led to many arrests and deaths.[74]

In the New World setting the role of African diviners such as Gullah Jack and Boukman assumed broader proportions. They were not only interpreters of the supernatural but had sociopolitical functions as well. The most active center of the Vesey conspiracy, aside from the African Church meetings, was Bulkey's farm where Jack's Gullah Society held its monthly meetings and planning sessions and also received intelligence from the country and city about the state of the rebellion. "Peter Poyas and others . . . came to the farm . . . and sang and prayed all night," confessed one informant. At another meeting Gullah Society members "roasted a fowl and ate it half-raw—as evidence of union." The sacrificial fowl is significant in African spiritualism. To kill a chicken, usually a white one, symbolically kept away bad spirits and ill will. In Santo Domingo on the eve of the slave rebellion, Boukman and his men uttered vodun incantations and sucked the blood of a "stuck pig." Both symbols of solidarity are reminiscent of Upper Guinea secret society initiation rites and BaKongo *minkisi* ritual, serving an expanded function. C.L.R. James reminds us that these prayers and supplications summoned forth courage against a powerful enemy:

The God who created the sun which gives us light, who rouses the waves and rules the storm . . . he watches us. He sees all the white man does. The god of the white man inspires him with crime, but our god calls upon us to do good works. Our god who is good to us orders us to revenge our wrongs. He will direct our arms and aid us. Throw away the symbol of the god of whites who has so often caused us to weep, and listen to the voice of liberty which speaks in the hearts of us all.[75]

Gullah Jack was also in charge of arms and referred to as "the general." He insisted that only African-born slaves could be trusted with information about weaponry, and even that group had to be limited. Jack consulted with other slaves who reportedly had divinely dispensated spiritual power. There was the "Old Daddy," with whom Jack met on Bulkey's farm, an aged African, "marked on both sides of his face." Though too old actually to participate in the rebellion, "Old Daddy" was privy to much information, and a source of inspiration for Jack, who visited him often. There was the old blind cartman, Philip, who could discern the expression on a recruit's face despite his blindness. Philip, a seer born "with a caul," was thusly empowered with ability to foretell the future and see spirits. Philip was also a preacher in the African Church. One recruit, introduced to the plot in the old man's presence, expressed hesitancy merely by his timorous facial expression and uneasiness, not by verbal utterances. Yet the recruit testified that the blind man perceived his fear and paraphrased scripture, asking, " 'Why should thy heart be troubled?' " The greatly alarmed man joined the movement, believing that his thoughts could be deciphered. Philip, as a fortune-teller encouraged the conspirators and at first foreshadowed victory. Later, however, he urged the rebels to " 'give up the business' " because " 'the white people could fire five times while they fired once.' "[76]

Jack's spiritual and political protégé was Tom, a blacksmith who reportedly made pikes and other weapons for Gullah Jack, and helped hide kegs of powder. The two were inseparable according to testimony. " 'When you don't see me and see Tom, you see me,' " Jack told his followers. Tom's blacksmith shop was a meeting place where a white youth who worked for Tom saw Jack frequently. Jack appeared even at mealtime according to the youth. And Tom's owner repeatedly warned him about associating with Gullah Jack but to no avail. They mostly "spoke in Gullah which I do not understand," reported the youth. He remembered watching Tom make a foot-long knife and this testimony alone sent the blacksmith to the gallows. Few people knew the whereabouts of the arms but all knew of their existence and many had seen weapons. Some were found on Bulkey's farm where the Gullahs met. Despite the small number, the discovery created a sense of terror. Yet because no one discovered a large cache of weapons does not necessarily indicate that it did not exist, but perhaps was well hidden. The Gullah Society was the most unified and trusted group of conspirators as well as the most resolute. They revealed nothing even as they approached death. The white youth testified that "Tom said that after the people were taken up, that he would not do as some had done, tell upon one another for money." Tom was true to his word. He remained at large for five days after his mentor was arrested, was confined for fifteen days before being executed, and probably endured torture. He never broke his silence.[77]

Tom may have been ordained by Gullah Jack to carry on the struggle if opportunity permitted, as Jack attempted to do when the first six leaders were arrested. For Jack decided to proceed with the rebellion after initial revelations prompted the first arrests. Originally a rescue of Vesey and the others was discussed. Realizing the unlikelyhood of success, the men opted for a move on the city to be led by Jack's Gullahs and those country slaves now commanded by Charles Drayton. In the short interim between the executions of the first six leaders on July 2, and the revelation that the danger was not past, Jack told his men to ready themselves. Hopefully if the Gullahs and other country slaves began the revolt, this would rally the urban slaves fearful of being named by those already "taken up." It was a bold attempt to salvage the rebellion and maintain unity. Undoubtedly Vesey and the others met death so audaciously because they knew the extent of the conspiracy and believed the rebellion would go on. It might have succeeded had not Jack been committed on July 5. The testimony of the state's chief witness was verified by others:

On Monday, 1st July, Charles Drayton told me that there would be an insurrection on the morning of 6th July, as soon as the guards were turned in—he said he commanded the country born company . . . Jack told me on the 1st July the same thing. . . .[78]

Gullah Jack's band was implicated more than any other group and most of the testimony against Jack and these men came to light only after the leader's reportedly undignified exit from life. The Official Report stated that for one professing such power and invincibility, Jack met his end uncourageously unlike the other leaders. At the pronouncement of the death sentence he reportedly begged for more time. When taken to the scaffold, "he gave up his spirit without firmness or composure."[79] This, perhaps more than any other factor, shook the faith of the insurgents and began a wave of confessions, implications, and accusations among some of the most deeply involved. It surely made faith in African spiritual prowess waiver and perhaps tied slaves closer to the slaveholders' religion, seemingly more powerful than theirs. Traditional beliefs had failed the insurgents as Gullah Jack's courage seem to fail him in the last hour. While he never revealed any information about the plot, his failed power symbolized the African-Christian cultural limbo of the slaves. Both traditions contained tactics suitable for liberation. Many Africans were members of the African Methodist church but feared and revered Gullah Jack as a diviner. "Until Jack was taken up and condemned to death," confessed one slave, "I felt as if I was bound up, and had not the power to speak one word about it. Jack charmed Julius and myself."[80] The power of Gullah Jack, however, did not withstand the test of indestructibility against white repression and force. Hence belief in the power of the old ways was visibly shaken though not immediately supplanted by Christianity. In passing sentence on Gullah Jack, the court mocked his power and his "gods":

Your boasted charms have not preserved yourself and of course could not protect others. Your altars and your Gods have sunk together in the dust. The airy spectres, conjured by you, have been chased away by the superior light of Truth, and you stand exposed, the miserable and deluded victim of offended justice. Your days are literally numbered . . . and all the Powers of Darkness cannot rescue you from your approaching Fate![81]

Yet Jack's boldness as an organizer and spiritual force had a deep logic within it. He warned the insurgents that African charms would not protect them against the treachery of their own color. This internal betrayal, distrust, and division among followers doomed the movement. The diviner's pronouncement was prophetic, for the seat of the slaves' undoing was found within themselves. Still, the 1822 conspiracy was an impressive collective militant effort, politically skillful and astute in its attempt to encompass all of the dispossessed blacks, even those who were quasi-free. Testimony conflicted, but a few free blacks besides Vesey were reportedly involved. Others may have gone undetected. Even the illustrious Morris Brown was implicated, although some witnesses denied this. Most testimony was second hand. But some insisted that Gullah Jack "had gone to Father Brown to ask him whether he would sanction the insurrection, and Morris Brown replied, 'if you can get men go on, but don't mention my name. I am going shortly to the North and I shall hear there, what you are about.' " Brown returned to Charleston to defend himself though eventually banished from the state. Another free black minister formerly harassed and brutalized because of his association with the African church reportedly approved of the plan, stating, a "little spanking with the sword was over due to the whites."[82] Most free blacks who were interrogated were released. The movement, clearly meant to be a slave revolt, nevertheless, attempted to achieve unity by bridging occupational, regional, and cultural barriers. The Vesey Conspiracy, though never pulled off, represented one of the strongest demonstrations of solidarity and racial unity in the history of North American slave revolts.

The argument of whether acculturated urban or isolated rural slaves were more given to rebelliousness has been addressed by a number of American historians.[83] In the case of the 1822 movement, the Conspiracy bridged these distinctions. Liberty for urban slaves was an illusion. Unable to reap the proceeds and benefits of their own labor, no longer able to look forward to purchasing their freedom or to free family members, these frustrated laborers and artisans provided an important leadership element. Although "privileged" to learn a trade, carry on the master's business, or allowed to become literate, they were still slaves. The modicum of flexibility and autonomy they were given only fed the contradiction. The rebel leaders were conscious men, aware of their worth yet no less bound than workers in the field. True they were spared the dull, degrading labors of field work, but as they used their opportunity to sharpen and cultivate their intellect their discontent became only more gnawing. Of course whites were incredulous at this logic and puzzled when "indulged" slaves sought open rebellion. For example, John the coachman of Elias Horry, was apprehended and implicated in the Conspiracy. The disbelieving master reportedly turned to his slave:

> 'Tell me, are you guilty? For I cannot believe unless I hear you say so.'
> 'Yes' replied the Negro.
> 'What were your intentions?'
> 'To kill you, rip open your belly and throw your guts in your face.'[84]

However, acutely oppressed African-born slaves, with strong ties to Africanity, formed the backbone of the rebellion effort. All of the leaders recognized their crucial role and knew that success depended on their assent and participation. Few doubted that it would be forthcoming. Planning and leadership came from the acculturated. But the rank and file were made up of plantation slaves. In this group the leaders placed the utmost confidence. "Let us assemble a sufficient number to commence the work with spirit and we'll not want men, they'll fall in behind us fast enough."[85] Also, the rural slaves, along with Jack's Gullahs, attempted to see the rebellion through before the capture of Jack.

The endeavor was a fusion of those at the bottom and those who could never aspire to the top, a lesson learned from Santo Domingo and Gabriel Prosser. The majority of African-Americans were at least united in their alienation from white culture and society. In the town the slaves met at class meetings and in each other's homes for planning sessions. As time for the rising neared, Vesey refused to work at carpentry and Jack refused to pay his mistress his wages. Both engaged themselves fully in the rebellion. Jack was instrumental in reaching rural and African-born slaves. But Vesey also traveled extensively in the countryside. As a free man and a respected carpenter, he traversed outside of the city limits without arousing suspicion. Lieutenants also worked the country parishes where kinship ties existed between those on the plantations and those in the city. Gullah Jack's haunt, Bulkey's farm, was on the outskirts of town, and the black overseer, Billy, was drawn into the insurrection. Jesse Blackwood, one of the first six leaders executed after the June disclosures, was expressly engaged in preparing and alerting plantation slaves. On one estate in St. John's Parish, forty miles south of

Charleston, all of the people were reportedly engaged, including the "trusted" driver. Most of the people apparently knew little of the details, but they did believe that their emancipation was at hand. The owner of the St. John's Parish plantation related that, from his knowledge of the means slaves used in "communicating intelligence from one plantation to another," he was convinced that "it was known throughout the neighborhood."[86]

The cause of failure cannot be placed on either the most exploited slaves who stood poised to move toward liberty or the urban laboring slaves who organized the rebellion but quickly defected. Most likely the bad judgment of Rolla Bennett who tried to recruit house servants and waiting men is largely responsible. This buffer group created by bondage was generally, though not always, composed of those who imbibed white culture and loyalty to white masters. Once again the wisdom of the black leadership was illustrated by the dictum of Peter Poyas, who warned leaders to be wary of those who worked in the house, particularly of those who wore the master's old clothes and ate the leavings from his table. Disclosures leading to the hanging of twenty-two men after the death of Gullah Jack came from urban slaves, which reveals the degree of disunion and distrust present among them. Significant also was perhaps a fear that they had rallied behind the wrong god and had trusted a fallible bastion of power. Living among whites as they did, urban slaves were between two cultures while isolated plantation slaves were able to keep more elements of the old one alive. Still, the Conspiracy was a supreme effort to break the chains of bondage in a spirit of nationalism, unity, and religious self-determination that would appeal to nearly all those of African heritage.

Testimony of informants gave credence to the magnitude, intensive planning, and geographical proximity of the conspiracy. The mainland country people to the south were under the command of Gullah Jack, the Island people around Charleston were led by Rolla Bennett, and those from the North by Ned Bennett. "I have spoken to Denmark and Peter about the people in the country," stated John Enslow, "and know they went into the country often and told me they had communications with all the islands—also in Columbia, Santee and different places in that direction." Estimates of numbers involved ranged from 600 to 9,000. Allowance must be made for exaggeration and for the leadership's persuasion tactics. Yet word of the intended insurrection or at least pending emancipation could have spread in a variety of ways, aside from direct information from an insurgent. Large retinues of slaves traveled from urban to country residences especially in summer months. Black boatmen traveled the creeks, rivers, and Atlantic waters frequently, carrying produce, white people, cotton, and, most significant for slaves, the latest information about kith and kin. Many "trusted" slaves had liberty to travel and do business in their master's stead, as did Rolla, Governor Bennett's "trusted" slave.[87]

Thus a network of communication was established that funneled gossip, news, and even secrets throughout the surrounding plantations. Such a network could spread news of rebellion once the first blow was struck in Charleston. That summer of 1822 the Lowcountry slave quarters were buzzing with news from Charleston. But it was not news of rebellion and freedom. The day of freedom never came. Instead, word indicated that a reign of terror was in full force and the black leadership was swinging from ropes in the Charleston jail yard. As far south as Beaufort and the surrounding Islands, planters readied themselves for an uprising. Beaufort's town council went into secret session and doubled the armed night patrol. Later that year Beaufort authorities were alarmed by rumors that a slave insurrection was planned in their town. But these fears were apparently unfounded.

During the trials of the insurrectionists, the official report singled out the religious practices of blacks as a leading cause of the intended rebellion. According to the chief investigator:

Religious fanaticism has not been without its effects on this project . . . the cession of a large body of blacks from the white Methodist Church formed a hot bed, in which the germ might be well expected to spring into life and vigor.[88]

Charleston clergymen of all denominations publicly alleged that blacks' recent religious practices were a major factor in spreading unrest. Respected Methodist minister Benjamin Elliott wrote a pamphlet deploring what he considered the exploitation of religion:

This description of our population had been allowed to assemble for *religious* instruction.—The designing leaders in the scheme of villainy, availed themselves to these occasions to instill sentiments of ferocity, by *falsifying the Bible*. All the severe penal laws of the Israelites were quoted to mislead them, and the denunciations in the prophecies, which were intended to deter *men* from evil, were declared to be divine commands which they were to *execute*.[89]

Edwin C. Holland of Charleston published a widely distributed pamphlet which contained the expressed opinions of those who denounced religious practices of African-Americans:

We are exposed to still greater perils, by the swarm of *MISSIONARIES,* white and black, that are perpetually visiting us, who, with the Sacred Volume of God in one hand, breathing peace to the whole family of man, scatter, at the same time, with the other, the fire-brands of discord and destruction, and secretly disperse among our Negro Population, the seeds of discontent and sedition. It is an acknowledged fact, that some of these religious itinerants, these apostolic vagabonds, after receiving the charities which the philanthropy and open-hearted generosity of our people have bestowed, have, by the means of Tracts and other modes of instruction, all professedly religious in their character, excited among our Negroes . . . a spirit of dissatisfaction and revolt. . . . Those . . . acquainted with the nefarious plot know, how blasphemously the word of God was tortured, in order to sanction the unholy butchery . . . and what a powerful agency was put into operation by the *dispersion* among Negroes, of religious magazines, newspaper paragraphs and insulated texts of scripture. . . . Religion was stripped of her pure and spotless robe, and, panoplied like a fury was made to fight under the banners of . . . Conspiracy.[90]

Many whites associated the African Methodist church, Christian instruction, and antislavery agitation with the rebellion attempt. Others saw African religion as the root cause of the conspiracy. Gullah Jack had pitted the gods of Africa against the Christian god. Even though Jack's courage failed him, revealing to his followers the vulnerability of his power and spirituality, his influence on the salves was frightening and incredulous to the court:

But no description can accurately convey to others, the impression which the trial, defence and appearance of Gullah Jack made on those who witnessed the workings of his cunning and rude address.[91]

Jack feigned ignorance until brought face to face with his accusers. In that situation his countenance instantly changed and "his wildness and vehemence of gesture, and the malignant glance with which he eyed the witnesses who appeared against him, all indicated the savage, who indeed had been caught but not tamed."[92] The "taming" of the "savage" and efforts to destroy the slaves loyalty to a "foreign" belief system occupied the minds of a few South Carolinians.

The depth of the planning and belief that the conspiracy covered most of the black coast accounted for the disproportionate terrorism and brutality. The Court employed the term "implicated" loosely. Aside from the leadership it included anyone with a weapon, anyone "named" with a horse or means of obtaining one, those "named" who met at Bulkey's farm, or who had been in the company of those with weapons and powder. Many families were affected. None was allowed to mourn or to recover the bodies. The July 26 executions were the most horrendous. Twenty-two men were brought to the gallows with the entire city watching. At the execution ground confusion ensued and a slave boy-child was trampled to death by horses. Another boy, white, watched the hanging from the safety of a third floor window of his King Street home. Later he described the spectacle as "a sight calculated to strike terror in the heart of every slave." It was a cold-blooded warning to would-be insurrectionists. But the death agony in the black community continued. On July 30, six more were executed. Additional men were thusly sentenced, but the stench of death began to sicken even white vengeance and these last thirty-six slaves were banished. The final victim to die for attempting to raise the insurrection was on August 2 when one William Garner was caught in Columbia where he had fled following the arrests.[93] It was a reminder of the power of the state and tenacity of slavery. Black leadership had fallen. The black Methodist church was destroyed. And in the eyes of many, African spiritualism had failed the test of service and invincibility against white might and white religion.

Despite apparent failings, many slaves were still tied to old ways, although drawn to the dominant religion as well. In both systems of belief they envisioned a means of attaining their heart's desire—liberty. But the immediate reality indicated that most whites were no more prepared to view Lowcountry slaves as spiritual siblings than as political equals. Yet at this time slaves may have decided that freedom would not come by the sword. The chances were too slim, the risks too many, and the price too dear. Much of the Old Testament militancy faded among the slaves familiar with its tenets. For the majority, who perhaps didn't fully grasp the association, it was not difficult to incorporate into their spiritualism a New Testament ideology which prophesied equality for all and the dignity of the sufferer. New Testament tenets became for them one banner under which to pursue their continued vision of freedom.

The Vesey Conspiracy prompted a lengthy debate and for a number of years afterward the subject of religious education was controversial in South Carolina. Most slave masters in the Lowcountry grew more adamant than ever in resisting Christian instruction of slaves. But among "thinking men" the belief emerged that a religious relationship between master and slave would have greater police power than statute. Two issued loomed in the minds of concerned South Carolinians. First, whites pondered the "falsification" of scriptures by the insurrectionists. Second, many slaves adhered to a spiritual tradition outside of white purview and capable of calling forth the instincts of freedom to a point of open rebellion. Governor Thomas Bennett, whose most trusted slaves were leaders in the attempted insurrection, lamented to Baptist pastor Richard Furman of Charleston that the projected insurrection had produced a backlash against the religious teaching of slaves. He urged that "humanity and religion" be advocated and laudably employed. According to Bennett, the Old and New Testament presented evidence of "Slaves and their Masters enjoying Membership together in the same Christian Church." As for the "religious" character of the "nefarious scheme," Bennett believed the scriptures were perverted by the insurrectionists. He observed that none of the "religious Negroes" in regular white churches were drawn into the plot because the conspirators were afraid to trust them. Bennett insisted that "religious Negroes" should not be punished for what others had done. Such Negroes were a safeguard to Southern society:

We have Reasons to believe they have a good Influence on the State of Society by the Promotion of good Morale as well as Piety among that class of People. This circumstance corroborates a Sentiment which has been long entertained by some who have been careful in making observations, as well as in informing on this subject . . . one of the best securities we have to the domestic Peace and Safety of the State is found in the Sentiments and corresponding Dispositions of the religious Negroes.[94]

Others felt moved to address the issue. In 1822, Richard Furman, representing the Baptist Convention of South Carolina, communicated to the new governor the expressed "official" views of the Baptists. South Carolina Baptist ministers reaffirmed the lawfulness of holding slaves. Some of them owned hundreds. Using scripture as evidence, Furman maintained, as had Bennett, that slaves belonging to regular white churches did not participate in the Vesey Conspiracy. He further admitted that Christian teaching among the slaves had been almost totally ignored. In that respect Furman recognized that masters had not done their "duty." Speaking for the Convention, he stated:

The interest and security of the State would be promoted, by allowing, under proper regulations, considerable religious privileges, to such of this class, as to know how to estimate them aright, and have given suitable evidence of their own good principles, uprightness and fidelity; by attaching them to principles of gratitude and love, to the interests of their masters and the State; and thus rendering their fidelity firm and constant.[95]

While Furman himself believed in a more active policy of religious instruction, the Baptists' statement was almost pure rhetoric. Baptists remained little concerned with religious instruction before or for some years after Vesey's Conspiracy. Wealthy coastal and Sea Island planters (nearly all Baptists and Episcopalians) viewed the attempted insurrection as an eerie vindication of their long-standing resistance to Christianizing slaves. In the midst of a large African slave population, they were the most vulnerable in case of an uprising. Still, every denomination was drawn into posturing on the conspiracy where religion and rebellion had been given the same meaning. The times stimulated much thought that would eventually lead to some implementation. Yet immediate reaction was not favorable to a liberal attitude. For whites the social trauma was too real. For blacks it was a time of anger and disappointment mixed with an overriding fear. Slaves were hanged for crimes that had previously brought lashes. Slaves set fires. In Georgetown in 1829 a conspiracy was discovered. Several slaves were hanged and the Lowcountry once again put on the alert. In Savannah and Augusta, disastrous fires prompted the Georgia governor to prepare a defense against slave revolt. In other states similar unrest occurred during this period. But Lowcountry slaves were particularly restless. The Southern situation was exacerbated by an incendiary document written by a black man from the North in 1829 and probably smuggled into South Carolina by black seamen. David Walker relied heavily on Christianity in his appeal to fellow blacks to take up arms against white masters. In the wake of these activities, the infrequent custom of teaching slaves to read was banned by statute. Runaway slaves robbed the mails and attacked travelers more than ever. Religious instruction, where it previously existed became unpopular. Slave meetings were disbanded and missionaries cut off from plantations. Masters previously indifferent became openly hostile to religious instruction. The few who once favored slave literacy disavowed it. The debate continued. But religious activity among the masses of slaves was, for a time, a closed issue in the South Carolina Lowcountry.[96]

A spiritual revival occurred in the first quarter of the nineteenth century. Societies were organized for spreading the gospel at home and abroad. In the South, before the Vesey Conspiracy, an impulse was given to religion mainly by Methodists, which awakened some to the "spiritual needs" of the black population. White churches began building galleries to allow for accommodation of free blacks and favorite or acculturated slaves. Eventually this limited exposure to Christianity would filter down to the masses of field slaves. But Vesey's Conspiracy and other factors delayed that. Even so, early nineteenth-century "revivalism" was mainly directed toward whites in newly settled regions, Indians, and missionary efforts abroad. By 1830 only a small minority of slaves regularly attended a church or heard a sermon. In the words of one slaveholding clergyman turned historian, "taking them as a class, their religious instruction was extensively and most seriously ignored."[97]

Still, some evinced concern and the issue began the "war of pens." A few planters and small number of statesmen felt the sting of abolitionist accusations and a gnawing contradiction as they piously embraced the evangelism of the 1830s and 1840s. The issue continued to breed anxiety. Most large planters deeply feared and distrusted the effects of Christianity on the servile population. It was a sore spot with the South Carolina clergy as well. Those who took their religion seriously were troubled by the dichotomy of the South. And even in South Carolina, though smarting from accusations, no denomination took their religion more seriously than the Methodists.

CHAPTER 6

"Religion of the Warm Heart": Plantation Missions and Methodist Impact

But when, in sight of our own doors, there were thousands of immortal beings, the slaves of a superstition as degrading, and an idolatry as dark as . . . the Pagans of savage lands; and when we observed that comparatively little was doing to guide them to purity to God, we have blushed for our own inconsistency. . . .*

In slabery, nigger go to white folks chu'ch. Slabe don't know nutting 'bout baptizing. W'en nigger dead, you can't knock off wuk for berry um. You berry um by de light ob torch. . . . Dey wasn't no nigger preacher on de plantation but dey been people to hold praise. (prayers).**

The Movement

The South Carolina Methodist hierarchy was apparently stimulated into action as a result of the Denmark Vesey Conspiracy and other events. Methodists came to view religious instruction of slaves as their particular calling. The mission was designed to Christianize the slaves on the one hand, and on the other, to demonstrate that Christianity would not foment rebellion or threaten the public peace. Rather than a two-edged

---

*James O. Andrew, "The Southern Slave Population," *MMQR* 13 (1831): 314–15.

**Sam Polite, former slave, in George P. Rawick, ed. *The American Slave: A Composite Autobiography*, 19 vols. *South Carolina Narratives*, vols. 2 & 3, in 4 Parts, (Westport, Conn.: Greenwood Publishing, 1972), III: (3)274.

sword, or a weapon of resistance, Methodists believed Christianity could, if "properly" taught, be the best insurance against insurrection. As far as Lowcountry slaves were concerned, the religion and some of those who brought it, had certain redeeming qualities. Selectivity was practiced on both sides. The Methodist hierarchy carefully chose biblical literature they believed suitable for slaves. And the Gullahs decided which features of the Christian doctrines could be serviceable to them.

Southern contemplation of the fears and horrors of slave insurrection and the pros and cons of slave conversion continued during the decade that had brought Denmark Vesey's Conspiracy. The Northern religious community grew more and more vociferous in denouncing the lack of Christianization efforts among bondspeople. At a time when American missionaries were "spreading the gospel" to American Indians, Africans, Asians, and Polynesians, some noticed that no such energies were spent on the African-Americans. In 1826 a leading Presbyterian journal, the *Christian Advocate*, published a query regarding the state of religious instruction among the slaves. Aiming at the Southern clergy, the writer asked:

Are there not 2,000,000 slaves in the republic of the United States?
Are not almost the whole of them denied the Word of God?
Are they not in full view of the American church, and yet in a great measure overlooked by that Church?
Is there any reason why they should be disregarded, especially while Greeks are remembered, and distant heathens commiserated?

The inquirer concluded that "It would doubtless be a work of mercy and relief to many who may have a conscience not justly enlightened, to furnish such fair and true answers to these questions, as would take away groundless apprehension that 'all is not right' in our own church and country."[1]

A Southern minister sent a prompt reply substantiating the validity of the criticism:

Should it be asked, "are not the greater part of them [the slaves] ignorant of the Word of God?" I should reply in the affirmative. Should it be again asked, "Are not many of them 'denied' the Word of God?" I should reply, yes. . . . Some slaves are, by their wicked owners, absolutely forbidden to use the Word of God. . . . Many slaves, owned by masters professedly Christians, are so neglected by them, as regards their spiritual interests, that they live and die in utter ignorance of the Word of God.[2]

Others expressed similar concerns. That same year the *Wesleyan Journal* published an article signed "Philander" which discussed the excuses offered for this "neglect" of "duty" in regard to the slaves. Some said slaves were "too ignorant" to understand doctrine and "too perverse" to regularly attend to matters of religion. Others, stated "Philander," insisted that masters would not allow Christian instruction of their slaves. Yet according to the writer, the "most significant culprit" was the Church, in this case Methodist. As "Philander" viewed the situation, the Church refused to broach the issue because it was unpopular. Thus the Methodist church was not fulfilling its duty as overseer of the spiritual welfare of the humanity within its own presence. "Philander" was followed by a letter of support from "Philemon," probably a slaveholder given the biblical reference of the name. "Philemon" suggested that the Methodist church "get on with the business." Christian instruction, he believed, would be a boon to *masters* and could be carried out effectively by the itinerant ministry.[3]

South Carolina Methodists have been credited with leading the slave states in motivating interest in Christian instruction among planters and other denominations. Certainly Methodists began discussion of the subject through the *Wesleyan Journal*, edited by William Capers, who became superintendant of the plantation missions. But the first major statement came in 1829 when Charles Cotesworth Pinckney, noted statesman and slaveholder, addressed the Agricultural Society of South Carolina. Pinckney had recently solicited the services of a Methodist missionary for his own plantations, and believed in the benefits to be derived from Christian conversion of bondspeople. His address skillfully approached the issue by disarming his listeners with an introductory defense of slavery. Settling fellow slaveholders at ease, Pinckney extolled them for concern with their slaves' physical well-being, juxtaposing the "happy" bondspeople with the "beleagured" laboring poor in Europe and the North. He further attempted to assure the audience of his proslavery commitment, defending the system from biblical example and citing passages well known to most upholders of the institution. Finally, satisfied with his own persuasive maneuvers, the statesman held forth on the business at hand, still cautiously speaking from the planters' position:

Nothing is better calculated to render man satisfied with his destiny in this world, than a conviction that its hardships and trials are as transitory as its honors and enjoyments; and that good conduct, founded on Christian principles, will ensure superior rewards in that which is future and eternal. A firm persuasion that it is both our interest and duty to afford religious instruction to the blacks, induces me to dwell on this subject.[4]

Many meritorious qualities existed in a Christian servile people as opposed to the "heathen" one that lived among them, Pinckney assured Society members. Christianity would elevate black behavior from its "deplorable state," and such amelioration was an asset to the planter. Pinckney held that black children learned from parents and elders mischievous tendencies that were counterproductive to plantation interests. From "his natural instructors," Pinckney related, the "little negro is often taught . . . that he may commit any vice he can conceal from his superiors; and thus falsehood and deception are among the earliest they imbibe." But if "true religion" were propagated, a sense of duty would undermine the slaves' reluctance to labor and,

diminishing the cases of feigned sickness so harassing the planter, would augment their numerical force and consequent production. . . . A greater proportion of domestic happiness would prevail, and render them contented with their situation, and more anxious to promote their owner's welfare. The absence, or diminution of theft, falsehood, and many other vices, would render the home of the Agriculturalist far more agreeable than it can be where guilt, which escapes human detection, knows not and fears not another tribunal.[5]

To those objecting to Christian instruction on grounds that it was "the cloak assumed to cover the nefarious designs of insurrection," Pinckney countered that such instruction would be "the best antidote to this very disease." He maintained that no arguments were entitled to so little weight as those condemning slave exposure to Protestantism because it was abused by some. So long as planters exercised their right of scrutiny and control over who taught slaves and kept a watchful eye on the content of the doctrines disseminated, Christian teaching would not lend itself to insurrection. The appeal was to group interest. To "ensure the security and comfort of the planter" slaves should be made "conscious of their advantages, and grateful to their Maker for his bounties." To accomplish this an efficient system of Christianizing was needed, especially in the country region, and every Protestant denomination stood ready and willing to send missionaries where plantation owners would permit it. These "white and Southern" missionaries Pinckney insisted, would only instruct slaves "orally" in the duties and principles of Christianity. "Such a state of moral culture," persuaded Pinckney, "would give us the advantage in argument over those of our Northern Brethren . . . whose objection to our system is partly founded on the deficiency of religious instruction." If said instruction and subsequent conversion were "more genuinely diffused," Pinckney assured, "our national character would be relieved from its only real opprobrium."[6]

C. C. Pinckney's address before the South Carolina Agricultural Society typified the concern of a few planters to make the masses of bondspeople culturally visible for the first time. While reminding slaveholders of their duty to provide spiritual and religious instruction to their slaves, his overriding argument in favor of Christianizing efforts centered on protection of the institution and a countermeasure support system against the influence of leadership in the slave quarters. Christianity, with its concepts of sin and rebirth, could conceivably contribute to the bondspeople's developing a sense of vulnerability and prostration. So long as slaves remained a somewhat foreign and even mysterious mass of laborers, outside the realm of human interest on the part of whites, such slaves were a threat. As Christians however, sharing the same beliefs and spiritual orientation as their masters, blacks would eventually come to feel part of the total society. To imbibe white religion as taught by the new wave of missionaries would, in the mind of Pinckney and others, allow slaves to accept their subservient role in society, making them not only physical dependents but spiritual and psychological dependents as well.

Pinckney's call for bringing Christianity to the slaves was a significant departure, coming as it did from a wealthy, highly recognized planter and politician. This was the first time a large group of South Carolina planters were addressed on the subject by an individual whose respectability was national and whose interests coincided directly with their own. Pinckney's method of approaching the issue was employed by others later. He saw the result of Christian conversion primarily in idyllic terms—happy, docile, "spiritually uplifted" darkies, and a peaceful plantation, free from theft, runaways, and bereft of artful means to avoid labor. The appeal also liberated the slaveholders from a sense of guilt—if they happened to have one—regarding their right to hold slaves. Pinckney reasoned that the doctrines of the Old as well as New Testaments upheld slavery and that scriptures, "if properly taught," would never undermine the slave system. Naturally, the best way to ensure "proper" instruction was to have "Southern men with Southern principles" as teachers. Finally, Pinckney's attempted evocation of the planters' sense of "moral duty" as patriarchs had its place. Certainly a thoughtful minority wished to view themselves in this light and Pinckney came as close to epitomizing the term of patriarch as any South Carolina slaveholder could. He gently admonished his listeners with a solemn if pharisaical appeal to conscience: "Is there no room for apprehension of future responsibility before a tribunal whose Judge has expressedly directed the dissemination of his doctrines?"[7]

Hence arguments aiding the erosion of resistance to slave conversion focused particularly around pecuniary concerns, desirability of public peace, a more submissive black population, and justification of slavery by holy writ. Appeals to cultural enlightenment and the slaves' spiritual ameloriation were of no consequence without the overriding rationale of a profitable economic venture. The sanction this slaveholding statesman gave to religious instruction paved the way for certain missionaries to go, unmolested, among slaves of the coastal region. Pinckney, supported by at least a small segment of influential slaveholders and clerics, had thrust the issue into the open. From there the South Carolina Methodist church adopted the idea as its own.[8]

The denomination long associated with antislavery activity in South Carolina and often blamed for stirring slave unrest had an opportunity to absolve itself. South Carolina Methodists became pioneers in the Christianizing effort. Despite Pinckney's boast, Methodists were the *only* denomination in 1829 that declared itself ready and able to send "laborers into the field" at the request of planters. Methodist leaders either took a cue from C. C. Pinckney's encouragement by both his public blessing and his employment of a missionary on his own plantations, or quite likely, Pinckney worked with the clergy in introducing the volatile issue to the Lowcountry master class. At any rate, in 1830 the South Carolina Conference organized a department specifically for the purpose of conducting missionary work among the slaves, pledging to "take up the cross" of preaching to African-Americans.[9]

South Carolina Methodists had not ignored plantation slaves before 1829 but neither did they especially seek them out as they did in the urban sector during early years of the connection. In the Lowcountry south of Charleston only a mere smattering of white Methodists resided, and consequently few slaves in the region were exposed to the denomination. In the Charleston District of the nearly 6,000 black Methodists around the time of Vesey's Conspiracy, most were slaves. But the up-country, frequented by circuit riders and stimulated by numerous revivals, contained the majority of the state's 18,460 black Methodists at the end of the third decade of the nineteenth century. Thus the coastal plantations, especially in the Sea Islands, were the main target areas during the thirty years of Methodist religious efforts among the bondspeople of South Carolina, and parts of Georgia.[10]

When the South Carolina Methodist Conference met in February 1830, its Missionary Society produced a stirring report entitled "The Southern Slave Population." Authored by James O. Andrew, a slaveholding bishop from Augusta, Georgia, the document noted the lack of missionary service to slaves and lauded the attention and encouragement given by C. C. Pinckney. More significantly, the report indicated a rising concern within the Southern Methodist church. In 1831 Andrew's report was published in the national Methodist journal, indicating that a movement was under way in the regional jurisdiction of the South Carolina Conference. Bishop Andrew acknowledged that in the face of "so many obstacles," a long period of negligence had characterized Methodist attitude. Yet he insisted that the Methodist church was not unmindful of the so-called irreligion of the slaves:

We saw the efforts made to send the Gospel to distant Pagans, and we heard of the success of those efforts with much gratification. But when, in sight of our own doors, there were thousands of immortal beings, the slaves of a superstition as degrading, and an idolatry as dark as . . . the Pagans of savage lands; and when we observed that comparatively little was doing to guide them to purity and to God, we have blushed for our own inconsistency, and longed to see put into operation such an instrumentality as should extensively and successfully, carry the Gospel to the large and increasing slave population.[11]

The difficulties and magnitude of the undertaking had until recently hindered the Church's commitment Andrew reported. But a new day was dawning. Of late, the Church was "cheered and strengthened" and much gratified by the expressed advocacy of the renowned C. C. Pinckney. The South Carolina Conference considered the words of so "notable and respected" a Carolinian to be a "valuable and powerful auxiliary" in the work undertaken. Speaking on behalf of the Methodists' missionary branch, the slaveholding bishop reiterated even more strongly themes pounded out by Pinckney: the "moral baseness" of un-Christian slaves had to be combated. Among bondspeople, stated Andrew, "the tender and hallowed ties of husband and wife are unknown," and the slaves' "love of strong drink" and "immoral spirit" was a detriment to the economic interests of the planter and tranquility of the plantation. In comparing these "vices" to the "virtues" of the "Christian Negro," Andrew noted:

The *Christian Negro looks to heaven.* He feels that this world is but a temporary home, and although his condition here may be a hard one, yet God can sanctify every hardship to an abundant increase of his spiritual comfort. He serves his master from *principle* not from *fear*. It is a service rendered to God; and he regards his master's interests as his own. They are therefore safe in his hands.[12]

The relationship between Christian instruction and socioeconomic control was not peculiar to "enlightened" elements of the South. British employers and Methodist clergy resorted to a similar analysis during the Industrial Revolution, which coincided with the period of American Methodist activity among the slaves. Some of the parallels are noteworthy. The values of a doctrine of submission with a spiritual base had its uses for both American slaveholders and British employers. British antislavery Methodists and reformers did not allow this "progressive" cause to interfere with the "demands" of a free market economy. Religion taught to slaves in the South, like that British laborers were encouraged to accept, reinforced the "blessedness of poverty," or the dignity of being a good slave. Both policies were viewed as essential for discipline to the machine in the case of England and to the fields in the case of the United States. Yet this "godliness" brought no temporal gain to the laborers. Thus E. P. Thompson, in writing about British workers, noted that the "first great lesson" taught to laborers was that their primary happiness was not in the present world, but in a future one. Labor then, was a *"pure act of virtue,"* according to British pro-Methodist ideologues of the nineteenth century. It was "inspired by the love of a transcendent Being, operating . . . on our will and affections." The *Power of the Cross* transformed the will, created a hatred of *sin* and love of *good*, as interpreted by employer and slavemaster through their missionary agents. The *Power of the Cross* was sacrificial. Sacrifice would remove the guilt of *sin*. The words of Dr. Andrew Ure from his *Philosophy of Manufactures* illustrate the functional use of religion as a means of work discipline. While specifically referring to British laborers, the analogy is comparable to the slaves. Ure maintained that the "transforming power" of the Cross was:

the motive which removes love of sin; it mortifies sin by showing its turpitude to be indelible except by such an awful expiration: it atones for disobedience; it excites to obedience; it purchases strength for obedience; it makes obedience practicable; it makes it acceptable; it makes it in a manner unavoidable, for it constrains to it; it is, finally, not only the motive to obedience, but the pattern of it.[13]

Still the Methodists boasted of spiritual egalitarianism rather than the elitism so traditional among Calvinist-oriented and Anglican sects in the United States and England. Methodism beckoned all. The elect could be legion if willing totally to prostrate themselves before the Cross. The South Carolina Methodist church declared itself ready to include the African-Americans on the Lowcountry plantations into their connection. Andrew concluded his address by calling for missionaries of a special caliber, particularly designated for such a work, and capable of feeling themselves charged with the slaves' spiritual interests. They must be men whom the bondspeople were willing to regard as *their preachers* but also men to whom slaveholders would look upon confidently, as the *appropriate* spiritual guides of their slaves. The appeal was moving and dramatic:

Here is a work which will require piety, prudence, patience in no ordinary measure. He who would enter upon it efficiently, must be willing to feel himself in a good degree an exile from the pleasures of society. He must be willing to be looked down upon by the rich and great about him as a *negro preacher*. He must be content to take up his abode amidst fogs and death, and *trust God* emphatically. . . .

Methinks we hear a goodly number starting from the different departments of the Church, and saying *we* are willing to sit down by the negro's cabin fire, and talk to him of Jesus and the resurrection and death; and take God as our portion and heaven as our final home. . . . Then we say to the Church, up quickly and send these men to their work.[14]

Impressive claims to apostolic fervor had their place in motivating the Methodist Church to Christianize the slaves in South Carolina. Yet the Methodists did not initiate the movement even though as early as 1824 they expressed a desire to create "a separate department" to address the slaves' "spiritual welfare." Lack of enthusiasm closed the issue until 1828. At that time two Lowcountry planters, Colonel Lewis Morris and Charles Baring of the Combahee region, asked Methodist circuit rider, George W. Moore, to give special religious instruction to their slaves. Morris and Baring were so pleased with the outcome that they determined to petition the South Carolina Conference, scheduled to meet early the following year, to send regular missionaries to their plantations. At the same time, but perhaps not independent of the former developments, C. C. Pinckney called on William Capers, Presiding Elder of the Charleston District, and asked him to recommend a "suitable exhorter" to oversee his plantations on the Santee River. Pinckney related that one of his Georgia friends employed a Methodist overseer, and was very happy with the "new piety" among the slaves and with the increase in plantation productivity. The Georgia planter credited these developments to his overseer's influence over the slaves. Capers informed Pinckney that he could not assist him in employing a Methodist minister as an overseer, but added that a full-time religious instructor could be provided by the South Carolina Conference upon application. Pinckney agreed to apply, and the South Carolina Conference of 1829 was historic. The Morris, Baring, and Pinckney requests were acted upon immediately, and the Conference sent out the first missionaries devoted exclusively to Lowcountry slaves. With the movement launched, a statement was appropriate. Pinckney's address favoring slave conversion came in August 1829. The Methodists began religious instruction in 1828. But no statement on the issue was forthcoming from the South Carolina Conference until February 1830. Thus Pinckney's approbation preceded the South Carolina Methodists' appeal, perhaps as a means of cushioning opposition and suspicion. In any case, the role of the Methodist church in initiating religious instruction among the slaves in South Carolina was not as bold a venture as some previous writers on the subject have stated.[15]

The Christian conversion movement, then, originated with an appeal from planters. After that initial step the Methodist church in South Carolina pledged active support and leadership. Possibly national pressure from the General Conference would have eventually forced the Southern clergy into action. Once the state hierarchy organized their missions to the slaves, the process was conducted with diligence and vigor. But as of 1829, no pressure from the national episcopacy induced such a movement, and the urgency which South Carolina Methodists expressed could easily have been prompted by the financial support from "concerned" planters. Furthermore, the source of South Carolina Methodist zeal for slave conversion was not found in the Church hierarchy. Most enthusiasm as well as commitment derived from the lay preachers, men of humble birth, for the most part non-slaveholders, sent among bondspeople in the isolated, unhealthy Lowcountry and Sea Island regions. Some of them were buried there. One wonders how long the question of slave conversion would have lain dormant except for the efforts intended to stabilize the plantation system. This primary goal, seasoned perhaps with some element of conscience, caused a few influential slaveholders to promote the experiment. A definite parallel existed between spiritual and temporal interests. And the view that Christianization would lead to a more efficient and submissive labor force slowly gained credibility.

Despite postulations about Methodist involvement in Vesey's Conspiracy, Southern Methodists were not antislavery, and Lowcountry planters had little real reason to suspect them as harbingers of black liberation. By their own admission they were a denomination whose Southern branch believed in slavery. The South Carolina Conference's reaction to the Vesey Conspiracy was to reaffirm their proslavery position. Andrew, in his 1830 report, stated that the church's responsibility was not to contemplate slavery as an institution. Such speculations, according to Andrew, brought much "evil" to the slaves without any corresponding benefits. "We look upon the blacks just as we find them," he wrote, ". . . hoping only to bring them into the enjoyment of freedom of a higher character; freedom from the bondage of Satan, from the control of passions and lusts."[16]

Yet such statements, undoubtedly sincere, could not immediately dispel suspicion and doubt. The burgeoning abolitionist movement, and the fact that some Northerners were already going south to do what Southern clergymen had heretofore left undone, made the task of the South Carolina Methodists even more difficult. Antislavery sentiment gained momentum among Methodists and other denominations in the North. Anxiety about the abolitionists disguised as "men of the cloth" going among slaves made any missionary a suspect until proven otherwise. One Sea Island missionary in the employment of the South Carolina Conference complained to the Missionary Society:

My success in getting access to the colored people, as far as I flattered myself in the early part of the year, has been in some measure obstructed, growing out of the excitement got up by the abolitionists.[17]

Sea Island and Lowcountry planters were surrounded by a dense black population as compared to a paucity of whites. White communities felt particularly vulnerable. A Northern Presbyterian minister, Courtlandt

Van Renssalaer, was forced out of Virginia as a missionary among the slaves. He then attempted to preach to the neglected bondspeople of the Sea Island and Savannah River regions in 1835 and 1836. His career was abruptly halted when a circular appeared stating that a gentleman of "high respectability" had information that Van Renssalaer held secret meetings with slaves, "and consulted with them on their means of revolt, their armies . . . when they expected to be ready. . . ." The "authorities" were alerted, and "Van Renssalaer would have been arrested but when sought for he had suddenly left." The missionary denied the charges from his Northern sanctuary and indicated they exemplified the opposition to the "work" which he and others endeavored to accomplish among the slaves.[18]

Allegations about antislavery activity being conducted by Northern missionaries, a distrust of so novel an experiment, and a traditional association of religion with rebellion evoked open hostility to Christian instruction in many cases. The idea of perfect strangers going among their "people" to preach was not one to which planters could easily adjust. The South Carolina Conference proclaimed repeatedly the official Methodist position on slavery: that it was an institution of "Divine Providence," that the issue of slavery did not fall within the jurisdiction of the Church but was "exclusively appropriate to the civil authorities," and that the Conference was resolved "not to intermeddle with it." Representing the South Carolina Conference in 1838, William Capers, Superintendent of the Missions to the Slaves, further affirmed the Methodist belief that "the Holy Scriptures . . . do unequivocally authorize the relation of master and slave." Capers, himself a slaveholder, affirmed:

> Our missionaries inculcate the duties of servants to their masters, as we find these duties stated in the Scriptures. . . . We hold that a Christian slave must be submissive, faithful and obedient . . . we would employ no one in the work who might hesitate to teach this; nor can such a one be found in the whole number of preachers in this Conference.[19]

In spite of such reassurances, skepticism among slaveholders continued and invitations to instruct Sea Island and Lowcountry slaves constituted a mere trickle in the 1830s. In a letter to William Capers, C. C. Pinckney expressed his own gratitude for the services of the Methodists. But he also stated that the majority of the seaboard planters were "still adverse to missionary efforts and give us ample cause to pray that their eyes may be opened." Nevertheless, missionaries increased their efforts yearly and other denominations applauded the undertaking. In 1838 an interdenominational group of influential clergymen met under the auspices of the Methodist Missionary Society and asserted their growing concern and commitment to slave conversion. They agreed that areas of the large cotton and rice plantations along the sea coast from the Savannah to the Pee Dee rivers in Georgia and South Carolina would receive the bulk of attention. In most of the state, churches existed in nearly every area, but the group admitted that even there, accommodations for blacks were insufficient. However, at least no one could say, "Negroes of the neighborhood are without the gospel." Such was not the case "on the Sea Islands, and in the delta of the rivers, where the Negroes are most numerous." These thousands had no churches accessible to them, and the interdenominational group confessed, "they are as destitute as if they were not inhabitants of a Christian land." The plantation missions were undertaken for the benefit of these slaves.[20]

Southern churches and seminaries were not long in taking note of the movement. Episcopalians and Presbyterians, as well as Methodists preached sermons on the benefits of the enterprise. Gradually, some planters, convinced of the desirability of Christian instruction, publicly declared their approval at agricultural meetings and in agricultural journals. Denominational newspapers also kept up arguments in favor of religious instruction. William Capers prepared a short catechism for the missionaries' use in instructing slaves. Arguments of appeal rarely varied. Although the interest of the plantation was preemptory, the security of the country and saving of black souls were also loudly proclaimed. The 1830s was a period of persuasion and promotion of Christian proselytizing, with the Methodist church directing the campaign and receiving widespread if not unified support from a number of quarters. In the words of one church association spokesman, discussing conditions in South Carolina and Georgia during this period, "The religious instruction of our slave population, entirely suspended in some parts of the country, through the lamentable interference of abolition fanatics, has proceeded with almost unabated diligence and steadiness of purpose."[21]

In the Sea Island region south of Charleston, Methodist missionaries acquired early access to some plantations. Two missionaries, George W. Moore and Thomas D. Turpin, arrived in 1833. Moore's appointment included Beaufort and the surrounding islands. His first charge consisted of two plantations and two preaching appointments in Beaufort (attended by slaves from several plantations), six plantations on Paris Island, and one plantation on each of the five remaining islands around Beaufort. Turpin's appointment in the Beaufort District, called the May and New River Mission, included Hilton Head, Bull's and Dawfuskie Islands, and the mainland between the May and New Rivers.[22]

The most successful method of gaining permission to evangelize slaves involved having a sympathetic local planter approach fellow slaveholders on behalf of the missionaries. In the Sea Islands Methodists were actively supported by William E. Baynard. The Baynard family were large slaveholders with plantation interests on Hilton Head and Edisto Islands as well as on the mainland. Baynard was a frequent intermediary between planters and missionaries. Writing to him in 1833, one Hilton Head planter expressed his confidence in the cause:

> I am anxious that the mission to the colored people in this community be continued . . . that the gospel should be preached to them in their cabins and the Scriptures explained in such a plain and simple manner that they may fully understand what true religion is.[23]

Baynard was not always so successful. While some slaveholders simply refused to allow missionaries on their plantations, others gave the experiment a try but found "results" discouraging. For example, William Pope, Sr., Baptist patriarch of a Sea Island family who owned the largest amount of aggregate acreage on St. Helena, Dawfuskie, and Hilton Head, answered Baynard's inquiry of 1834 in the negative. Pope felt that Thomas Turpin, sent the previous year, had gained few converts. He wrote:

> If I am not deceived one or two of them [the slaves] will long remember him with gratitude . . . but am inclined to think he has not met with decided success . . . he has had to encounter some difficulty, discouragements and prejudices which he has not been able to fully overcome—tho' he has certainly laboured faithfully, and been zealous and diligent in the discharge of his duty.

Pope concluded his letter by stating that the missionary's services would be discontinued since the "means and opportunities" of religious instruction had improved; there were "now two churches on this Island [Hilton Head] in which there is service at least twice a month."[24]

There appeared to be a consensus among certain planters in the May and New River Mission to withhold cooperation from Turpin and the Methodists. James Sealy, also a planter on Hilton Head Island, wrote to

Baynard in a letter dated the same day as Pope's. Sealy expressed hope that "the people" had profited from the missionary's presence, but he "could see nothing of it." Sealy, like Pope, withheld consent for the missionary's coming within the confines of his plantation.[25] Denominational rivalry may have been a factor in decisions to deny Methodists access to the slaves, and Baptists expressed the most skepticism toward missionaries. But more significantly, the Methodist-Baptist controversy provides insight into religious activity among the slaves prior to the missionaries' coming.

Thomas Turpin, assigned to the May and New River Mission in 1833, had his own opinions about the state of religion in the Sea Islands, and defended himself regarding his unsuccessful efforts among the bondspeople. Turpin had access to about 1,000 adult slaves, one third of whom were in the Baptist church and in the "Negro societies, and all of them under Baptist influence." Yet these slaves rarely saw the pastor of the church or attended its services. Instead, Turpin related, the slaves had "societies organized among themselves." According to the missionary, "these societies were very corrupt." Turpin described a scene at one black society gathering on Bull's Island in which a particular type of penance, drawn from African traditions, was engaged in as punishment for sin:

They had three degrees of punishment, and . . . the punishment was inflicted agreeably to the magnitude of the crime, according to their view of the crime. If the crime was of the first magnitude, the perpetrator had to pick up a quart of benne seed . . . poured on the ground by the priest; and if of the second, a quart of rice; and if of the third a quart of corn; . . . they also had high seats and low seats, but incorrect views relative to those who ought to be punished; . . . it was also a rule among them never to divulge the secret of stealing: and if it should be divulged . . . that one had to go on the low seat or pick up the benne seed.[26]

The rite the slaves engaged in is remiscent of high-low seats and a pyramid of degrees in the Poro and Sande in Upper Guinea, and some secret societies in Angola. The Poro inner circle was a social regulating as well as religious body. It stopped quarrels, caught, tried, condemned, and punished social criminals. In Poro-Sande culture, high seats belonged to a few old religious leaders of high degree.[27] But the way Gullahs employed the use of high-low degrees was unique and reflected their ability to adapt a past tradition to the organization of their slave community. The association of the communal and the spiritual is evident,

since this regulation took place within a religious context, ostensibly under the rubric of Christianity. High and low seats in Gullah society assumed a meaning different from African Poro-Sande society. But the
function of regulation and community control was still present. The
Gullahs reserved the "low seat" for those who betrayed community interests by divulging "the secret of stealing," undoubtedly from the master. This demonstrates the seriousness of solidarity among the people.
Thus picking up the benne seed was reserved for the worst of crimes
"according to their view of the crime." While the Methodist missionary
believed the slaves had incorrect ideas about who should be punished,
slaves themselves were using an internal logic with little reference to
Protestant conceptions of sin. This Gullah interpretation of sin was at
variance with their Christian instruction. A sense of contrition for the
safety and peace of the plantation or out of fear of the Christian God
was not a motivating issue. For the Gullahs, moral guilt fell on those
who forsook socioreligious authority and loyalty in the slave quarters.
The presence and influence of black leadership was also revealed as the
"punishments" were administered by a "priest." This implies no relationship to the Christian church to which some of the slaves belonged.
Missionary Turpin believed the rites strangely akin to Catholicism. Obviously they were not. But in West Africa Poro-Sande priests and priestesses were responsible for administering justice and punishment. Thus
this role had some cultural-historical continuity. Slaves saw nothing incongruous about adopting elements of Christian religion and adapting
those to aspects of their traditional spiritual heritage still serviceable in
the New World setting.

The penance for the "sin" of divulging the secret of stealing was no
brief activity, but a rather trying feat. A "gentleman" residing on Bull's
Island informed Turpin that an individual usually could not pick up all
the scattered benne seeds in one night. And "if it was not done in one
night they had to continue until they did it." Thus while the benne seed
ritual was not comparable in degree to African punishments instituted
by the Poro Council for community crimes, there is a symbolic reference. While representing a form of censure for erring members, it was
not the way "Christianized" slaves were expected to interpret the concept of "sin." Turpin stated in his report that having to contend with
"all this superstition and ignorance, together with their prejudices against
Methodism," he had added few church members. Nor, reported Turpin,

did he strive to do so, "but rather . . . to beat down their prejudices and to establish a better principle of religion among them, all of which I should not presume any person in this low country would attempt to contradict."[28]

Planters in the May and New River Mission region were offended by statements implying that they tolerated practices such as the one Turpin discussed. Sea Island Baptists felt under attack for not instructing black converts in "true" principles of Christianity and for baptizing slaves without scrutinizing their religious life. Turpin was smarting from the cold reception he received from planters. Turpin did in fact infer that some planters were aware of and permitted un-Christian practices among slaves baptized as Baptists. It was after all a "gentleman" of the Island who had explained to Turpin the workings of the benne seed penance he had observed. Methodist unpopularity among Sea Island planters was recognized at the Missionary Society Headquarters. Soon after the report was circulated, Turpin was removed from the May and New River Mission, and assigned to the John and Wadmalaw Islands Mission in the Charleston District. Turpin insisted, however, that he did not intend to discredit the planters. Nor, he said, did he mean that planters knowingly sanctioned "corrupt" practices among the slaves. Turpin merely wished to point out how irreligious so-called converted slaves were. Through the pages of the *Southern Christian Advocate*, he made a somewhat cynical apology, which undoubtedly did little to assuage the ire of Sea Island planters:

But it [the report] appears to have injured the feelings of many of the Baptist friends. I did not intend to injure their feelings, nor any other persons, notwithstanding though, it has been said that I have "shot a ball particularly at the Baptists, and in its glance it was hit the Episcopalians." If it has made any mortal wound by its being received in a light different from what I intended, I feel it my duty to heal the wound.[29]

Turpin had indeed offended the planters, especially his comments on the slaves' lack of "truly religious" training, despite Baptist church membership. He believed that the "converted" slaves made a mockery of Christianity. These slaves who "scarcely ever saw the pastor" of their church were members of the First African Church in Savannah. Andrew Bryan's nephew, Andrew Marshall, was the pastor. In 1830, church membership was 2,417. Although a black church, whites were responsible for control and for the conduct of its members. Whites came to the

church at will, and randomly sat in on conferences or any other meetings
the blacks held. Nor could black ministers preach or officiate at the church
without the endorsement of at least two white Baptist ministers. Thus,
the black church was separate physically but dependent upon white favor for its existence. Turpin's critics reminded him that Marshall was
"nothing more than a Negro," implying that the black minister need not
be taken seriously. Turpin disagreed. Marshall may be a "Negro," said
the Methodist, but one authorized to baptize and preach, "and he has
baptized a great many many in this low country." Slaves in the May and
New River area were among Marshall's converts, but Turpin said, "he
never comes to see them . . . nor any other Baptist minister." Therefore, as far as the Methodist missionary was concerned, his observations
were grounded in the fact that slaves in the Sea Island region were practicing "corrupt," "superstitious" rites under a rubric of Christianity.[30]

Membership in Andrew Marshall's Savannah Church was for these
slaves a contact with Christianity, perhaps the only contact. It provided
them with a sanctuary for continuance of spiritual independence, though,
like the ill-fated African Church of Charleston, probably serving a number of roles for various groups of African-Americans. By joining the church
Gullahs became nominal Christians yet practiced religion relatively free
from scrutiny. Church attendance was not an every Sunday occurrence
even for white Baptists, who might attend once a month. Turpin believed the slaves had no contact with the Savannah Church, yet they
must have had some. But undoubtedly most slaves who could join did
so because it was an African-American spiritual organization as well as a
Christian church. Membership would also hopefully keep the Methodists
away. Planters *and* slaves probably wanted this at first, although for different reasons.

The Turpin report exemplifies the Gullahs' own method of putting
the new religion to use. The "discouragements and prejudices" he encountered were not as much a *preference* for Baptist worship, as implied
by slaveholder Pope's letter. Certainly elements of Baptist practices appealed to the slaves, just as elements of the missionaries' "method" did
not. Methodism took a more persistent attitude toward its converts and
its doctrines. Conversion was a serious solemn matter. Doctrine had to
be memorized, and scriptures were lectured on and discussed extensively
by the missionary. Preaching among the slaves was more didactic than
inspiring, and "true" believers had to demonstrate a reasonable under-

standing and acceptance of Christian teaching as presented before they became church members. Furthermore, during this early period, Methodist religious instruction among the Gullahs was entirely conducted by whites, and caused problems for a slave population unaccustomed to seeing any whites except slave masters and overseers. Gullahs did not readily adapt to Methodist concentration on learning and reciting church discipline. They were even more resistant to efforts to shift spiritual leadership out of the slave quarters and from black to white influence.

Most Gullahs wanted to to construct their own socioreligious system and not without its "Christian" elements. Few were actually affiliated with any Baptist churches during this period as compared to later. But for those who were, religious activities through association with a church acceptable to slaveholders facilitated approval of the slaves' own independent "Negro Societies." These societies were reportedly organized by the slaves themselves. As long-distance Baptists, Gullahs deviated from little-understood orthodox practices without being closely observed.

The straightforward, illuminating approach detailed in Turpin's report provides insight into the religious practices he found among the Gullahs. But his "Missionary Sketch" further increased Methodist unpopularity with planters. Nor apparently was it favorably received by the South Carolina Missionary Society, since Turpin was removed in midyear, following circulation of the report, and a circuit rider from the Orangeburg area sent to replace him. Furthermore, subsequent missionary reports never assumed the pointedness and frankness which characterized Turpin's statements in 1833. During the remainder of the period of Christian conversion in South Carolina, vivid descriptions of "superstitions" encountered by the missionaries no longer found a place in public print. Yet there were undoubtedly many. One missionary suggested that preachers write down the nature of these slave beliefs in order to provide a history of the Methodist plantation movement. Evidently nothing came of this effort. Missionary reports were first carried by the *Christian Advocate and Journal*, a widely read Methodist newspaper published in New York. By 1837, the growing schism between Northern and Southern Methodists led to the founding of the *Southern Christian Advocate* published in Charleston. But Northern religious presses, also interested in the progress of slave conversion, often published the missionary reports even after the New York based newspaper was superseded in the South.[31]

The South Carolina Conference wanted favorable, optimistic reports. In their efforts to absolve the Southern Church from Northern reproach, Methodists expected missionaries to cease concentrating on the nature of "superstitions" among the slaves, on "moral degradation," or sect rivalry. Such emphasis suggested that the enterprise was not successful. Also to focus on planter impropriety undermined the confidence the Methodist church hoped to instill among the slaveholding class. Perhaps as a result of Turpin's unpopular "Missionary Sketch," late in 1833 William Capers published a notice to missionaries stating that the sort of information then being received was unsatisfactory. "General remarks," wrote Capers, "by no means furnish the requisite information." The Superintendent of Missions instructed each missionary to provide a quarterly report which, if nothing else, answered the following types of questions:

—how many preaching places have you
—how many schools, teachers, scholars, how many of these are natives
—how many since the last report
—Revivals.[32]

After Turpin's controversial report, statistics and discussions of Christian-type experiences dominated missionary information from the field. It was more significant to detail the conversion of an old African-born slave than to outline what appeared to be latent types of "Roman Catholic" ceremonies. The former type of religious experiences were dramatized in the pages of the *Southern Christian Advocate* in the 1840s and later.

Missionaries assigned to the Sea Islands and coastal regions maintained a healthy optimism, but reports were often discouraging. Early support from slaveholders was spasmodic and intermittent, and bondspeople took a lax attitude toward Methodist discipline. In 1835, John Coburn reported from Beaufort that, while his charge had increased to include twenty-one plantations with 400 children under catechetical instruction, "the prospects of this mission are not considered flattering." He blamed "interference" and "foreign intermeddling" for his lack of success, yet recommended that the station be continued for at least another year. In 1836 Coburn indicated that improvement had taken place, yet church membership dropped considerably because of many expulsions and the fact that some planters had withdrawn their slaves from the mission. His work was also greatly hindered because the islands, separated by wide waters, were frequently impassable for small boats.[33]

The "interference" and "foreign intermeddling" discussed by Coburn came from two sources. First, Gullah leaders continued to exert influence and they resented as well as resisted supersedence of their authority. Secondly, a growing number of slaves professed affiliation with Baptists of the region. Many missionaries complained that these alleged black Baptists were unfamiliar with Christian doctrines. Thus from the missionaries' point of view, the complexity was actually three-tiered: a powerful black leadership holding sway through beliefs and practices apart from Protestantism, a conflict with black "professors of the faith" whom missionaries considered mere "pretenders," and both problems compounded by the skepticism of Baptist and Episcopalian slaveholders. The missionaries admitted that religious instruction under such circumstances was a formidable task.[34]

Methodist Sea Island missionary activity experienced various periods of growth and decline. Methodism was persistent, but there was never a massive moment into the church on the part of the Gullahs. By 1839, the May and New River Mission had been discontinued and the limited number of converts absorbed by the Beaufort and Savannah River organizaiton. Also by 1839 Methodists created a new mission in the Beaufort district, called Pocotaligo, and another in the Charleston district called Edisto Island Mission, including Jehossee and Fenwick Islands. Edisto was by far the most prosperous of the Sea Island missions. By 1842 Beaufort Mission embraced thirty plantations but contained only 310 members, with 370 children under instruction. The Pocotaligo missionary ministered at nine plantations, had 295 church members, and 156 children under catechetical instruction. Progress was slow in these areas compared to other missions north of Charleston and in the upcountry. For example, the North Santee Mission embraced only fifteen plantations but had 528 church members and the Black and Pee Dee Rivers Mission covered twenty-five plantations with 1,180 church members. By the time of national division within the Methodist church in 1844, the Beaufort Mission had dropped to twenty plantation appointments, and Pocotaligo still served only nine. The Edisto Mission however, maintained steady progress.[35]

Figures relating to church membership are not impressive considering the thousands of slaves in the coastal and Sea Island region. Still, Methodist missionaries remained active there until 1861, even after it became apparent that Baptist influence would predominate. Not only were white

Baptists already in the area, but many were large slaveholders. Hence Baptists had the power to control the type of contact, religious or otherwise, to which slaves were exposed. Organization of the Methodist Episcopal Church South and the Southern Baptist Convention in 1844–45 gave a new impetus to the movement of slave conversion. But by then Methodist missionaries were employed mainly by Episcopalian Sea Island planters. In 1844, island appointments south of Charleston included Port Royal, Paris, Dawtaw, Coosa, Ladies, and Beaufort. However, even during these years, missionaries indicated that the "spiritual state was not encouraging." By 1855, Sea Island appointments had dwindled to preaching places only on Ladies and Paris Islands, and a tiny Methodist chapel erected in Beaufort. On the mainland around the Sea islands, Beaufort Mission continued to increase in terms of plantations served and preaching appointments. Yet even here it was clear that while Methodists seemingly provided Gullahs with their first organized exposure to the doctrines of Christianity, they rarely gained a large number of new or lasting converts for their own denomination as occurred in other regions of the state.[36] Nevertheless, despite the distrust manifested by a number of Lowcountry and Sea Island planters, and the problems with black leadership, Methodism left its impact on these slaves who ultimately adopted the Baptist faith.

The Response

Gullah response to Methodism is partly related to the nature of slavery in the Lowcountry. Plantation bondage in the Sea Islands and coastal regions of South Carolina and Georgia was a complex phenomenon. Similar to the West Indies, it contributed to growth and development of cultural autonomy among the slaves because visible aspects of Africanity could remain. At the same time, however, the region proved ultimately to be fruitful ground to plant seeds of Christianity among the slaves. One finds little of the paternalism which some historians claim was the determining ideology in the relationship between master and slave. Sea Island slavery was generally absentee. Planters might have several tracts of land on one island, as did the large Fripp family, or have holdings in several regions of the coast, as did the Popes, Fullers, Jenkinses, and Butlers. The real family home was usually in Beaufort, Charleston, or Savannah, in some cases as far away as Philadelphia, Newport, or England. Industrious masters might remain near their plantations during the "sickly season" by building homes on a high bluff. From these retreats, such as St. Helenaville, they directed plantation affairs through their drivers and overseers. The enormous black population working in the fields rarely saw a white except for overseers and their families, or through brief sometimes seasonal contact with slave masters.[37]

Bondspeople were under the direct supervision of black drivers who might report to a head driver, also a black man. Slaves recognized these supervisors' powerful position as coming from an outside oppressive force. The Gullahs had little affection or even genuine respect for black drivers. Although exceptions existed, the interests of slave drivers and those of the slave community were inimical. Francis Kemble, an English resident on the Georgia Sea Island plantations of her husband Pierce Butler, described drivers in their role:

> At the upper end of the row of houses, and nearest to the overseer's residence, is the hut of the head driver . . . The negroes, . . . are divided into troops or gangs, . . . at the head of each gang is a driver, who stands over them, whip in hand, while they perform their daily task, who renders an account of each individual slave and his work every evening to the overseer, and receives from him directions for their next day's task. Each driver is allowed to inflict a dozen lashes upon any refractory slave in the field, and at the time of the offense.[38]

Laura M. Towne, a Philadelphia osteopath who went to the Sea Islands as part of the Port Royal experiment, observed the Gullahs' attitude toward slave drivers. Towne noted that the people complained of one driver in particular named Gabriel. " 'How, boys,' " he answered, " 'You know I cut and slash you for ole Massa. Ain't you know I no do dat Massa do worse.' " The men smirked at him scornfully. Certainly the black drivers' position was unenviable. They did not usually seek the role, yet were bound to do the master's bidding or face punishment themselves. Nevertheless, antipathy toward black drivers was observed on many occasions. Yankee cotton agent, Edward Philbrick, stated that their position over the masses of slaves did not seem to derive from intelligence or respect. As soon as the artificial element of force was removed by masters and overseers fleeing, "these black foremen generally dropped back to the level from which they had been temporarily raised." They had no useful authority over the slaves and attempts to reinstate them in the management of crops "generally met with singular failure." Antebellum Methodist missionaries stated the slaves believed drivers would never get to heaven. Gullah soldiers sang a song about the black driver during the Civil War. White witnesses thought the song appeared "quite secular in its character, yet its author called it a 'spiritual' ":

> Fust ting my mammy tell me,
>   O' gwine away!
> Tell me bout de nigger-driver,
>   O' gwine away!
> Nigger-driver second debil. . . .

The relationship between the missionary's observation and the "spiritual" further illustrates how Gullahs viewed slave drivers. One driver, "noted as a good Negro, and a Methodist," had heard since his childhood that no driver could ever get to heaven, "and they need not try, for none . . . could see God's face in peace." The distraught man told a Methodist missionary, " 'to that tree every night I want to pray; at last God, for Christ sake, pardoned my sins.' " The black driver became fully convinced that " 'Christ is able to save a driver as well as anybody else.' " And he hoped, said the missionary, to hold out faithfully so that " 'people will see at least one driver in heaven.' "[39]

The type of bondage experienced by the Gullahs was related to the Lowcountry's settlement as well as the staple crops produced. The colony of Carolina was settled by West Indian planters who created a system of slavery notorious for maltreatment of black laborers. One individual, a German, traveling through the Carolina Lowcountry after the American Revolution, observed that:

The condition of the Carolina negro slaves is in general harder and more troubulous . . . wretched food, more work, tedious work, harsh and cynical treatment at the hands of owners and overseers. There is less concern here as to their moral betterment . . . proof is in the fact that they do not multiply . . . numbers are refreshed thru importations.[40]

The continued harshness of the system was maintained. After indigo cultivation, both South Carolina and Georgia became absorbed in cotton culture. Although not as backbreaking as indigo, Sea Island cotton extracted a heavy toll from black workers in many ways. The staple needed a tremendous amount of labor and laborers, especially after 1820 when the international market value of fine cotton soared. On an average plantation, fifty to sixty days of labor per slave were required to produce one bale of fine Sea Island cotton. The crop required more hoeing than short-staple cotton, a different type of picking, which had to be done from only slightly opened bolls, and a painstaking preparation for the staple market in the ginning process. Men were usually responsible for seed extraction of Sea Island cotton. Jenkins Mikell of the Peters Point Plantation, Edisto Island, gave an account of this activity on his father's estate:

> The operation was long, tedious and fatiguing. It was done on gins operated by foot, a crude plantation, or domestic device for getting out the seed from the lint—one man to a gin. He would stand on his left leg and work a crank-like arrangement, somewhat like a crank that drives a sewing machine, first with his right foot, then when he got tired . . . he would hop on his right foot and work his gin with his left foot—never stopping his gin as he changed. . . . As each man has thirty pounds of lint cotton to gin out for his day's work, he has no time to loaf.[41]

Sea Island slave women also performed arduous, monotonous, and fatiguing work on the plantations. The crop was harvested from late September through December, a cold, damp part of the year on the coast. Women and boys were considered the best pickers, though all field hands would be ordered out at first harvest. As soon as enough cotton was gathered, ginning began which took many men away from the fields. Women pickers worked rapidly yet carefully, so not to bruise the delicate fibers for this would affect the grade. Sea Island planter William Elliott maintained that "the greatest care is used by them to separate from the cotton, all dried leaves or other substances that may impair or discolour." While "prime, young and strong" women engaged in this activity, the elderly, "less sturdy" women and those near their time of childbirth worked in the gin house. They thrashed or "whipped" seed cotton to further remove loose sand or dirt then passed it on to "assorters." This group of women stood before long tables and divided the lint according to color and fineness. From there men received the "assorted" seed cotton for seed extraction. Once this was accomplished, women "moters" inspected and divided the cotton once again, removing fibers stained by the black cotton seed crushed by the gin. Finally, before packing, the cotton was subjected to one final inspection at the "mote table."[42]

The whole process created a tenseness which everyone experienced. A driving momentum was kept up, but quality work was insisted upon since that was the key to the lint's value. Activities were coordinated so that cotton did not lie around or be stored after picking since too much exposure injured the product. Some overseers worked the slaves at night and on Sundays. The rawness and wetness of the weather did not deter managers and planters from ordering all "available" hands out to the fields. Though work in the gin house was considered "light" work, this "cotton barn" offered little relief from cold and dampness. The air inside was so unhealthy that slaves preferred the openness of the fields. Workers breathed flying lint and dust during the long hours as they labored in standing positions.[43]

The labor had a telling effect on the slave women's physical health. A callous attitude developed toward needs of pregnant women, postpartum illnesses, infant care, exhaustion and exposure to inclement weather. Bondswoman Susannah, in relating to Laura Towne, the tragedy of having all three of her living sons sold away, mentioned that she had actually had twenty-two pregnancies. Another defiant Gullah woman who worked in the house was beaten frequently by order of the mistress and retaliated by bringing "not one nigger" to Maussa. Another woman was buried up to her neck in earth as punishment, a few days after she had given birth to a stillborn child. Laura Towne, who saw signs of illtreatment, recorded various accounts:

> On this place, the Oaks, Loretta showed me her back, arms and breasts today. In many places there were ridges as high and long as my little finger and everywhere marks of the whip. She said that her children had been killed in her by whipping. She says it was because when "heavy with child," she could not do the full task of a field hand. I suspect also being rather apt to resist and rather smart in speaking her mind, poor thing. She has suffered terribly and it is no wonder that she is more indifferent about her clothes and house. . . . She says this was "de cruelest place."

Loretta lived on the plantation of Daniel Pope, a member of the Sea Island Baptist "aristocracy" who "gave no shoes, salt, molasses, nor Sunday clothes . . . neither would he allow the field hands any meat, nor permit them to raise pigs." In the year before the Civil War Pope determined to make the people work as much as possible, "so he kept them in the field from morning till night and lashed them every day."[44]

Francis Kemble noted on her visit to the Georgia Sea Islands that the principal hardships fell to the lot of the women. She wrote of her first visit to the "Infirmary":

Women lay prostrate on the floor, without bed, mattress or pillow, buried in tattered and filthy blankets. . . . I stood in the midst of them, perfectly unable to speak. . . . Here lay women expecting every hour the terrors and agony of childbirth, others who were groaning over the anguish . . . of miscarriages— here lay some burning with fever, others chilled with cold and aching rheumatism on the hard cold ground, the draughts and dampness of the atmosphere increasing their sufferings, and dirt, noise, and stench, and every aggravation of which sickness is capable, combined in their condition.[45]

Conditions among the female population affected Kemble deeply. She spent much time trying to alleviate deprivation and discomfort. For her concern she faced the resentment of Pierce Butler, who considered her interfering with plantation "discipline." An antislavery Englishwoman, Kemble claimed she married Butler without knowledge of his human property. Their divergent views caused dissension between them. On one occasion, Kemble wrote of Butler's reaction to the petition of a group of slave women:

Mr. _____ was called out this evening to listen to a complaint of overwork from a gang of pregnant women. I did not stay to listen to the details of their petition, for I am unable to command myself on such occasions and Mr. _____ seemed positively degraded in my eyes as he stood enforcing upon these women the necessity of their fulfilling their appointed tasks . . . as a *duty*.[46]

The conditions of labor under the "peculiar institution" hindered longevity and a natural increase in birth rate survival among the slaves. Both races paid in different ways because cotton planters did not usually attend to their estates personally, and because they too often judged managerial quality by the magnitude of cotton profits. But illegal imports still contributed to the increase in slaves. The last slave vessel to arrive in the Sea Islands, the ship *Wanderer*, was in 1858. Sea Island planters had opposed reopening the slave trade in South Carolina in 1803, apparently because it might have decreased market value of their own slaves at a time when these planters were economically vulnerable. However, after the close of the African trade to North America in 1807, and the rise of Sea Island cotton, planters engaged in smuggling. Illegal importations continued to contribute to the native African population.[47] Even more significantly, many American-born slaves were only one or two generations from African ethnicity, because many were imported into the Sea Islands during the last two decades before the War of Independence.

Thus Methodist missionaries found very oppressed but tightly knit communities of African-Americans still clinging to patterns of social behavior and modes of worship, largely a mystery to whites, having developed through African cultural convergence. Their pattern of speech was one example of this. "Their language," wrote one missionary in 1840, "though . . . understood by themselves, cannot be by one unaccustomed to them, without great study and application." It was a peculiar creation—an English patois. As previously discussed, Lorenzo Dow Turner's linguistic study of Gullah, conducted over a fifteen-year period, involved many former slave informants. He views Gullah as a creolized form of English with elements of survivals from African languages spoken by ethnic groups brought to South Carolina and Georgia. Turner found most retentions present in vocabulary but also in elements of sound, syntax, morphology, intonation, and word formation. Yet as previously mentioned, Gullah was even more than a distinct pidgin English or dialect, but a means of expressing oneself in the most graphic and sometimes literal sense. Arthur Sumner, a Northern teacher on the Sea Islands during the Civil War, found it "easier to understand a foreign language":

'Talk we get dinner,' means 'do you mean that I shall get dinner?'
Byron came to me this morning with a message from his mother.—'Ma says, if you give her some trade. . . .' Can you make it out? Oh, dull girl! The meaning is clear. Ma wants to know if you will give her some thread.[48]

William F. Allen, another Northern teacher, also wrote about the Gullah's peculiar interpretations and usage of English. For instance, "stand," referred to the state or condition of a person, place or thing. On one occasion, Allen, teaching sentence structure to a class of children, had them go over to the window and then asked them the color of the sky. "Nobody could tell," and most of them "stared straight ahead at Jimmy, who was in the yard, and I half expected them to say 'black.' " Finally "Abraham" ventured "white," then "red." Dick, a former house man, passed by the window and Allen expressed his frustration, to which Dick replied promptly, " 'lick'em":

"Well Dick," said I, here's a chance for you to lick Tom, who was appearing around a corner of the barn. "Tom, what's the color of the sky?" Tom stared at the sky, but said nothing. Dick grinned. "Tom, how sky *stan'*?" "Blue" shouted Tom.[49]

Missionaries categorized black spirituality as "curious superstitions" or as types of worship reminiscent of Catholicism. Gullahs had their own religious leaders who sometimes professed Christianity and solicited sanction from planters and overseers as the "spiritual elders" of the people. One St. Helena planter who spent little time on the island, wrote to the Methodist missionary assigned there in 1833 that he hoped the Methodists could improve the religious condition among the Gullahs. The biggest problem according to the planters was the black leaders whose control had to be broken.[50]

Thus missionaries vied with black spiritual advisers for religious leadership in the slave community.[51] There was no way for the Methodists to counter the influence of slaves whom the Gullahs regarded as spiritual advisers but who made no claim to Christianity. Methodists felt that under Christian instruction customs and practices perpetrated by this leadership would die out in time. But the missionaries believed black leaders who fused "paganism" with Christianity were most detrimental to the Methodist cause. These leaders had either to be set on the "true" path or their influence undermined. The competition proved difficult. Everywhere they went among the Gullahs, missionaries found black leaders successfully impeding Methodist influence. From Beaufort Mission, T. E. Ledbetter reported in 1836 that although some "pious" Episcopalian planters allowed missionaries to preach to slaves, he saw no evidence of progress:

. . . we combat a great many false notions, and . . . fatal doctrines which have been elderly imbibed by the colored population through the instrumentality of ignorant and superstitious teachers among themselves. And nothing is more difficult to overcome than a strongly prejudiced understanding . . . many among them are opposed to us.[52]

Some missionaries, even without planter approval, attempted completely to halt black spiritual leadership. Others hoped to communicate with Gullahs by recognizing or even appointing certain "elders." Both tactics often bred frustration. From Pocotaligo Mission in Beaufort District, John N. Davies reported in 1840:

A black man, one of them [the slaves] whom they claim for their spiritual father, and, as they say, "had brought them through the spirit," became corrupted and inflated with self-importance—I gave him a close talk, with a design of moving him, when he held up the wand of his sweeping influence by asserting that all the children [the people] would follow him. As we have no authority to visit them at the plantation we chose the only mode of saving them, . . . to select and appoint a zealous and upright man, of their number to be with him as an aid and guard; meanwhile a noise came from abroad of large depredations being committed which implicated this and several plantations . . . nearly all have ceased to attend and we fear they are rushing to ruin—Lord have mercy upon them and upon me.[53]

This missionary's report typifies one significant aspect of white attempts to usurp black leadership — that of replacing an individual who could not be subordinated with one seemingly more controllable. Undoubtedly, the "zealous and upright" man was more cooperative than pious. The audacious missionary had no access to the plantation where his spiritual rival lived, nor apparently did he have the good wishes and confidence of the planter. Some planters left it completely up to the Gullahs as to whether or not they attended missionary services, and others specifically forbade it; this contributed to the continued presence and influence of black leaders. Moreover, as the Davies' account reveals, slaves given passes to attend preaching appointments often found other more lucrative or entertaining means of utilizing their temporary mobility. Fear of this limited movement and assembly was a continual obstruction in obtaining unified support for religious instruction from the slaveholders. When Christian conversion took on a new seriousness in 1845, large slave gatherings for religious purposes, never popular, were discontinued and the emphasis shifted to individual and family instruction on plantations. The latter type of religious teaching eventually brought the Methodists more success.[54]

Still many Gullahs displayed skepticism toward the Methodists and resisted offending their own leaders. From Pocotaligo, John N. Davies continued to inform the public of his problems:

We have had some trouble at another preaching place, occasioned by the puffing up of father S., as he is called, but plantation authority forbids his guiding the people. They have appeared spellbound, not to move or think without him. He a poor creature of dust imagines himself to be the Great Shepherd whose voice alone "the sheep know," and whom alone the true sheep will follow. . . . We visit the plantations and explain as far as possible. God grant us brighter days and better times.

But despite only marginal encouragement from both planters and slaves, the missionaries continued to "suffer and rejoice and pray and labor." And from the beginning, though suspicious and cautious, some slaves came to hear the missionaries by choice. The fact of their attendance was considered progress as expressed by one optimistic missionary in 1835:

Although the colored people were generally in a lukewarm state and inattentive to preaching when I commenced, there has been an encouraging improvement, whether it is the novelty of the thing that has drawn them out, or the special regard had to them by their owners in getting a preacher exclusively for them, I know not, but one thing is certain . . . they attend the appointments very regularly and a deep concern is manifested in the congregation generally.[55]

The Gullah's increasing attention to Methodist presence can be understood on a number of levels. In the life of a slave any occasion which brought a cessation from labor was welcomed. One can imagine the excitement as well as skepticism in the quarters when news spread of the coming of a white "spiritual man" whose sole purpose was to administer to slaves. Certainly their interest was measured. Yet for these isolated African-Americans the special attention itself was something new. Furthermore, preaching places facilitated gathering of bondspeople from various plantations, providing opportunities to visit with friends, relatives, and probably lending a gaiety and sense of freedom to the event. Missionaries recorded little lasting progress of a religious nature as a result of their preaching at these large assemblies. Planters insisted the gatherings produced more harm to the system. But these occasions appealed to the slaves for reasons other than the spiritual content of the sermons. Preaching stations provided many with their only opportunity to be away from the plantation. Monthly meetings became convivial holiday-type excursions, adding to the few outlets in a life too often dulled by pointless, profitless toil. The gatherings provided a reason for attending to personal hygiene, to don whatever their "best" attire consisted of—faded though colorful turbans and caps; their one pair of shoes; tattered, coarse and worn, yet carefully laundered gingham skirts and breeches of iridescent check. Missionaries reported with frustration that slaves readily engaged in the singing and attentively responded to the prayers, but many slept through whole sermons although at the meeting's end they heartily shook hands and thanked the missionary "fur de Wud."[56] Gullah gratitude was probably not so much for the Word as for what it represented in terms of offering an alleviation of routine. Such comments may have been expressions of cynicism. Yet some missionaries evinced a genuine concern and imparted to the Gullahs a different sense of worth and dignity. The most positive and uplifting principles of the "religion of the heart" seeped through the lessons on obedience, subordination, and prostration. And the Gullahs came to recognize a relationship between Christian imagery and their own historical position. This was the triumph for which the committed amongst the missionaries labored. They added but few "true" Methodists to church rolls but won the "heart" of many slaves. Nevertheless, even at its soul searching, heartrending best, slaves employed Methodism as an exculpation from bondage. Those preaching among the slaves imparted a spiritual ideology founded upon this premise. The dualism of the religion was not lost on the Gullahs.

In the period before the national division of the Methodist church, missionary activity was circumspectly observed by slaveholders who feared that antislavery doctrines, inadvertently or otherwise, might be disseminated. The South Carolina Conference instructed that the content of sermons emphasize the "duty" of servants to masters, not because it would avert suspicion, but because the state episcopacy sincerely believed this was the most important element of Christianity to be taught to slaves. In any case, the textbook prepared by William Capers for the use of plantation missionaries, referred to as a catechism, reflected an interpretation of the Christian religion to an enslaved people. The introductory section consisted of hymns, prayers, commandments, the Creed, and portions of the scripture having to do with duties of husbands and wives, parents and children, and servants and masters. The remainder of the little book was in question-and-answer form, obviously designed for slave children. This portion of the text covered parts of the Bible that the South Carolina Conference specifically wanted pointed out, namely, the creation, the fall, and the life and death of Christ.[57]

For sermons, St. Paul provided the missionaries with favorite subjects and was also the apostle most quoted by proslavery elements. Other scriptural texts used ostensibly relegated blacks to a fate of perpetual bondage and aimed at convincing them to accept enslavement as the natural order. Slaves were taught a selective Christianity—a doctrine of contentment and humility. No text espousing such scriptural tenets as "The truth shall make you free" or "The laborer is worthy of his hire" could be preached. There was of course none of the militant Christianity discovered and expounded by the black rebels in Charleston years before. Most of the Old Testament was ignored except when certain passages could serve as a conduit further to reinforce white domination.

One account of the narrow latitude of preaching was left by Lundsford Lane. Lane, born a slave in North Carolina, purchased his freedom and became an abolitionist lecturer. He wrote:

> I often heard select portions of the Scriptures read. . . . On Sunday we always had one sermon prepared expressly for the colored people, which it was generally my privilege to hear. So great was the similarity of the texts that they are always fresh in memory: "Servants, be obedient to your masters—not with eye-service, as men-pleasers." "He that knoweth his master's will and doeth it not, shall be beaten with many stripes"; and some others of this class. Similar passages with but few exceptions, formed the basis of most of these public instructions. . . . I will not do them the injustice to say that connected with these instructions there was not mingled much that was excellent . . . one very kind-hearted clergyman . . . was very popular with the coloured people. But after he had preached a sermon from the Bible that it was the will of Heaven from all eternity that we should be slaves, and our masters be our owners many of us left him, considering, like the doubting disciple of old, "This is a hard saying, who can hear it."[58]

Steady outpourings of sermons stressing obedience and duty would not win slaves to Christianity. Black laborers as a group refused to accept a religion filled with aphorisms that emphasized their perpetual subjugated role in the human family. But implementation of other more personal approaches brought Methodist missionaries some success. Catechizing of children, for instance, was ardently attended to, for they were the hope of the enterprise. Church emissaries were encouraged by the children's eagerness and brightness. They learned quickly, if not always perfectly, and they expressed more enthusiasm for the individual missionary than for his religion. Nevertheless, slave children of the 1830s and 1840s were expected to provide the Lowcountry with a future generation of black workers who, from an early age, imbibed and personalized Christianity as taught by white missionaries. Yet while catechism taught to children might be insurance for the future, adult slaves, considered to have "grown up in ignorance," did not readily respond to that learning process. Nor did slaveholders usually provide time for such instruction. But Methodists determined to awaken enthusiasm for Christianity among the adult slaves, otherwise not only would black laborers remain "heathen," they would not encourage Christianity among the young. Thus the efforts of slave conversion would be undermined. The Gullahs' confidence had to be acquired, and the more dedicated missionaries pursued this end diligently.[59]

The "class meeting" was an important method of personal instruction and among the slaves its function was broadened in an effect to quicken their interest in Christianity. In "class," adults were given instruction, doctrines were explained, and general check-ups were made on the progress of individuals. Here the missionary asked and answered individual questions and slaves related the nature of their religious experiences. Also, through examinations in "class meetings" missionaries ascertained the state of Christianity on the plantation, and decided who was ready for church membership. Furthermore, since "class" was held on individual estates, the missionaries could have more impact than at the preaching places. In "class," the missionary could, if he chose, be less didactic and more intimate. Some missionaries elaborated on the most dramatic portions of the Bible, hence capturing the Gullahs' imagination. Through these gatherings the missionary became acquainted with his large "flock," usually getting to know the adults and children by name. He ultimately became a familiar face on the plantations he visited, sometimes welcomed and sometimes resented. William Capers wrote to the slave missionaries:

> Class meetings are especially ours. A missionary should emphatically be these three things—a preacher, a catechist, and a class leader. He must be the class leader, whoever may engage to assist him. . . . Unvaried pains should be taken to instruct them in the nature of Christian experience, both by remarks to the class in general, and to each individual. . . . Organization is a main thing in Methodism, and a main thing for missions. Without it there can be no efficient training, little permanent instruction, no order, no discipline.[60]

But "organization," "order," or "discipline" did not impress the Gullahs as much as the sincerity of motive some missionaries conveyed as they acquainted themselves with their charges. Preachers were required to attend the pastoral needs of their widespread congregation. Although some neglected this feature of their duties, others engaged in the work with deliberate gravity. Many missionaries felt more able to open the slaves' heart to Christianity by this method. Some of the most interesting "Missionary Sketches" printed in the *Southern Christian Advocate* were written by A. M. Chreitzberg, stationed on the Beaufort Mission and elsewhere in the Sea Island region. Chreitzberg wrote from the Sea Islands, summarizing his duties outside the pulpit. He provided illuminating insights into the ways some missionaries merited gratitude and confidence from some of the bondspeople:

It is not only the duty of the missionary to catechize the children and preach to the adults, but also to visit the sick and aged, and it is here that many a triumph has been achieved for his Lord. Many a dark and benighted soul has been brought into the light and liberty of the Gospel. Here, too, does he frequently prepare himself for the exercises of the pulpit, for it is here that he learns the way to the negro's heart, and becomes acquainted with his ideas of God and religion. The negro knows that his minister is not ashamed to enter his smoky cabin, to take him by his rough and toil-hardened hand, and talk to him about the way to heaven, or to kneel beside his bed, offer prayer in his behalf, and to pour into his heart the consolation of God's word. It is this that frequently takes his heart captive, and binds him to the cross.[61]

Here then was the religion of the warm heart at its spiritually redeeming best among the Gullahs. A disarming warmth of feeling, an effort to bridge, spiritually at least, the gap between black and white, slave and free was to serve a definite purpose. Such acts, seemingly prompted purely by human kindness, deeply affected the Gullahs, so unaccustomed to being objects of concern among whites except in matters related to labor. Gradually, the more seasoned missionaries like Chreitzberg began to stimulate a "change of heart" in the slaves. Especially affecting was the adaptation of some sermons and lectures to the daily lives and fortunes of the Gullahs. Hence they came to identify elements of Christianity with their own circumstances. Skillful variation of preaching methods, coupled with a fraternal spirit which the missionaries demonstrated toward the Gullahs, was effective. By the mid-1840s a goodly number of slaves had "professed" their conversion to Christianity under Methodist tutelage.

Missionaries such as Chreitzberg took full advantage of opportunities to service their black congregations in the hope of winning more converts. Below Chreitzberg describes the value to be derived from officiating at a Gullah night funeral:

"What" says the not-to-be-disturbed-at-night Pastor of a Chapel of Ease, "put yourself to the trouble of burying a *dead* negro?" Why not? We have unsuperable objections to burying a *living* one, but see no reason why the last sad office of the Church should not be performed over the remains of the black man. Has he no affections, are there no weeping friends to be consoled. . . . But apart from this, may not the living be effectually warned? When the dead man lies before them in all his helplessness, stricken down in his prime and (as in this case) suddenly called to the final account,—what better time to read to them a lesson on the uncertainty of life.

These were golden opportunities for the missionary. The entire plantation gathered to see a body laid to rest in "its narrow house." The preacher
first consoled the sorrowful widow, bidding her to trust God, "the husband of the widow and father of the fatherless." He then addressed the
dead man's fellow servants on the necessity of preparing for death: "In a
word I preached Jesus and the resurrection, and by the glimmering of
the lightwood fire, was the burial service read and the body committed
to the dust." Upon leaving the plantation late that night, the missionary
was moved by thoughts which were probably not very different from
thoughts which the slaves who had just witnessed the burial might have,
"thoughts on life, on life's duties, on life's end: of the wants and woes of
the world."[62]

Once again the missionary capitalized on an opportunity to involve
himself in the black community and the slaves' experience. His efforts
to share in and add meaning to life and death among the bondspeople
helped make him a presence in the quarters even if he came but twice a
month. He was, for his caring, often looked upon fondly. Although the
missionary represented the same forces of oppression as did the master,
the slaves perceived the spiritual arm of the dominant society as perhaps
its one redeeming quality, a contradiction to serve the slaves' interests.
Still the fondness was more on an individual level. A well-meaning
Methodist like Chreitzberg was accepted though all he preached and taught
was not. From the slaves' vantage point it was unwise to completely
relinquish that which had previously provided spiritual solace and replace it with something new and as yet untried. For missionaries able to
secure access to plantations, spiritual rewards might be inspiring if short-
lived. Through catechism, "class meeting," and carrying out of pastoral
duties, Methodists experienced some triumphs for Christianity. Missionaries never succeeded in dethroning black leadership and felt that this
influence continually created obstacles to Christian conversion.[63] Nevertheless, Methodists proved to be relentless in the dissemination of their
doctrines. As Gullahs grew more attentive to the preachers' words, they
discarded the incongruous and discordant features of the instruction and
fashioned the religion of slaveholders into something peculiarly their own.

One of the most significant effects that Methodism had on Gullahs
was in the creation of the religious music of these slaves. Some scholars
argue that the actual source of Gullah religious songs can be traced to
Methodist hymns and tunes sung at camp meetings. Certainly Methodist

hymns were adopted by the Gullahs and other slaves. Francis Asbury traveled the seacoasts of Georgia and South Carolina frequently. While he gained few white converts, he was impressed with the black response to his preaching. During the Civil War, musicologists and others, fascinated by Gullah songs, noted that what was sometimes called a "Negro song," was of white origin, especially the so-called religious songs. But to these white melodies, the Gullahs added their own "spirit and relish," giving a "peculiar individuality and nationality" to the music. Thus it is pointless and probably inaccurate to insist that whites and blacks did not create sacred music together when they worshipped together. Such was the case at camp meetings and revivals. Still these gatherings were not as common in the Lowcountry as they were elsewhere. Some writers argue that the camp meeting was distinctly a pineland and upcountry institution. Although evidence indicates that a few camp meetings were held in the rice communities—the hinterlands of the Sea Islands—we find no record of its presence on any of the Islands. The influence of the domestic slave trade, black-white cultural borrowing, and diffusion were all factors in the creation and development of African-American music. Nevertheless, a unique continuity in religious songs can be found in the Sea Islands and coastal lowlands. There were indeed two types of religious music among the Gullahs who adopted Christianity: those songs and hymns learned from white religious instructors and mainly Methodist in origin, and those representing the product of the Gullah's own creativity and imagination, generally referred to as spirituals or prayer songs.[64]

The primary influence of Methodist preachers on the development of spirituals was in providing Gullahs with raw material for their songs. From past spiritual traditions these African-Americans inherited a mysticism, sense of drama, and creative antecedents that aided them in expressing and interpreting through song the apocalyptic and miraculous elements of biblical narration already rich in symbolic imagery. Also, New Testament biblical lore was not unlike the Gullahs' own oppression and suffering. From the Sea Islands in 1843, A. M. Chreitzberg provides examples of the spontaneous creation of spirituals. In delivering his message, the missionary enforced the concepts of "repentance toward God, and faith toward our Lord Jesus Christ." At the conclusion of the meeting, the group was "much affected" by a "soft female voice" singing:

> Dis berry same Jesus, dis berry same Jesus,
> We heares dese people de talk about;
> Dis berry same Jesus . . .

Chreitzberg finished his labors and headed back to Beaufort by boat. Undoubtedly the black boatmen had heard his sermon. It was a dark night and the effect of the scene was heightened by "one of those thundergusts, so frequent in our latitudes." Chreitzberg and his associate sat at the stern of the boat, comfortably "gazing at the clouds." The lightening gleamed in the distance, "with the sullen roll of the distant thunder":

We were sitting at ease in the stern of the boat, suddenly a sound struck upon our ear, that we can liken to nothing save the shriek of a lost spirit. This we found to be the chorus of a song the boat hands were preparing to sing, the chorus we cannot write; it was something between a groan and the cry,—"have mercy"; and was sung at the end of every line.

> O Lord, O Lord! what shall we do?
> What shall we do, what shall we do?
> What shall we do for a hiding place;
> No hiding place for sinner here.
> We run to de sea—de sea run dry;
> We run to de rock—de rock da sink;
> We run to de tree—de tree ketch fire;
> We run to de grave—de grave bus open;
> We run to de door—de door shut close;
> We wring we hands, we grine we feet,
> We cry O Lord, O Lord, O Lord,
> No hidin' place for sinner here!

The words written, may only serve to excite a smile, but when sung, the effect is directly the reverse; as in the intensity of excitement, one holds his breath to catch every intonation of the voice; he will, in spite of himself, be affected to tears.[65]

The Gullahs sense of their own human frailty was expressed in their spirituals. Illness, floggings, fatigue from overwork, and the ubiquity of death were features of daily existence. The harsh Sea Island bondage must have contributed to a longing for a better world at best or for another one at the very least. For some slaves an eternal reward would justify a life that was often painful and joyless yet not without hope. Some conscious rationale regarding a future being might ease a portion of the strong sense of injustice felt toward the present, and fill gaps left by features of traditional African religion and philosophy not transferable or appliable to the New World situation. In this way the Gullahs gradually developed a holistic religion with components of both experiences. The helplessnss implicit in the Christian motif was a central ingredient of Methodist teaching. But one need not seek an explanation for identification with Christianity in Methodism alone, with its prostrating sense of fatalism. Aside from biblical example, and need for a complete world view, the Gullahs' own ill-fated lives and the frequent occurrence of untimely deaths were often sufficient to bring forth the poetry from within. The following Sea Island torchlight burial is an example of the kind of tragic scene that might well motivate the creation of a spiritual:

On one occasion of burial, I have reason to believe much good was done. A woman, who was a member of the Church, and who had died in full hope of immortal life, was to be buried at night, it being the most convenient time for the people to be together. Accordingly I met the people at the time appointed. The plantation being large, many were present. The corpse was conveyed about a quarter of a mile to the burial ground, the procession moving slowly and silently along, with lighted torches interspersed through the ranks. This presented a solemn scene; but after we arrived at the burying place it was still more solemn. A grove standing in the midst of a large clearing, which had been sacredly kept for years as belonging to the dead, undisturbed even by the footsteps of man, except when another was to be laid in the earth, and under the shade of the cedars. Here we all met in the midst of the grove, around the grave. It was a dark night, but in the midst of the grove it was still more dark. All was silent, except the thrilling note of the whippoorwill, who had made this lonely retreat its home; all around us lay the graves of the dead of all sizes. The reflection from many torches presented them full in view in every direction, as though they had but just been closed; so thick was the shade above that no grass grew on that spot. I have attended many of my fellow beings to the grave; but never did I witness a more solemn time, and yet I felt it a blessed time. I felt it a duty to try and improve the occasion of our being together; and indeed it was a time of weeping—some of the most stubborn were melted into tears. The husband of the deceased and her infant child were near the grave; he, before a careless man, now wept aloud—and since that period has shown his grief was not of a worldly kind; he has offered himself to the Church, and his child he has had baptized. Many others on the plantation have become serious, and are now on trial.[66]

The spectacle of this young woman's funeral and the presence of the white missionary preaching the prospect of life after death aroused thoughts of the finality of human life and generated desires to transcend reality and be projected into a peaceful future existence. More than likely a burial scene such as the one above prompted the creation of a most poignant Gullah spiritual. It was recorded during the Civil War by Thomas Wentworth Higginson, Commander of the First South Carolina Volunteers. He considered it "the most poetic of all their songs."

> I know moon-rise, I know star-rise;
>   Lay dis body down.
> I walk in de moonlight, I walk in de starlight
>   To lay dis body down.
> I'll walk in de graveyard, I'll walk through de graveyard,
>   To lay dis body down.
> I'll lie in de grave and stretch out my arms;
>   Lay dis body down.
> I go to de Judgment in de evinin' ob de day
>   When I lay dis body down.
> And my soul and your soul will meet in de day
>   When I lay dis body down.[67]

Certainly Gullahs wanted to believe in a bondless futurity, and many accepted assurances of the missionaries, if not their discipline. Undoubtedly, a number of Gullahs felt that their existence on earth offered so little and mortal doom was so certain that nothing was gambled by adopting Christianity. Their imaginations and aspirations were quickened by inspiring parables, stimulating renditions of undeserved agonies of the long-suffering man-god, his earthly demise, and ultimate triumphant rebirth. The parallels were clearly hard to resist.

Thus it might appear that the hopes and expectations of planters such as C. C. Pinckney were realized—that as professors of Christianity, slaves resigned themselves to their circumstances in return for the hope of a heavenly future. Yet it is a mistake to interpret the Gullahs' acceptance of some Christian teachings as a reflection of negative attitudes toward earthly life. Nor did such teachings instill a sense of futility and resignation. Christianity as interpreted by the slaves did not induce them to disavow the present as much as it served to mitigate the inhumane features of their existence as slaves. For the Gullahs, Christianity was a spiritual release from anxieties, frustrations, and animosities, providing a frame of reference to understand their position as bondspeople. In this sense the religion of the slaveholders was diluted, becoming for the slaves a source of strength embodied in their use of Christian ideology as a personification of their will to freedom. Major emphasis of slave religion was not "otherworldly." What Gullahs accepted in Christianity did not prevent the kind of defensive acts which the planters anticipated would cease. Flight, theft, and reluctance to labor were means of undermining plantation order and were acts of resistance that continued to plague planters although more and more blacks became "converted."[68] True, they did not rise in revolt. Memories of the consequences of failed rebellion attempts and strong kinship ties encouraged another type of resistance involving less individual risk while creating more collective energy. The goal after all was freedom. Doctrines of the New Testament exposed the Gullahs to a kind of freedom in a spiritual sense but also upheld their right to physical liberty and equality.

Gullah reaction to Christianity under Methodist tutelage was complex. On the one hand, the slaves responded to the warmth and tolerance demonstrated by missionaries. Acts of sincerity and kindness induced the slaves to take an interest in Methodist teachings. Once Gullahs applied Christianity to their own daily lives, they grasped how its tenets could, in some ways, reflect the nature of their experiences as a people. On the other hand, the paradox inherent in Christian teaching as presented by the Methodists did not escape them. Gullahs rejected doctrines instructing them to be dutiful and obedient to slave masters, but embraced the teachings about the suffering of Christ, the resurrection, and the impartiality of a future judge who would right past wrongs. One finds no evidence of spirituals applauding an obedient slave, admonishing a disobedient one, or warning a slave against the retribution extracted by God for "crimes" against a slave master. The benne seed ritual evinced just the opposite implication. Contrary to the planter's desire, slaves did not fear "another tribunal," and as "Christians," continued stealing corn and rice, burning cotton, and fleeing to the swamps and marshes. If anything, the introduction of Christianity among the Gullahs enhanced their justification for deploring the system of bondage, and provided sound arguments for what was sensed all along—the equality of humankind.

The strongest reaction against Methodism existed because of the cultural barrier between missionaries and Gullahs. Although early white Methodism accepted emotional expressions as signs of godliness, missionaries among the Gullahs emphasized a primarily stodgy instructional approach to Christianity. Methodists permitted and applauded the emotional outpourings characterizing Gullah spirituals. But other physical manifestations were often viewed as "ungodly." Missionaries noted that

Gullahs were "easily excited," and claimed that it was necessary "to instruct them in distinguishing between animal feeling and a real work of grace." Methodists frowned upon Gullah paroxysms, not viewing these as manifestations of Christian fervor but as non-Christian or "natural" means of expressive outlet, born of older traditions. In any case, black impetuosity had to be eradicated just as the violins and banjos had to be silenced. Generally speaking, Methodism among the Gullahs can be partly described as E. P. Thompson implicitly viewed it among British workers—a religion of the heart that sometimes attempted to stifle spontaneity of the mind and soul.[69] Slaves were rarely allowed to be themselves in the presence of Methodist emissaries. This fact, coupled with Gullah preference for a presentation of religion (or a religious presentation) in more original and familiar terms, lost the Methodist church many black converts.

Acceptance of Christianity by the Gullahs, as presented by their Methodist instructors, was more of a process of coming to terms than a total commitment. Christianity was incorporated into, but did not immediately supersede, all of their previously held beliefs and practices. The missionaries realized this, reported it with disappointment, and hoped for a better day. Such was the case with the adult generation of Gullahs in the 1830s, and this continued to be a major factor in the 1840s as well.[70] On the isolated Sea Islands a certain Old World cultural similitude contributed to the retention of communal and cultural components. Traditions inspired by Africanity and infused with Gullah folk Christianity remained identifiable well past the antebellum years. Nevertheless, Africanisms outlasting the capture, the long march, and the culminating humiliation of foreign servitude had to be preserved in a vestigial state. In addition, commingling of various ethnic groups indicates that cultural diffusion was also an important factor as native ceremonies and customs were renewed and exchanged. Therefore, what was retained of African religion and spirituality was culled from the customs, beliefs, and practices of a number of West African peoples. Thus Gullah-English dialect may be a pidgin influenced mainly by Tshi (Gold Coast), KiKongo (Kongo-Angola), and Mande (Upper Guinea) linguistic patterns. But Gullah spiritual and communitarian features bear strong resemblance to traditions of Upper Guinea and BaKongo peoples. When the Methodists arrived among the Gullahs, they probably found a syncretism of African customs and practices sprinkled with snatches of Protestantism borrowed from Baptist and Episcopalian masters, and limited contact with black preachers.

The Methodists' systematic religious instruction provided Gullahs with the first opportunity for a uniform type of religious culture. This socio-religious nexus did not vary from plantation to plantation or from island to island. It was based on a moral philosophy, not precluding the preservation to some extent of a continued faith in the customs of African-born forebears. The emerging religious association resembled and gave expression to a world view brought from Africa, common to the Gullahs, and suited to their circumstances. More than any other features of the Christian religion, the Gullahs embraced its moral virtues—humanity, humility, fairness, a sense of the dignity of the sufferer, and belief in the merit of all people. No matter how one regards these values, they are celebrated in Christianity, and it was this spirit in Methodist teachings that the Gullahs accepted. The letter of the law, in a strict Mosaic form, and the Pauline sanction of servitude were rejected. There was little room for internalization of the dogma present in Christianity as taught by whites. That would have negated Gullahs' previous belief patterns and their hatred of bondage. Gullah folk Christianity was an ardently felt religion. It was a religion which elevated them above their masters' efforts to make them contented slaves. Far more than Methodism perhaps, Gullah folk religion was a religion of the heart. Their spirituality helped them channel what was expected to be hopelessness, helplessness, and prostration into the forging and further enrichment of a culture. Through individual stamina, collective faith, and cultural development they merged as a people. Their collective faith kept them spiritually free in spite of physical bondage. Their collective faith, together with spiritual freedom, and matched with natural gifts and talents, provided Gullahs with a will to create, the courage to persevere, and power, as a "prepolitical" people, to use religion as a progressive force and shield against white psychological and cultural domination. This collective faith allowed them to believe in themselves and in their dream of ultimate freedom.[71]

The year 1845 was momentous for the history of slave conversion in South Carolina and for the nation as a whole. At that time the Methodist Episcopal Church South and the Southern Baptist Convention were organized. Both denominations pledged to make a more zealous thrust in Christian instruction of the black population. Also, in May of that year,

South Carolina statesmen and clergy called a meeting in Charleston, inviting slaveholders either to attend or submit in writing information on the state of religious instruction among slaves on their plantations.[72] After that time, Christian conversion of bondspeople occupied a more prominent position in antebellum life and thought. It became an issue with social, economic, political, and even moral implications. What was previously viewed as a movement of questionable value soon transformed into a crusade. As the national scene became more and more polarized because of the slavery issue, it was incumbent upon Southerners, as a defense against their "national character," to see that bondspeople received some type of Christian instruction.

Although efforts to Christianize slaves became widespread, Methodist presence in the Sea Island region receded. By the late 1840s Methodism there was more symbolic than effective. Even at the time of the Charleston Meeting, Episcopalian planters most actively solicited the services of Methodist missionaries. However, the fact remains that for nearly fifteen years Methodists were the major Christian influence among the Gullahs, planting a foundation for the growth of Christianity among slaves of the Sea Islands and coastal regions. However, the Baptist denomination, once it engaged in religious instruction, claimed the harvest of "converted" slaves.

CHAPTER 7

To Make Them Better Slaves: Baptist Persuasion, 1830-1861

Lizzy, Excommunicated, running away and insolent to owner.
Charles, Excommunicated, stealing corn and breaking into corn house.
Nell, Excommunicated, theft.
Joe, Excommunicated, drunkenness and running away.
Bacchus, Suspended, selling whiskey in violation of the law, publically
punished for it in stocks.*

. . . All de time, dey'd lick you. After dey'd like 'em until de blood come
out, den dey'd rub de red pepper and salt on 'em. Oh, my God! Kin you
say dem as done such as dat aint gone to dere reward? My uncle was whip
so he went in de woods, an' live dere for monts. Had to learn de independent life. Mr. Aldridge was de overseer. Old Mr. Aldridge gone now. But
dere can't be no rest for him. Oh my God no!**

"Christian" Masters

In 1845, concerned clergymen called a three-day meeting in Charleston,
inviting planters, ministers, and statesmen to discuss religious instruction of the slave population. A "chief mover and supporter" of white
Baptist activity in the Sea Island region was St. Helena patriarch William Fripp. Fripp reported that on St. Helena Island "the gospel has

---

*Committee on Discipline, *Minutes, Beaufort Baptist Church*, July 8, 1842, 34, BC.
**Solbert Butler, former slave, in George P. Rawick, ed., *The American Slave: A Com-
posite Autobiography*, 19 vols., *South Carolina Narratives*, vols. 2 & 3, in 4 Parts, (Westport,
Conn.: Greenwood Publishing, 1972) II (1), 162.

been preached for many years to our Negroes." The boast needs quali-
fication and amplification. Certainly as far back as Whitefield and the
Bryans periodic spurts of whites *preaching* to blacks occurred. Also the
more recent and protracted Methodist presence in the Lowcountry is
another illustration. Moreover, some slaves could occasionally take advantage of the few existing white-controlled black churches in the Savannah and Augusta, Georgia area. Most Baptist churches in the region
were members of the Savannah River Baptist Association organized in
1803 by Georgia and South Carolina. In 1818 the Association divided,
including only churches north of the Savannah River and within South
Carolina. Jurisdiction was in the districts of Beaufort, Barnwell, and
Colleton, but most member churches were concentrated in Beaufort District. By 1830 the Savannah River Association consisted of thirty-two
churches. Back rows and galleries seated free blacks, as well as domestic
and artisan slaves. Thus despite assurances of William Fripp, prior to
1830 the masses of slaves were not included in Baptist apostolic activity
and only nominally represented in a few white congregations.[1]

In 1831 and 1832, a short-lived but prolific Lowcountry revival occurred and reportedly stirred a number of planters in the Sea Island
region to accept a religious affiliation. The effects of this "remarkable"
religious awakening were most visible in Baptist congregations, and records of the Savannah River Baptist Association indicate a comparatively
large membership increase in these churches. By 1831 the largest Beaufort District churches were Euhaw, Pipe Creek, Black Swamp, Beaufort,
St. Helena, and May River. In 1830, just prior to the revival, the combined number of baptismal candidates for these churches was 164. Toward the end of 1831, a total of 228 baptisms were reported. In 1832
Black Swamp and Pipe Creek made no reports, but the other four larger
churches reported a total of 619 baptisms.[2] Considering the paucity of
whites in these areas the numbers represent significant increases. Early
records had no racial breakdown, but evidence indicates that some of the
converts before 1831 were black.

Both Episcopalian and Baptist planters "smitten" during the famous
1831 revival reportedly took new interest in Christianizing their slaves.
The former denomination allowed Methodist missionaries to preach and
teach among bondspeople. No missionary movement for slaves was organized by the Baptists, however. And rather than allow Methodists on
their plantations, most Baptist planters who favored the enterprise preferred to accept "converted" slaves into their own churches.[3]

Even some time after 1831, general Baptist concern for the spiritual well-being of their slaves was limited. Only a small number of churches showed significant increases in church membership in about a ten-year period following the revival. This gradual progression itself was unique to older Sea Island churches. Leading Baptists stimulated to "duty" by the "revival spirit," and mindful of the currents affecting church and state nationally, attempted to generate more Christianizing activity through their influence in the Savannah River Baptist Association. In 1832 the Association formed a committee to seek funds from member churches to hire Baptist missionaries for the slaves. Since this effort was a slow process, the Association further recommended that ministers devote a certain part of their time exclusively to the slaves. The organization went on record as "feeling a deep interest for the spiritual improvement of our colored population, who have hitherto been neglected."[4]

The committee was composed of large slaveholders, many of whom were also deacons or pastors of the more prosperous churches at Beaufort, St. Helena, Black Swamp, Hilton Head, and Euhaw. These congregations had comparatively large black memberships, and the committee members were known for their "good works" in general and for the interest they took in converting their own slaves. But the resolutions expressed more of the committee's own sentiments and personal concern than a real plan of action. Baptist congregations were autonomous, and slaveholders in the Sea Island region resisted efforts of individuals in the denomination to create a Christian instruction movement. For a variety of reasons, Baptist efforts at slave conversion met with some success where it existed. But if measured in terms of church membership and frequency of exposure, such endeavors, were not extensive.[5]

About a third of South Carolina's Baptist laymen and two-fifths of the ministers were slaveholders. Baptists in the Sea Island region, the most numerous sect since 1820, counted the wealthiest and largest slaveholders among its numbers. Consequently, antislavery sentiments were never expressed there despite early debates elsewhere in the South. On the contrary, the official opinion of South Carolina Baptists was expressed in 1822 following the Vesey Conspiracy, by Richard Furman of Charleston. "Slavery," wrote Furman, "was clearly established in the Holy Scriptures by both precept and example."[6]

Nevertheless, South Carolina Baptists confronted strong abolitionist sentiment from church members in other regions. As with Methodists, the controversy dominated national meetings in the 1830s. Abolitionists' primary target was Baptist home and foreign missions. There antislavery elements labored to obtain official condemnation of their Southern brethren not only for slaveholding but for hypocrisy in attempting to spread Christianity domestically and abroad while ignoring their own bondspeople. Accusations prompted some prestigious Baptists to encourage more attentiveness to slave conversion. However, abolitionist recriminations also infuriated Southern congregations. Sea Island Baptists raged over the presence of abolitionist-oriented home and foreign mission "agents." They also denounced abolitionist dissemination of religious newspapers. One such newspaper, *The Christian Reflector*, which argued against a scriptural interpretation of slavery, was sent to Sea Island churches. Not all Northern Baptists were antislavery. Even some of those who were did not advocate abolition, nor propose interference with slavery. Yet the situation was perceived as threatening in the Lowcountry, and it was impossible to procure a consensus on instruction from congregations whose only tie with the regional association was voluntary. Yet, larger churches continued to scrutinize and contemplate the situation. In 1837 further proclamations were used to stir congregations into activity. The Euhaw Church representatives spoke out on the "spiritual destitution of our colored population," and urged the Association to act. The committee previously formed in 1832 had apparently met with little success, and offered three resolutions on the issue. First, emphasizing the duty of ministers to pay "especial attention" to the slaves' spiritual condition. Second, that the "Domestic Missionary" preach to slaves whenever an "opportunity may be offered him." Third, that the General Committee consider the subject and adopt measures to "best secure to our colored population spiritual instruction."[7]

Clearly no real commitment was as yet outlined. A few individual churches were already engaging in evangelism among the slaves and attempting to persuade others. The message was one of urging a sense of responsibility, since the Savannah River Baptist Association lacked power to bind churches to a strong general policy. the Association's resources allowed them to employ one missionary, but mainly to serve whites. He ordained officers, preached at the various established churches with no regular ministers, generally superintended the constitution of new churches, and preached to "destitute" whites. Although not specifically precluded from preaching to slaves, the missionary's other extensive obligations prevented his going to plantations where he was needed or accepted. The Association did not gain approval to hire a missionary for the bondspeople until 1839. But he encountered so much opposition that by the end of that year, he had no progress report to make and refused to continue in the position.[8]

Among Northern and Southern Baptist clergymen scriptural arguments over slavery were hotly debated and further hindered Baptist planters' involvement in Christianizing activity. According to planters, Northern Baptists were attempting to "procure the massacre of our wives and children" by preaching that all people of the South had a God-given right to freedom.[9] Certainly slaveholders realized that the Bible denounced bondage as well as supported it. Why else would clergymen emphasize "oral" instruction as a means of Christian instruction? Faced with the double meaning of scriptures and fearing the impact of an egalitarian interpretation of the teachings of Christ, religious instruction of the slaves remained unimpressive in the 1830s among most Baptist churches within the jurisdiction of the Savannah River Baptist Association. The Association attempted to meet the issue head on. To pave the way for a Baptist missionary enterprise, the question of the biblical sanction of slavery needed to be firmly and convincingly laid to rest. In 1841 Association ministers issued their position, hoping the resolution would be accepted as official so the work of Christian conversion could commence:

> Resolved, that the subject of slavery has been discussed until all men who seek candidly for truth must be satisfied. The whole Bible, and all history concur to settle this point, there where Christianity finds slavery existing as one of the institutions of a nation, it tolerates it, and seeks not to disturb the relation of master and servant by violence—but to infuse the spirit of love into each of these parties, and prescribes their respective duties—duties which it becomes us to perform on our part, and which, if performed, would render our slaves the happiest and most contented peasantry on earth.[10]

Thus the spirit of Christianity would inspire "love" and stimulate both master and slave to perform their "duty." For the slave, this duty entailed acceptance of a Christianity that taught meekness, subordination, docility, inferiority, and recognition of the rights of master over slave. The master was "burdened" with the "duty" or instilling these "virtues" in bondspeople to make the slaves' "happiness" and "contentment" complete. Some Baptists became reeducated to this manner of thinking, for the resolution was followed by a request from two Sea Island congregations for the services of a missionary, approved by the Association of course.

> The Hilton Head Church, and Dawfuskie Church, request your body to send a missionary to preach on these islands. We want, say they, a man of piety and talents suited to our colored population. Your committee recommend that your messengers to the Sunbury Association be requested to solicit our Br. Farley R. Sweat, of Savannah to engage at once in this work, and to occupy this post. These churches have had their desires turned towards this brother, and God has so clearly intimated his will as to Br. Sweat, that your committee cannot believe he will refuse to yield himself to the call of his master. These churches will contribute liberally to the support of their missionary.[11]

Here we observe the close relationship between the Sunbury Association in Georgia and the Savannah River Association in South Carolina. The African Baptist Church was part of the Sunbury Association, and as previously discussed, South Carolina slaves sometimes joined or attended the black church in Savannah. The proximity of Hilton Head and Dawfuskie Islands to Savannah made this possible. Thus in some areas of the coast, slaves not regularly instructed by white Baptists, were exposed to the faith through members of their own race. This contact went further back than the first Baptist missionary to Hilton Head and Dawfuskie.

These two churches' requests did not stimulate a large-scale movement to hire missionaries, but other Sea Island congregations began individually to engage in spreading Christian influence among the Gullahs. Some Southern religionists and "enlightened" planters had, since the Vesey Conspiracy, been convinced that Christian inculcation of slaves was the best security for the plantation system. But when the Northern and Southern churches severed relations in 1844, such approaches were pursued in earnest. While a sense of obligation was expressed, the prominence which secular motives received in the course of the Christian conversion movement was evident at the Charleston Meeting in 1845. Notables who gathered there to champion the cause of Christianizing African-Americans specified their major concerns:

> The degree of benefit apparently derived by the Negroes generally from the instruction imparted, and particularly as it regards their morals—their tempers and their conduct . . . their regard to truth—the rights of property—and their observance of the Sabbath.
> The influence of this instruction upon the discipline of the plantation and the spirit and subordination of the negroes.[12]

Emphasis shifted away from old arguments related to a fear of militant principles within Christianity and toward the pacific features of that religion. The idea that Christianity could serve as the safeguard of the Southern white community was a minority opinion in the 1820s when, because of the Vesey Conspiracy, Northern clergymen were blamed for inspiring and encouraging religious teachings inimical to Southern survival. However, after 1845 arguments favoring Christian instruction of slaves as a societal safety valve became the pillar of clergymen's reasoning in attempting to awaken planters. Now religious instruction was undertaken and accomplished without interference from non-Southerners. Slaves were instructed in a manner that planters believed did not weaken the South's socieconomic structure. On the contrary, the training was expected to strengthen and solidify the master-slave relationship. By employing a selective type of teaching and promoting Christianity as an individual not a collective experience, Baptists and others felt they quelled concerted rebellious attitudes.

In their published sermons intended for black audiences, ministers of all denominations emphasized the life of "meek and lowly Jesus," his ability to quietly bear personal suffering, his abhorrence of violence and of disorder. Missionaries and ministers concentrated on miraculous aspects of Christianity, parables, and historical events such as the lives of holy and profane men to illustrate doctrine and practice. Catechisms stressed discipline, especially the Ten Commandments. Presbyterians and Episcopalians became leaders in articulating the positive aspects of Christianizing slaves, by publishing catechisms, sermon books, and penning suggestions on the methods to be employed in this endeavor. In 1850, James Thornwell, a prominent Charleston Presbyterian minister succinctly capsulized the most "progressive" attitudes among clergy regarding how well the teachings of Jesus suited the condition of people in bondage. Thornwell sermonized in support of a separate church building in Charleston for black communicants of all denominations, because "the galleries of the white churches could not contain more than one-fourth of their numbers." Those supporting the enterprise met with strong opposition because the plan brought back memories of the Vesey Conspiracy and its relationship to scripture as perceived by the rebels, away from the watchful eye of whites. But Thornwell counseled that none need be afraid of the lessons of Jesus, "who was no stirrer up of strife, no mover of sedition." On the contrary, insisted Thornwell, the religion taught by Jesus was "the pillar of society, the safeguard of nations, the parent of social order." This religion alone possessed the power to curb passions and to accord each group their rights: "to the laborious, the reward of their industry; to the rich, the enjoyment of their wealth; to nobles, the preservation of their honors, and to the princes, the stability of their thrones." Jesus, said Thornwell, did not teach insurrection, anarchy, bloodshed, or revolt against masters. "Christian knowledge inculcates contentment with our lot," he preached, and "renders us comparatively indifferent to the inconveniences and hardships of time." Christian knowledge, persuaded Thornwell, subdued the "passions and prejudices" responsible for endangering the "social economy."[13]

In 1848 delegates of the Savannah River Baptist Association took definitive action, making Baptists of the Sea Island region among the last to engage in the religious instruction enterprise. Even then only "two or more" missionaries were approved to go among the slaves, and money to support the preachers was solicited not guaranteed. As if planter and congregational opposition were not enough, filling missionary posts also proved a trying task. Ministers often refused to accept the charge. This reluctance can be partly explained by the lack of financial support, which is an index for gauging the degree of earnestness. Contributions were never large, generally ranging from thirty-five to fifty dollars annually, but on several occasions were as low as fifty cents. Not until 1853 did Sea Island slaves receive a missionary through the Association. Yet the cause was not totally lost. The Savannah River Baptist Association succeeded in creating interest in the Sabbath School movement for the young after 1849, and some churches as well as individual planters furthered the Baptist cause through this institution while they spurned organized efforts. Other Baptist slaveholders periodically employed their own missionary, or hired Baptist "exhorters" as overseers.[14]

Considering conditions among white Baptist churches during the antebellum era, it is not surprising that so little enthusiasm was expressed over the religious welfare of slaves. Many churches met infrequently, once a month, and shared the same pastor. Often a congregation was without a pastor for whole seasons, and the only services were provided by the Association missionary whenever he had the opportunity. This dearth of spiritual ardor was matched by internal strife in various congregations and general unruliness on the part of members. The missionary was sometimes given the task of settling disagreements which disrupted a church. He was often unsuccessful. The Savannah River Baptist Association consistently commented on the languid condition of the majority of churches in the 1830s. During the 1840s and 1850s the Association promoted Sabbath Schools not only as a means of instructing slaves, but also to combat the "declension and prevailing coldness" as well as "lack of grace" in white churches. It is surprising that slaves ever received Christian instruction considering the circumstances of Baptist churches without "grace" or filled with "paranoia" about abolitionists. Yet some planters provided plantation meetinghouses for the slaves especially after 1845. Here African-Americans met among themselves under supervision of some "trusted" black elder. Through these "invisible institutions" slaves received some Christian instruction. More significantly, they used these opportunities to interpose their own interpretations on Protestantism. Nowhere was this development more evident than in the Sea Islands. Congregations there were far ahead of their sister churches in terms of wealth, stability, leadership, and an early though gradual commitment to ostensibly integrating Gullahs into the Christian religion.[15]

Two significant events occurred in the Sea Island region in 1831. First, the presence of Methodist missionaries among the slaves. Second, the appearance of a fiery revivalist named Daniel Baker. Both happenings were determining factors in initiating a "change of heart" among Sea Island Baptists about teaching some Christian doctrines to the Gullahs.

Baptist planters of the Sea Island region laid claim to a tradition of religious dissent that began long before American independence. Some Baptist founders in the region were early disciples of George Whitefield when the established church refused to admit him to the pulpit.[16] Prominent Beaufort District Baptists of the 1830s, such as the Fripps, Fullers, Lawtons, Chaplins, and Robertses, were descendants of pioneer homeseekers, and identified with a legacy of an evangelism older than American Methodism. Given such claims to revivalist tradition and considering the apostolic dictates of the Faith, Baptist planters may well have experienced some degree of guilt and embarrassment as Methodist "knights of the saddle bags" descended upon the Sea Islands to undertake what thier spiritual brethren had neglected.

Further pressure was brought to bear in 1831 and 1832 as Beaufort District quaked under the forceful impact of a revival initiated by a cultivated and spirited evangelist. Daniel Baker was a Southern Presbyte rian and former pastor of the Second Presbyterian Church in Washington, of which both John Quincy Adams and Andrew Jackson were members. He left the Washington Church to accept a pastorship in Savannah and there heavily engaged in evangelical preaching. The impact of Baker's sermons was reportedly felt along the entire seaboard of Georgia and South Carolina. Wherever he preached a steady stream of converts came forth. His was not a mass revival since the seaboard white population was sparse. But hundreds attended the protracted meetings which Baker conducted in "the little sea coast towns and villages" mainly inhabited by planter aristocracy. And his sermons reputedly "moved whole communities." Baker wrote in his autobiography that his South Carolina efforts led to "important results" in places such as Gillisonville, Grahamville, Robertville, May River, and Beaufort. The meetings at Beaufort he deemed "the most remarkable." There was no Presbyterian church so Baker preached alternately in the Baptist and Episcopalian churches. "Oh, what blessed meetings we had!" he wrote. Baker preached three times a day "to full houses," and the numbers "hopefully converted amounted to about eighty." [17]

In regard to the number "hopefully converted" in Beaufort, Baker apparently took only white converts into account. Another section of Baker's autobiography quotes the Episcopal minister as stating that there were "two or three hundred conversions in Beaufort under Mr. Baker's ministry," consisting of "a number of whites," seventy of whom presented themselves for confirmation at the Episcopal church, and "very many blacks," who united with the Baptists. [18] Thus at least some of the slaves from the town of Beaufort participated in the Baker revival.

At the time of Baker's appearance the two houses of worship in Beaufort were described by one of thier "eminent laymen" as "little better than masonic lodges." The churches had the form of godliness but were "destitute of its power." The "layman" observed that "frequenters of the race-course and the theater found their places at the communion table," and that not even the duelist was excluded. Baker was credited with stimulating religious enthusiasm among "decadent" members of the planter class. An observer of the 1831 revival noted that in at least one instance derision of Baker's mission was transformed into contrition. Notice of Baker's services was sent from house to house. The announcement was received at a whist club during their weekly meeting. The notice was read aloud "amidst shouts of merriment." The group ridiculed the religious meeting and decided to attend, "confident of their ability to withstand all the preacher's snares." They attended Baker's meeting and found themselves "overcome" by a force stronger than they, and stripped "of the armour wherein they trusted." Before the revival ended, eight of the party of eleven "were found sitting at the feet of Jesus." One became a bishop, and another a presbyter of the Episcopal church.[19]

Word of the spiritual awakening in Beaufort District was carried to other parts of the state and even attracted coverage in national religious presses. The Methodist *Christian Advocate and Journal* printed an article illustrating the pitch of regeneration fervor aroused in Beaufort. The correspondent, one of those converted, stated that "no one can conceive who was not present," the effects of the revival on the resort town. Schools were closed, businesses, shops, and stores were shut—even politics were forgotten. The church was "filled to overflowing—seats, galleries, aisles, exhibited a dense mass of human beings from hoary age to childhood." Yet despite the multitude, "breathless silence" prevailed, broken only by the preacher's "reproving, persuading, imploring, thrilling" voice. Crowds reportedly came forward, and fell prostrate at the feet of the altar, as the musical voices of hundreds rose over the kneeling multitude. The scene was compelling, related the participant-observer, and "it was not in human hearts to resist the influence that awoke its sympathies, and spoke to its purest and most elevated feeling."[20]

Residents insisted that Baker was responsible for bringing new life to many Lowcountry churches. This rebirth was most visible in Beaufort. Citizens there claimed that even twenty years later there was a "a higher moral and religious tone, and a more intelligent and consistent profession of Christianity maintained."[21]

The Beaufort Baptist Church recorded a sizable white membership increase over a period of about ten years following Baker's appearance. And the augmentation of black members was unprecedented. According to membership lists, only 62 whites united with the church from 1804 (the year of its establishment) to 1831. From July 1831 to October 1840, 110 whites joined the congregation. Thus the majority of Beaufort Church's over 2,000 member increase from 1831 to 1840 consisted of black converts. Increases at other Beaufort District Baptist churches participating in the revival, though not as impressive, were nevertheless considerable compared to the majority of other churches in the Savannah River Baptist Association.[22] Thus, emerging zeal in some of the Baptist churches in the Sea Island District inspired more attention toward the spiritual welfare of the Gullahs.

Daniel Baker's conversion of Richard Fuller in 1831 had significant implications for Christianizing efforts in the Sea Islands. Under Fuller's ministration the Beaufort Church became the largest, most influential congregation in the Sea Island region. Fuller was greatly moved by the reformer's cry to instruct the slaves and was largely responsible for the comparatively phenomenal growth of the Beaufort Baptist Church.[23]

Richard Fuller was a member of the Fuller-Middleton family, long-time residents of Beaufort District. Fuller's personal holdings consisted of plantations on St. Helena and Cat Islands as well as the mainland. At the time of Baker's appearance in Beaufort, Fuller was a wealthy, well-established, Harvard-educated attorney not yet thirty years old. His parents were Baptists, but at birth Fuller was baptized an Episcopalian. Following his "moving" conversion in 1831, Fuller was rebaptized and he united with the local Episcopal church. But, not finding the "peace of mind" nor the "inspiration" he sought, Fuller was baptized again, this time in the Beaufort River, and as a Baptist. As further evidence of his reformation, Fuller immediately relinquished his lucrative law practice and declared himself called to the gospel ministry. In 1832 he was ordained a Baptist minister and accepted pastorship of Beaufort Church, where he remained until 1847. He then accepted a call to the Seventh Street Baptist Church in Baltimore where he was pastor until 1871.[24]

Late in his career, Fuller confided to a friend that when he was initially "called" to the ministry he resolved to confine his labors wholly to the slave population. But, Fuller claimed, he "was prevented by the hand of God." Although he did not devote his entire career to religious instruction of bondspeople, as a minister in Beaufort Fuller spent much of his time to preaching among the Gullahs. The attention and interest he gave represented a turning point in the religious history of Sea Island blacks. The immense African-American population, previously ignored by Baptist planters and churches, gradually, under the administration of Fuller, became objects of concern from a spiritual standpoint. As white membership increased, slaves of these new members were baptized and the Beaufort Church became a training ground for black Baptist converts at liberty to attend services. Fuller insisted that galleries be given over to the bulging black membership. A special lecture room was also added where black church members could be instructed before and after Sunday worship as well as during the week. Slaves attending Beaufort Church were sometimes instructed by their own masters who were also prominent church elders. Aside from scripture, church discipline and rules of conduct were emphasized.[25]

As a Sea Island planter and a favorite son of the community, Fuller could combat some resistance to religious instruction of the slaves. By 1840 he had organized a system of preaching places on the Islands where he or a member of his staff made periodic appearances. Establishment of these preaching stations furthered the Baptist cause, leading to "conversion" of many plantation slaves. While pastor of Beaufort Church, Fuller was respected among the whites as a sincere, inspiring, and effective minister. He was also popular with the Gullahs. Fuller was one of the very few planters who openly denounced the separation of families. He considered this morally wrong and against biblical law. He refused to sell or divide his bondspeople, an important consideration to black people accustomed to seeing "pious" planters disregard slaves' familial ties at a moment's notice. In addition to observing (like a true patriarch) this fundamental principle of humanity, Fuller adopted an evangelical style of preaching said to be filled with "earnestness, fire and melting pathos." An associate who often heard Fuller preach wrote:

His whole mien was imposing. When he rose to address a congregation, his very attitude was that of a man conscious at once that he had a most important message to deliver, and that he had the capacity to deliver it worthily. . . . His voice was singularly sweet and of great compassion and managed with such exquisite skill, that his softest whispers were distinctly heard in the remotest parts of a crowded congregation; while his loudest tones did not jar upon the ears of those nearest the speaker. His gestures were always graceful. . . . He subdued others, because, in the loftiest flights of his imagination and the deepest feelings of his heart, he was master of himself.[26]

Apparently a skillful and arousing speaker, Fuller captured the imagination of the bondspeople, something few white preachers could do. The Gullahs also viewed him as a kind and sensitive man whose "good works" were equal to his "faith." No doubt these considerations explain the eagerness with which he was received and accepted by the Gullahs as a preacher and for the warmth with which they remembered him to the Northern missionaries during the course of the Civil War. The Gullahs even created a stanza for Fuller in one of their most revered spirituals: "Massa Fuller on de Tree ob Life, Roll, Jordan, Roll."

After Fuller left for Baltimore in 1847, attempts to bring slaves into Sea Island churches were not persued with the same enthusiasm. But in 1853, through efforts of the Savannah River Baptist Association missionary and an energetic new pastor at Beaufort Church named I.M.C. Beaker, Gullahs again became a focal point of concern. During the last seven antebellum years, slave baptisms in the Beaufort River again became frequent. A record was set in 1857 when 220 slaves received into the Church "were all on Sunday morning . . . Baptized by our Pastor . . . in 1 hour and 45 minutes and in the presence of a very large number of spectators." The total number of slaves baptized for that year was also a record—556.[27]

The first phase of Baptist efforts to Christianize slaves, from 1830 to 1845, roughly corresponds to a period of growth in Sea Island churches and, most spectacularly, the Beaufort Church. In 1833, Beaufort District had a slave population of around 30,861. For that year the nine largest Beaufort District Baptist congregations reported a total membership of around 4,419. That was over two and one-half times the total membership of the remaining twenty-eight Baptist churches in the Savannah River Association (whose combined memberships was only 1,666). We cannot be certain about the number of slaves these figures represent, since racial designations were not yet in use. But the majority of these church members were slaves, a hypothesis supported by membership returns of later years for which there are racial designations.[28]

By 1845, when the Southern Baptist Convention was organized, the largest Beaufort District Baptist churches at Beaufort, St. Helena, May River and Hilton Head for instance, reported a total membership of around 5,914. Most of this increase is attributable to slave baptisms and over half of those to Beaufort Church. Total membership for all forty-three churches within the Association was about 8,529. This trend indicates that the most active area of religious instruction was in the Sea Islands. St. Helena Parish, with a slave population of 6,740 in 1845, had two Baptist churches. While St. Helena's Brick Baptist Church was accessible to the several thousand slaves living there, Beaufort Church drew its membership for a forty-mile radius that included six Sea Islands and parts of the mainland. The adult slave population in Beaufort District was around 22,000 in 1840, out of a total slave population of 29,682.[29] Thus approximately one in every five slaves in Beaufort District was a Baptist church member.

In the latter and generally most vigorous period of the movement for Christian instruction from 1845 to 1861, Baptist involvement continued to center in areas where evangelizing efforts were already in progress, such as the Sea Islands. Although several Lowcountry churches did increase their black membership during the period, such augmentation was numerically insignificant. Most membership returns submitted to the Savannah River Baptist Association had racial designations by 1848. These reports indicate that a few individual Sea Island churches maintained fairly large memberships and Beaufort Church had unusual increases. But the majority of Baptist churches in the Lowcountry south of Charleston seemed to fall short of the goal of religious conversion of bondspeople. Actually neither Sea Island Baptists, Baptist missionaries, nor lukewarm Baptist churches adequately "served the spiritual needs" of so large a black population. In 1859, as civil conflict approached, the total black membership of the Baptist churches within the jurisdiction of the Savannah River Baptist Association was not yet 7,000.[30] In some ways these figures are unimpressive, but they nevertheless demonstrate black exposure to Christianity through Baptist efforts. We can also surmise that black church members were the best conduits of the faith in the slave quarters. When this is considered, Baptist influence is even more manifest, for few Gullahs actually joined the Methodist church. Most Gullahs "converted to Christianity" or even adherents of it accepted the denomination of their masters, a preference that continued even after bondage. This raises questions about the nature of Baptist activity among the Gullahs, and why the denomination of slaveholders so strongly appealed to slaves.

Superficially, Lowcountry planters appear to represent "paternalism" par excellence. Those "young and refined" citizens of the Sea Island communities who claimed Daniel Baker for their spiritual patron included such men as C. C. Pinckney, William H. Barnwell, Robert Barnwell Rhett, Stephen Elliott, and Richard Fuller. These men represented the quintessence of South Carolina Lowcountry aristocracy, dominating landholdings and counting their slaves by the hundreds. Beaufort was the chief place of residence for most Baptist planters. But some of the stauncher Baptists such as the Lawtons, Robertses, Bosticks, and Nortons shunned "iniquitous" recreations offered by the Sea Island resort town and created their own manorial splendor at Robertville, Lawtonville, and Gillisonville. These planters reportedly excelled in erudition as well as wealth, and during the Civil War Northerners occupying their homes found extensive libraries. Sons were often educated at Harvard, at Princeton ("very popular" because "no Negroes" were ever allowed), and Yale. Daughters were sometimes taught refinement of manners and grace of carriage at exclusive Northern finishing schools. According to a contemporary who resided in Beaufort, nowhere on the continent was "family hauteur and pride carried to such extremes," and nothing in the largest cities North or South could "equal the display of carriages and equipages with the servants in livery" seen on a pleasant afternoon in Beaufort, "when the mothers and daughters of these cotton lords took their accustomed airing."[31]

An Island planter's occupation, then, was both remunerative and often conducted by proxy. And, since his education was usually unsurpassed by others in the state, the question may be asked, what did he consider his *raison d'être?* According to Jenkins Mikell of Edisto Island, the planter seldom pondered this question. "He followed the path of least resistance and enjoyed life after his own idea." "But," Mikell added, "if forced to be specific," the planter "would assert that politics and the Church stood out most prominently and more generally occupied his attention than other things. It was either one or the other—sometimes both at one time." Some of South Carolina's most illustrious statesmen and clergymen hailed from the Sea Islands. Naturally, since the wealth of these individuals directly depended upon continuation of their "peculiar institution," they were bound to its protection and defense against governmental encroachment. The Sea Islands, then, were also a hotbed of Southern nationalism and the home of the most vociferous South Carolina fire-eaters. When statesmen met in 1861 to discuss and vote on secession from the Union, one tempestuous Sea Island patriot declared impatiently, "If South Carolina does not secede from the Union, Edisto will!"[32]

The concern manifested toward religious matters by some of these "first families" of the South was noticed by Northern observers during the Civil War. The deserted mansions "were generally found strewn with religious periodicals, mainly Baptist magazines."[33] Implicitly then, the letter if not the spirit of Christianity occupied the minds of these slave-holding Baptists at one time or another. And, in keeping with their aristocratic affectations, some probably had an esoteric flair for leisurely contemplation of theology and doctrine. More significant for the slaves, some planters practiced a self-fashioned mode of paternalism through religious instruction. The example of Richard Fuller is a case in point.

As a large slaveholder, Northern-educated lawyer, and Southern Baptist preacher, Fuller's position on slavery was curious and filled with the dialectical trappings that reveal the nature of paternalism as a self-serving, conscience-assuaging ideology of a dominant group. Fuller upheld the right to hold slaves and used scripture to support his arguments. Yet he spoke out against slavery in the United States and against some evils of the system, insisting that its existence be limited. Like other slaveholders such as Henry Clay, Fuller was an avid member of the American Colonization Society. The stated goal of the Society was colonization of free blacks in Africa. Many Southerners such as C. C. Pinckney abhorred the organization, seeing it as seeping antislavery sentiment. Yet others, such as Fuller, supported the scheme mainly as a vehicle to channel reformist evangelical zeal, since black Americans could convert Africans, and as a public example of concern for black welfare. In 1851 at one of the organization's most important meetings, both Fuller and Clay addressed the members. Fuller's statements attracted wide national attention, temporarily alienating him from many of his slaveholding friends and former white parishioners in Beaufort. Fuller lauded missionary efforts among slaves in the South and condemned the North for its impatience. His address, though certainly not abolitionist, seemed antislavery in tone, and much of it was directed at fellow slave masters. Fuller stated that "we of the South" should make concessions, and candidly admit that while slavery "enriches the individual, it impoverishes the State." Slavery, said Fuller, fostered indolence and luxury, "the bane of governments." Additionally, he appealed, the South should consider, as "honest," "Christian" men, "whether, when Jesus Christ says 'What, therefore God hath joined together, let no man put asunder,' husbands and wives ought to be separated; whether labor ought to be received without compensation." Recalling a conversation he once had with recently deceased John C. Calhoun, the latter insisted that planters did "pay fair wages for the labor of our slaves." But it was not "the calculation," said Fuller, nor "the dollars and cents: it is the principle I am contending."[34]

But several years earlier, while still pastoring in Beaufort, Fuller had engaged in a dialogue with Francis Wayland, President of Brown University. Fuller argued in favor of slavery from the Old Testament and while he found nothing explicit to support slavery in the New Testament, Fuller maintained that this silence was tacit approval. "What God sanctioned in the Old Testament and permitted in the New," Fuller proclaimed, "cannot be a sin." [35]

Also, despite Richard Fuller's "professed" views against slavery, he maintained his plantations after leaving Beaufort for Baltimore. During the Civil War he was loyal and remained in Baltimore. Following the outbreak of the war he went to Washington, D. C., and called upon Salmon P. Chase, Secretary of the Treasury, to inquire about his rights "in regard to his plantations and slaves in Port Royal." Chase wrote:

> Told him that, as a loyal man, he was Proprietor of the land. "How about the Negroes?" he asked. "They were free," I replied. He thought his right to them was the same as his right to the land. Told him opinion would differ on that point, and that, for one, I should never consent to the involuntary reduction to slavery of one of the Negroes who had been in the service of the Government. Told him further what I thought of the character of the rebellion and its results, etc.

The conversation concluded with Fuller indicating his willingness "to acquiesce in the experiments of the Government," but having "grave doubts" about the ability of the Gullahs to behave responsibly as free people. Fuller quoted Machiavelli's saying, "Next to making free men slaves, it is most difficult to make slaves free men." [36]

Richard Fuller may have been antislavery in "principle" and in theory. But in reality he upheld American slavery as a white man's right. Yet, while his theoretical position on slavery was ambiguous, he was unwavering in efforts to expose the black population in St. Helena Parish to Christianity and in his support of such endeavors all over the state.

At a glance, it appears that during the apex of the antebellum era, Sea Island Baptists combined the qualities of material wealth and an exhibition of missionary zeal. The small white memberships and disproportionately large black galleries ostensibly imply that in the wake of paranoia about abolitionists and general inertia among most Lowcountry churches, Sea Island Baptist planters were exemplary in Christianizing slaves. Yet to what extent did Sea Island Baptist planters actually further the cause of Christianity among the Gullahs? And, insofar as they did, were such teachings instituted out of an acknowledgment of Christian duty? Without denying the individual motivation and limited sense of moral obligation expressed by one such as Richard Fuller, Baptist con-

cern for religious instruction was mainly superficial. Possibly some wished
to ease a sense of conscience aroused by the 1831 revival and to neutral-
ize criticism from Northern quarters. But more significantly, Baptist interest in Christianizing the Gullahs was prominent where doctrine might
be a means of exerting influence over personal behavior and social relationships to further the existing status quo.

"Christian" Slaves

Mostly town slaves and house servants were first accepted into Baptist
churches. Certainly, in the early phase of the movement, these African-
Americans had access to the "privilege" of becoming church members.
Since Beaufort was the chief place of residence for Sea Island planters,
their retinue of house servants had the opportunity, and sometimes were
forced to attend Baptist worship. As church membership increased, the
next group of slaves in plantation hierarchy, the artisans, were also represented. Field workers were not completely excluded from the churches,
especially Beaufort Church. When a slaveholder and his family joined a
church, his slaves might be required to join as well. Richard Fuller, for
instance, was diligent about accepting his slaves into Beaufort Church
and encouraged this among his slaveholding neighbors. Yet few Sea Island Baptists allowed their field slaves the mobility needed to attend
preaching places. This rule must have applied particularly to slaves wishing
to attend church service in places like Beaufort or Bluffton that necessi-
tated leaving the Islands or vicinity of the plantations for long periods of
time and usually required some means of water transportation provided
by the planter. Furthermore, these country churches were modest-sized
structures, built mainly with the small white population in mind. Not
all churches even had galleries. Among those that did, once the more
"privileged" slaves and house servants were seated, there was obviously
no room for the field hands. According to one former Beaufort slave:

> Didn't have no colored churches. De drivers and de overseers, de house-serv-
> ants, de bricklayers and folks like dat'd go to de white folk's church. But not de
> field hands. Why dey couldn't have all got in de church. My marsa had three or
> four hundred slaves, himself. And most of the other white folks had just as many
> and more.

Even with favored slaves, concepts of white spiritual egalitarianism did
not go far. Beaufort whites insisted in 1841 that the inside stairs leading

to the slave galleries be moved to the outside so that the two races would not have to pass each other, or use the same entrance when they met to worship God in common.[37] One can thus imagine the disdain that "gentle" white folk felt at being in close quarters with field slaves.

Some whites considered it a dangerous practice to allow slaves to leave plantations to attend church no matter what their status. Thomas Fuller, Episcopalian brother of the venerable Richard, reported on the state of religious instruction at the Charleston Meeting. Fuller complained that the habit of black church members descending upon the town of Beaufort was deplorable:

> Removed as so large a number are, every Sunday from the control and discipline of the plantation, and impossible as it is for the Church to know and control their conduct, they use their liberty in ways and for purposes adverse to their morals. Nothing seems to me more essential in order to their becoming a religious people, than that they be subjected to the supervision of the plantation, of the minister of a Church, that will investigate and correct their wrong views and bad habits. . . . It is owing, I think, to the want of religious instruction and discipline on the plantations, that the influence of religious instruction and the spirit of subordination among the negroes is so little seen and felt.[38]

Baptist planters themselves recognized and attempted to confront these problems. As church memberships increased, a means of superintending the widespread congregation and keeping slaves on the plantations was needed. Black church members were organized into plantation associations under the jurisdiction of the church.

These "black societies" were the nucleus of the Gullah socioreligious community. They existed even before preaching stations were established and were reportedly religious bodies which slaves entered into voluntarily, although the nature and origin of these societies was unknown. Methodist missionaries found them already organized and a hindrance to Methodist authority among the slaves, especially when their practices were under the rubric of Christianity. In 1833, John Field, a St. Helena planter, wrote to the Methodist missionary assigned to the island. Speaking for himself and "others," Field expressed his disapproval of the societies, and of the slaves' association with the Baptist Church on St. Helena. According to Field, the slaves who joined the church were "almost entirely under the control of Negro leaders." The Methodist missionary's preaching on the island prompted "constant application" of slaves for "tickets to get baptized," and join the Baptist Church. The slaves derived no Christian benefit from their association with the church, said Field, but used it as "a place of resort." Field "suspected an influence decidedly contrary to vital godliness," but added that it could not be prevented "unless I resided on the place myself."[39]

If the benne seed ritual is an example,[40] these societies had some characteristics similar to African associations. It is later argued that the black societies were, like the African societies, units of organization that regulated conduct and served to integrate individuals into the plantation community. Within these societies Gullahs practiced their own version of Christianity, and created their religious folk-culture. Baptist planters apparently intended to alter the "corrupt" elements within these slave associations and use them to promote a Christianity, suitable to their own ends. Slaves' familiarity with concepts of secret society, membership, and social regulations suggest a relationship to African institutions that Christian ideas of a community of believers reinforced. Like the formation of Gullah language, the syncretic evolution of African Christianity was a gradual process. It began when diverse African groups framed a spiritual commonality and belief system into which Christianity, at various times and with varied intensity, was incorporated, reformulated and appropriated. For many years, Gullahs heard of "Christianity" mainly from black rather than white teachers, and this contributed to the persistence of African norms, thought, and ceremony. But, as the benne seed ritual suggests, the presence of black "Christians" in the slave quarters undoubtedly produced debates, challenges, acknowledgments and selective adaptation even before 1830.

While Methodist missionaries were "suspicious" of the black societies, for Baptists they were a medium for religious service and discipline among the slaves. Thus the black societies served one function for slaves and embodied another for slave owners. At Beaufort and other churches, slaves professing conversion as Baptists had to unite with a society. Beaufort Church, with its large black membership and extensive records, illustrates how whites expected these societies to function. At first black leaders had charge of the societies, but subject to the superintendence of a resident planter. The black leaders reported at the monthly church meeting. According to the Minutes of Beaufort Church for November 11, 1840:

The Committee on discipline are requested to obtain if possible the presence
of all the colored elders, at their meetings; as from them and them alone [the
elders] must they expect to receive legitimate reports, of Deaths, the prosperity
of their societies or backsliding members.[41]

When societies first came under jurisdiction of the Church each one
bore the name of their black leader in charge. But by 1850 societies were
under governance of a white brother living on the island and the organizations named after their locations. Rather than attend the white church,
the black membership was directly affiliated with black societies for purposes of "religious instruction and worship."[42] Thus, black societies were
the vehicle through which the Gullahs as Baptists participated in the
Christian experience.

Although white brethren ultimately were ostensible leaders of black
societies, the structure and supervision of the organizations still provided
the slaves with some autonomy. Ideally the white brother in charge of a
given society held monthly meetings with society members, scrutinized
the slaves' activities, conducted religious exercises, and examined candidates for church membership. Each white brethren was assisted by one
or more blacks (depending upon the size of the society) called "watchmen," "elders," or "deacons," appointed by the church at the suggestion
of the "brother in charge." In reality, however, the black deacon continued to direct the society. He was responsible for "general watchcare"
over the society, and conducted society meetings "to inquire into and
report . . . cases for discipline that may come to his attention." He was
also at liberty "to hold meetings for worship and exhortation . . . on
such plantations as he may have received special permission," and to
administer communion. The black elder was in turn aided by "help" on
each plantation with a sufficient number of society members. The help
supervised members on the plantation, held prayer meetings, and reported weekly to the elder, naming those slaves desiring to join the society. According to a former Sea Island slave, a black exhorter would
preach "to de field hands down in de quarters. . . . Meet next day to de
Marsa's and turn in de report, how many pray, how many ready for
baptism and all like dat."[43]

Gullahs had a measure of control in terms of internal structure and
worship within black societies. How they transferred that into community cohesion is discussed later. Planters primarily wanted plantation discipline preached, breaches of discipline punished, and corrective retri-

bution administered in the name of Christian commandments. Beyond that superintendence, slaveholders spent little energy on Christian doctrine. Planters probably welcomed opportunities to provide slaves with a "safe" outlet for releasing pent-up hostilities and emotions. After 1845, many plantations had rude structures where the Gullahs could "hold prays" on weekday evenings as well as Sundays. Northern missionaries were appalled at the condition of the "Prays" or Praise Houses. "The owner furnished a better stable for his horses than a house of worship for these sons and daughters of the King of Kings," wrote Mansfield French from Port Royal.[44] Yet for Gullahs the Praise House was a plantation community hall where they related secular experiences, directed their religious life, openly expressed among each other their innermost frustrations, longings and expectations.

The white brother in charge of a society was generally a large slaveholder sometimes with several plantations on the Island he superintended. In other cases a Baptist overseer, but slaveholder in his own right, was assigned to a society. The names of Fripp, Chaplin, Barnwell, Baynard, and Fuller dominate Beaufort Church Minutes as "brethren in charge" of black societies. Most of these planters rarely spent long periods of time on their island plantations, preferring the comforts of their Beaufort townhouses. Most knew little about their slaves' activities (except house slaves) unless some depredation was committed and reported. In the early period of church superintendence of societies, white brethren were lax about meeting with the organizations, often leaving this responsibility with the black elders. In 1842 the Beaufort Church Business reminded white brethren of their duties:

Resolved . . . that *Brother Chaplin be requested to attend himself in person as the Church deems it important that the Brethren appointed and responsible be themselves instructors of the societies confided to them.*

The Church had difficulty retaining a white brother in charge and resignations were frequent. Most Baptists apparently did not want the responsibility of overseeing black church members.[45]

Thus, black societies primarily accommodated the slave membership of large Baptist churches with little or no Christian instruction being imparted by white society leaders. The other sources of exposure to white Christian teachings came from Methodist missionaries, from preaching places established by Richard Fuller (though supplied less rigorously after he left), and late-coming Baptist missionaries who brought the last surge of slave baptismal activity in the mid-1850s. Apparently little screening occurred prior to uniting with Baptist churches, except examinations imposed upon the slaves by black leadership. Slaves were accepted into the Church from the societies, and admission was based on a profession of faith, evidence of "good character" from the slavemaster, and recommendation from the white brother in charge, who relied on intelligence received from the black elder.[46]

This lack of a meaningful conviction to teach Christianity raises the question of why some slaveholding Baptists accepted such large numbers of slaves into the churches at all. Neither a revival spirit nor Northern agitation fully explain the motivation. But activities of the Church Committee on Discipline perhaps express the manner in which Baptists expected Christianity to best serve them as slaveholders. Their change in attitude reflected the general shift away from paranoia about Christianizing slaves. After 1845 many believed that practical Christianity could work for the slave system. And although the majority of Gullahs had little or no contact with the Baptist church itself, church members felt the restraining arm of the faith through the Committee on Discipline.

Church discipline is an old concept, dating as far back as the sixteenth century. Early Baptist discipline was similar to the English Separatists' 1696 "Confessions of Faith," and integral to views of Christian fellowship for believers. This spiritual and communal sense revolved around creating a "true and orderly gospel church," with members conducting personal behavior according to Old Testament biblical tenants. Later, London Baptists' "Confessions of Faith" reflected concern for "order and discipline," and this was emphasized by their American counterpart, the Philadelphia Baptist Association, when in 1742 they composed their confessions and annexed a particular discipline code to it. In 1769 the Charleston Baptist Association adopted the Philadelphia model. Not all, probably not most, American Baptist churches had explicit discipline references in their confessions although discipline was a reality in the churches. But Charleston Baptists and their Lowcountry congregational extensions were products of the Calvinist-Baptist tradition as is reflected in their patent emphasis on discipline, and in other ways previously discussed.[47]

Nineteenth-century Southern and frontier evangelical congregations fostered a sense of community through worship, revivals, camp meetings, prayer meetings, and discipline. Church discipline kept alive the "heavenly pattern" which each church personified. This "city set on a hill" meted out censure and excommunication regularly to offending members who paled its self-image of purity and piety. As the country expanded, church discipline was used to control the raw excesses of new communities struggling against such "immoralities" as "drinking, fornication, gambling, dueling and profanity." Evangelical churches grew increasingly more powerful and espoused an increasingly conservative theology in the South and perhaps elsewhere. This trend toward religious conservatism was tied, though not exclusively, to political and social developments in the South, most notably to slavery. An obvious manifestation of this was the national polarization of church denominations.[48] In the Lowcountry, another significant and more immediate expression of efforts to protect the existing social and political order through religion is found in the function of discipline committees on plantations. Every Lowcountry church examined for this study with a large black membership had such a committee. The nature of this committee's concern with the slaves' activities reveals how Baptists intended to make Gullahs "good Christians" mainly insofar as Christianity made them better slaves. The work of the Committee on Discipline in the largest Sea Island church amplifies this thesis.

Once attention focused on slave conversion, the most pressing church business was discipline of slave members. The Committee existed previously, but was reorganized and restructured in 1840, and its function broadened. According to the Minutes, the disciplinary body governed behavior of all church members, "both bond and free," but was specifically charged with looking into breaches of conduct committed by bondspeople. This committee of eight brethren investigated a few white cases, mostly involving social lapses. But in the "inquiry and investigation" of slaves, the "Committee on Discipline" had "broad" but "conservative powers."[49]

As with white "brethren in charge" of black societies, prominent Sea Island slaveholders, such as Benjamin Chaplin, Saxby Chaplin, William Fuller, James Fripp, and Edward Fripp dominated discipline of the Gullahs. Furthermore, members of the Discipline Committee might also double as superintendents of a black society. Sea Island planter Benjamin Chaplin, for example, was a member of the disciplinary body and also superintendent of the Beaufort Society. Noted for cruelty to his slaves and intemperance, even Chaplin's peers admitted that his "violent temper" which was "so entirely ungovernable," disqualified him as a religious teacher.[50]

Discipline Committees met once a month. Prior to 1845 black elders met at the church with the Committee and reported on the state of religion in their societies. Later, this procedure was discontinued. Instead, white brethern in charge of a given society met with black members one Sunday in the month and subsequently reported to the Discipline Committee, providing a list of recommendations for action. The responsibilities of the brother in charge were elaborated in the Minutes of Beaufort Church. Should any "private or personal offense be reported," he could take such action as "he may think proper." If the offense was of a "more serious character, involving immorality," it was the duty of the brother in charge to carefully investigate "the facts," report these to the church at its regular discipline meeting, and offer his recommendations. The white brother was also "authorized and expected to examine applicants for restoration" of their membership, "and if satisfied," to recommend action to the church.[51]

Thus only the "more serious" offenses got to the church discipline level, and all manner of "lapses in moral conduct" and plantation "crimes" were considered serious enough to warrant censure by the church. Slaves were suspended and excommunicated as often for "crimes" against plantation authority as for "moral" breaches. Frequently mentioned were offences such as "killing beef," "hog stealing," "barn burning" and simply "theft." Additionally, flight appeared consistently as a reason for excommunication. In 1841 for instance, bondswoman Betty was "suspended for running away," and the same action was taken against Tom for "harboring above Betty." Other reasons for excommunication were "impudence," "Sabbath breaking," "fornication" and "adultery." Occasionally slaves requested "permission to marry."[52]

The word of plantation authority subjected a slave to church discipline. As in a white court of law, a bondsperson's word was worth nothing in a white church. Monthly society discipline meetings were public. They were meant to dishonor and humiliate the slaves before each other, to admonish others against "wrong doing," and to prostrate the "guilty" before "church" law. The Gullahs were confronted with their "sins" by their earthy masters as they would face a "heavenly father" in the future. Interests of both "masters" were represented as the same so a crime against a slaveholder was a "sin" in the eyes of God. This outlook was pressed on children who, after 1845, sometimes received instruction on Sunday mornings in the form of oral catechism, recitation of the Ten Commandments, and prayers. Rebecca Grant recalled that in Beaufort her former owners "wouldn't miss de catechism," and they [the children], "was taught they must be faithful to the Missus and Marsa's work like you would to your heavenly Father's work." Slaves on St. Helena Island discussed "Good Billy" (William) Fripp, a Baptist master who was referred to as "good," not because of his benevolence toward his slaves, but for his avowed piety and strict sense of biblical discipline. According to the Gullahs this "leading Baptist" carried his Bible out to the fields, showed slaves "Moses' law," and then flogged them "accordin'."[53]

Baptist slaveholders applied selected scriptures to the Gullahs' daily life struggle. Planters hoped a general spirit of contrition, via a "fear of God," would prevail in the slave quarters and subvert independent thought and action. They viewed discipline meetings as having a purgative effect on the Gullahs and defeating their efforts to resist the most degrading aspects of bondage. Double jeopardy existed for these black church members. If discovered committing acts against slaveholding interests, they suffered bodily punishment. But worse perhaps was expulsion from black society, the Gullahs' primary source for freedom of expression. An excommunicated or suspended church member would receive no pass to attend a preaching place or "society" or be allowed to "hold prays." Slaveholders tried using Christianity to exercise psychological dominance over the minds of Gullahs as they employed brute force to maintain physical control. No other spiritual activity detracted from or competed with these religious tribunals. When they occurred, plantation authority insisted on the slaves' undivided attention. From the Beaufort Church Minutes we find that even the Methodist missionary's limited activities had to revolve around these assemblages:

> The Pastor to write to the Rev. Mr. Moore [Methodist Missionary] and request him to appoint any other Sabbath than the first in the month to preach on Ladies Island—as that is the day appointed for the discipline of that Society attached to this Church.[54]

White Baptists' use of church discipline to undermine the Gullahs' active indignation and struggle against bondage is evident when considering the nature of the "sins" of which black church members were found "guilty." Theft, for instance, brought many Gullahs before disciplinary tribunals. Of course slaves did steal for consumptive purposes, obviously because provisions were often insufficient and monotonous. To keep cotton at maximum yield, planters sacrificed cultivation of food staples for their workers. Provision acreage was not determined by the slave community's size, but by the numbers of food-acres workers could attend while working cotton. Sam Mitchell, a former bondsman on one of John Chaplin's Ladies Island plantations, considered his master one of the more tolerable slaveholders. Yet Mitchell recalled that slaves received only a weekly peck of corn except at potato-digging time when they also received potatoes. Sam Polite, of John Fripp's plantation on St. Helena Island, also remembered a grim picture of subsistence:

> On Sattiday night every slabe dat wuks gits peck of corn and pea, and sometimes meat and clabber. You nebber see any sugar, neider coffee in slabery. You has straw in your mattress but dey gib you blanket. Ebery year in Christmas month you gits fur or eider fibe yaa'd cloth. . . . You wears hit winter en summer, Sunday en ebery day. You don't git no coat.[55]

Understandably, Gullahs felt no particular bond toward a "Thou shalt not steal" edict despite supposed spiritual and assured physical reprisals. Certainly the Gullahs realized the sham of such dictates given their peculiar circumstances and oppression. Still Gullahs were not immoral on the subject of theft. Among themselves they took a serious attitude toward theft, considering it a breach of trust. Yet Gullahs felt no compunction about such acts directed toward the slave system. In the American Freedmen's Inquiry Commission Interviews, conducted in 1863, Robert Smalls and Harry McMillan, two soldiers, Sea Island residents and former bondsmen, explained the slaves' attitude toward theft. They testified that while the majority of Gullahs stole from their masters and deceived them, these slaves would not steal from each other and were truthful in their dealings with one another. During the Civil War a white officer of the First South Carolina Volunteers told Charlotte Forten, a black Northerner, that he never saw a regiment where men were so honest. "In many camps the colonel and the rest of us would find it necessary to place a guard before our tents. We never do it here," he said. "They are left entirely unguarded. Yet nothing has ever been touched." Similarly, Laura M. Towne wrote in her diary: "The men and women come crowding here at all times begging to be allowed to buy clothing, and though they stand about for hours in the sun, we have never missed the slightest thing."[56]

In the benne seed ritual, Gullahs dealt with theft in a spiritual context, under the guise of the Baptist faith. But the moral judgment was the opposite of Christianity. "Sin" was not upon the slave who stole from the master, but the individual who "divulged" the act. Gullahs possessed a keen sense of communal morality which, in this regard, was not subverted by dogmatic features of Christianity. While stealing from "Maussa," was a sin, it was wrong—that is, against elements of collective interests and values—to steal from a fellow slave and hence betray community confidence. Gullahs extended their moral philosophy further than race or condition however, by refusing to steal from whites simply because they were white. But, the Gullahs were not naive. Their shrewd analysis of justice helped them distinguish between friend and oppressor even among white Northern "missionaries." And some white Northern Baptist ministers sent to the Sea Islands during the Port Royal experiment were more avaricious than cotton agents. One Reverend Phillips, on full salary from a missionary organization, also drew a salary from the government as a superintendant of plantations, and was provided with "house-rent and rations." Still, Phillips "demanded," from St. Helena Island Gullahs, "half-a-dollar from every church member for the half year ending January 1." Since some one thousand blacks on St. Helena, claimed membership in Brick Baptist Church, Phillips expected to collect quite a sum. But the Gullahs refused to pay. Other ministers "of like kidney" were dismissed for "lying" and for "stealing" contributions sent to the Gullahs by Northern congregations. On one occasion, Gullahs discovered that James McCrea, a minister representing the American Missionary Association was cheating them. They refused to attend McCrea's religious meetings and refused to labor in the cotton fields he supervised. Likewise, when some government cotton agents on St. Helena charged over 100 percent more for store items than was being charged in Beaufort, these stores were broken into "and robbed of a good deal of clothing."[57]

Flight, another problem continually plaguing Sea Island slaveholders and punished by both church and state, was usually provoked by some extreme act of cruelty, or gross injustice. Sometimes slaves left because of a strong desire to visit a loved one. Gullahs rarely ran away with intentions of "going North" for instance. Aside from the near impossibility of such an accomplishment, an intense love of family and deep attachments to familiar surroundings kept runaways nearby. Perhaps even more than any other slaves in the United States, Gullahs maintained a clan-type kinship community, and in their isolation clung tenaciously to these relationships. This attitude was also expressed toward their plantations. Those Gullahs able to purchase small twenty-acre plots of land during the Port Royal experiment, resisted buying on any plantation other than their "own." They thought "it was as bad as slavery if they had to leave their old homes." Yet as slaves, Gullahs ran away frequently and bad treatment was the leading cause for absence. Treatment was also a recurring theme in Gullah songs, as indicated by this slave worksong related by Sam Polite:

I wuk in field on Maussa Johnnie Fripp plantation. Sometime we sing w'en we wuk. One song we sing ben go lak dis:

> "Go way, Ole Man
> Go way, Ole Man
> W'ere you bin all day
> If you treat me good
> I'll stay 'till de Judgment day,
> But if you treat me bad,
> I'll sho' to run away."[58]

Not all masters were cruel. For example, the Gullahs represented "Capt. John" Fripp as a kind man. Still, his "whipping post" was within twenty feet of the "drawing-room." The tree, "a sprawling Asia-berry," covered with grey moss, "looked wiered enough." "Capt. John" reportedly never "licked" hard nor struck "in the same place twice." Fripp's houseman, Dick, only recalled getting one "hard" flogging, when he watered the old man's garden with seawater. However, his wife, the cruel one, liked "to stand at the window to see the floggings," administered by "Driver Moody," when "Capt. John" was away. Thomas Chaplin of Tombee Plantation was tough enough, and threatened his slaves a great deal. He was also an insensitive master in regard to selling slaves, unable to believe blacks had the same familial loyalty as white people. He wrote in his Journal, "cowhide was all talk with me." But one must take such a comment skeptically since he frequently had his drivers do the flogging. Chaplin was not remembered by his slaves for excessive cruelty nor for kindness.[59]

Rarely could a Sea Island slave boast, as one did, that their backs "stan lak white man's," that is, with no marks of the whip. "Talk o' lick um sar?" answered one slave when queried about floggings, "yes, sar, nebber did noffin but lick um sar." He insisted that they were whipped when they didn't work and "when we work, hard lick um all same sar." A "devil" for cruelty was Alviro Fripp who "before he got religion use to cuss and cuss and cuss." But when he joined the Baptist church, he could no longer cuss, "so he used to lick 'em instead." The "richest man on St Helena," Edgar Fripp, was reportedly the meanest, and his temper knew no bounds at "full moon." He also worked his slaves all night in full moon at cotton-picking time. The Gullahs went out of their way to avoid him for if a hat was not tipped quick enough or a bow low enough, Fripp would "lay his horsewhip on them well."[60]

Of the many cases of harsh treatment and sometimes actual barbarity, few compared with the 1849 incident recorded by Thomas Chaplin in his Journal. Chaplin's neighbor, James Sandiford, was brought before an inquest of planters regarding the death of his slave, Roger. In examining the slaves' remains, Chaplin wrote that "such a shocking sight never before met my eyes." The slave, a born cripple who "used his knees more than his feet," had been instructed, on a "cold and bitter day," to paddle a boat downriver for oysters and then to cut a bundle of mud marsh. Roger, instructed to return before "high water," did not show up until "ebb tide." But he brought back seven baskets of oysters and a small bundle of marsh. "That," commented Chaplin, "was more than the primest of my fellows would have done." But Sandiford gave Roger thirty lashes for not returning sooner, for not cutting more marsh, and for hollering loudly while being flogged for the first two offenses. Sandiford later eavesdropped on a conversation Roger had in the kitchen with another man. Two versions of the exchange were reported. According to the planter, Roger stated that if he had "sound limbs" he would shoot down a white man before he took a flogging. The man to whom Roger spoke denied this, informing the jurors that Roger said "he would turn his back on them if they shot him down," which Chaplin believed was the truth. Neither comment, in Chaplin's opinion, warranted the punishment Roger received:

For these *crimes*, this man, this demon in human shape, this pretended Christian, member of the Baptist Church, had this poor cripple Negro placed in an open outhouse, the wind blowing through a hundred cracks, his clothes wet to the waist, without a single blanket & in freezing weather, with his back against the partition behind him, & fastened on the other side—in this position the poor wretch was left for the night. . . . The wretch [Sandiford] returned to his victim about daylight next morning & found him, as anyone would expect, dead, *choked, strangled*, frozen to death, *murdered*.[61]

That same day the jurors reached a verdict—the slave met his death by choking on the chain his master put around his neck, "having slipped from the position in which he was placed." The verdict, Chaplin wrote should have been Roger died from "inhumane treatment," for he not only strangled from trying to disengage himself, hence becoming entangled in the most "shocking position," but was also "stiff dead" from the cold. In Chaplin's "individual" opinion, the act was deliberate, but unpremeditated murder. Whether Chaplin attempted to convince the court of this is unknown. The case, like many such situations was certainly murder, but it behooved slaveholders to protect their position. The "witness" against Sandiford was a slave, the planter was related to at least four of the eight jurors and property rights were supreme in the South. Whatever Chaplin felt in private, his public posture was another matter. Furthermore, five years later, he defended an overseer who killed a runaway slave for stealing watermelons.[62]

Since Sandiford was a Baptist planter, his conduct came before the Beaufort Church where he held membership. The crime apparently occurred on February 18, 1841, and the inquest was held the next day. However, not until March 31 was the incident was brought to the Beaufort Church's attention according to the Minutes. At that time it was discussed at the "Business Meeting," and Sandiford ordered to appear at its next session. On May 5, after receiving "a letter" from Sandiford, his case was "postponed for further consideration." On June 30, "the case of Brother Sandiford was again postponed," and never mentioned after that time. Sandiford's letter was not part of the Minutes and its contents are unknown. Undoubtedly he defended his actions, and though the case probably made him an unpopular communicant, he was never "disciplined." He eventually sold his property and left the region. But more significant, this rawly violent, not to say un-Christian act went uncensored by the Baptist Church.[63] One can imagine what a stir it caused among the slaves, some of whom probably had sanguine expectations that at least ecclesiastical action would be taken. Such occasions reinforced for slaves the fact that even in matters of "Christian" justice, a double standard applied.

Thus during the Civil War, observers commented on a "total absence of any trace of feudal affection among these people." Even on supposedly "model" plantations with well-built, neat-appearing cabins like the Smith Estate on St. Helena, slaves related tales of white cruelty and black defiance. One slave who did not salute his master "respectfully enough," was ridden "down and over and left in the road until night." When brought back to his cabin, the man was "more dead than alive." Another man helped his wife finish her task after doing his own. He was ordered to flog his wife but refused. For his "obstinance," slaveholder Smith, a "kind" master, gave the man "500 lashes with his own hand." The slave, previously one of the strongest workers, was "completely broken down." Susannah, the sickly but high spirited seamstress on the Oaks plantation, told Laura Towne she once raised pigs but her harsh, domineering master, Baptist patriarch Daniel Pope, forbade this and threatened to shoot them. "'I don't mean impudence Massa, but you cawn't shoot my hogs. What can I do for my children's winter shoes and our salt.'" Pope's slaves were some of the worse off, ill-clothed, ill-housed and ill-fed. However, Susannah's mistress, though full of threats and scoldings, never lashed her seamstress. Susannah attributed this good fortune to "my pride and principle." Another bondswoman, Celia, told Towne how "Driver John" abused the people and how she once "clutched him by the throat when he whipped her husband and two children."[64]

Gullahs who took "to de swamps and marshes" usually either returned voluntarily or were caught. Sometimes "patterollers" apprehended Gullahs as they returned from or embarked upon some innocent but unauthorized personal errand. Brutal corporal punishment and church censure were certain, yet no amount of flogging, stays in the stocks, ball and chains, sermons, suspensions, or excommunications could daunt the Gullahs' high spirit or their natural inclinations to independence. Incidents of flight express these slaves' refusal to accept their masters' conceptions of moral behavior. Although no reliable avenues of physical escape from bondage existed, Gullahs resisted servitude instinctively, undermining plantation and church discipline. When Northern forces occupied the Sea Islands and masters fled, chances for freedom did seem imminent. Masters endeavored to take as many slaves as possible with them to the mainland, telling the Gullahs that the Yankees intended to carry them to Cuba, take their children, and "knock out der brainses against de treeses." Few Gullahs went willingly with their masters to the mainland, but many were taken forcibly. Gullahs risked and often lost their lives to flee, telling horror tales of death and suffering inflicted upon anyone suspected of desiring either to remain on the Sea Islands or to escape from the mainland where the planters "refugeed." The fact that they continued to flee under these circumstances is the best testimony to their sense of independence and will to freedom. One such incident was told to Laura M. Towne:

> A woman today just escaped from her owners on the Mainland. She said she had hard work to escape, sleeping in the marsh and hiding all day. She brought away her two little children. Her master had just whipped her oldest son almost to death because he was suspected of trying to join the Yankees.[65]

Although the Battle of Port Royal ended in an easy Northern victory and occupation, the rest of South Carolina remained in Confederate hands. Planters fled the Sea Island region but returned, sometimes under cover of darkness, hoping to force slaves back to the mainland. Blacks and whites picketing the region could not place men at every landing spot and Gullahs lived in apprehension of the slaveholders' return. Susannah's master returned several times, once telling slaves to burn the cotton. "Why for we burn de cotton? Where we get money then for buy clo' sho' and salt?" So instead of burning cotton, they guarded it nightly. Women kept watch and men stood ready to defend their interests when the alarm sounded. At the Oaklands plantation of rebel Baptist Dr. Sams, a field hand named Cupid told Charlotte Forten how his master had daringly returned to St. Helena, risking capture by Northern soldiers, solely to retrieve slaves. Sams attempted to cajole Cupid into cooperation:

> He ordered the people to get all the furniture together and take it to a plantation on the opposite side of the creek, and to stay on that side themselves. "So," said Cupid, "dey could jus' sweep us all in a heap, an' put us in de boat. An' he told me to take Patience—dat's my wife—an' de chil'en down to a certain pint, an' den I could come back, if I choose. Jus' as if I was gwine to be sich a goat!" added he, with a look and gesture of ineffable contempt. He and the rest of the people, instead of obeying their master, left the place and hid themselves in the woods; and when he [Sams] came to look for them, not one of his "faithful servants" was to be found.[66]

To the end Baptists had "faith" in the "faithfulness" of their slaves, apparently believing that the white church had secured fidelity among the Gullahs. Just how far some whites took this assumption is illustrated by a statement issued by Prince William Baptist Church as late as May 20, 1865:

Found the following coloured members have deserted their homes, the homes of their owners and their church and we fear the Cause of God. They were excommunicated. Boston, Amy, Sallie, Jane, Hannah, Jerry, Ellen, Ransom, Rina, Abraham, Annie, etc. . . .[67]

In attempting to regiment male-female relations in the slave quarters Baptist slaveholders demonstrated the most hypocrisy and cynicism. Masters separated families by whim and will regardless of religious convictions. Baptist planters sold "Christian" slaves without trying to rationalize such sales in correspondence with the laws of God even when these sales fragmented families. "I give to my son Alec, a son of my wench, boy named Jimmy," wrote Joseph Lawton, the "illustrious" pastor of Black Swamp Church at Robertville where elaborate galleries for slaves and free blacks were constructed in 1824. Slaves lived in constant dread of separation. "Every slave know what, 'I'll put you in my pocket sir,' mean" said former Robertville slave Isaiah Butler. A Northern Baptist published an appeal to slaveholding Baptists which contained an 1835 advertisement taken from a Southern newspaper. It was a notice of an auction telling "its own sad tale," and was a comment on Southern clergymen's rationalization about slavery. The "property" of the estate of "the late Rev. Dr. Furman," prominent Charleston Baptist and supporter of religious instruction for slaves, was for sale. Aside from three lots of land and a library, there were: "27 Negroes, some of them prime, two mules, one horse and an old wagon."[68]

Yet despite frequent forced family breakups, the church was particularly pharisaical in pretending that slaves were free agents. Gullahs considered "guilty" of "adultery," for example, were excommunicated as a general rule, for according to biblical law it was a sin to "put away" one's wife or husband. This ludicrous issue was debated, however, and the charge rescinded if an individual went before the church via the black watchman or white brother in charge and asked permission to "remarry."[69] Few Gullahs took this step, seeming to prefer exercising their independence insofar as they could within a forced situation. The folly of this supposed violation of scripture was not lost to their intelligence, and they usually ignored such censures.

Slaves' wishes in choosing a mate were sometimes ignored, and unions were neither sanctioned in law nor respected by slaveholders. Still Baptist churches "devoutly" passed sentence upon Gullahs for "adultery" and "fornication." Perhaps this gesture aimed at giving Gullahs a false send of equality—the same laws for both races regardless of circumstances, as implied by the Savannah River Baptist Association.[70] Possibly this an attempt to demoralize and humiliate—main ingredients of Christianity as taught to slaves. In the interest of "order" and cupidity, masters sometimes denied legitimacy to slaves' emotional inclinations, forcing couples to live together against their will because of convenience and profitability. According to Sam Mitchell, on the Chaplin plantations a slave had to tell the master as soon as he began to "cote." Mitchell added, "If Maussa say 'no you can't marry dat gal' den dat settle it, you can't marry um. He don't lak his slave to marry on nodder puson plantation." In like manner, Harry McMillan testified before the Freedom Inquiry Commission:

A man saw a young woman and if he liked her he would get a pass from his Master to go where she was. If his owner did not choose to give him the pass he [the master] would pick out another woman and make him [the slave] live with her whether he loved her or not.[71]

Under these oppressive circumstances, where personal preference was ignored, Gullahs understandably had no respect for the church edict establishing rules of conduct about marital status and decisions.

Among Gullahs no stigma was attached to sex without marriage as defined by white society. When asked what proportion of young women had sexual intercourse prior to marriage, Robert Smalls replied the majority did but "it was not considered an evil thing." When individuals settled with mates of their choosing he added, such unions were considered binding. Smalls explained male-female relations among the Gullahs:

If a woman loses her husband she mourns for him and will not marry again for a year and a half, unless she is driven to it by want and must have somebody to help her. . . .
. . . You hardly ever find a husband will separate from his wife except he finds her going with another man. . . . very few . . . married women are carried away by sexual passion if their husbands can take care of them.[72]

Church minutes, then, belie the actual situation by stressing stealth and immorality among the Sea Island region's black population. Gullahs simply operated under a different moral code. Thomas Chaplin, noted how strange it was that his first wife's two maids, who married in 1849, were still on "his place," in 1876. But what to Chaplin was even "stranger," was that these "girls" still "have the very same husbands." Undoubtedly many slaves kept the same mates if circumstances permitted. But Chaplin was aware of this fidelity only because the slaves were house servants. In a letter to Wendell Phillips Garrison, Laura Towne expressed "indignation" about articles appearing in the *Nation* concerning "immorality among the people of these islands." No one, said Towne, saw more of the islanders than she, "in every relation." Towne gave "an utter denial" of Gullah "immorality." Slavery "did what it could to confuse the minds of slaves with regard to conjugal relations." But added Towne, "a native fidelity—instinct perhaps," made the slave marriages "sacred in their own eyes and kept together without legal obligations." On the contrary, Towne stated that in her school of large boys and girls, there was "less impropriety—more purity— I may truly say— than is always met with among whites." When "immorality" occurred, it was "strictly dealt with by the church and by general reprobation in social life.[73]

Northern missionaries reported cases of slaves legalizing their unions out of respect for each other and also probably because of their love of ceremony and "title." Many couples having grown old together, went before "de parson." Elizabeth Botume witnessed the occasion of the civil ceremony between of Smart and Mary Washington who lived together for forty years. Smart and Mary shared a great deal through the years, and had nineteen children, only one of whom survived the antebellum years. According to Botume, the couple were very happy over the recognition their enduring relationship was given:

They walked away together side by side, for the first time endowed with the honorable title of husband and wife. Smart chuckled well when we congratulated him, saying—
"Him's my wife for sartin, now. Ef the ole hen run away, I shall cotch him sure."
We thought there was no danger of good Aunt Mary's running away after so many years of faithful service.

During and directly after the Civil War, the situation wrought by slavery often led to much unhappiness. Husbands and wives who were separated and forced to take new partners returned to claim their old mates. Baptist discipline did not proscribe slave sales or interfere in any way with the "property" rights of slaveholders. "There was often great disappointment," wrote Botume. "Sometimes two men claimed the same woman, whilst she coquetted not a little, evidently disposed to take the one that bid the highest." But, Botume added that this "rarely if ever" occurred when children were involved.[74]

Although the Committee on Discipline within Baptist churches operated as a religious tribunal, efforts to use Christianity to control the Gullahs was largely unsuccessful. Nevertheless, Gullahs seemed almost unanimously to prefer religious affiliation through Baptist membership rather than Methodist. Methodist missionaries displayed a more sincere and human interest in the slaves than their sometimes ruthless, Puritan-oriented Baptist masters. "This seems to be a very unpromising portion of our field of labor," wrote one Methodist missionary, "all owing to the prejudices of the negroes." He continued:

> We cannot . . . find fault with the negroes in this portion of our mission field, for preferring another communion to our own; but our voice will ever be lifted against them, for refusing the bread of life, because, forsooth it comes not to them on a silver salver, or from the hands of one who has not "gone down into or come up out of the water."[75]

The cermonious manner in which Baptists initiated converts into church fellowship impressed the Gullahs. Also, despite Calvinist orientation, Baptists were nonheirarchial, worship was less formal, and church structure less legalistic. But, such considerations were not as significant in influencing Gullah acceptance of the Baptist denomination as were other factors. Baptists slaves exercised a religious autonomy the Methodists would not hear of, and this, coupled with the fact that Sea Island slavery was a quasi-absentee type, contributed to the Gullahs' opportunity to control their own religion, to a point. Moreover, in their endeavor to keep blacks under civil control and to keep them on the plantations, slaveholders allowed spiritual permissiveness by legitimizing already existing black societies and leaving them in the hands of black leaders with only minimal white supervision.[76]

The extent to which spiritual autonomy influenced Gullah culture and social organization is most evident in the prominence of black leadership. Baptist planters recommended black watchmen who were supposedly "tried and true," and slaveholders apparently had great confidence in those chosen. Such elders were usually staunch church members, but also influential and respected in the quarters. Methodist missionaries were skeptical about employing blacks even as helpers. William Capers insisted that "helpers" only be "a feeble staff—not leaned upon. They can no more do the missionary's work than a staff can walk." On the other hand, Sea Island Baptists placed much Christian teaching on the shoulders of black leaders. Methodists were consistently confronted with the problems created by this difference in tactical approach. After 1845 most black elders operated with the approval of slaveholders. Some, according to Methodists, had rudimentary knowledge of Christianity. But most, said the missionaries, represented "the very essence of ignorance and superstition." Some slaves came to Methodists' preaching and "precious seasons" and "effusions of tears would ensue." But Methodists lamented that slaves immediately deserted them for "one of their own":

Let it be known that one of these [slaves] is to preach on such a day and there is such a rush . . . that they may have the pleasure of hearing one of their own color . . . what else than mischief can be expected from the teaching of an ignorant enthusiast who knows nothing of God's word, and puts his own delusions in the place of divine truth? . . . and they say that whenever they come to hear me, it is from duty . . . because I am employed by their owners.[77]

Wherever Baptists authorized Christian instruction, Methodists found black leaders and black societies. "The society exerts its influence against us which is remarkably strong," wrote the missionary at Pocotaligo in 1844. "This 'society' is altogether in the hands of the colored people who are actively engaged against us." Thus black leaders struggled to maintain their position among their people and continued preaching and practicing their own version of "Christianity." Methodists hoped the establishment of missions would fragment the influence of black teachers and thus foster the cause of "true" religion. A lengthy editorial was printed in the *Southern Christian Advocate* in 1846 where the author discussed the "deplorable exhibition of pseudo religion" among slaves of the large plantations in coastal South Carolina:

The superstitious notions prevalent here and there, are probably the reflects of—more ancient superstitions, handed down by tradition and propagated by so called *leaders*, who prior to the preaching of the gospel by . . . the missionaries . . . wielded a fearful amount of spiritual influence among their followers, and the negro communities of the plantations generally. And it is what with remarkable tenacity these superstitious actions still maintain their hold in spite of a better teaching. Instead of giving up their visionary religiónism, embracing the simple truth . . . our missionaries find them endeavoring to incorporate their superstitious rites with a purer system of instruction, producing thereby a hybrid, crude, and undefinable medley of truth and falsehood.[78]

Many missionaries saw slave children as the future of the enterprise. Others were even skeptical about that. According to one Methodist, "so far does prejudice extend, even the children on some of these places refuse to be instructed, because of the example of their parents and the older ones." Many Baptist planters left instruction of the young in the hands of plantation "help" who taught the children prayers and whatever else their religious instruction consisted of. Gradually, Methodists were forced to admit that despite their consistent though infrequent preaching and catechizing, they could not successfully compete with black leadership operating clandestinely or with the approval of Baptist churches and slaveholders.[79]

The Episcopalian mission established in 1849 on the Sea Islands took away the near monopoly that Methodist missionaries previously had among a number of Episcopalian planters. Episcopalian slaveholders observed the same uninterested attitude among the slaves as Methodists witnessed. John Edwin Fripp, a St. Helena Episcopalian, allowed his slaves to attend the preaching of a diocese missionary while Fripp himself was in residence on the plantation. But given a choice, few showed up to hear "Mr. Welch" when the minister was on the plantation. According to Fripp's Journal:

Sat. Dec. 19th—Rev. Welch is down tonight lecturing to the Negroes. Will go to Seabrooks in the Morning. The Negroes appear very backward in coming to hear him. They are getting tired of religion I expect.

No doubt "religion" was not what tired Fripp's slaves, but the dry "lecturing" which often characterized missionary sermons. Gullahs realized that planters were not truly concerned with their spiritual welfare and the they recognized the one-sidedness of their situation. An old coachman on the same Fripp plantation stated "massa been unjust to we. Take all we labor and get rich, then say we lazy, Can't care for we self, give us two suits a year, dat our wages."[80] No one need wonder about the degree of enthusiasm Gullahs had for the religious emissary of such masters.

Thus, a key to understanding the appeal of the Baptist faith for Gullahs lies in recognizing the slaves' rationale. Methodist emphasis on order and hierarchy left little room for internal flexibility in the denominational structure. Baptists on the other hand had separate congregations, loosely bound together. Baptists sanctioned black associations that were relatively independent of the church and largely dominated by the slaves themselves. In some cases Baptists even provided Gullahs with a place to hold society and "prays" meetings among themselves, however humble such places were. Moreover, Baptist planters authorized religious leaders from the quarters with whom the Gullahs readily identified. Not surprisingly then, to the extent that Gullahs adopted Christianity, they considered themselves Baptists. The Baptist faith became the Gullahs' own personal religion, one they molded and fashioned away the watchful, critical eyes of the forces of spiritual "superiority" and physical exploitation.

Why did the Baptist slaveholders permit this flexibility and modicum of freedom to their slaves? The answer probably lies with the slaveholders' capacity for self-deception and belief in the power of their ability to dominate (for which as a class they are well known). Thus they were confident that black leaders' presentation of Christianity would not jeopardize plantation interests. In keeping with the merging Southern religious vogue of the time, slaveholders ultimately believed in the soothing effects of Christianity on a slave population's mentality. Furthermore, a limited degree of personal commitment had an effect on some slaveholders' attitude toward Christian instruction. For if "duty" and Christian instruction harmonized in bringing more order and discipline to the plantation, clearly nothing was at risk. The primary reason for Baptist involvement with Christian instruction was its potential for perpetuating power and cultural ascendancy over the slaves, to maintain the "Southern way of life" for the dominant class. The Gullahs, however, perceived the situation differently.

Sam Polite, the Praise House elder. From the Penn Historical Collection. (Permission granted by Penn Community Services, Inc., St. Helena Island, South Carolina.)

Susannah of the Oaks Plantation. From the Penn School Historical Collection. (Permission granted by Penn Community Services, Inc., St. Helena Island, South Carolina.)

Brick Baptist Church, St. Helena Island, S.C. From the Penn Historical Collection. (Permission granted by Penn Community Services, Inc., St. Helena Island, South Carolina.)

"MARCHING ON!—THE FIFTY-FIFTH MASSACHUSETTS COLORED REGIMENT SINGING JOHN BROWN'S MARCH IN THE STREETS OF CHARLESTON, February 21, 1865.—[See Page 172.]

The Fifty-fourth Massachusetts Colored Regiment. Harper's Weekly.

Gullahs and Sea Island Cotton. (Personal collection.)

PART IV

The Socioreligious Community: An African–Christian Synthesis

CHAPTER 8

Elements of the Head and the Heart: Gullah Interpretations of Christianity

Do not pass we by, My Jesus, as you go on de road from Jericho to de new Jerusalem, but tarry at de door and speak de word of hope to we heart and blow de breeze of blessing upon us. Almighty and eternal Father, we de prisoners of Hope, turn to de stronghold and begs oona (you) fur give we de long look and de over-coming patience dat we could have 'couragement fur go forward and see de truth dat will make us free. Do God, if it so please you, Massa Jesus, Gib me de long look like Moses, so I could see into de Promised Land from de mount, if my weary feet ain't neber guine to walk in de New Jerusalem with my people. . . .*

"Let me lib wid de musket in one hand an' de Bible in de oder,—dat if I die at de muzzel ob de musket, die in de water, die on de land. I may know I hab de bressed Jesus in my hand, an' hab no fear."
"I hab lef' my wife in de land o' bondage; my little ones dey say eb'ry night, whar is my fader? But when I die, when de bressed mornin' rises, when I shall stan' in de glory, wid one foot on de water an' one foot on de land, den, O Lord, I shall see my wife and' my little chil'en once more."**

Sam Polite lived to become senior elder on the Benjamin Fripp plantation. Polite did not know his age, but had "ben a man fore 'gun shoot'" (Battle of Port Royal, November 1861), and became the most respected and sagacious elder on St. Helena Island. Those who knew and observed

---

*Prayer of Sam Polite, "The Long Look," n.d., misc. corr., Penn School Papers, SHC.
**Gullah soldier's prayer, in Thomas Wentworth Higginson, *Army Life in a Black Regiment* (New York: Collier Books, 1962, repr. from 1870 ed.), 48.

him for many years insisted that his "wisdom" and "vision" were "God's free gift" for a service of faith and hope that "Prophet" Polite had rendered his people. In old age, as a free man, he addressed the Praise House congregation probably the same way he did on other occasions throughout the years after slavery. The words of Sam Polite demonstrates that the Gullahs, in freedom as in bondage, viewed their religion as a special gift with a unique essence:

> God done gib de white folks a heap of things, but he ain't forgotten us 'cause He gib us Religion and we have a right to show it out to all de world. De Buckra [white people], deys got de knowing of the whys and hows of religion, but dey ain't never got de feel of it yet. I think God ain't have much respect for no kind of religion without de feeling. De Book say, 'They that worship me must worship me in spirit and in truth.' There might be some truth in deys-all religion, but there ain't much spirit in a religion that's all in de head.[1]

The Gullahs' capacity to maintain psychological and spiritual autonomy in the face of degrading implications of their historical circumstances was usually attributed to their faith. The ostensible basis of this faith was Christianity. Certainly one source of Gullah religion and spirituality is found in Christian example, enabling them to see their enslavement in heroic terms. Yet Gullah roots sprang from an African world view that emphasized affirmation and celebration of human life, with religion representing the highest expression of that existence. Additionally, their African heritage familiarized Gullahs with the power and supremacy of a collective spirit over individual experience. Thus, while planters valued religious instruction as a means of manipulating the actions and thinking of Gullahs, the slaves' discretionary adoption and adaptation of certain features of Christianity was a way of articulating and manifesting their common oppression in terms significant for them and also either acceptable or esoteric to slaveholders and missionaries.

Most Gullahs cared little about didactic features fundamental to Christianity. And while their exposure to the religion was primarily superficial, their acceptance and reinterpretation was essentially practical, reinforcing older traditions. Their limited understanding of Protestantism was observed by antebellum travelers and Methodist missionaries right up to the time of civil conflict. Aptitude had nothing to do with the Gullahs' failure to grasp a firmer knowledge of Protestantism. They shrewdly did what was expected of them without actually internalizing doctrine. When given the opportunity, they fashioned their own religion. For instance, slaves in the wealthy coastal parish on the Waccamaw peninsula had the atypical experience of receiving, from about 1835 to 1861, very concerted Christian instruction. The rector of All Saints Episcopal Church at Waccamaw was Alexander Glennie of England, who, with several assistants, spent thirty-three years preaching and teaching bondspeople on numerous plantations. Glennie's parish and church were showplaces of the Carolina Coast whenever planters and Southern clergymen wanted to demonstrate how fully they were meeting the spiritual needs of their "people." Glennie himself published a popular book of sermons designed especially for slaves. Hundreds of Gullahs were communicants at All Saints, and "thousands of colored children recited the catechism, intelligently." Observers were impressed with Glennie's effectiveness:

He has been with them so long and is such an amiable kind man that the negroes love him very much and his example has as much influence over them as his preaching. We all went to the negro church one P.M. . . . the congregation responsed and sang the Te Deum with Mr. G. . . . . When he preached he would go on a while, then stop and ask them questions about what he had gone over and they answered very well.

Yet after the Civil War, returning residents witnessed what they termed "religious deterioration" among the former slaves:

Chapels were taken over by the negroes and soon resounded with barbaric shouting, the accompaniment of the debased Christianity of the emancipated slave. . . . They have forsaken the way which they had learned, and taken to themselves teachers of their own color. Fanaticism and extravagance rule in their assemblies. . . . There are indications of a return to African barbarism.[2]

During the Yankee occupation, representatives of the American Missionary Association noted that Gullahs were a "religious people," easily inspired to sing and pray profusely. Jesus was "a common theme in their conversation." But observers also noted that Gullahs knew little of "practical religion." Northern teachers commented on how quickly Gullah children memorized their school lessons. Yet the children's knowledge of religion was strangely confused with the current events in which they were caught up. One teacher, after "plainly" explaining to a Sunday School class of large boys the origin of the Ten Commandments and how they were given to Moses, then asked the children who wrote the Ten Commandments. She received such answers as "Uncle Sam," "General Saxby" (referring to General Rufus Saxton, Commander of the Department of the South), and "Columbus." On another occasion, a group of students were quizzed by officers in General Sherman's army. The question "Children, who is Jesus Christ?" was at first received with "paralyzed silence." Finally, a small boy loudly ventured, "General Saxby sar." An older boy responded by giving his classmate "a vigorous thrust in the back" and proclaiming, 'Not so, boy! Him's Massa Linkum."[3] So much for the effectiveness of Methodist catechism and Baptist Sunday School.

Yet the children were heard singing of Jesus constantly. Even at school children consistently sang such "spirituals" as the following:

> Patrol around me. Tank God he no ketch me
>   O Lord, yes my Lord
> . . . .
> In de mornin' when I rise,
>   Tell my Jesus Huddy oh, . . .
> . . . .
> I would not let you go, my Lord,
>   I would not let you go,
> . . . .
> I can't stay behin' my Lord,
>   I can't stay behin'[4]

Even adult knowledge of Christianity was severly limited despite their attraction to "things of the spirit." One example was their attitude toward Christmas. Although the Gullahs revered Jesus, few understood the significance of Christmas, the day of Christ's birth. Still it was a joyous season, viewed in slavery primarily as a rare occasion, when fresh meat was allocated, labor ceased for two or three days, and possibly a new suit of clothing was received. Mary Ames taught among the Gullahs on Edisto and Wadmalaw Islands where Methodism was reportedly particularly effective. Yet Ames expressed surprise that the people knew so little of the life of Christ, "not knowing even of his birth." But, she related, "they are all familiar with his sayings." Elizabeth Botume, a Hilton Head teacher, remembered one jubilant Christmastime among the Sea Island "Contrabands," when she was asked to preach:

I replied that there was but one sermon fitting for the occasion, and I read the whole of Christ's Sermon on the Mount, first explaining to them the meaning of

the evergreens, typical of Christ's life and teachings. They gave breathless attention to all this, ejaculating from time to time, "My Lord! is dat so?"
I know now they understood very little of all I said, but no speaker ever had
more interested and attentive listeners. When I sat down, one of the leaders
chanted rather than spoke a touching prayer, in which he styled me his "dear
imperial preacher."
Then the white friends sang,—"Joy to the world, the Lord has come."
By this time the entire audience was aroused and ready to pray and sing all
night. In each prayer the speaker tried to introduce, in his uncouth phraseology,
some of the passages of Scripture he had heard read.[5]

Though lacking a basic background regarding the teachings and historical importance of Christ, Gullahs strongly identified with his suffering, crucifixtion, and resurrection. This, to them, was Christianity, and
since they felt their earthly lives so closely paralleled that of Jesus, becoming "Christians" was for Gullahs somewhat of an apocalyptic fulfillment. In fact, much of the essence of their understanding of Protestant
religion centered around Jesus and His followers. Other writers have
suggested that African-American slaves saw themselves primarily in the
same light as the Children of Israel. This association certainly inspired
some of the Charleston rebels in 1822, as already discussed. Also, the
commander of Gullah troops, Thomas Higginson, stated that the men's
memories were a "vast, bewildered chaos of Jewish history and biography," and that most great events from the past, up to "the American
Revolution, they instinctively attributed to Moses." How the experience
of the Jews aroused the Gullahs was witnessed by a Civil War missionary:

Last week I read to the *church full* the account of the escape of the Children of
Israel from Egyptian bondage. I was amazed at the impression it seemed to make.
The remarks the old men made were graphic and eloquent. It made them re-
count with praise to God their escape. The little church seemed like dreamland
to me almost when they got stirred to talk.[6]

Yet most Gullahs conceptualization of Christianity centered on the
experiences of Jesus rather than the Jews, as is evident in their songs,
prayers, and conversations. The militant nationalism so strongly associated with the Jewish struggle was a prominent ideology of Christian-
oriented slaves during the Vesey Conspiracy but was not a major orientation in Gullah religion. Instead, as far as Christianity was concerned,
Gullahs relied on a conviction that a moral wrong had been committed

against them, as against Christ, and the transgression would ultimately be rectified. Not that they refused to struggle against bondage, but rather the Gullahs actively expressed their resistance and opposition through cultural tenacity, collective strength, a deep identification with Christ, and a conviction that with Him they had a covenant of freedom.

In any case, Christianity largely contributed to helping Gullahs consciously find a reason for being, and much of what they embraced in that religion conformed to this purpose. Thus, while it was difficult for them to grasp the concept behind the Ten Commandments, the story of the Jews being led out of Egypt could be easily internalized. More significantly, although intellectual perceptions of Jesus Christ caused some problems, and Gullahs did not totally comprehended the words of the Sermon on the Mount, nevertheless they saw their wordly existence as closely harmonizing with that of Christ's. They, as a people, were very much within the philosophical drift of the Sermon.

The Gullahs earnestness and simplicity in matters of religion left little room for doctrinal trappings that made Protestantism a religion fashioned to suit the needs of various social groups within Anglo-European society. From the teachings of Methodists and Baptists, Gullahs critically extracted that which gave meaning to their life-struggle, often devising novel interpretations of Christianity. The example of Christ provided uniqueness to their oppression since he too was a great sufferer. The comparison encouraged them to persevere because he was also the embodiment of a life-giving symbol. A ninety-two-year-old former slave recounted the experience of her mother, who along with her five children was sold away from their plantation. The mother was in a very distraught state when a man, "white and shining" appeared with whom she had the following dialogue:

"Sarah, Sarah, Sarah!"
"Yes Sir."
"What is you fretin' bout so?"
"Sir, I'm a stranger here, parted from my husband, with five little children and not a morsel of bread."
"You say you're parted from your husband? You're not parted from your husband. You're jest over a little slash of water. Suppose you had to undergo what I had to. I was nailed to the Cross of Mount Calvary. And I am here today. Who do you put your trust in?"[7]

The observations of black Northern teacher Charlotte Forten provide a further example. Forten was a frequent visitor at the Praise House and

witnessed the Gullahs' spiritual enthusiasm at these meetings. She noticed an old blind man, Maurice, who led the singing with a remarkable
voice, and sang with special forcefulness the favorite "New Jerusalem."
According to Forten, his voice rang out "a glad, triumphal sound," but
Maurice's story was a tragic one:

His blindness was caused by a blow on the head from a loaded whip. He was
struck by his master in a fit of anger. "I feel great distress when I become blind,"
said Maurice; "but den I went to seek de Lord; and ebber since I know I see in
de next world, I always hab great satisfaction."[8]

Undoubtedly the pathos was eased somewhat by the Gullahs' ratio
nalization that no matter how painful life was, someone had endured
more than they, by their belief in the efficacy of salvation, and their
expectation of immortality. Also, a great source of sustenance and faith
in themselves derived from the Gullahs' presumption that they, like Christ,
were historically guiltless. Gullahs reportedly possessed a "piety" of the
heart. And they displayed an intuitive knowledge of the moral teachings
of Christianity based upon practical experience, the socioreligious influence of African religion, and their own sense of collective survival.

Northern missionaries and teachers were impressed with how much
Gullah religious expressions "sparkle with rich genius." Their belief in
the noble nature of their circumstances helped to inspire creative inclinations. Gullahs called themselves a "peculiar people," and the words of
an old Baptist deacon, recorded by Laura Towne, poignantly illustrate
their communal spirituality. After planters deserted the Islands, Gullahs
were compelled by Yankees to continue working in the cotton fields,
often for little or nothing. Bondspeople wanted to cultivate provisions
for their families, and just as the Gullahs were beginning to trust some
white Northerners, another calamity befell them. In May 1862, Gullah
men were, at bayonet point, conscripted into the Union Army by General David Hunter. The Gullahs feared the worse, that as their masters
had warned, they were being sent to Cuba. All gathered together before
the men were herded off. Fathers took children in their arms. Women
gave way to expressions of grief that touched the hearts of the strongest
observers of the scene. According to Towne, this was an exceedingly
low point for the Gullahs, who had already withstood so much:

We, anxious and depressed, talked in low tones over this extra ordinary proceed-
ing. . . . That evening we ladies went to the praise house and heard good, old
Marcus exhort, Dagus pray and all sing. Marcus said he had often told all the

brethren they must be just like birds when the gunner is about, expecting a crack every minute. "Dey ain't neber know what gwine to befal dey, pore black folks must wait and hab faith, . . . Massa laff one day. Ask me if I tink Christ want black nigger in heben. One ting I sure. We'uns gwine to be where de crucify Lord am. And if dat place be Hell, He gwine make it heben for we."[9]

Gullah religion was not quiescent, nor an enslavement of the mind, despite the "Christian" and long-suffering attitude seemingly responsible for their sensitiveness and lofty, visionary approach toward oppression. Many observers were appalled at what they interpreted as resignation among Sea Island African-Americans. Arthur Sumner wrote from St. Helena Island in 1863, "I am astonished that they should be fit to live after such generations of mere animal life. A higher race would have lost all moral sense." Even one of the Gullahs' staunchest advocates, Elizabeth Botume, believed that "the patience of the freedpeople in sickness was so general and remarkable, it seemed like apathy." If what Botume observed was only resignation, it probably was a function of Gullah affiliation with Christianity. Yet their coping capacity was also possible because of the sense of protection that spiritual association offered, with religious and community membership forging ties that strengthened the Gullahs' resolve. Thomas Wentworth Higginson was surprised to find Gullahs so little demoralized and he accurately attributed this to religion:

I learned to think that we abolitionists had underrated the suffering produced by slavery among the negroes, but had overrated the demoralization. Or rather, we did not know how the religious temperament of the negroes had checked the demoralization. Yet . . . it must be admitted that this temperament, born of sorrow and oppression, is far more marked in the slave than in the native African.[10]

Higginson perceptively realized the lack of "demoralization" wrought by slavery. But the personality and "religious temperament" of Gullahs owed much to a non-Christian tradition, and was not "born of sorrow and oppression" or as foreign to the "native African" as Higginson imagined. As previously suggested, African religion and philosophy emphasized the celebration and affirmation of human life, and within this scheme, while God was the apex of the theory of being, humankind was the center, or pivotal point, of earthly existence. Gullahs were very much a part of this world view. Even though on the conscious level the pillar of their faith rested on their association with Christ, this may have primarily provided Old World ideology with an organized, plausible New

World perception. Anthropologist Paul Radin has written that the Christian God provided African-American slaves with a "fixed point," and that they converted God to themselves.[11] Of the Gullahs at least it might also be more aptly stated that they converted Christianity to their African world view. Gullahs used religion as a justification to combat objective forces, to collectively perpetuate a rich sublimity in cultural form, and as a spiritually liberating ideology. It was not so much that Christianity instilled a sense of resignation because of belief in future rewards, though admittedly for some this was a determining factor, but that an African philosophical tradition was asserted in the slave quarters.[12]

For slaves, acceptance of Christianity did not imply negation of earthly life. The supreme example of this was their desire for liberty. Freedom was a continuous topic of conversation among them. Robert Smalls, who grew up in antebellum Beaufort, remembered that as a boy he first heard of Frederick Douglass in the slave quarters of one of his owner's Ladies Island plantations. Three people in the slave quarters could read and every scrap of printed matter was given to them to translate. One of the literates, a recent arrival from Charleston, secured a copy of one of Douglass's speeches and read it to the slaves. Between the three literate field hands, the bondspeople of the McKee plantations kept abreast of the "politicking" over slavery. An old slave woman of Edisto Island told Northerner Mary Ames, "I heard for a long time of war and the coming of the Yankees, and I spects my bones be white before I see that time, but I did live to see them, bress de Lord." On one of the St. Helena Island plantations, a black carpenter held a secret night school for the men during bondage.[13] Thus did the Gullahs attempt to apprise themselves of events affecting their future.

The most obvious testament of the Gullahs' will to freedom is their participation in the Civil War, once it became a liberation struuggle. In May 1862, when General Hunter drafted the men without authorization, there was no desire to fight. The Gullah men, having "smelt a very large rat," took to the woods to "split rails,"but were soon rounded up. They were taken to Hilton Head, drilled, kept until after the harvest, placing an extreme hardship on their families, then discharged without pay or freedom. Thus, in the fall of 1862, when the authorized draft was called, with the provision for emancipation, many hesitated. The memories of the previous impressment were still fresh, and "weakened their confidence" in "promises for the future." Enlistments were slow at first. But the pledge of freedom won them over, and by January 1863, formation of the "First Regiment of South Carolina Volunteers" was complete.[14]

Many whites either doubted the African-American slaves' capacity to fight the slaveholders, feared the consequences of an armed black population, or simply expressed racialist convictions in their attitude. But exigencies of war turned slaves into liberators, and black soldiers demonstrated what freedom meant to people in bondage. The "enthusiasm," "alarcrity," and sense of duty among men of the "First South" was reportedly unmatched. Rather than fearful, they were impatient to fight. Their commander, Colonel Higginson, insisted that "braver men never lived." Accustomed to bearing pain, some did not even report injuries after battles. Frequently susceptible to pulmonary disease, some refused to report to sick call unless their officers insisted. Gullah soldiers fought all the more fiercely because of a particular grievance. Blacks were not recognized as soldiers by Confederates, but as fugitive slaves. Thus black soldiers and their white officers fought "with ropes around our necks." Confederates ordered that, if captured, blacks and their officers would suffer a "felon's death." Gullahs were especially sullen when North and South raised truce flags, saluted each other "courteously," exchanged cigars, and negotiated "usually to send over to the enemy, some family of Rebel women." While showing no disrespect in word or deed, according to Higginson, the blacks hated these women "from the botton of their souls." "Deres no flags ob truce for us," said the Gullahs, contemptuous of such proceedings, "When de Secesh fight de Fus' Souf', he fight in earnest." But Gullahs also fought in earnest. In the words of Sergeant Prince Rivers, former Beaufort slave and coachman, they could, as "men, look our old masters in de face." "Now," he said, "we ain't afraid, if they meet us, to run the bayonet through them."[15]

In their frequent prayer meetings, Gullah soldiers prayed for victory, mixing "the warlike" with "the pious." They spoke of "a religious army," and a "gospel army." According to Higginson they even "evangelized" the chaplin, who previously was "rather heretic." Higginson found that their "faith," "love of freedom and of their families," together with their sense of pride, combined to "make them do their duty." They were confident in the rightness of their cause and that "God would watch over them." Their religious leaders encouragingly assured them that eternity awaited the fallen hero. When the "First South" prepared for an expe-

dition to Florida, one of the black preacher's exhortations was reportedly
"worthy of a place in 'American Oratory.'" He urged the men to seek
the post of danger and fight bravely. "He who is de fust man to get on
de boat," he rallied, "and de fust to jump on shore, him, if he fall, will
be de fust to get in heaben." Then, as if himself in the midst of battle,
and aroused by the occasion, he added fervently:

'An' when do battle comes—when you see de Kunn'l put his shoulder to de
wheel, and hear de shot and shell flying all around like de rain drops, den remember dat ebery one ob dose shot is a bolt of de Almighty God to send dem
rebels to deir eberlasting damnation.[16]

Sacrifices for freedom were not only made by Gullah soldiers, for the
war effort was a community enterprise. The men's absence from the
plantations placed the burden of breadwinning solely on the women,
who shouldered it admirably. Gullah men had at first objected to the
women working in the fields because this labor had taken such a heavy
toll on female health. But women insisted on working "fur pay," and did
so "with a will," sometimes working two tasks in one day. Thus, while
the men went off to fight or to work as laborers for the army, field work
continued. Women, boys, and girls worked side by side, planting, hoeing,
picking, sorting, ginning, and packing the cotton. They also raised veg-
etables and poultry for consumption and to sell. The women were am-
bitious and disciplined, laboring with "tireless energy" when working for
themselves and their families. Sometimes they even managed to attend
newly established schools in order to "catch a lesson." As a way of further supporting loved ones away with the regiment and the army, the
women wrote letters. Many of the Northern women's "spare time" was
spent writing words of love and encouragement dictated by the freed-
women.[17] It was a period of optimism, when social relations knitted over
generations proved tenacious and steady. This was also a time when the
faith of the bondspeople seemed to bear fruit.

The subject of freedom was often symbolically and thematically expressed in Gullah spirituals. While these "prayer songs" appear to be a
portent of the future in a Christian context, they contain ambiguity that
implies otherwise. Double meanings and surrogates abounded, and
Gullah spirituals could often be interpreted in several ways. For example:

Jesus make de blind see,
Jesus make de cripple walk,
Jesus make de deaf to hear.
Walk in, kind Jesus!
No man can hinder me.[18]

When Laura Towne heard this impressive spiritual, she believed the refrain "no man can hinder me" meant that "nothing could prevent access
to Jesus." Yet Charles Nordhoff, a journalist sent to Port Royal in 1863
to write about Sea Islanders, heard the song and immediately attributed
it to "an aspiration for liberty."[19] Certainly there were elements of truth
in both interpretations—a combination of mystical belief in the miraculous powers of the Christian God and a deep, sense of freedom—a heritage from the African past. Higginson heard Gullah soldiers sing the
song and noted that they sometimes substituted "hinder me" with "hinder
we." But he failed to attach any significance to this, merely stating that
it was "more spicy to the ear, and more in keeping with the usual head-
over-heels arrangement of their pronouns." Despite the perception and
usefulness of Higginson's book, it also contains a disturbing air of condescension toward the Gullahs which was typical of some abolitionists.
Although he attested to the Gullahs' daring and coolness in combat, thus
affirming their equality with whites in terms of courage, he failed to
credit them with having any intellectual complexity in their modes of
expression. He recognized Gullah soldiers' physical strength but overlooked aspects of their character which bespoke of higher emotions, unless these could be interpreted in a strictly Christian sense. Hence Higginson viewed the Gullahs' songs as "thoroughly religious," and the
attitudes contained in them as "always the same, and, as a commentary
on the life of the race, . . . infinitely pathetic. Nothing but patience for
this life,—nothing but triumph in the next."[20]

Gullahs were a proud people who did not indulge in self-pity and
would have resented being seen in a piteous light by their friend and
supporter. Life for the Gullahs was an uphill battle but not without
grace and nobility. Higginson sometimes failed to grasp this, despite his
close relationship with Gullah soldiers and their families. One can imagine the thoughts of Gullah soldiers as they sang and contemplated that
their treasured expectation was becoming a reality. Substitution of "we"
for "me," possibly represented feelings of nationalism which had developed over a period of generations when social and cultural traditions

merged under slavery and created one people with common interests, ambitions, beliefs, and sense of oppression.

The Gullahs' Marseillaise was the exhilarating spiritual "New Jerusalem":

> De Talles' tree in Paradise
> De Christian calls de Tree ob Life,
> an' I hope dat trumpet blow me home
> To my new Jerusalem!
>
> Blow Gabriel! Trumpet, blow louder, louder!
> An' I hope dat trumpet blow me home
> To my New Jerusalem!
>
> Paul and Silas jail-bound
> Sing God's praise both night and day,
> An' I hope dat trumpet blow me home
> To my New Jerusalem! [21]

This favorite "shout" song of the Gullahs was triumphant rather than tragic. Thus it was not one of those to be sung with a "heavy heart" or a "troubled speerit." "New Jerusalem" was an uplifting, infectious tune. Its symbolic range could harmonize with a number of situations, circumstances, and experiences. When freedman Maurice, who had been blinded by his master in a fit of rage, sang "New Jerusalem" at the Praise House, his mind turned toward heaven and the prospect of gaining his sight in a future world. But when the freedpeople sang "New Jerusalem" at the Emancipation Jubilee on New Year's Day in 1866, it was their earthly future and enthusiasm for their long-awaited freedom that filled their thoughts and expectations. The tree of life was the tree of liberty, as paradise was a land free of bondage. The meaning behind this spiritual was not lost on Northern teacher Elizabeth Botume:

The streets of the city were filled with happy freed people. According to their spiritual, they had "fought for liberty," and this was their "New Jerusalem,"of which they so often sang. Even the poorest, and those most scantily clothed, looked as if they already "walked that golden street," and felt "that starry crown" upon their uncovered heads. It was indeed a day of great rejoicing, and one long to be remembered. These people were living their "New Jerusalem." [22]

Spirituals sung during the Civil War attest to Gullah creativity and further demonstrate that the desire for freedom was as strong a motivation as relgious piety. Songs such as the following grew out of the war years:

We'll soon be free,
We'll soon be free,
We'll soon be free,
    When de Lord will call us home.

My brudder, how long,
My brudder, how long,
My brudder, how long,
    "Fore we done suffrin' here?

It won't be long (thrice)
'Fore de Lord will call us home.[23]

Slaves in Georgetown were jailed at the outbreak of the war for singing this spiritual. As a little drummer boy explained to Higginson, "Dey
tink *de Lord* mean for say de Yankees." Higginson doubted that the slaves
made the same association of which their masters thought them capable.
Once again he reveals his nineteenth-century "romantic racialism." But
no one could mistake the plaintive meaning in the following song, first
heard at Hilton Head Island and said to have been a song "to which the
Rebellion had actually given rise":

No more peck o' corn for me,
    No more, no more,
No more peck o' corn for me,
    Many tousand go.

No more driver's lash for me,
    No more, etc.

No more pint o' salt for me,
    No more, etc.

No more hundred lash for me,
    No more, etc.

No more mistress' call for me,
    . . . .
    Many tousand go.[24]

Thus, while God, personified as Jesus, offered Gullahs an explanation
for life and provided a model of virtue, as did their African God, this
was not an abjuration of human existence. Their religion contained a

fervent zest for life. As slaves, the cornerstone of their faith rested on confidence that freedom on earth would not be denied them and their progeny. One missionary wrote of how the Gullahs expressed this:

> As they spoke of their trust in the Savior, his assurances, by the application of the promises to their hearts, that "a good time was coming" when their own vines and fig trees would cast their shadows around them in quietness and safety, and no more parting of families be known, our hearts dissolved in sympathy and gratitude in their behalf.[25]

Christianity can be interpreted in fatalistic terms. But to believe Gullahs totally accepted a submissive Christian posture suggests that they did not struggle against the cultural domination that masters attempted to impose through religion. To say, on the other hand, that an element of patience was not present in their form of Christianity would be a denial of historical reality. Resolution of the contradiction may come through understanding the limited role of doctrinal Christianity in Gullah life and thought, and taking a fuller cognizance of the influence of previous traditions. Practically and theologically speaking, Gullahs were not resigned to their condition, and not uncritical of religious teachings. Nor were they beguiled by insipid attempts to "make them better slaves." From their African heritage Gullahs retained optimism—a proclivity to make the best of their near-tragic situation for the sake of communal spirit and future generations. This was more meaningful than blindly striking out and committing racial suicide. The simple issue of the practicality of insurrection must also be considered. They had learned from Vesey and others, perhaps implanting the Charleston insurrection attempt in their memory. They believed armed rebellion was impossible as long as they were enslaved. Higginson stated that he often pondered over why the Gullahs' "daring and endurance" in combat had not manifested itself in armed insurrection against the slavocracy. Predictably, Higginson attributed the lack of large-scale rebellions to "the peculiar temperament of the races, in their religious faith, and in the habit of patience that centuries had fortified." But Higginson added that to have kept "the land in a perpetual flame of insurrection" would have been impossible for a number of reasons:

> The shrewder men all said substantially the same thing. What was the use of insurrection, where everything was against them? They had no knowledge, no money, no arms, no drill, no organization. . . . They had no mountain passes

to defend like the Maroons of Jamaica,—no impenetrable swamps, like the Maroons of Suriname. Where they had these, even on a small scale, they had used them,—as in certain swamps round Savannah and in the everglades of Florida, where they united with the Indians, and would stand fire—so I was told by General Saxton, who had fought them there—when the Indians would retreat.[26]

Priceless energy and humanity would have been the fruits of rebellion as far as the slaves were concerned. Such physical confrontations would have left little enthusiasm for cultural creativity. Thus does the quest for examples of physical courage often overshadow a valiant spiritual temper. Gullahs maximized their creative talents, developing a socioreligious collective derived perhaps from the most edifying features of two traditions. In this way they maintained their dignity and provided a legacy of the truest examples of valor and vitality. They maintained a passionate love of humanity so that they could confront their former masters with an absence of revenge. But as Higginson noted, they also possessed a deep sense of progressive rationalism in their calm realization that masters and slaves are natural enemies. In observing the Gullahs' capacity to endure pain and tendency to look beyond their own individiual situation, the surgeon in Higginson's black regiment referred to the men as "natural trasncendentalists."[27] This was true to some extent. Yet a more accurate characterization could be that these African-Americans were natural humanists. For them, integration of the human personality on a collective level was central, so that cultural considerations received primary attention sometimes at the expense of practical ones.

While the African tradition from which Gullahs descended emphasized preservation, protection, and enrichment of life, the phenomenon which unified this anthropocentric philosophy was religion. Hence it is not difficult to understand why Gullah life was expressed from an essentially spiritual perspective. Christianity and traditional African religion combined to provide them with an ideology of freedom, and a noble, mystical explanation for their existence as a people. They internalized the optimism in both religions and both orientations were necessary ingredients in the creation of Gullah culture. Slavery did not erode the African sense of pride, of community, love of home, and of family. Yet who knows how long these attributes could sustain cultural life among slaves, no matter how much their spirits struggled against degradation? Christianity offered the additional cohesion needed to develop a homogeneous people and a society based upon a progressive religious nationalism. Consequently, religion cannot be viewed only or primarily as a source of visionary, spiritual fulfillment. Nor can religion be mainly viewed as manipulative. For Gullahs it offered a politic for collective consciousness and group conformity within an African-Christian synthesis.

Freedom was not attained as the 1822 conspirators had invisioned. When freedom came, years later, a New rather than Old Testament ideology partly gave meaning and fruition to that liberty. As Leon Litwack points out, few triumphs in the spirit of freedom could equal the day in 1865 when in Charleston, a cornerstone was laid for a new African Methodist Church. It was over forty years after the old wooden structure in Hampstead had been destroyed. The new church was to be built by black hands. The architect was Robert Vesey, son of Denmark.[28] In 1822 freedom under the banner of "A Chosen People" eluded black South Carolinians through no fault of those who made the supreme sacrifice. Yet who could fault the Gullahs and perhaps other African-Americans in 1865, as they regarded themselves if not as a chosen people, at least as the "chosen generation" of a "peculiar people?"

CHAPTER 9

Folk Religion in the Slave Quarters

All was silent on the plantation. The sun had gone down and the chill December wind which blew crisply from the tide-river had driven the people into the cabins. Here and there all over the plantation, like the throbbing stars which night had called to light her world, the red glow of the fireplaces flashed out into the darkness through the open doorways, as if to mark the heart of a home. Suddenly a sharp persistent jingle broke the silence. It was the Praise House bell calling the people of the plantation together for their evening "Praise". . . .*

The secret societies are an embodiment of . . . supernatural power. Collectively, they provide an institutional structure which bears . . . similarities to the medieval church in Europe. . . . They lay down various rules of conduct, prescribe certain forms of behavior and are the sole agency capable of remitting certain sins.**

On the Sea Islands, one rarely saw a plantation home that did justice to the name "big house," since most planters maintained their more elegant residences elsewhere. But there was always a large, airy "main house," sometimes inhabited by the planter and his family during the spring and cold season. The main house was situated about half a mile from the overseer's abode. Not too far away from the overseer's residence were the yards and outbuildings, followed by the slave quarters. Gullahs called their quarters "the street," and it was described as "a real street in the

---

*"The Long Look," n.d., misc. corr., Penn School Papers, vol. 1, SHC.
**Kenneth Little, "The Role of the Secret Society in Cultural Specialization" American Anthropologist 51 (1949): 199.

middle of a sandy cotton field, with cabins on each side in a row." The first building on the street was the Praise House, a paintless, cheerless-appearing building of boards that "looked as if a heavy gale might lay it low." Some antebellum Praise Houses were equipped with a bell (not to be confused with the driver's horn). Several nights during the week, as well as on Sundays, its welcoming, soothing sound brought the people on "the street" together for assembly. The following description, although a post-Civil War one, could easily fit the antebellum scene:

. . . soon dark figures moved along those countless little footpaths that intersect the plantation in all directions.

The Praise House filled slowly. It was a small one-roomed cabin that looked weirdly alive as you approached it through the darkness. The numerous cracks in roof and walls gave the outlines of the building sketched in streaks of light against the background of the night.

The room was filled with rough backless benches, and at one end was a little table for the leader. Behind this stood a long bench where several men, officers of the Praise House sat facing the people in motionless silence with half-closed eyes and bowed heads.[1]

Most planters erected these meetinghouses after 1840 to afford the slaves a place for worship and to deprive the inhabitants of various plantations of an opportunity to mingle. Yet the Praise House also offered Gullahs a means to free expression. It was not only a place for religious gathering and spiritual solace but was essential to their community structure. At the Praise House, among fellow slaves, Gullahs publicly professed what they considered a satisfactory spiritual experience, as it was necessary to obtain approval from the Praise House congregation before petitioning the master and the Baptist church for membership. If the religious experience was not inspiring enough, or if the elders and the membership doubted the candidate's sincerity, the individual was not recommended for baptism.[2]

In addition to being a means of bringing conformity and spiritual harmony to the slave quarters, the Praise House was very much like a town hall where members of the plantation gathered, using prayer, song, and exhortation to comfort each other. J. Miller McKim, a Northern observer very much interested in Gullah music, wrote in 1862:

I asked one of these blacks . . . (Prince Rivers, Sergeant, 1st Reg. S.C.V.)—where they got these songs. "Dey make 'em, sah." "How do they make them?" After a pause, evidently casting about for an explanation, he said: "I'll tell you, it's dis way. My master call me up, and order me a short peck of corn and a hundred lash. My friends see it, and is sorry for me. When dey come to de praise-meeting dat night dey sing about it."[3]

The slaves' loyalty was to the Praise House rather than to the Baptist church few of them ever attended. Even during Northern occupation and after the Civil War, Gullahs continued to gather at the Praise House whenever trouble befell their community. Despite the fact that white Baptist churches were almost completely under black control during the war (in terms of both structure and organization), the source of power on the plantations was still the Praise House. And after the war, Gullahs continued to see it as the center of group life and to conduct themselves according to Praise House customs and regulations.[4]

Since the Praise House congregation consisted of families who knew, through daily contact, the personal life of a candidate, it was possible to scrutinize behavior and to ostracize an individual, not so much on purely religious grounds as for breaches of trust within the quarters. Elders and members exerted great disciplinary power over plantation hands, having the right to "turn dem outen de Pray's House if dey ain't fur walk right." Hence, while the Gullahs probably attached little significance to church disciplinary measures instituted by the master, but which they, as Praise House members, were forced to implement, a crime against one of their own was a different matter. Long after slavery, the Praise House continued effectively to hold its members responsible for good behavior, and the influence of these small units of the church has long been credited for the fact that crimes were rarely committed among Gullahs. In the 1920s the Beaufort sheriff stated that the Praise Houses kept Gullahs law-abiding even as freedpeople, "because the Negro fears the Lord more than he fears the law." Yet it was not "fear" so much as a desire for harmony and a sense of love and respect for each other that allowed Gullahs to maintain integrity in the community. The significance of Praise House loyalty and community membership as a social regulating force has been observed by researchers as late as the 1970s.[5] Existence of these plantation meetinghouses conformed to the desires of slaveholders, but they also served to strengthen bonds of kinship and a sense of common-wealth among the Gullahs.

Gullahs often expressed time in terms of before or after they "had sense." The concept puzzled Northern teachers who worked among them during the Civil War. "Catching sense," as the Gullahs called it, a term still used today on some Sea Islands, refers to the time when a person completes the process of joining the Church and Praise House. According to Patricia Guthrie who did field work in the Sea Islands, "entrance into the religious and the politico-jural domains parallels the time when plantation membership becomes fully realized," or when a person "catches sense." Joining the Praise House formally expressed this initiation into the plantation domain. An individual was no longer merely a member of a household but a citizen of the plantation community, and a member of the Church. Thus personhood was attained through "catching sense." All members had to answer to the religious court system when discord arose. The Praise House law was considered the "just law," and when disputes arose, settlement was reached in the religious court. Praise House membership demanded that all grievances go before this "Committee." The "unjust law" was essentially white law.[6] This raises questions about how plantation membership functioned before widespread Christian teaching by whites, and before freedom. The benne seed ritual indicates that before Methodist missionaries came, plantation depredations against the master did not warrant censure in the slave quarters. It is doubtful that this changed even after slaves "accepted" white Christianity. Internal association among any group is more significant than outside forces, especially if the outside element is an oppressive one. Also, community leaders did not go about seeking wrongdoers. Instead, cases were reported by other church members or by individuals involved in the grievance. Obviously a case brought to the leader's attention by the planter had to be acted upon. But the Gullahs did not view plantation "discipline" from the master's perspective, or as "just law."

The religious court heard both sides of a dispute and encouraged the parties to reach an agreement without input from the Praise House leader or other church members. Usually cases were settled at the first level. If not, the case went to the leader and then to the membership. The religious court system was respected and taken seriously. The small amount of crimes after slavery indicate that few Gullahs came before it and few wanted to be censored for misconduct. The ultimate aim of the religious court was to maintain "peace and harmony" in the community. The Gullahs believed this was best accomplished by settling disputes within the group. There was strong disapproval of anyone who went to the master or, after slavery, to the secular authorities. Such a person did not want a settlement, but to merely create more trouble for the group.[7]

The same attachment to religion and community membership that existed among West Africans was observed among the Gullahs. At the time of the Civil War, over half of the adult population of the Sea Islands were church members. Many others were baptized during the Northern occupation, some stating that "they had desired for years to join the church, but could not get leave from their masters." Francis Kemble noted that on the Butler estate on St. Simon's Island, slaves were forbidden to go to church and ministers were not allowed on the plantation. Yet some slaves were willing to endure corporal punishment and were baptized without approval. An American Missionary Association minister observed in 1863 that "the colored people think a good deal of belonging somewhere. This is alright but I fear many of them have been taught to think that joining church was the principal thing." Arthur Sumner recorded an incident that gives insight into the Gullahs propensity to equate communal and secular concerns. The following conversation occurred between Sumner and his housekeeper Patience:

"How many children you got, Misser Sumner," said she.
"Not one, thank the Lord."
"No Chillun?"
"I'm not married."
In sheer amazement she sat down and stared at me as little boys do at the museum.
"Oh, you'r joking."
"Fact."
Then she rolled over, and laughed till she was sore.
"Not married! Why," said she, "you look settled!"
She went off, finally, muttering to herself. . . . The next morning she returned to the charge.
"You a member sure."
"Eh?"
"A member, a church member."
"Neither married nor a member," I replied with solemn voice. She almost dropped my breakfast. She has been trying I see, to comprehend this double phenomenon; but she makes bad work of it. Sometimes I find her looking at me with wonder and commiseration; and if I ask her what she is thinking about she avoids a direct answer.[8]

Sumner's was a kind of individualism which Patience apparently could not fully comprehend. No wife, no children, no membership meant alienation—no place in the community. Gullah religion was not only a contract between God and the individual. It was a mutual agreement among themselves which implied that they could not love God without loving each other. While their common oppression bound them together in one sense, the Gullahs' decision to see themselves as contracting with each other to live as "one body" also allowed them to operate collectively and ward off the demoralizing effects of exploitation. A central element in their religious attitude was a sense of individual honor. Love for their fellows, and a respectful disposition would find favor with God. This orientation was often expressed in terms of "manners." "A Christian is mannerable," the Gullahs were fond of saying. One Gullah soldier, in his supplications to heaven, implored, "Let me lib so dat when I die I shall *hab* manners." Northern teacher Harriet Ware described an old Gullah woman, Widow Bedotte, who had been driven insane by watching her master whip her daughter to death; "very sad it is to hear her talk," wrote Ware. Yet, although Widow Bedotte's epithets against her master and the rebels were voluble and denunciatory, "she prides herself upon her good manners, which she says she gets because she belongs to the church, which every now and then she joins again." Charlotte Forten observed the Gullahs' attitude toward each other:

These people are exceedingly polite in their manner towards each other, each new arrival bowing, scraping his feet and shaking hands with the others, while there are constant greetings such as, "Huddy? How's yer lady?" ("howd' ye do? How's your wife?") The hand-shaking is performed with the greatest possible solemnity. There is never the faintest shadow of a smile on anybody's face during this performance. The children, too are taught to be very polite to their elders, and it is the rarest thing to hear a disrespectful word from a child to his parent, or to any grown person. They have really what the New-Englanders call "beautiful manners."[9]

Despite enslavement and poverty, the Gullahs maintained a generous attitude, never allowing one of their number to go without food or shelter. Kinship was important, but the Gullah concept of a household did not necessarily mean filial attachment, but all those living within a family and community structure, with the rights, duties, and privileges therein. While there were many children without parents because of the ravages of bondage, reportedly there were no orphans on the Sea Islands. Gullahs were also fond of bestowing presents upon their Northern benefactors, or anyone whom they considered a friend. Gifts of sweet potatoes, peanuts, and eggs which had a special spiritual significance and were rather expensive, were often offered to visitors. "They feel hurt if their presents are refused," wrote Laura Towne. "Old Susannah often sends to table, fish and other extras. They don't want pay. No indeed."[10]

While the Christian example contributed to inspiring a kindred spirit, the Gullah's sense of charity also had another source. African peoples have a tradition of politeness. Among the Limba of Sierra Leone for example, "shame" (Kulaku) and "honor" (yiki) are spoken of often. According respect to leaders, strangers, one's wife, and her relatives, is of great importance. Fear of shame is a very real sanction in everyday life. Rudeness or abusive behavior also brings shame, which only an apology can erase. Ceremonious welcomings involving hand shaking are greatly stressed among Africans. Thanks, greetings, and farewells are often reinforced by a gift, approved of as much for its token value of "giving the words weight," as for its economic worth. A gift of a fowl, eggs, or rice is commonly offered when guests arrive. A physician assigned to the colony of Sierra Leone in the late eighteenth century, wrote that the people possessed a "great share of pride, and are easily affected by an insult." They could not even bear a harsh expression, or raised voice without distaste. One of the severest insults toward an African was to "speak disrespectfully of his mother," which the Africans called "cursing her." More recently, a researcher in the Kongo was told that there were two things he should know right away about BaKongo peoples. "The first is that we all came from Mbaza Kongo. The second is the importance of good manners." [11]

Aside from a spirit of cooperation, Gullahs used their religion to foster a sense of justice. Undoubtedly, since they were exploited so unjustly on all quarters, it was important that among each other fairness predominate. The power of the community and the extent to which slaves could pursue their indignation against erring members was not always peaceful, and could reach extreme proportions. Jenkins Mikell's recollection of a grisly event on Edisto Island represents a case in point. Crimes within the slave quarters were infrequent, but they did occur:

Early one morning, we were awakened by the repressed excitement we felt around the dwelling. We soon found that all the people on the home place were in a terribly wrought up state and waiting for the Master to appear. A murder had been committed among them. A man had killed his wife in anger. The poor woman had been found dead hanging by her neck to the rafter of the cabin, and the guilty husband had run away and left her there. He was caught during the day . . . he was tried and convicted and remanded to the scene of his crime for execution. . . . On the day of his execution very little work was done in the community by the negroes. All attended the tragic scene. His coffin was made on the plantation and placed in a wagon. The doomed man, tied, seated upon this coffin rode six miles to the place of execution, and by his side seated on the same gruesome seat was his companion in guilt—a woman. She was made to witness at close quarters his dreadful end. She returned to the place of burial, on the plantation, seated on the box containing his dead body, and as the body was lowered into the grave, she was seized by a frenzied mob, forced into the open pit and every effort was made to bury her alive. These efforts nearly succeeded. But wiser counsels prevailed and she was at last released.[12]

In this situation moral judgment within the slave community was not in keeping with the Christian doctrine of forgiveness that usually characterized the Gullahs' disposition. Instead, it indicates how African influences continued. Apparently, Gullahs believed that some violations should not be summarily dismissed or forgiven. Among the Windward Coast peoples, no concept of sin seems to have been present. Yet among some, the Mende for example, there was a sense of guilt in two areas of government—breaches in communal laws and regulations, and violation of the rights of those unable to help themselves. The BaKongo considered sin to be a wrong against society, not God, and thus should be punished by society. The above Gullah crime could be viewed as betrayal of communal trust, an individual violation, and as an immoral act against the people as a whole. Such violations called for punishment, not only for the offender, but for those closely related to the act.[13] Such irrevocable behavior among the bondspeople could possibly undermine their collective strength and organization, and no doubt Gullahs felt that depravity should be rooted out in a drastic manner as a warning to others who might be driven to commit such violence. Yet the fact that the example was an atypical incident demonstrates that adoption of a common socioreligious connection among Gullahs had more of a restraining effect on deviant social behavior than threat of violent retaliation.

In the Gullah slave community the most important people were religious leaders, comprising two groups. One consisted of black elders, and the others were spiritual parents, or the black elders' "help." Black elders were chosen by whites, often by Baptist planters. These black leaders, referred to as "deacons" or "watchmen" were responsible for "watchcare" of members of the plantation societies. They were the experienced church members in the quarters, having some knowledge of Christianity and probably taking their religion more literally and seriously than their fellow bondspeople. Black elders maintained relatively close contact with the Baptist churches during the last thirty years of bondage, and were exemplary people, managing to walk a thin line between securing the trust and confidence of both masters and slaves.[14] Undoubtedly, to the slaveholders black elders embodied those features of Christianity which, they hoped, would encourage obedience, docility, humility, and a "turn-the-other-cheek" attitude. The elders' judgment was important to planters, who realized the influence these leaders exercised. Masters probably depended upon the reasoning power of elders, expecting them to use Christianity as a soothing influence in the slave quarters. Although law forbade black religious gatherings without three slaveholders being present, this edict was grossly violated in the Lowcountry, as probably elsewhere, and black societies were rarely visited by whites supposedly superintending black worship.

Thus, black elders' duties of oversight, direction, watchcare, and advice were extensive. Since they ultimately had the last word on whether or not the "Christian" character of a "seeker" of religion warranted that individual's being accepted into "de Ark ob Safety," the supremacy of these leaders was considerable.[15] Yet black elders undoubtedly used their position of power with measure, fairness, and to benefit of the slave community, for they always maintained respect among the bondspeople. Their message was one of encouragement and their capacity to inspire moral confidence largely depended upon their verbal ability, gravity of deportment, and consistent record of honesty and correctness. As guardians of the community and articulators of group values, they may have counseled patience and been the main proponents of the Christian attitude of "resignation," which observers attributed to some Gullahs, as a form of protection. Above all, black elders were firm about depredations within the slave quarters, watching closely "to detect some delinquency" or "any shortcomings," yet ready to forgive an errant member.

They visit, pray with and exhort the sick, rebuke the impenitent, counsel the weak, conduct social meetings for prayer, whenever such meetings are permitted by the proprietor of a plantation, and especially have vigilant watch over the young, striving to keep them in the path of rectitude.[16]

The other group of religious leaders, spiritual fathers and mothers, were not white-sanctioned leaders of the Praise House, but among the Gullahs they were recognized as legitimate and reportedly had "the most absolute authority over them." They were a continuous foil to Methodist missionaries and often disliked by planters because these religious leaders successfully incorporated non-Christian elements into white Protestantism. From this group came Praise House leaders and the "committee' that acted as the religious court. Thus on an individual plantation, the "help" who held Praise House membership, conducted religious services, and oversaw local religious activity was actually more significant than the black elder who might oversee several plantations. Like the elders, spiritual leaders were loved, respected, and faithful in those things pertaining to the welfare of the religious community. The spiritual leaders' influence belonged to a tradition older than the black elders' role.[17] They undoubtedly adjusted to Christianity by making a place for themselves in the heart of it as practiced by Gullahs. Also Baptist elders, though having the interests of the community at heart, may have imbibed too much of the new religion and been too willing to preach and teach conservatism. Thus for the Gullahs, the power of and respect for plantation spiritual parents exceeded that of Baptist-sanctioned elders. The former were healers, interpreters of dreams, signs, and visions, all of which were central to Gullah conceptions of religion and infused with their impressionistic form of Christianity.[18] The functions of the two types of religious leaders may have overlapped to some degree and also complemented each other. They represent different aspects of the Gullahs' spiritual existence—one Christian, the other African—and an element of syncretism within slave religion.

Examination of Gullah methods of admission to church membership is one key to understanding the significance of the spiritual leader's role, Gullah socioreligious spiritualism, and links with a West African past. A candidate's acceptance into the church and subsequently into the Praise House depended upon relating a satisfactory experience, which was the result of a soul-grappling, traumatic confrontation between the individual and a higher power, culminating, if successful, in a sensation of rebirth and full membership in the religious community. The period of transition between the time a desire to become a Christian was expressed and the acceptance by elders of the religious experience was called "seekin'."

The name, "seekin'" was introduced to the Gullahs by Methodist missionaries. At meetings with slaves, after preaching and teaching, the Methodists would then inquire if anyone would like to come forward and "seek Jesus." Those who professed such a desire would then go "on trial" and remain in this limbo status until the missionary deemed them ready for baptism. Probationers, or "seekers of religion," were required by Methodists to know the Creed, Sacraments, and Lord's Prayer, and they were "not eligible for baptism until they had learned them understandingly."[19] It was an impractical expectation, and few of the slaves attempted to provide the missionaries with an "adequate" explanation of religion. Yet true to their adaptive genius, Gullahs embraced the term and devised a unique interpretation of "seeking Jesus" that had little to do with the Methodists' idea, but which the Baptists accepted as proof of "Christian" conversion. A critical and frustrated Methodist missionary provided the *Southern Christian Advocate* with a revealing illustration of the slaves' method of determining religious conversion and their "seekin'" process:

> When one of these people becomes serious, or "begins to pray" as he would say,—and this is seldom the result of preaching, but most commonly a "warning in a dream,"—it is customary for him to select, by the direction of "the spirit" of course, with some church member of influence, as his spiritual guide. Females are often chosen. Soon after the "vision" in which his teacher is pointed out, he makes known to him his revelation and puts himself under his instruction. These are of a two-fold nature, answering to the two-fold character of the teacher. He is now a prophet to teach him how to conduct himself, and particularly how to pray. He is also "an interpreter of visions" to whom the seeker relates all his *"travel."* This word *travel* . . . is one of the most significant in their language, and comprehends all those exercises, spiritual, visionary and imaginative, which make up an "experience." . . . These travels may differ in some things; and in others they all agree. Each seeker meets with warnings—awful sights or sounds, and always has a vision of a white man who talks with him, warns him, and sometimes makes him carry a burden, and in the end leads him to the river.
> When the teacher is satisfied with the travel of the seeker, he pronounces "he git thru"; and he is ready for the church. This decision is never questioned by the neophyte. "I prayed under him," says the latter; "he is my spiritual father." Thus the case is settled. The man's religion is endorsed by an authoritative *imprimatur* and heaven is sure. Meanwhile perhaps there has been no solitary conviction of the true nature of sin, no genuine repentance to embitter sin to the soul, no distant apprehension of the sacrifices of the Savior and the merit of his death as the atonement for sin, and the great procuring cause of pardon: in a word, no distant element of Christian experience involved in the whole affair.[20]

The lengthy account failed to mention several other paramount aspects of the "seekin'" experience. First, the seeker was expected, as far as possible, to shun all "social or worldly pleasures." Second, the seeker was required to "go into de wilderness," where the "visions" usually appeared to the candidate and where the travel took place. Solitude and meditation were essential features of the seeking period. Approved and unapproved night vigils were common. Such places as the graveyard,

normally an absolute taboo for Gullahs (except for the occasion of burials), cotton or corn fields, and the marshes were favorite praying grounds
for seekers. Gullahs believed that "Notin' won't hurt you while you bin
seekin'." Yet no matter where one prayed, "in de fields and pine woods,"
"in de bush," "out doors," or "under live oak," all was defined as "de
wilderness." It was not generally possible for slaves to withdraw in the
literal sense. Often as a gesture of going into the wilderness they would
refrain from social interaction, sometimes not even speaking to family
members or friends unless it was absolutely necessary, communicating
only with their spiritual leader. It was a time of utter prostration for the
seeker. Untidy and exceptionally ragged clothing was worn. Female seekers
often covered themselves with ash. Seekers wore a "little white cloth or
string," around their heads, "jus to mark deirself diffun'." This had to
be worn, unwashed, for the duration of the seeking period. During
Northern occupation, despairing teachers remarked that children were
taken out of school when they became seekers, and since "de trabbel"
usually lasted for months, sometimes the entire school was disrupted.
From Hilton Head Island, Elizabeth Botume wrote:

> In the winter most of the children were "seeking and praying." The older
> people said, "They do hang their heads and pray"; and they were not allowed to
> do much of anything else for fear they would "be turned back.". . . .
> These religious revivals were a source of much disturbance in school rou-
> tine. . . . We cannot call these "religious excitements"; the young seekers were
> in a stupid and lethargic condition. Some children were not allowed to come to
> school for fear they would be turned back.[21]

It was not only essential for seekers to relate a satisfactory emotional
experience, they also had to declare themselves free of malice toward
anyone and ready to abide by rules of the church via society control.
Hence the Praise House operated as the extending influence on behavior
in the slave quarters. While the seekers' dream experiences varied, they
first had to be bad, fearful dreams, which the spiritual parent explained.
As the seeker's "experience" neared an end, metamorphosis was indicated by, among other things, a profession of charity for others. This
was always an important part of their spiritual affirmation:

> "You think you are converted?"
> "Yes, . . . I' so lovin! I loves ebery body—all de trees, an' de chicken, an' de
> peoples; I loves ebery ting an' ebery body. . . ."[22]

More important than feelings of guilt and sinfulness, so fundamental to Christian conversion, was the seeker's desire to become a part of the community. The more intense the "trabbel" or "vision," the more dramatic the integration into society.

The mystical nature of the slaves' conversion experience involved a travel during which seekers often prayed and spoke to religious nature objects rather than to God.[23] As the Methodist informant noted, this was not linked to a Christian tradition. Literature on the previously discussed secret cultural associations of the Windward Coast peoples is limited, since even today ethnic groups generally refuse to discuss them. Nevertheless, there is enough existing material on this tradition to suggest secret society link with Gullah concepts of conversion, personhood, and group membership as practiced within and reinforced by Christianity.

Initiation into the Poro and Sande contained two central components—contact with spirits and extended instruction, both aimed at socialization of the individual and preparation for an active communal role. Among the Kuranko, Mano, Limba, Mende, Temne, Gola, and other ethnic groups, withdrawal from organized society into the bush was clearly related to a type of release through transcendence, commonly expressed as a lonely, spiritual journey or travel on which the initiate becomes acquainted with death. The Poro and Sande were the universal male and female cultural societies of Sierra Leone, Liberia, and parts of Gambia. Boys and girls usually entered the bush school at puberty, but at separate periods and for different lengths of time. Sande initiates, like Gullah females, wore a white head tie, called "the white thing," and covered their faces with white clay while Gullah female seekers used ash. The *Mazowo* (high priestess) always wore white and was envisioned thusly by initiates. Withdrawal from village society was a ritualistic death. Initiates were taken into a sacred designated area of the bush by Poro-Sande priests and priestesses, called altar mothers and fathers. Here they symbolically took leave of earth and journeyed down into the spirit world, the world of the dead. Among some groups, the Mano, for example, these spirits were ancestors. For others, the Kuranko and Limba, they were spirits the initiates encountered, spirits who were nameless, capricious, quais-human nature beings sometimes occupying streams, rivers, and mountains. In any case, contact with these spirits represented a form of demise and in their realm initiates dwelled during the entire period of segregation. The boys and girls conversed with the spirits and related these conversations to the altar parent, who interpreted them. Little is known of the initiates' experiences while on the journey through the spirit world. But their soul was considered to be in a state of anxiety and confusion, seeking to "recover balance and collect itself." The encounter with "nameless spirits" in the sacred grove was manifested in dreams and prayers since these were common forms of revelation and communication. The symbolic travel to the world of death and subsequent return, if successful, represented an effort to reduce the all-pervading spirit world to an organization in which humans could not only participate, but where people could actually become spirits. Among the Mano, a noninitiate was called a shadow, an image, or imitation—that is, not really a member of the village. During the initiation process the initiate was a "little spirit of the bush," indicating godhood but not membership. After graduation, the neophyte was known as "citizen," a full-fledged Poro or Sande member.[24]

This journey to the world of ancestors or nameless spirits, and the return, represented the death of individualistic tendencies inimical to group survival. A successful travel also indicated an eclipse of family ties, particularly with the mother and immediate kinship group, so that one's responsibility to the group exceeded the powers of immediate or extended family. Among the above-mentioned ethnic groups, the wild (the bush) was considered to be the direct opposite of village or domestic life. Animals, especially predatory beasts and scavengers, were associated with antisocial behavior. A libelous form of insult was to refer to someone as a "bush person," implying that he or she had no ability to grasp principles of correct social conduct associated with collective living. Thus, the bush was occupied by hostile or estranged natural and supernatural beings. The initiate had to overcome a fear and dread of these beings who represented forces of alienation and destruction. West Africans believed that the community could control or at least rise above fear of life and death forces by successfully confronting the wild. Since life in the bush was viewed as antisocial, predatory animals and selfish nature spirits living there were not given communal recognition. To symbolize their animal state while in the bush, initiates were often required to engage in antisocial activities, such as stealing their food. Thus a graphic distinction was made between the two types of behavior. Entering the bush and returning as a social being was a way of conquering the environment and combating deviant individualistic tendencies. Laws and traditions of the group, duties, and proper relations with the opposite sex were taught. Withdrawal into the bush—into the spirit world—and the dissimilarity between that situation and village life made the individual experience disorientation and prostration. The initiate was in the power of the cult leader, far removed from kin who might condone or overlook frailties. The initiate entered the bush helpless, irresponsible, and with no social sense. Guided by the altar parent, he or she underwent a thorough physical, mental, and moral test in which unsuitable traits were eliminated. At the end of a session the neophyte experienced either profound transformation or death. Weaklings and homosexuals were killed or allowed to die.[25]

The cult association represented an attempt to control the forces of social life, and the common theme was regeneration and integration. Social existence was "life" and its absence represented collectively unacceptable attitudes or death. To ensure a continuation of life, that is, the perpetuation of the group, ideals of social behavior within the community had to be maintained. Yet individual existence was also a condition of social life rather than apart from it. Everyone had a specific and useful place in the village and this was taught to the initiate while in the bush. Individual life could complement social existence, but this relationship was made imperfect by the unpredictability of death, the precariousness of nature, and human variance. The bush initiation was an effort to transcend or to place under human control these elements of division. Hence destructive personal inclinations had to be rooted out. The experience itself represented opposing human tendencies. Exclusiveness, secrecy, isolation, a hierarchy of power, and a lonely sojourn were all manifestations of individualism. Thus, the ultimate end was not total destruction of one's uniqueness but the coexistence of individuality and collectivity in African communal society, so long as personal considerations did not sacrifice organic structure. A triumphant bush experience bolstered self-esteem while it served collective ends.

The Grand Master of Poro was usually called *Dazowo*, which means Father *Zowo*. The Grand Lady of Sande was the *Mazowo*, or Mother *Zowo*. Their assistants in the bush were referred to as zo. The zo people were the actual spiritual leaders of the Poro and Sande, and were called altar parents. Respected and demanding members of the community, they could not be dismissed from their high office for any misconduct regardless of gravity, although "certain punishments" in the unwritten code of the society could be imposed upon leaders by society members. The zo were the principal characters in the society, and were charged with protecting the traditions and institutions of the group. The zo people had a "majestic status." They were respected by chiefs and elders, and "honored with intense devotion by the youth of the land." In personal characteristics a zo was "chivalrous, courteous, public spirited, law-abiding and fearless." The zo was also a teacher of "native lore, arts, and crafts." He or she had full knowledge of the history and traditions of the people. Above all, the zo were "authentic" judges of all matters pertaining to the people's welfare.[26]

As role models these African leaders correspond to some extent with Gullah elders. But there is an even closer relation between zo and Gullah spiritual parents to whom the slaves looked for guidance and who maintained such "absolute authority" over them. Laura Towne wrote:

I went to-day to see Maum Katie, an old African woman who remembers worshipping her own gods in Africa but who has been nearly a century in this country. She is bright and talkative, a great "spiritual mother," a fortune teller, or rather prophetess, and a woman of tremendous influence over her spiritual children.

Similarly, Harriet Ware was acquainted with "Old Peggy, the 'leader' from Fripp Point." Ware was told that "Old Peggy and Binah" were the two "whom all that came into the Church, had come through, and the Church supports (takes care of) them." Thus the Methodist missionary correctly assessed the role and power of women diviners in Gullah church membership. A further example of female influence in the sacred-secular world of slaves is provided by Francis Kemble. An old woman on the Butler plantations named Sinda, reigned as a prophetess among the slaves for many years and acquired as ascendency over them. When she declared the world would soon end, "her assertion took such possession of the people on the estate that they refused to work, and the rice and cotton fields were threatened with an indefinite fallow in consequence of this strike on the part of the cultivators." The overseer, realizing the impossibility of attempting force, waited until the appointed day arrived. Sinda' prediction proved false and no emancipation was forthcoming. The people went back to work and Sinda, in a fallen state, was "tremendously flogged."[27]

It is difficult to discern where one type of socioreligious leadership began among the Gullahs and the other ended, or if in slavery a shared authority and governance was practiced. Among Windward Coast Africans authority rested with two bodies—the chief and his elders, and cultural authority, which consisted of Poro and Sande leaders. The latter was called the Poro Council. "All grave and problematic questions touching the interest of the section or tribe in general were handled by this Poro Council, and their decisions, after due deliberation, were preemptory." Among the BaKongo, governance was far more centralized and hierarchical. Authority was in the hands of a king, and on the village level, a chief, who might have advisers, among whom was a medicine man *(Nganga Nkisi)*.[28] But the importance of the priest in all African societies may explain the continued presence of the spiritual parents. Because spiritual parents, like their African counterparts, held their positions for life, and since they comprised the "religious court," they possibly represented the communal soul of the people while the elder personified the individual soul in a more Christian context. From the spiritual leader a Gullah candidate not only received religious guidance but also instruction in conduct or "manners," thus preserving values as well as maintaining authority. Different social conditions make it impossible to actually compare types of instruction given to African and Gullah initiates. But in both situations such qualities as good conduct, allegiance, generosity, and group responsibility were emphasized. Secret society initiates received a rich background in physical survival, social interaction, instruction in ethnic-group history, and art. They were also schooled in their particular occupation for the future. For Gullah "seekers," instruction was probably a mixture of Christianity, Africanisms, and practical information. Candidates were taught how to pray, an interpretation of the nature of God and Christ, concepts about death, and especially about the realities of life, all within a context relevant to their circumstances as bondspeople.[29]

When African initiates left the bush, they returned to the village as "reborn," and were said to have "crossed the water." Their former existence was obliterated—old animosities, debts, even crimes no longer existed. The person was entering a new life with new responsibilities. Neophytes were expected to take their place in the village, to serve it when called upon, and to obey its regulations as interpreted by the Poro Council. When initiates were led back to the village, they underwent a washing ceremony in the creek or river. After "washing," new members were dressed up for their final return. Parents publicly expressed pride in their offspring, sparing no expense in efforts to make the neophytes as radiant as possible. After initiates were dressed in their new finery, they gathered in the meetinghouse with friends and family, "where in a public ceremony they are handed over to their parents with great acclamation."[30]

Among Gullahs, a "seeker" related an acceptable experience to the spiritual leader and declared a profession of faith to the Praise House members. At an appointed time, the church elder and his "help" would then further examine the individual to determine readiness for baptism. Laura Towne witnessed such a prebaptismal examination on St. Helena:

> . . . father Tom and his bench of elders examined candidates for baptism and asked Ellen to record their names. Each candidate clad in the oldest, dirtiest clothes, with a cloth band round their forehead stood humbly before the bench. Father Tom, looking like Jupiter, grave, powerful and awfully dignified put the most posing questions to which the candidates replied meekly but promptly. They asked the satisfactory candidate at last, "how do you pray." Then the soft, musical voice made the coaxing, entreating kind of prayer which they use so much, and a nod dismissed the applicant. Another was called up at once. There were seventy to be examined.[31]

Following examination, the candidates were ready for their water burial, which took place on communion Sunday morning. Teacher David Thorpe wrote of one occasion in 1863 when "upwards of one hundred and forty people," of all ages, were baptized. It was for him a "strange and picturesque scene." The people gathered from "far and near," in all manner of vehicles and "in every kind of attire." The candidates arrived "dressed for the water," according to Thorpe, "in miserable looking clothing," with their heads tied up in handkerchiefs. Nearby, among the bushes were mule carts loaded with garments for the converts to put on after the baptism. The white minister, Mr. Phillips, read off each candidate's name, and "Old Pa Tom" nodded his approval of their examination. All headed down to the water:

> The ceremony was performed by the roadside near a bridge where the road crossed the creek. "Siah" "leader" at "Good William Fripp's" took the arm of Mr. Phillips and together they entered the water. Around on every side were hundreds of people arrayed in their Sunday best. Their shiny black faces surmounted by bright turbans and white turbans. . . . They presented a beautiful sight today. Truly the sun shone out on a beautiful scene. . . . On the bridge in the crowd a few eager white faces could be seen peeping out, while on the grove near the water were other white friends . . .—near the water stood a large

band of singers and they sent up hymn after hymn during the exercises. Mr. Phillips and Siah went into the water. The Pastor extended his hands and his whole flock of candidates went forward into the water. Each one seemed to be attended by several friends or relatives, who besides being bodily support carried dry clothing, shawls, cloaks and overcoats. . . . They all gathered about the minister and Siah. Mr. Phillips took them in turn—each by one shoulder while Siah laid hold of the other and together they immersed them, over one hundred and forty. As fast as they had been baptized they stepped to the shore, though before they reached there, their friends received them and shuffled them up . . . and hurried them off into the bushes. It took a long time to get through with so many, but after a while it was over and we all went back to church. All the candidates came out in shiny robes. . . . There was a great difference in their looks when they came into the church the second time. Then we had a long service after which the right hand of fellowship was given and . . . the sacrament was administered to them.[32]

Resemblance is noted between the African secret society candidates' "turning out" and the Gullahs' "baptizin'." Both situations represented the emergence of a new individual whose status as a full member of the community was illustrated by a water burial. This new position was not only expressed by immersion but by the wearing of new garments and partaking of a communion service with family, friends, and, in the case of Gullahs, only "true believers" of the Baptist faith. In both instances the event was as impressive as it was significant. Like the new Christians, African initiates returning from the bush were considered "newborns from the belly of the Devil." All claims against them were forgiven and they were not responsible for any contract or behavior displayed prior to being devoured by the devil and reemerging as new beings.[33]

No ceremony symbolized an individual's initiation into the church and community more than baptism. For Gullahs, this had to be total immersion. Even those salves who joined the Methodist church usually insisted on total immersion rather than "mere sprinkling." Perhaps this preference was a latent memory of secret society initiation, with total immersion representing absolute commitment to the Gullahs' socioreligious culture. It is also possible that, as some Methodist missionaries believed, Gullahs were confident that "baptism by total immersion is a means of a present, full and eternal salvation; and that after you have been baptized, it is impossible to sin or fall from grace."[34] Yet the most significant feature of the Gullahs' attachment to total immersion may have been that this black community interpreted performance of the rite as symbolically

adding to a collective attitude in the quarters. Total immersion was exclusively their way of being baptized and, although a Christian service,
the pomp, color, and ceremony was original to the slaves. The Gullahs'
method of baptism, with its solemn pageantry, had African antecedents
as well as Christian form. But more important, from the slaves' point of
view, the rite was uniquely a prerequisite for community stature within
their own society.

Gullah efforts to construct an organized harmonious social system was
further illustrated by the fact that, while collective affiliation in the slave
quarters was most significant, a sense of individual fulfillment was also
essential. Hence, while "seekin'" culminated in acceptance of socialization through church membership, the experience itself was a private one
and the desire to "seek Jesus" was a slave's personal decision, although
not devoid of community pressure. The travel, the visions, and the solitude possibly represented a bondsperson's inner reflection and recognition of "self" as opposed to his or her treatment as "thing" by the master.
Efforts toward acquiring a valuable self-image is related in the slave's
dependence on the spiritual parent who listened to and interpreted individual experiences. The significance of individual experience also had its
source in the personal attachment to and identification with Christ,
prophets, and disciples rather than to perceived abstractions and inappl-
icable doctrines within Christianity. Moreover, Gullah cultural achieve-
ments represent manifestations of individual creativity as well as collective will and fortitude.

In the Gullah socioreligious community, exclusiveness served collective goals perhaps in the way that secrecy in Poro and Sande expressed
loyalty, solidarity, and trust. One illustration of this was the practice of
close communion among Gullahs. Close communion was actually an elit-
ist doctrine which the slaves apparently adopted from their Calvinist-
oriented Baptist slavemasters. American Missionary Association ministers stated that the Gullahs practiced close communion before they came.
"I find that the colored people understand the doctrine of 'close communion' perfectly well," wrote the Reverend Augustine Roots from Port
Royal in 1863. "I have however said, myself nothing about the matter of
communion." This was not the opinion of Laura Towne. She related
that a white Baptist minister, Mr. Horton, informed the Gullahs that no
one "who taught different doctrines" had any right "even to stand in the
pulpit." Horton further told the Gullahs that those with different reli-

gious persuasions "had no right" to come to church communion. Many Northern teachers were Unitarians. Others followed no faith. Still, they enjoyed the Gullah church services and felt that the bondspeople wanted them at communion. In any case a denominational feud erupted in the occupied area. Some Gullahs did not agree with the exclusion practice, and insisted that white antebellum Baptists and Episcopalians even communed together in the Sea Island region, and no doctrinal proscription was made. "So," wrote Towne, "Mr. Horton has not the excuse he gave for his course, that it was already established." After creating the issue Mr. Horton left the region and Mr. Phillips came in his place. Phillips sided with Northern teachers and missionaries. Towne, a Unitarian, stated that the "Reverend Mr. Phillips was here today and says the elders asked by what right we stayed to communion." Phillips interceded on behalf of the teachers, but met firm resistance. "Mr. Phillips . . . says the elders decided to exclude us from communion," related Towne. Later, the teachers continued to press the issue with an influential Gullah leader:

Nelly had today, I think, a long talk with Demas upon close communion, but he was immovable, as might be supposed. He did not think much of the theological arguments of a girl like Nelly; and he is perfectly unbending by nature.[35]

For a people whose knowledge of Christian doctrine was marginal, and whose spiritual nature was one of warmth and generosity, it was uncharacteristic of the Gullahs to embrace staunchly such a rigid theological doctrine. If close communion was not a concept introduced to the Gullahs by Baptist masters, their use of the concept is even more interesting and further illustrates their adaptive capacity. Yet it was practiced all over the region. Gullahs continued to follow the close communion model, scolding members who worshiped outside of their religious structure. While they frequently invited and always welcomed white Northern missionaries and others to "jine praise wid we," the Gullahs remained adamant about refusing communion to those not of their faith. Perhaps Gullahs interpreted the ritualistic sacrament as a private ceremony among church members and believed that its usefulness in fostering unity and harmony among believers was best served by keeping others out of fellowship. This included white non-Baptists as well as black nonbelievers. The one construct resembling law, custom, practice, and system that Gullahs could consider their own was their religious societies and the beliefs contained therein. Black societies were indeed "invisible institutions," and they were controlled from within. While confusion and vacillation occurred in other areas, within Gullah black societies there was organization, structure, and a cameraderie transferable to the slave quarters. Religion was their "fixed point" and the one realm where they needed authority if a group attitude was to be maintained. The concept of close communion was not completely new, given the African heritage. And black elders insisted that only members of the societies had a right to fellowship, for probably no event more symbolized integration of the individual into the socioreligious connection than acceptance of the elements representing the mystical blood and body of Christ. This ritual bound members of the various societies. The more exclusive the event, the more it impressed upon the communicants the responsibilities entailed. By joining society, Praise House, and church, an individual became a full participant in the community. Communion service epitomized this relationship. Communion was not only a method of initiating new converts into the socioreligious connection, but a way of reminding old members of their commitments. In addition to being "de Ark ob Safety" in the spiritual sense, communion was possibly a conduct agreement, restricting antisocial behavior yet inspiring a feeling of personal status very much in the way that Poro and Sande did in West Africa. Gullahs and Africans used their religion to fulfill sacred and secular communal needs in similar ways. In both instances the main emphasis was on community preservation. In each case an institution evolved that initiated individuals into society and committed them to abide by the customs, beliefs, and practices of the group for the sake of unity and order, while not ignoring the members' need to maintain a sense of self.

Once the candidates were baptized and given communion, they were then members of the black society and the plantation Praise House. This new status gave former candidates the right to participate in the ring shout which was held at the praise meeting or in the home of the individual considered to be the most pious. One of the earliest available antebellum description of the ring shout was provided by Charles Lyell, who traveled through the South Carolina and Georgia Sea Islands in 1848. According to Lyle, on the Hopeton plantation of James Hamilton Couper, over twenty violins were silenced by the Methodist missionaries. Thus was music and dancing, the slaves' chief form of merrymaking, prohibited. Yet Methodists did allow slaves to engage in a form of physical exercise after prayer meetings, hence the origin of the "shout":

At the Methodist prayer-meetings, they are permitted to move round rapidly in a ring, joining hands in token of brotherly love, presenting the right hand and then the left, in which maneuver, I am told, they sometimes contrive to take enough exercise to serve as a substitute for the dance, it being in fact a kind of spiritual boulanger.[36]

Physical expressions of religious fervor had been a feature of eighteenth-century Methodism. But the phenomenon had for the most part disappeared by the time of the Methodist slave conversion movement. While most Methodist missionaries frowned upon slaves' religious expressions, others heeded the instruction of William Capers, superintendent of missions, to allow the slaves to "be themselves" in matters of worship, so long as they abided by the discipline.[37] Hence, although worldly entertainment was forbidden, in some cases religious exercise was not. Baptist planters may have permitted the shout to exist because they saw no harm in such behavior and recognized the therapeutic effects of such "periodic releases." Thus, the shout ritual, among other things, can be seen as a cathartic which enabled slaves to act out tensions, anxieties, and suppressed facets of themselves in an approved manner.

While Gullahs considered the shout to be a religious, even Christian practice, it was their own creation. At the Praise House, shouts only took place after service had ended and the benediction announced. Also, while Gullahs sang Methodist and Baptist hymns at the praise meetings, when time came for a shout, the slaves sang only their own spirituals.[38]

Some accounts of the shout indicate that three or four people stood and sang, clapping and gesticulating, while others shuffled along on their heels, following each other in a circle, bending the knees slightly. The movements began slowly, a few going around and others joining in vocally and kinetically, while the song became faster and faster, "till at last only the most marked part of the refrain is sung and the shuffling, stamping and clapping get furious." According to Laura Towne, the floor shook dangerously, swaying rhythmically in time with the song. The dancers would get out of breath only after long periods of time, rest for awhile, and begin again, as the several outside of the ring kept up the singing. Charlotte Forten, a black teacher from the North, added color and imagery to the shout scene she witnessed:

. . . at the close of the Praise-Meeting, they all shake hands in the most solemn manner. Afterward, as a kind of appendix, they have a grand "shout" during which they sing their own hymns. . . . The first shout that we witnessed . . . impressed us very much. The large gloomy room, with its blackened walls—the wild whirling dance of the shouters,—the crowd of dark, eager faces gathered around,—the figure of the old blind man, whose excitement could hardly be controlled, and whose attitude and gestures while singing were very fine—and over all, the red glare of the burning pine-knot, which shed a circle of light around it, but only seemed to deepen and darken the shadows in the other parts of the room,—these all formed a wild, strange, and deeply impressive picture, not soon to be forgotten.[39]

Only members of the Praise House could join in the ring shout. Children were taught the shout at a very early age but never allowed to participate in or attend religious gatherings where the shout was performed until they became Praise House members. Once membership was attained, the new converts were welcomed into the Praise House by the opportunity to lead the ring shout and illustrate their ability.[40]

Most Northern teachers were at first appalled when they observed the shout. "I never saw anything so savage," wrote Laura Towne. "They call it a religious ceremony, but it seems more like a regular frolic to me." "The shout reminds one of a pagan performance," wrote a Ladies Island teacher. Arthur Sumner referred to it as "a strange, barbaric Central-African dance and song." Yet Gullahs insisted that the shout was religious and that each movement and step had spiritual significance. The steps never changed and even after freedom the shout was not altered by maneuvers that might have been learned at a "worldly dance." A watchful leader made sure that the feet were never crossed. Some whites, after coming to know and understand the Gullahs, reversed their initial critical stance. Laura Towne spent the rest of her life with the Gullahs after going there during the Civil War. She grew to love and respect the Gullahs enough to appreciate their forms of expression. "Went to a fine shout today," she wrote in her diary after a few years' stay on the Sea Islands.[41]

The Gullah ring shout, like the travel and the vision, involved an altered state of consciousness and had the attributes of "possession." It represented either an unusual behavior inspired and controlled by an outside agent, in this case the Holy Spirit, or the outside agent displaced the individual's personality and acted in its stead.[42] The background of the Gullah ring shout, a manifestation of possession trance, was West African in origin and an important characteristic of the initiation process.

African initiation, beginning with a symbolic death, a journey to the spirit world, and complete rupture with one's past life and personality, was a time of lethargy, isolation, and prostration. As a result of contact with the spirits (nameless objects or ancestors) while in the bush, the novice's personality was modified in the image of a deity, and the individual was said to have become godlike through association—hence the Mano term "little spirits of the bush." Spirit possession took place during bush-life, itself represented as a period of unconsciousness when the initiate departed the domain of reason. The neophyte emerged from the experience "reborn," with a secondary spiritual personality inculcated as a type of conditioned reflex. When cultural and environmental forces interacted with these individual personalities from similar traditions, a psychological, collective process that was rarely conscious could be stimulated. The baptism or "sacred bath" purged the initiate's mind of previous attitudes, and future behavior would be an emulation of the true spirit within, or "little me."[43] Hence possession behavior can be interpreted as part of a society's efforts to incorporate into a coherent system the natural and supernatural worlds. Since possession was a public ceremony, where one demonstrated his or her individual spiritual presence in a sharing experiental manner, the phenomenon can be seen as solidifying human collectivity and providing a further basis for the participants to create a socioreligious network of communication and interaction. In the following description of a shout recorded more than fifty years after slavery, it illustrates possession in full force among Sea Island blacks, and suggests how certain African religious cult themes could have been retained. This shout, in a St. Helena Island Praise House, involved "welcoming and initiating" three teenage boys baptized into the church that morning. The Praise House leader announced that, "After givin' de right han' of fellowship to dese t'ree boys," the benediction would take place, after which "we'll gib dese boys de opportunity to exercise deyselbes wid de shout." The new converts were allowed to begin and demonstrate their ability to "exercise deyselbes." As people pushed back the benches, there was laughter and conversation as the shout began. The three youths stamped the floor, clapped their hands rhythmically, and moved around and around the open space in the center of the floor, "which was walled in by encouraging older people and other young people, all singing "De bell dun rung." The people commented on the shouters, such expressions as "Yoner look at Johnny, he exercise fur tru enty?"

or "Com' on, let's git indey widdem." The others joined in, now paying little attention to the new members. The three initiates, while no longer leading the shout, were "determined boys in their teens," and seemed bent on holding the center of attention. They clapped and stamped louder, and again assumed leadership of the group of shouters:

Clear, distinct, and strong their treble voices took up the shout song. Above all the voices in the room theirs could be heard singing "De bell dun rung, de bell dun rung, de bell dun rung." Catching the contagious enthusiasm of these youthful voices, the others in the ring and those around the wall sang louder and louder. Yet above the rhythmic thud of the heels of the shouters as they jerked themselves around the circle in perfect two-four time, above the deafening din of the hand clapping, above the boisterous laughter and giggling of those who had stepped outside to "cool off" and were pressing one another against the quivering window sill of the open windows was heard the initiates with a note of frenzy in their shrill clear voices as they screamed the shout song, "De bell dun rung, de bell dun rung, de bell dun rung," which many of their associates in the circle were incoherently muttering with apparently little effort toward articulation. Just as a whirling dynamo generates a magnetic field, so this vibrant circle varying in diameter according to the endurance of the participants turning on, and on, seemed to create a desire which could not be satisfied until each one yielded to the irresistible urge to "git in dey widdem."[44]

The shout as a form of expression may have been a way of reconciling contradictory tendencies among individuals. Certainly not all of the participants were identically inspired, but probably had a number of different, authentic, subjective motivations and sought an outlet in a similar type of collective behavior. Hence, on the conscious level, the West African tradition notwithstanding, engaging in a ring shout had a variety of appeals for the Gullahs as slaves. It was a form of entertainment, a substitute for the social activity they were forced to relinquish, an individual release for pent-up frustrations and hostilities, a dimension of their religious spirit which linked them to natural and supernatural forces, and a mode of liaison among themselves. The following antebellum account of a Christmas shout on one of the Barnwell Sea Island plantations provides insight into the multifaceted meaning of this ceremony for the Gullahs:

The Negroes never went to sleep on the night before Xmas. They held prayers all night in the largest house at the settlement. This was Daddy January's house. Jack (foreman) could read and also August Baker our houseservant. Our mother had given both of them Testaments and Prayerbooks. I can still recall very distinctly the scene. The benches had all been taken outside to make a clear floor. The table with the books was shoved into a corner. A brilliant fire of lightwood was blazing in the chimney and a torch of the same hung in a tin bucket in a corner. Under this bucket the leader stood. She was a visitor. She was 50 or 60 years old, black and scrawney, only a few teeth left in her head. She had been singing for hours but still went on like one possessed. Gleaming with perspiration from head to heel—her dress at the bosom thrown wide open her head thrown back eyes closed, teeth prominent, head kerchief loose and hanging arms bare, clapping and shouting with a shrill ringing voice. I can recall in most of the other Negroes each with a different step, individual and characteristic. Some very much in earnest almost reverential, some heavy and stupid and some enjoying the fun. My grandmother's coachman "Sam" particularly, very black, good looking, smart and mischievous. I can recall the gleam of his eyes as he grinned at us in passing and improvised some peculiar contractions for our special benefit.[45]

For the Gullahs, then, the Christian experience was a means of communal fulfillment on the individual as well as collective level, and plantation life had aspects of an African village in microcosm. Gullahs attempted to exert control over their environment just as their African forbears had. For Africans it was a hostile natural ambiance that most threatened the group. For slaves it was an oppressive socioeconomic system that challenged their will to develop self-esteem and social cohesion. Gullahs successfully met that challenge and rose above bondage in a spiritual and communal sense. By combining the edifying features of Christianity and African culture and philosophy, they created a practical folk religion that served them well, under the travail of slavery.

The Plantation "street." (Personal Collection.)

Women and children in the evening after "Maussa's" task is done. (Courtesy of the New-York Historical Society, New York.)

Gullahs working for themselves. (Courtesy of the New-York Historical Society, New York.)

Laura M. Towne, Dick, Maria, and "seeker" Amoretta, February 1866. From the Schomburg Center for Research in Black Culture. (Courtesy of the New York Public Library.)

Gullah decorated grave. (The Library, University of Oregon.)

CHAPTER 10

Gullah Attitudes Toward Death and the Supernatural

"En when I trabbles de deep woods, whey de moss wabe low en Mr. Cooter lib en Mr. Moccasin crawl en de firefly flicker—meh packet fer load.

Yas'm. I'm ready fer em. Gunpowder en sulpher. Dey es say Plat Eye can't stan dem smell mix. . . . So I totes meh powder en sulper en I carries stick in meh han en puts meh truss in Gawd."*

Gullah's attached a tremendous significance to death, but there was little evidence of apprehension at the prospect of dying. Slaves lived in the presence of death so constantly that they seemed to consider the phenomenon as much a part of living as was their continuous labor. That they often reflected on the subject is evident in their spirituals. Yet these songs do not indicate that Gullahs thought of death with fear, foreboding, or morbidity. Perhaps it was partly this stoicism in the face of earthly demise that some observers viewed as resignation or the effects of demoralization. All African ethnic groups believed in life beyond physical death. Possibly Gullahs retained the West African bush-initiation experience in their attitude toward death. This idea of a symbolic journey to the world of the dead and a triumphant return might explain the Gullahs' ability to transcend feelings of dread about death and to disavow its ultimate power over them. But perhaps an equally strong influence was the BaKongo, since these societies had the most elaborate afterlife beliefs. The BaKongo four moments of the sun, as previously discussed,

---

*"Truss Gawd." South Carolina Folklore Project #1655, D-4-33, WPA, SCL.

implies that earthly death is the setting of the sun, or the third moment. Death was not the end of life, nor the cemetery a final resting place, but a door *(mwelo)* between two worlds. The fourth moment is midnight on earth when the sun is shining on the world of the dead. Here rebirth takes place. In any case, no matter what the unconscious motivation, what many considered to be a weakness among these bondspeople was actually a source of strength. They overcame a fear of death in light of the reality of its dominant presence among them, and through their realization that they, more so than most people, were often powerless to alter its course. Thus, while Gullahs did not shirk from death, they were sensitive to the degree to which their lives were exploited, and aware that oppression often caused an untimely end to life. The depth of their understanding of their position was sometimes grippingly demonstrated. Teacher William Allen was struck by how much the children sang of pain and death. Little "Margaret" came to the well to draw her pail of water. Putting it on her head, she walked off singing "shall I die—shall I die." She was followed by Tom and Abraham "galloping along on bamboo horses and shouting, 'my body rock 'long feber.' " Charlotte Forten was much affected by one of the hymns which she heard Gullah children singing:

> I wonder where my mudder gone;
>   Sing, O graveyard!
> Graveyard ought to know me;
>   Ring, Jerusalem!
> Grass grow in de graveyard;
>   Sing, O graveyard!
> Graveyard ought to know me;
>   Ring, Jerusalem!

It is impossible to give any idea of the deep pathos of the refrain,—
"Sing, O Graveyard."[1]

The pathos is there certainly, but the sense of hope, so characteristic of the Gullahs, is also present in the words "Grass grow in de graveyard." This could indicate that, in the BaKongo tradition, although there was death, there was also life and rebirth. The refrain "Graveyard ought to know me" might refer to the slaves' previous journey to the world of the dead as "seekers." The phrase could also recognize the omnipresence of death among the slaves.

Another spiritual expressed a sense of optimism and a superior attitude toward death:

> O Massa Death,
> He's a very little man,
> He goes from door to door;
> He kills some souls,
>   and he woundeth some.
> Good Lord remember me;
> Good Lord remember me;
> Remember me as the years roll round,
> Good Lord, remember me.[2]

In Christian belief the finality of death was often negated. One of the most appealing aspects of Christianity for Gullahs was the expectation of a better life after death. This afterlife was not visualized in the African sense, that an individual's status would not differ from one's mortal position. Instead, Gullahs strongly adopted the Christian concept of heaven, where all "true believers" would sit on "Christ's right side." For obvious reasons, this was one of the tenets of Christianity they most cherished.[3] While their African world view encouraged Gullahs to take a rich, positive attitude toward life, through Christian influence they expected a better life as payment for their suffering. As one person expressed it:

De harder me cross to bear down here de better I go be prepare to tek me place in dat Happy Land where all is 'joicin, an' when I git dere, I want de Lord to say, "Ophelia . . . come an' rest wid de elect ob de Lord!"[4]

There was little in Gullah prayers or songs to indicate they feared the tribunal expected to reward the "faithful" and damn the "sinners." Thus they disregarded that portion of their religious instruction which strenuously emphasized a judgment day where "every theft or falsehood" would be brought to light and held against them. What was more important to the Gullahs was a change in their conditions. Just as Baptist slavemaster Daniel Pope queried Marcus, the Praise House elder, as to whether the Gullahs really believed Christ wanted "black nigger in heben," so were slaves convinced that the "Kingdom of God" would have almost no white subjects. Gullah Christianity was one of recompense. Slaves accepted the Christian doctrine of eternal life but modified it so that heaven was an exclusive place, primarily available to sufferers of the right hue as expressed by a former slave:

It is impossible to reconcile the mind of the native slave to the idea of living in a state of perfect equality, and boundless affection with white people. Heaven will be no heaven to him, if he is not to be avenged of his enemies. I know, from experience, that these are fundamental rules of his religious creed; because I learned them in the religious meetings of the slaves themselves. A favorite and kind master or mistress may now and then be admitted into heaven, but this rather as a matter of favor, due to the intercession of some slave, than as a matter of strict justice to the whites, who will, by no means be of an equal rank with those who shall be raised from the depths of misery, in this world.
The idea of a revolution in the conditions of the whites and the blacks, is the cornerstone of the religion of the latter; and indeed it seems to me, at least, to be quite natural, if not in strict accordance with the precepts of the Bible.[5]

Although the Gullahs did not fear death, they recognized its power, and the passing of one of their number had a profound effect on the community. As has been noted, Methodist missionaries observed this and often tried to use the drama of death among the Gullahs to "bind them to the cross."[6] But while the Gullahs' perception of life after death was essentially of Christian origin, many practices associated with the dying and the dead were derived from African antecedents.

When death was expected, the plantation community felt compelled to enter into the spirit of the event and vicariously involve themselves in the death throes of the individual, lest when their time came they have to face the ordeal alone, or the deceased, dissatisfied with the send-off, would return and bring evil. The dying person was surrounded by the community, who offered comfort and support. "We got tuh help him cross de ribber," the Gullahs would say. Friends of the dying were expected to bring gifts even though the sufferer could not use them. Such offerings were usually edibles "tuh taste de mou't," but never flowers. Singing, praying, and pious conversation filled the cabin nightly. It was not a solemn time unless sad or obscure circumstances caused the death, but rather was somewhat cheerful, and the subject of death itself was not neglected. Everyone was expected to hold forth as part of the ritual of coaching the dying person to report a heavenly visit or some other evidence of "dying good." When the sufferer drew the last breath, everyone present gave a loud shriek as notification that another soul "done crossed ober." Many Northern teachers were repulsed at the Gullah "death-watch":

This practice of sitting up all night with the dying, H. W. [Harriet Ware] justly enough condemns as "heathenish." "The houses cannot hold them all, of course,

and they sit round out-of-doors in the street, the younger ones often falling asleep on the ground, and then they 'hab fever.' "
But of course it was useless to expostulate with them; to their minds the omission of the watch would be a mark of great disrespect.[7]

Like their African forebears, Gullahs believed in the presence of evil almost as much as they believed in the forces of good, and their attempts to please both God and the "powers of darkness" explain much about their customs regarding death. Even though they professed to believe that God "called" his servants to heaven, death was still looked upon as an instrument of the powers of darkness. Thus night vigils, singing, praying, and preaching around the bedside of the dying was supposed to strengthen the person as they "passed death's door." The loud shrieks as the last breath was drawn were said to be a formal announcement of the death, but also "scares off the spirits of hell who are always lurking around to get possession of another soul."[8]

Gullahs believed that one could not always know whether demise had come through natural causes because "God called," a "good" death, or by witchcraft, considered a "bad" death. This was also true of many African peoples. Among those of the Windward Coast, death reportedly came to people because God or the ancestors wanted them or because of witchcraft. If witchcraft was suspected, a rather gruesome postmortem was performed. Among the Mende and other groups, a "probing man" would be given permission to search the deceased's abdomen for evidence of witchcraft. The spleen was removed and placed in a pot containing a solution of certain leaves and water. If the spleen sank to the bottom of the pot, the deceased was declared a witch. If the spleen floated, the deceased was free of witchcraft. Among the BaKongo, the concept of "a bad or a good death" was also important. Characteristics indicating a bad death were the sick person quarreling with those present, having severe pains, or a prolonged death agony. If a person could not speak properly when dying, or turned his or her head toward the wall, a bad death was also suspected. A bad death meant a person was "shot with nkisi-guns," and was considered a *ndoki* or witch. A good death was a calm ordeal, peaceful and easy, with the person lying on his or her back.[9] Gullah attitudes about "good" and "bad" deaths were infused with African customs, though the death watch was viewed in a Christian context.

An individual was said to "die good," that is, of natural causes with no sorcery involved, by praying out loud, reporting a heavenly vision or giving some evidence that peace had been made with God on the death-bed. A pious life counted for little if this was not observed. Nor did an evil life mean damnation, if the dying could satisfy spectators with an appropriate heavenly vision. What was probably more important to Gul-lahs was that the deceased be at peace with the world, hence assuring the community that he or she was not a witch, or bewitched, and would not return to "haant" the living.[10]

Those spirits destined for hell did not actually go there until judgment day, according to Gullahs. Instead, these "on-easy speerits" roamed the earth, having no resting place, and tormented the living. Some Gullahs believed that good spirits went straight to heaven, but most seemed to think that even these spirits remained on earth, close to the place of their burial. Unlike those who "died bad," good spirits would normally not harm the living, nor would they roam. They appeared only in dreams, giving messages and warnings to the living. Thus Gullahs had a real concern for coaxing an individual to "die good," and a real superstition about those who "died bad." The slaves devised various mechanisms of defense against the latter spirits.[11]

Much of the Gullahs' attitude toward death and belief in spirits was inherited from the African respect for and honor of the living dead, and from the African belief in the power of sorcery. Consider, for instance, a description of death among the Mende:

When a dying man is panting for breath, the Mende say "Taa ha ha yiyei le ma" ("he is climbing the hill of death"). As soon as death is announced, the members of the family all begin to wail. The body of the deceased is then washed, and messages are sent to call the absent members of the family. . . . Members of the family will bring money, cloth, wine and rice as their contribution towards the funeral expenses. . . . On the fourth day for a man (the third day for a woman), the "crossing-the-river" ceremony takes place. . . . If these ceremonies are not properly performed, the evil will fall on those responsible.

Similarly, for Temne people, the underlying idea of funeral rites is to appease the spirit of the dead so they will not trouble the living. Mende also believe that separation of good and bad people takes place after their crossing the river. While there is no clear-cut idea as to who bad people are, they are chiefly thought of as those who dealt in "bad medicine or witchcraft." These evil ones in their spirit form will vent their feelings by sending disease and will manifest themselves by haunting the living and taking possession of them. Among the BaKongo, the curse of the dying is much dreaded, especially that of a relative, for the deceased will soon enter the spirit world. A dying person may admonish those around to take care of his or her affairs. "If you do not, I shall fetch you, and you will not become old here on earth." The dying one may also request the living to "wrap me well in the cloth that I leave," may insist that the living hold many lamentations after the death and care for the deceased's family. If not properly buried, the deceased might bring *kindoki* (evil).[12]

A curious example of the application of both African and Christian practices among the slaves is provided by a former South Carolina bondsman. According to the informant, a good-looking and very popular slave girl named Mary became ill and died after a lingering illness of four or six months' duration. The slaves on the surrounding plantations were sure that Mary had been conjured (poisoned) by a rival in a love triangle. The plantation proprietor, a Methodist minister, had Mary treated by his brother, a practicing physician. While the doctor was attending Mary, the slaves appealed to their own doctor, a plantation slave who also treated the young woman. But Mary died, and, according to the author, her funeral, which as was traditional took place at night, "was the largest ever held in all that region of the country":

The coffin, a rough home-made affair, was placed upon a cart, which was drawn by an old Gray, and the multitudes formed in a line in the rear, marching two deep. The procession was something like a quarter of a mile long. Perhaps every fifteenth person down the line carried an uplifted torch. As the procession moved slowly toward "the lonesome graveyard" down by the side of the swamp, they sung the well-known hymn of Dr. Issac Watts:

> "When I can read my title clear
> To mansions in the skies,
> I bid farewell to every fear
> And wipe my weeping eyes."

Mary's baby was taken to the graveyard by its grandmother, and before the corpse was deposited in the earth, the baby was passed from one person to another across the coffin. The slaves believed that if this was not done it would be impossible to raise the infant. The mother's spirit would come back for her baby and take it to herself.

After this performance the corpse was lowered into the grave and covered, each person throwing a handful of dirt into the grave as a last farewell act of kindness to the dead, and while this was being done the leader announced that other hymn by Dr. Watts:

> "Hark! from the tomb a doleful sound
> My ears, attend the cry;
> Ye living men, come view the ground
> Where you must shortly lie."

. . . A prayer was offered. . . . This concluded the services at the grave. No burial or commital service was read. . . . At a subsequent time, when all the relatives and friends could be brought together a big funeral sermon was preached by some of the antebellum negro preachers.

The presence of a plantation slave "doctor" is reminiscent of the Ba-Kongo *nganga*, who employed life-affirming *nkisi* to heal and ward off bad medicine or *kindoki*. The charm did not work for the plantation slave, and the large funeral turn-out may represent the people's desire to protect themselves from whatever evil had caused Mary's death as well as to express their respect. Passing the woman's baby back and forth over her coffin was a well-known Gullah graveside custom. "Dead moder will hant de baby," Gullahs explained, and "worry him in his sleep." A similar custom among the BaKongo was women crossing back and forth over the graveside of a woman who died in childbirth, hoping that such a fate would not befall them. Singing at the grave was also part of the BaKongo send-off. The funeral, a lavish affair, would take place when all members of the clan could gather and when enough food could be collected.[13]

Thus another aspect of Gullah religion was a syncretic blend of belief in the efficacy of Christian salvation, the prevalence of the living dead, and the awesome powers of conjuration. It was sometimes difficult to determine where they believed the most power rested. At any rate, their expression, "Love God and fear the devil" indicates that, as a precautionary measure, they preferred to respect the authority and domain of both. For Gullahs saw no contradiction in being firm proponents of the Baptist faith and protecting themselves against forces of the supernatural as well. In spite of the Gullahs' strong profession of Christianity, Laura Towne noted that "They believe in the evil eye, and also in the power of a good eye for healing," and that "they are afraid of being alone at night, or of sleeping alone, for fear 'the hag will ride we.' " A slaveholding South Carolina minister remembered Elihu, a "devout, old creditable deacon" of the church and highly respected exhorter in the slave quarters. Upon passing the old man's cabin, the owner observed an inverted horseshoe over the door. Since Elihu's skill as a hostler was well known, the owner assumed that the horseshoe was a "professional sign." However, the insignia was instead a charm against supernatural agencies:

"What is that over your door Elihu?"
"Dat for witches, Massa."
"For what?"
"Witches, Massa. Nebber sleep, no how, widout horseshoe to keep out de witches.[14]

Thus, besides the Christian version of immortality, elements of African tradition also accounted for the Gullahs' attitude toward death, as indeed it did in their attitude about life. As previously stated, existence of spirits of the deceased was not only central to African ontology, but these beings constituted the largest group of religious intermediaries. Hence, Africans viewed death as perhaps the most important rite of passage rather than as the demise of life. Death was a momentous transition, requiring demonstrative evidence that the physical presence of the deceased would be missed. But it was just as necessary to celebrate this passage into the spirit world in a manner that indicated a continued existence. Africans believed that the spirit which survived the body was conscious of all earthly events and had the power to exercise influence over the destiny of the living. Consequently, the death of a clan member was observed with greatest respect and the death commemoration had to be expressed collectively.[15]

Ancestors were said to retain their normal human passions and appetites which had to be gratified in death as they had been in life. Ancestors felt hunger and thirst. They became angry or happy depending on the behavior of their living "children." If neglected, the living dead were vindictive, but propitious if respected. Just as filial loyalty prevents one from allowing a parent to go hungry, "so must food be offered to the ancestors." Among the BaKongo, food was put out immediately after the burial and palm wine poured over the grave. Survivors believed the deceased would eat the food, and bless those who placed it there.[16]

Among the Gullahs, even for one who "died good," the spirit could not rest if something had been left behind which it desired. It was observed that the Gullahs and other African-Americans placed articles on newly formed graves. These objects were usually personal belongings, broken pottery and porcelain, playthings, lighting utensils, objects pertaining to medicine, food, and water. According to the antebellum memories of Telfair Hodgson, a number of her father's slaves came directly from Africa. The slaves' graves were "always decorated with the last articles used by the departed, and broken pitchers, and broken bits of colored glass were considered even more appropriate than the white shells from the beach nearby." Sometimes the slaves also carved "wooden figures like images of idols," or put a "patchwork quilt" on the grave. One twentieth-century investigator, Samuel Lawton, was told by a number of Sea Island ministers that it was also a common custom to bury articles along with the dead:

> You must not think that just because you do not find anything on those graves that the relatives did not put some things in there. It is most likely that they have a number of things buried with the body. I have often, at the burials I have conducted, seen the relatives pour hamper baskets full of things right down on top of the coffin before the dirt is shoveled into the grave.[17]

The custom of putting objects both in and on top of graves can be traced to African origins. The Ovimbundu place articles such as baskets, gourds, and instruments used in the burial on top of grave sites. Peoples in the Kongo were said to "mark the final resting-places of their friends by ornamenting their graves with crockery, empty bottles, old cooking-pots, etc." Many ethnic groups of the Windward Coast believed that it was necessary to provide the dead with various gifts, domestic articles, and clothing that could be of use in the life beyond the grave. Such articles, along with food and water, would be left at the grave, so that the spirit of the deceased would come and claim them.[18]

Although the Gullahs believed in two spirits, it was the "trabblin" spirit rather than the heaven-going spirit which caused the greatest concern. The reasons given for grave adornment clearly indicate the African precedent. One informant related:

> Yo' see, suh, everybody got two kinds ob speerits. One is der hebben-goin' speerit. . . . Den dere is de trabblin' speerit. . . . De hebben-goin' speerit don't gib you no trouble, but de trabblin' speerit, 'e be de one dat gib you worriment. E come back to de t'ings 'e like. E try fur come right back in de same house.[19]

Some Africans regarded their essential being as divided into "little me in the big me." Apparently "little me" existed before life and would continue to exist after death in the spirit world. This relates to the Gullah informant's idea of two kinds of spirits. The heaven-going spirit, "little me," depending on how one died, would, after death, rest in the spirit world while the traveling spirit would torment the living. Hence, Gullahs asserted that the last used articles were buried with the deceased to "keep de speerit outen de house." This would go along with the Gullah practice of thoroughly cleaning the deceased's house to break earthly ties. Another explanation which the Gullahs offered was "to satisfy de speerit at de grave." It was said that the spirit desired to be near objects that it loved before death. "Yessuh," stated one informant, "dey puts t'ings on de grave so dey be handy fur de speerit and he be satisfy."[20]

Like Africans, Gullahs had a definite revulsion against the return of the deceased in the form of "trabblin' speerits" regardless of the kind of life the individual had lived. These spirits were considered evil, similar to *kindoki* among the BaKongo. Every effort was made to pacify these "speerits." This is further illustrated by the presence of whiskey bottles on the graves in churchyards. A Gullah minister provided the following explanation:

> When a man is living it take liquid whiskey in he stomach to make him drunk, but when a man is dead he don't hab a stomach to hol' de liquor, but it don't take nuttin' but de fumes from whiskey to make a speerit drunk. Dose dat bin used to gittin' drunk fo' dey dies, dey will keep on gittin' drunk after dey dies, so dey t'ink dat de speerit ob a drunkard will hover right in front ob de mout' ob a livin' person when he bin drinkin' so he can whiff de fumes ob de whiskey on he bre't an' dat will make de speerit drunk. But ain't no livin' man want no speerit hover right dere in front ob he mount', so dat is why dey puts whiskey bottles on de drunkard's grave. De whiskey bottles on de graves is empty 'cause de smell is enough to satisfy de speerit an' make 'en drunk.[21]

Gold Coast Africans believed that the spirits made use of all offerings left by friends and relatives after death. Mende carried to the graveside cooked chicken together with rice and red palm oil. This mixture was placed on a banana leaf and laid by the side of the grave. Sometimes soil was dug out and the red rice placed in a hole. Then a little water was placed on the grave and words were spoken: "Here is water, wash your hands, eat your rice, drink your water." The family then ate the remainder of the chicken and rice and offered a prayer, indicating that the family had done right by the deceased and expected the dead to remain there and to protect them:

We are leaving you as we have finished your last ceremony. We want you, from now on, to look after your children (other members of the family may be mentioned). May no bad thing fall on them.[22]

Similarity of beliefs and motives regarding grave adornment is best illustrated by the types of articles found on graves in the Sea Islands. Such objects as partially filled medicine bottles, mirrors, broken pitchers, saucers and cups, mayonnaise jars, pickle jars, vaseline, cold cream, tobacco, and black pepper were placed on graves. Seashells were also commonly placed on graves. Other personal items included shaving brushes, toothbrushes, mirrors, combs, and belt buckles. In addition, twelve Gullah ministers reported to Samuel Lawton that other articles of food such as grapes, oranges, apples, bananas, bread, and cake were often placed on graves and soon eaten by animals and birds. Further efforts to satisfy the spirits of the dead consisted of pouring water on the grave during a drought. This custom could have been for the purpose of quenching the thirst of the spirit so that the dead would not disturb the living by seeking water.[23]

Gullah decoration of graves indicates a firm belief in the return of ancestors from the world of the dead. Offerings on graves were statements of homage and in these graveyards, one finds the strongest expressions of African-inspired memories. Many objects are associated with or used to hold water. In BaKongo religion, deceased ancestors became white creatures called *bakulu*. They lived in the village of the dead, referred to as the land of all things white. This village was located under river beds and lakes. *Bakulu's* white spiritual transparency allowed them to return to the world of the living undetected. Sea shells, used on Gullah graves, for instance, are an important theme in BaKongo metaphysics. One BaKongo prayer which addresses the shells states, "As strong as your house, you shall keep my life for me. When you leave for the sea, take me along, that I may live forever." The essence of this prayer is recaptured by the late Bessie Jones of St. Simons Island, Georgia. She related:

The shells stand for the sea. The sea brought us, the sea shall take us back. So the shells upon our graves stand for water, the means of glory and the land of demise.[24]

Just as sea shells and pottery express immortal existence, and the significance of a water underworld, so the glittering, iridescent mirrors and porcelain on Gullah graves reflect the light which represents the spirit. These objects, like water when struck by sunlight, are intimations of the flash of the separated spirit in symbolized flight. Mirrors, lamps, porcelain, and glass are spirit-embodying once they are placed on the graves.

Their presence keeps the spirit away from the living. The significance of spiritual proximity in brilliance gave rise to the BaKongo custom of lighting bonfires on graves to lead one's soul to another world. Similarly, Gullah torchlight burials may have had a deeper meaning than simply lighting the path. Certainly the presence of lamps on African-American graves indicates that perhaps this was a means of lighting the way to the world beyond, and keeping away the deceased's spirit. Furthermore, the decorations imply the deceased's entrance into the fourth moment, a spiritual existence where all is light and brilliance. Breaking pottery and porcelain was perhaps not done to prevent theft, as some researchers believe, but may indicate the deceased's spiritual release and break with earthly life.[25]

Another interesting continuity between Gullah and African traditions in regard to burial is the position of the deceased. In Central West Africa, the coffin is placed so that the deceased faces eastward. Folklorist Elsie Parsons noted that Gullah graves were "invariably dug east to west, with the head to the west." Thomas Higginson wrote in his diary of a "very impressive" funeral for two black soldiers in his regiment. Just before the coffins were lowered, "an old man whispered to me that I must have their positions altered,—the heads must be towards the west." Higginson complied without asking why. Gullahs and Africans shared a concept of the cosmos. The world followed the sun from east to west.[26]

Sea Island slaves retained a belief in the power of agents of evil and easily included the Christian devil in their hierarchy. Ghosts, hags, plateyes, conjurers, and others were all instruments of Satan. At times their faith in God may not have surpassed their fear of the devil.[27] On other occasions God could, for the sake of "the faithful," take the role of a conjurer and bring evil instead of good. Although Gullahs believed that Satan and his cohorts were mainly responsible for evil, they also felt that God was sometimes willing to bring evil down upon an adversary of one of His own. In the following illustration, God reportedly used His power in this way. July Brown was a high officer in one of the churches on Edisto Island. When he was interviewed in the 1930s for the Federal Writers Project, he related the story of how he once prayed a man to death:

I been on de Savannah train goin' to Charleston. My wallet been jam down deep in my hip pocket. Must ob had 'bout twenty dollars in um. Lo and behold when I git to de Union station, I feel in my pocket to git street cyar money, and my wallet done gone! I notice dat when I come out ob de train uh black, shaap face nigger been press close to me. I say: "Dats de bery man steal my money." I'quire roun de station and find out who he be. Dey say he uh man from John Island and dey call 'e name to me.

No, I ain't make no 'temp to call de police. Dat man done spend de money anyhow. I jest say: "All right. I goin' to leave yuh wid God."

When I git home, I shet my door and put de whole ting 'fore God. I tell um my trouble and what dat man done 'gainst me. In two week time dat man jest as stiff and cold as uh piece ob iron.[28]

This may be similar to the power of *nkisi*, essentially a positive force working for the good, to ward off *kindoki*, and thus doing an evil deed. Generally speaking, however, the deity represented forces of good. Gullahs believed in the power of God and saw that power as a form of protection. This may perhaps explain why interviewers for the Federal Writers Project observed that nearly all the doors and windows of Gullah cabins were painted blue, the color of the heavens. One theory was that the custom of painting doors and windows blue was an unconscious holdover from the early days of slavery in the Sea Islands when Gullahs were given the residue from indigo vats to use on the doors and windows of their cabins. However this does not explain the fact that Gullah conjurers concocted pills for their "patients" the color of which was usually blue also. Perhaps then, the shade blue was effective in keeping out "speerits." Spirits were said to be afraid of blue because it reminded them of heaven, hence evil beings could not stand the sight of blue. But the Gullahs themselves would not verify either notion regarding their preference for blue. If asked why they painted their doors and windows blue, Gullahs would smile wryly and say some people "jest lak dat color."[29]

Thus, while Gullahs turned gratefully to the Christian God, whom they regarded as a warm, personal friend, this did not prevent them from retaining some of their ingrained customs and beliefs, as is observed in their attitudes toward life, death and the supernatural. And, even in the Gullahs' approach toward death, a sense of community prevailed. The ritual was observed with respect and responsibility. There was a feeling of satisfaction that, while the individual had to cross the river alone, the right impetus had been given before the deceased left the earth, and thus the living had done their part by fulfilling their collective obligation for the last time.

A direct relationship appears to exist between the African and Gullah theory of being. In both, God (Jesus for the Gullahs) was the apex, representing honor, constancy, harmony, and perfection, while humanity occupied the center, ever striving to be godlike through a sense of love, community, kinship, and cooperation. In addition, the good and bad of the spirit world existed in both traditions although it was far more complex for Africans than for Gullahs. These beings included superhumans, animals, and objects without biological life.[30] Gullahs applied the African ontology, adapted Christianity and bondage to it, and created a religion that employed spirituality as a means of self-preservation and as a vital component of community life. It is, then, to the Gullahs' credit that though circumstances prevented them from rising up against slavery, they did not succumb to white cultural domination. Instead, they successfully rose above many of the negative ingredients of Christianity while assimilating certain other attributes which were synthesized with African culture. In bondage, Gullahs achieved elevation on the level of personal culture and the molding of community values. The edifying qualities of Gullah religious belief must be seen as having contributed much to that achievement, just as an element of truth must be recognized in the assertion that insofar as people develop their own culture they are not slaves.[31]

Epilogue

Slavery chain done broke at last!
Broke at last! Broke at last!
Slavery chain done broke at last!
Gonna praise God till I die!

Way up in that valley,
Pray-in' on my knees,
Tell-in' God a-bout my troubles,
And to help me if He please.

I did tell him how I suffer,
In the dungeon and the chain;
And the days I went with head bowed
    down,
An' my broken flesh and pain.

I did know Jesus heard me,
'Cause the spirit spoke to me,
An' said, "Rise, my chile, your children
An' you too shall be free."

I done 'p'int one mighty captain
For to marshal all my hosts;
An' to bring my bleeding ones to me,
An' not one shall be lost."

Now no more weary trav'lin',
'Cause my Jesus set me free,
An' there's no more auction block for me
Since He give me liberty.*

The Thirteenth Amendment, which ended all slavery in the United States, barely slipped through the House of Representatives with the necessary two-thirds vote on January 31, 1865. But for the Gullahs, the "Year of Jubilo" was January 1, 1863, when Abraham Lincoln's Emancipation Proclamation declared them "forever free." It was the first truly Happy New Year the Gullahs ever had, and they marked it with a festive occasion organized by General Saxton. The celebration took place in Beaufort. The multitude consisted of the "First South" Regiment, many "white visitors," superintendants, officers, dignitaries, and the band of the Eighth Maine. From the Islands and surrounding mainland came the now for-

* Quoted from Leon Litwack, *Been in the Storm So Long: The Aftermath of Slavery* (New York: Alfred A. Knopf, 1979), 167.

mer slaves, "chiefly colored woman with gay handkerchiefs on their heads, and a sprinkling of men" (since most able-bodied males were in the army). All the blacks reportedly "had the bearing and distinct respectable look they always had on Sundays and holidays." The services began with a prayer. The Emancipation Proclamation was read by William Brisbane, a South Carolinian who freed his slaves before the war. Then the chaplin presented the colors to the regiment—all according to program. After the chaplin's introductory remarks, and just as Higginson "took and waved the flag," but before he began to speak, the "unexpected," and "startling" occurred. A "strong" but "cracked and elderly" male voice was heard. Instantly, two female voices blended in as if by "an impulse too strong to be repressed." They sang:

> My Country, 'tis of thee,
> Sweet land of liberty,
>   Of thee I sing!

They went on "verse after verse" as the people on the platform appeared stunned. "It seemed the choked voice of a race at last unloosed," Higginson wrote. The rest of the blacks joined in and the whites also began, but Higginson motioned the latter to silence. "I never saw anything so electric," he wrote. "It made all other words seem cheap." "Art," wrote Higginson, "could not have dreamed of a tribute to the day of Jubilee . . . history will not believe it . . . tears were everywhere." Corporal Robert Sutton, a favorite of Higginson's, spoke, vowing that no black soldier would rest until all his brothers and sisters were free. "Boys," he vowed, "we will take Christ for our Captain who never lost a battle."[1]

The moment of freedom, more than any event, bound African-Americans to Christianity. Their deliverance from the house of bondage "by no man,"[2] as they believed, did more to instill faith in Christianity than any doctrines taught by whites.

Although religious instruction was intended as a conservative element in slave life, and clearly it did not provide the bondspeople with a successful ideology of revolt, slave religion, a synthesis of African and Christian traditions, was used in a progressive manner by slaves. Their application of collective moral principles under the guise of Christianity illustrates how religion can be used effectively to keep a community spiritually alive and culturally creative during a period of historical crisis. Although religion was at the heart of the Gullahs' process of socialization in the slave quarters, this did not imply total acceptance of a Judeo-Christian concept of reality. The Gullahs broadened the meaning of Christianity, organizing and integrating it into past beliefs and practices. Two traditions formed the basis of the Gullahs' struggle against slavery. The example of Christ allowed them to take a superior attitude toward their oppressors. But they also exerted spiritual and psychological autonomy by clinging to Africanity. In their isolation, the Gullahs remained an uprooted people whose acceptance of Christianity was sometimes outward, selective, and subject to reinterpretations which would not force them to relinquish old ways entirely. Of course, African beliefs, where these remained, accommodated the slave situation just as Christianity, to some extent, accommodated African religion and philosophy. Where Protestantism did not tolerate Africanity as a separate expression, Africanisms sometimes continued through secretiveness or by finding a place at the center of Protestantism as practiced by the slaves.

As Lawrence Levine notes, freedom placed the slaves in a culturally marginal situation, and weakened their "cultural self-containment." No longer were values and cultural standards determined from within the group. African-Americans found themselves in a bicultural situation, absorbing elements of the dominant society in order to obtain recognition and privileges. Perhaps at the moment of freedom the period of accommodation began as a significant factor in black life. Nowhere is this more pronounced than in the organization of the black church. This point may be most easily illustrated by the motif of the gospel songs and their otherworldly context, whereas the slave spirituals were full of camouflaged prayers for freedom. As Levine points out, the period after bondage reflects a changing consciousness.[3] Slave religion bred radicalism in the early years, and progressivism later. The institutionalized black church, formed after freedom, was far more powerful and independent, but often counseled conservatism.

Sam Polite lived long past bondage. He was over one hundred years old when he prayed the prayer of "The Long Look." He had grown up in slavery, lived through emancipation, reconstruction, restoration, and into the twentieth century of segregation. Still he prayed the prayer of hope. Still he asked for a sign—a look at the future for his people. Polite's prayer implied what history has revealed—that the "New Jerusalem" evaded the African-Americans after freedom. The emancipation experience, born of hope and optimism, brought a new kind of bondage.

Gullahs and other African-Americans were to readjust to the new religion that served them so well in bondage. Slave religion was an adaptive and vital spiritualism, a guide for living and for struggle. Acceptance of Christianity had little to do with accommodating slavery. Acceptance of segregation after freedom, without a struggle, owed much to the creeping conservatism within the black church.

One hundred years after the Emancipation Proclamation took effect, a black religious leader spoke out that "the Negro is not free." Outside forces that prevented black equality are well known. Historical forces within black society, on the leadership level, have been analyzed but little. Gullahs and other African-Americans did not come out of bondage unscathed. But they did emerge, for the most part, psychologically and communally intact. Though toughened by generations of bitter servitude, they maintained an optimistic spirit. Gullahs were not accommodationists in 1863 and 1865, but a community hoping and eager to take their place as citizens. They were aware of their strength as a people. What happened to erode the African-American sense of worldly confidence was not so much born of slavery as it was the product of unfulfilled promises from the national sector and perhaps disappointed leadership from the black institutional religious community in the years of the first freedoms and afterward. As W. E. B. DuBois stated, the greatness of black religion can only be found in its link with the "spiritual strivings of the black masses," as it takes a stand on social and political issues affecting African-Americans.

Gullahs and the Carolina Lowcountry. (Personal Collection.)

Ethnic Origins of Carolina Slaves

This appendix explains my own tabulations for ethnic origins of Carolina slaves. A valuable source of information for studying African origins was published in four volumes by Elizabeth Donnan. Her works are based on primary sources consisting of ships' records, newspaper advertisements, records of the Royal African Company, the correspondence of Henry Laurens and other merchants, and various documents illustrating the pattern and magnitude of the international slave trade. Donnan's volume on the Southern colonies was particularly useful for examining the slave trade to Carolina because the records of that colony were so well preserved and because white Carolinians made a fetish of regional provenance where human cargo was concerned. From these data we obtain an impression of the coastal origins of many cargoes entering Charleston harbor, and it appears that Africans of the Windward Coast and Senegambia regions provided South Carolina with the majority of its forced laborers for nearly forty years.

Table A.1 represents my calculation of the ethnic origins of slaves entering South Carolina during the middle period of the international slave trade. It was compiled from a tabulation of lists of cargoes published by Elizabeth Donnan. Table A.2 is a rough numerical calculation of slaves identifiable by African origins entering Charleston during the middle period of the trade. Since many cargoes did not indicate size, our estimate for this unknown was based upon the average number of slaves on vessels which did indicate the size of their cargo. Deliberately ex-

TABLE A.1

Number and Percentage of Cargoes of Identifiable Origin Imported from 1749 to 1787 (Middle Period)

Coastal Region of Origin	No. of Cargoes	Percentage
Senegambia	102	32.4
Windward Coast	90	28.6
Gold Coast	54	17.2
Bight of Benin		
Bight of Biafra	25	7.9
Angola (including Gaboon and the Kongo)	35	11.1
Others: Whydah, Bance Island, Isle de Los	9	2.8
Total	315	100.0

Source: Elizabeth Donnan, *Documents Illustrative of the History of the Slave Trade to America,* 4 vols. (Washington, D.C.: Carnegie Institution, 1935) vol. 4, passim; and *South Carolina Gazette.*

TABLE A.2

Numerical Estimate of Slaves Identifiable by Origin Imported from 1749 to 1787 (Middle Period)

Coastal Region of Origin	Cargoes with Numerical Count		Cargoes without Numerical Count		Total Cargoes	Total Slaves (Est.)
	No. of Cargoes	No. of Slaves	No. of Cargoes	Est. Slaves		
Senegambia	66	10,499	36	5,724	102	16,223
Windward Coast	65	11,135	25	4,275	90	15,410
Gold Coast	37	6,240	17	2,856	54	9,096
Angola	33	7,480	2	454	35	7,934
Bight of Benin						
Bight of Biafra	18	3,343	7	1,302	25	4,665
Others	7	956	2	274	9	1,230
Total	226	39,653	89	14,885	315	54,538

Source: Elizabeth Donnan, *Documents,* vol. 4, passim.

cluded from tables A.1 and A.2 are those vessels which indicated only the West Indies as the source of origin. Such listings meant the slaves were purchased in the West Indies from an arriving African cargo, or that the ship had stopped in the West Indies and disposed of most of its African cargo. Cargoes listed as simply from the West Indies were usually quite small and often contained Creole New World-born slaves.

As discussed in the text, research indicates that the majority of slaves in Carolina by 1740 were chiefly from Kongo-Angola. This was also the largest group imported into South Carolina during the entire slave trade as illustrated in table A.3, which was taken from Philip D. Curtin's *Atlantic Slave Trade*. However, Curtin's percentages may be misleading for purposes of examining African cultural influence in coastal Carolina because he lumps the entire slave trade period together. Up to 1740, the end of the first period of the Carolina trade, Kongo-Angolans were the majority. But as evident from tables A.1 and A.2, during the period of high economic growth and large-scale slave importation in the Sea Island region, these Africans composed a relatively small percentage of total cargoes with known coastal origins. Africans from the Kongo-Angola region do not again figure heavily in South Carolina trade until the nineteenth century. Curtin has no separate breakdown for these years (1804–1807), when many Kongo-Angola peoples were imported (see tables A.4 and A.5) chiefly, but not exclusively, for the benefit of up-country plantations and new territories. At the time, South Carolina was the only state importing slaves and supplied other states as well. In the nineteenth century, despite the emergence of Sea Island cotton as an export of growing significance, many coastal and Sea Island planters were well supplied with slaves and expressed strong hostility to reopening of the international trade in 1803. Concerned about the depreciation of their own slave property, as well as the prospect of slave revolts, these planters were instrumental in the near-defeat of the bill to reopen the African slave

TABLE A.3

Percentage of Slaves of Identifiable Origin Imported from 1733 to 1807

Coastal Region of Origin	Percentage
Senegambia	19.5
Windward Coast (including Sierra Leone)	23.1
Gold Coast	13.3
Bight of Benin, Bight of Biafra	3.7
Angola	39.6
Mozambique, Madagascar	0.7
Total	100.0

Source: Philip D. Curtin, *Atlantic Slave Trade: A Census* (Madison-University of Wisconsin Press, 1969), 157, Table 45.

TABLE A.4
Percentage of Cargoes of Identifiable Origin Imported from
1804 to 1807 (Final Period)

Coastal Region of Origin	No. of Cargoes	Percentage
Senegambia	11	7.5
Windward Coast	44.5	30.5
Gold Coast	23.5	16.0
Bright of Benin, Bight of Biafra	3	2.0
Angola	55	37.7
Others	9	6.3
Total	90.0	100.0

Source: Elizabeth Donnan, *Documents*, vol. 4, passim.

TABLE A.5
Numerical Estimate of Slaves Identifiable by Origin Imported from
1804 to 1807 (Final Period)

Coastal Region of Origin	Cargoes with Numerical Count		Cargoes without Numerical Count		Total Cargoes	Total Slaves (Est.)
	No. of Cargoes	No. of Slaves	No. of Cargoes	No. of Slaves		
Senegambia	4	290	6	73	10	435
Windward Coast	33	4,374	16	2,096	49	6,470
Gold Coast	16	2,416	7	1,057	23	3,624
Angola	50	14,440	5	1,694	55	16,134
Bight of Benin Bight of Biafra	6	1,809	1	301	7	2,412
Others	2	473	—	—	2	473
Total	111	23,802	40	5,221	151	29,023

Source: Elizabeth Donnan, *Documents*, vol v. 4, passim.

trade in South Carolina. Thus, Philip Curtin's percentages, which cover the years 1733–1807, are too broad chronologically to adequately represent the pattern of the slave trade in regard to cultural geography.

In *The Myth of the Negro Past*, Melville J. Herskovits provided what appeared to be a good source of ethnic information. Using raw material supplied by Elizabeth Donnan, Herskovits developed a numerical tabulation of slave imports into South Carolina for the years 1733–1785 in

TABLE A.6

*Number of Slaves Identifiable by Origin Imported from
1733 to 1785 (Middle Period)*

Coastal Region of Origin	No. Imported
Origin given as "Africa"	4,146
From the Gambia to Sierra Leone	12,441
Sierra Leone	3,906
Rice and Grain Coasts	3,851
"Guinea Coast" (Gold Coast to Calabar)	18,240*
Angola	11,485
Congo	10,924
Mozambique	243
East Africa	230
Total Imported from Africa	65,466
Total Imported from the West Indies	2,303
Total Number of Imports	67,796

*Herskovits notes that of this number only 1,168 slaves were brought in ships sailing from "Benin," "Bonny," "New Calabar," and "Old Calabar." Melville J. Herskovits, *The Myth of the Negro Past*, p. 305 n.

Source: Melville J. Herskovits, *The Myth of the Negro Past* (Boston-Beacon Press, 1958; repr. from 1941 ed.) p. 48.

order to determine ethnic origin and influence among Africans imported into that state (see table A.6). However, Herskovits' computation somewhat confuses the issue of provenance in regard to the Sea Island region because it is based only on the available number of slaves from various regions rather than on the number of cargoes as well, and the percentage of cargoes from a particular area. In many cases, neither Donnan nor the Charleston newspapers (which were her main source) reported the number of slaves in a given cargo. Donnan's information on total yearly imports was not based on individual computation but derived from annual figures printed in newspapers that did not distribute imports on the basis of coastal origin. Thus, Herskovits apparently tabulated only cargoes which listed the African *coastal origin* and indicated the *size* of the cargo as well. This makes his numerical tabulation unreliable.

Another problem with Herskovits' tabulation for this study is that his estimates partly cover the period in which the Sea Islands were only sparsely settled (the early period). Hence, we cannot obtain a clear indication of the ethnic origins of Sea Island Gullahs from Herskovits' information. It seems that a more reasonable estimated of sources of origin can be obtained by using the *number* of cargoes of known African origin, as is done in table A.1, rather than using *cargo size* as a primary indicator. Yet, both table A.1 and table A.2 illustrate that during the middle period of the slave trade a large, new migrant group was added to the African-Carolinian population.

Excerpts from a "Missionary Sketch" Written by Thomas D. Turpin to the Christian Advocate and Journal, January 31, 1834.

. . . the number of adults to whom I had access in preaching were about 1,000, one third of whom were in the Baptist Church and in the negroes societies, and almost all of them under Baptist influence; and that a great many of those lived on an island who scarcely ever saw the pastor of the Church to which they belong. Hence they had societies organized among themselves; and that those societies were very corrupt, and appeared to be very much under the influence of Roman Catholic principles; and that they did penance, and the following was a specimen, viz; that they had three degrees of punishment, and that the punishment was inflicted agreeably to the magnitude of the crime, according to their view of the crime. If the crime was of the first magnitude, the perpetrator had to pick up a quart of benne seed poured on the ground by the priest; and if of the second, a quart of rice; and if of the third, a quart of corn; and that they also had high seats and low seats, but incorrect views relative to those who ought to be punished; and that it was also a rule among them never to divulge the secret of stealing; and if it should be divulged by any one member, that one had to go on the low seat, or pick up the benne seed. I observed, having to contend with all this superstition and ignorance, together with their prejudices against Methodism, that I had added very few to the Church; and I had, moreover, strived very little to do this, but rather strived to beat down their prejudices and to establish a better principle of religion among them, all of which I should not presume any person in this low country would attempt to contradict.

But it appears to have injured the feelings of many of the Baptist friends. I did not intend to injure their feelings, nor any other persons. Notwithstanding, though it has been said, that I have shot a ball particularly at the Baptists, and in its glance it has hit the Episcopalians. If it has made any mortal wound by its being received in a light different from what I intended I feel it my duty to heal the wound.

In regard to the words Baptist influence, it has also been observed, that it has generally been received as intending to mean that the whites have knowledge of those corruptions among the negroes, and tolerate them. I had no such meaning. I simply meant that the negroes were under the peculiar influence of the Baptist tenets. Now, unless the Baptist tenets tolerate the doing of penance (which the world knows to the contrary), it could not mean that they tolerated these things among the negroes. It is notorious that almost all of the negroes in the bounds of my mission are prejudiced in favor of the Baptist Church.

As it respects the picking up of the benne seed, it has been said that it was not a very likely thing that it could be done in one night. In answer to this, I heard a gentleman say, no longer than last week, that the rule was, if it was not done in one night, they had to continue until they did it—Again, as regards those of whom I spoke, who scarcely ever saw the pastor of the Church to which they belong, they were a set of negroes belonging to Andrew Marshall's church of Savannah. It may be objected that Andrew Marshall is nothing more than a negro. If he is, that does not derogate at all from the truth of the assertion made in the letter stated above. The negro has been authorized by the Church to preach and baptize.—He has done it, and he has baptized a great many in this low country; and those of whom I spoke are in that number. He is the only pastor that those negroes have on the island. He never comes to see them, nor any other Baptist minister. Therefore the facts remains, there are many negroes on Bull's Island that scarcely ever see the pastor of the Church to which they belong. This is the light in which I intended it should be received . . . the little negroes improve on the mission, but the adults are about the same as represented in the above statement.

APPENDIX C

Baptist Churches

TABLE C. I

State of the Churches within the Savannah River Baptist Association in 1833

Churches	Constituted	Number Baptized	Membership
* 1 Euhaw	1745	43	841
2 Beach Branch	1759	65	132
3 Healing Springs	1772	7	143
* 4 Pipe Creek	1776	38	287
5 Treadaway	1776	6	66
6 Columbia	1780	2	115
* 7 Black Swamp	1786	11	294
8 Great Saltcatcher	1793	59	127
9 Barnwell	1803	13	126
10 Springtown	1803	66	244
*11 Beaufort	1804	239	1,292
12 Rosemary	1804	11	114
13 Willow Swamp	1805	0	34
14 Union	1805	7	220
15 Little Saltcatcher	1807	21	50
*16 St. Helena	1809	138	536
*17 May River	1811	36	621
18 Beulah	1811	0	20
*19 Prince Williams	1813	70	140
20 Steep Bottom	1814	3	44
21 Cypress Creek	1814	41	144
22 Double Ponds	1825	1	58
23 Philadelphia	1827	9	75
24 Kirkland	1827	12	162
25 Black Creek	1827	69	111
26 M't Pleasant	1828	4	38

TABLE C. I *(continued)*
State of the Churches within the Savannah River Baptist Association in 1833

Churches	Constituted	Number Baptized	Membership
27 3 Mile Creek	1829	29	64
28 Matlock	1830	0	33
29 Bethesda	1830	8	30
30 Steel Creek	1830	23	71
31 Joico's Branch	1831	3	30
32 Ebenezer	1831	3	21
33 Coosawatchie	1832	34	196
34 Beach Island	1832	0	38
*35 Hilton Head	1832	86	212
36 Sardia	1833	14	33
37 Pleasant Prospect	1833	0	43
Total		471	6,805

*Beauford District churches with large memberships and which are on or near the Sea Islands.
Source: *Minutes of the Savannah River Baptist Association,* November 23, 1833, 11, BC.

TABLE C.2
State of the Churches within the Savannah River Baptist Association in 1842

Churches	Number Baptized	Membership	By Whom Supplied
*Euhaw	. . . No Report . . .		W. A. Lawton
Beach Branch	0	71	E. Estes
Healing Springs	1	104	D. Peeples
*Pipe Creek	12	131	I. Nicholes
Treadaway	1	31	H. D. Duncan
Columbia	17	141	L. M. Brown
*Black Swamp	13	278	George Kempton
Great Saltcatcher	18	130	James Fant
Barnwell	2	140	D. Peeples, M. Shoares
Springtown	0	183	L. B. Brown
*Beaufort	152	1,947	R. Fuller
Rosemary	0	111	D. Peeples
Union	8	240	H. Z. Ardis
Little Saltcatcher	0	70	George Walker
*St. Helena	61	762	W. Hall
*May River	30	888	W. A. Lawton
*Prince Williams	. . . No Report . . .		L. G. Bowers

Churches	Number Baptized	Membership	By Whom Supplied
Deep Bottom	1	33	C. J. Robert
Cypress Creek	0	37	I. Nix
Philadelphia	4	87	L. M. Brown
Smyrna	3	207	M. Shoares
Black Creek	. . . No Report . . .		(No Pastor)
Mount Pleasant	. . . No Report . . .		(No Pastor)
St. John's	1	3	George Walker
Matlock	0	9	(No Pastor)
Bethesda	0	57	William Baxley
Steel Creek	19	131	H. Z. Ardis
Joico's Branch	25	73	H. D. Duncan
*Coosawhatchie	. . . No Report . . .		H. D. Duncan
Beach Island	5	189	H. Z. Ardis
Friendship	0	66	(No Pastor)
*Hilton Head	. . . No Report . . .		(No Pastor)
Sardia	9	34	John Youmans
Pleasant Prospect	. . . No Report . . .		(No Pastor)
Sandy Run	11	61	J. Fant
Gent's Branch	9	32	(No Pastor)
Beaver Dam	1	43	John Youmans
M't Temperance	. . . No Report . . .		(No Pastor)
Long Beach	. . . No Report . . .		J. Munch
Beulah	14	51	J. Fant
Union, Colleton	0	20	W. Price, B. Ferguson
Mount Aaron	2	33	Joseph A. Lawton
Three Lower Runs	2	39	Joseph A. Lawton
Doctor's Creek, Colleton	0	76	(No Pastor)
Total	421	6,508	

*Beaufort District churches with large memberships and which are on or near Sea Islands.
Source: *Minutes of the Savannah River Baptist Association*, November 26, 1842, 16, BC.

TABLE C. 3

State of the Churches within the Savannah River Baptist Association in 1851

Churches	Baptized	Black Members	White Members	Total
*Euhaw	8	442	32	474
Beach Branch	12	70	64	140
Healing Springs	0	23	31	54
*Pipe Creek	20	No Breakdown		179
Columbia	0	No Breakdown		146

TABLE C.3 *(continued)*
State of the Churches within the Savannah River Baptist Association in 1851

Churches	Baptized	Black Members	White Members	Total
*Black Swamp	10	259	64	323
Great Saltcatcher	0	43	106	149
Barnwell	1	71	3	105
Springtown	8	73	107	180
*Beaufort	32	2,477	196	2,673
Rosemary	3	20	98	118
Union	6	148	39	187
Little Saltcatcher	4	17	162	179
*St. Helena	16	866	34	900
*May River	25	510	30	540
Steep Bottom	9	54	38	92
Cypress Creek	0	14	46	60
Philadelphia	9	120	10	130
Smyrna	7	223	43	266
St. John's	0	6	30	36
Matlock	20	26	70	96
Bethesda	9	11	91	102
Steel Creek	2	64	11	75
Joico's Branch	0	1	57	58
*Coosawhatchie	29	258	38	296
Beach Island	19	22	38	60
Friendship	0	No Breakdown		90
*Hilton Head	1	106	2	108
Black Creek, Colleton	0	No Breakdown		104
Pleasant Prospect	5	No Breakdown		57
Sandy Run	17	44	56	100
Gent's Branch	0	7	38	45
Beaver Dam	0	1	40	41
Long Beach	3	12	75	87
Union, Colleton	0	No Breakdown		25
Mount Aaron	0	3	37	40
Lower Three Runs	1	No Breakdown		38
Doctor's Creek, Colleton	8	No Breakdown		47
Round O	0	No Breakdown		48
Great Swamp	0	15	18	33
Blackville	0	15	55	70
Sand Hill	10	No Breakdown		35
Bedon's	0	No Breakdown		44
Peniel	12	No Breakdown		66
Mount Olive	2	6	17	23

Churches	Baptized	Black Members	White Members	Total
Cypress Chapel	0	0	22	22
Bethel	0	No Breakdown		12
Beulah	0	25	7	32
Total	308	6,052	1,805	9,282

*Beaufort District churches with large memberships and which are on or near the Sea Islands. These churches claimed 4,918 members out of a total black membership return of 6,052. Most of the 4,918 blacks were members of the Sea Island congregations at Beaufort, St. Helena, May River, and Hilton Head.

Source: Minutes of the Savannah River Baptist Association, November 22, 1851, 20, BC.

The Deity

The Gullahs' concept of the deity was not that of a God of wrath, but one of love and mercy. In Gullah music, phrases such as "Kind Jesus," or "In the mornin' when I rise, tell my Jesus Huddy ho," indicate that for these slaves Christ was a warm personal friend, as well as a fellow sufferer. Similarly, the Gullahs' prayers also express how they viewed their relationship with God. Prayer was considered actual communication with Jesus, and He was expected to listen and hopefully answer the appeal in some way or another. In such verbal expressions the supplicator reveals inner ideas of the deity. In a study done among the Gullahs in the 1930s, it was observed that by far the most prominent attribute of the deity in prayers was merciful, being mentioned 189 times as opposed to a total of 119 times for all the other attributes ranging from loving to glorious. No description suggesting wrath or vengeance was among the characteristics attributed to the deity.[1] In the following prayer, recorded during the Civil War, one is able to observe the Gullahs' poetic imagery, spirituality, sense of community, and their attitude toward the deity:

Aunt Jane's Prayer

Der Maussuh Jesus, we all uns beg Ooner (you) come make us a call dis yere day. We is nuttin' but poor Etiopian women and people ain't t'ink much 'bout we. We ain't trust ask any of dem great high people for come to we church, but do' you is de one great Maussuh, great too much dan Maussuh Linkum, you ain't shame to care for we African people.

Come to we, dear Maussuh Jesus. De sun, he hot too much, de road am dat long and boggy (sandy) and we ain't got no buggy, for send and fetch Ooner. But Maussuh, yo' 'member how yo' walked dat hard walk up Calvary and ain't weary but t'ink about we all dat way. We know you ain't weary for to come to we. We pick out de torns, de prickles, de brier, de backslidin' and de quarrel and de sin out of yo' path so dey shan't hur Ooner pierce feet no mo'.

Come to we, dear Maussuh Jesus. We all luns ain't got no good cool water for give yo' when yo' t'irsty. You know, Maussuh, de drought so long, and de well so low, ain't nuttin' but mud to drink. But we gine to take de 'munion cup and fill it wid de tear ob repentence and love clean out ob we heart. Dat all we hab to gib yo', good Maussuh.

An' Maussuh Jesus, you say you gwine stand to de door and knock. But you ain't gwine stand at we door, Maussuh, and knock. We sets de door plum open for yo' and watch up de road for see you.

Sisters (turning to the other women in the church), what for you'all ain't open de door so Maussuh know He welcome? (One woman rose quietly from her knees and set the church door wide.)

Come Maussuh Jesus come! We know you is near, we heart is all just tremble, tremble, we so glad for hab yo' here. And Maussuh, we church ain't good 'nuff for yo' to sit down in, but stop by de door jes' one minute, dear Maussuh Jesus, and whisper one word to we heart—one good word—we do listen—Maussuh.[2]

Gullah Folkways

Because they occupied a position of servitude, the Gullahs had to accept outwardly, points of view, customs, and beliefs to which they were exposed by the dominant society. Nevertheless, through sublety and secretiveness they were able to retain some of their previously held beliefs and practices. After slavery, the Gullahs were occasionally willing to share some of their beliefs, customs, and "superstitions" with those readily identifiable as friends, or with those who would not censure the Gullahs for their ways of thinking. Thus a wealth of information about Gullah culture was collected from various sources, but particularly by WPA workers. The following information related to Gullah folk religion and supernatural beliefs provides a mere sample of the material. Unless otherwise stated, this information on Gullah folk beliefs was taken from the WPA files at the South Carolina Library, University of South Carolina, Columbia. Although more research is needed in this area, it was nevertheless possible to trace some of these beliefs to African origins.

Folk Beliefs

Spirits show themselves to babies more often than to grown people. When babies smile or cry out in their sleep, it is because some spirit is amusing or troubling them.

If there is a baby in a house of death, pass the baby over the coffin. This will prevent the spirit from returning to trouble the baby.

People born with a caul or veil over their faces are supposed to have strange powers, to foretell the future, see spirits, etc.[a]

Spirits lift their feet high off the ground when they walk. If they come around your bed when you are sick and stay for some time, it means you are going to get well. The spirits belong to your dead relatives, who have come back to earth to see how you are. If they come and then go away again, it means that they have come for you and you are going to die.

Spirits come back to the earth sometimes in the shape of animals. They do this because they are evil spirits and want to worry humans. It is easy to tell whether a dog or cat that crosses your path is a natural animal or spirit. If it is a natural animal you won't feel anything, but if it is a spirit, the hair will stand up on your head and the goose bumps will rise on your skin.[b,c]

To prevent a dead person's spirit from returning to "Hant you," sprinkle turpentine on the floor behind the body as it is taken out of the house. The turpentine carries the spirit with it.

To keep "hants" (evil spirits) off when there is a death, burn sulphur at the four corners of the house.

If a person who has voodooed another looks in the face of the corpse when he is in his coffin, blood will gush from the mouth of the corpse and everyone present will know who "fixed" him and caused his death.

There are certain persons among the Gullah Negroes who are known as "conjurers," these are very dangerous people and not to be trifled with. A conjurer can "put bad mout" on people or things, give them bad luck and keep them from prospering. A "spell" cast by a conjurer can cause a person to become ill and slowly waste away until he dies.

A conjurer is a very secret thing. Negroes will not discuss it with a white person. It is black magic and to treat it lightly is to invite disaster. They will admit quite readily however, if they have had a particularly bad run of luck, that somebody has "put bad mount" on them.[c]

Negroes of the South Carolina Sea Islands seldom employ the word "witch" in describing an old woman who is versed in the art of witch-craft. Accurately speaking there are no witches among the Negroes—at least in the usual sense of the word. The blacks generally speak about "hags"—beings who have all the powers ascribed to witches and a great deal more. A hag is the disembodied spirit of an old woman who practices witchcraft. She is able to slip off her skin at night and roam about, under the earth, on the earth or above the earth, without anyone being able to see her. A person without skin is always invisible, but it is possible to feel them.

When darkness sets in, the hag who has been in the body during daylight hours, frees herself from the flesh, and proceeds to pursue her dread calling—that of "riding" persons against whom she has spite, or plaguing individuals she has been paid to worry. She is able to slip through the smallest cracks of your house while you sleep. She deposits her skin in the chimney corner. On your back, she pummels you to exhaustion, then sucks your blood. Upon leaving, she cries, "Kin, Kin, you know me," until the skin has fitted itself to the hag's body.

Anybody with common sense knows when he is being ridden by a hag. First he will have unpleasant dreams and every night they become more alarming. Insomnia is a sure sign, as is worrying at night. If the hag is not called off the person will lose his mind.

A hag will ride your enemy for a small pittance.[d]

Supernatural Beliefs

"The Negroes who live down on the salt in the Sea Island region of South Carolina are firm believers in a motley variety of supernatural beings. To them the earth is filled with ghosts, plat-eyes, boo-daddies, boo-hags, drolls and spirit animals. Only the educated Negroes who have contact with the big cities of America deny the existence of these outerworld creatures. The rest of the Sea Island blacks are steeped in the same superstitions that their forefathers held in Africa."

Ghosts—A ghost is very real thing to the Negroes of Edisto and Wadmalaw Islands. A ghost, the materialized body of one who is dead, may be said to have the same dignity as a human being as far as its existence is concerned. The Gullahs say that they know exactly where ghosts could be seen, their familiar haunts, the time they have to leave their graves and their time of return.

For instance, all ghosts leave the graveyard at twelve midnight and return at "fust fowl crow"—all but one who is left on guard. They walk ten feet high off the ground, and cover long distances at a surprisingly short length of time. They like certain trees and certain houses. They have never been known to attack a human being physically, but are able to scare one to death.

These spirits are the "on-easy" spirits who are destined for hell on judgment day, but who roam the earth and "hant" the living for they have no place to rest themselves. These "ghosts," "speerits", or "hants" fall into the following categories:[e]

Plat-eye—There are a number of beliefs regarding plat-eye. One is that plat-eye is the spirit of some of "those old timey people what been dead a long time." Another is that plat-eyes come into being when one buries a treasure and places the head of a murdered man in the hole with the valuables. If an intruder approaches the spot, the plat-eye will arise out of the ground in the guise of a six-legged calf or headless hog and frighten the trespasser away.[g]

Boo-hags—are spirits of hags. They are sent to plague and pester the enemies of the voodoo practitioner, or the enemies of the conjure man's clients. The spell can only be removed by a charm made by another doctor-nigger or witch who has superior knowledge of black magic.

Boo-daddies—are the spirits of doctor-niggers and conjure men released from the body of the living at night for dread purposes.

Drolls—are the spirits of young children who died a painful death. They can be heard, the Negroes say, crying piteously at night in deep swamps and deserted marshland.

Spirit-animals—are numerous. One particularly fearsome cat, which sometimes reaches a height of ten feet and explodes before one's eyes when the Lord's prayer is recited backwards, can be seen at Hamilton Hill on Edisto Island, when the moon is young.[b,f,g]

Conjure-horses and *Spirit-bears*—have not been heard of since the War between the States. Old-time Negroes say that a conjure-horse could follow a haunted person for miles, traveling well over the tree tops all the way. They breathed fire out of their nostrils, and when they passed by, the sound of hooves beating against some ghostly substance filled the air. Spirit-bears had long shaggy black hair, and mouths like caverns from which enormous red tongues, dripping with blood, protruded. They could climb the tallest tree on Edisto.

LETTERED REFERENCES

[a] The Kuranko also believe that such places as the bush, rivers, and mountains are the domain of the "Nyenne" spirits. The nyenne are quasi-humans, some of whom are sympathetic toward humans while others are harmful. Certain individuals are reputed to have special gifts of vision that enable them to see and make contact with the nyenne and even to secure their help in some undertaking. Similarly, the Limba believe that the bush is the domain of a group of spirits who cannot be seen except by those people who are born with "double eyes" or a special "clear spiritual vision." Michael Jackson, *The Kuranko: Dimensions of Social Reality in a West African Society* (London: C. Hurst, 1977), 34–35; Ruth Finnegan, *Limba Stories and Story Telling* (London: Oxford University Press, 1967), 22.

[b] Among the Kuranko of Sierra Leone, there is a belief that certain people have the power of transforming themselves into animals in order to harm others. These "shape shifters" are greatly feared and embody all of the anti-social behavior which the Kuranko people try to combat. See Jackson, *The Kuranko*, 22.

[c] In African society, certain men are considered very proficient in the curative art. They are said to have more power over spirits than others have and do not necessarily use this power for positive ends. They can heal, foretell the future, and "change a thing into something else or a man into a lower animal, or a tree or anything." Their medicine is said to consist of charms, grasses, herbs, and barks taken from the bush. It is the spirit dwelling within these men which gives them their power. The Africans say that without the spirit these "magicians," "healers," and "fortune tellers" could do nothing. Allen Wolsey, *The Natives of the Northern Territories of the Gold Coast, Their Customs, Religion and Folklore*

(London: George Routledge, 1920), 46; Brodie Cruickshank, *Eighteen Years on the Gold Coast of Africa*, 2nd ed. (London: Frank Cass, 1966; repr. from 1853 ed.), 146–148.

[d]The Vai of Liberia have a belief that witches come to your house and ride you at night. The witch comes in through the door, and deposits its skin aside in the house until ready to leave. It is believed that the witch rides the person, then puts its skin back on and leaves. The witch may be killed by sprinkling salt and pepper in certain portions of the room, which will prevent it from putting its skin back on. Just before they go to bed it is a common thing to see Vais people sprinkling salt and pepper about the room. George W. Ellis, *Negro Culture in West Africa* (New York: Neale Publishing, 1914), 63.

[e]Among certain Kongo peoples, the spirits of the dead are termed "abambo," and "whether they are positively good or positively evil, to be loved or to be hated, or to be courted or avoided, are points which no native of the country can answer satisfactorily." The abambo appear "anywhere and at anytime and to anybody," although they have no message. They rarely speak and their most common effect on humans is to frighten. "Indistinctly seen, its appearances are reported as occurring mostly in dark places, in shadows, in twilight, and on dark nights. The most common apparitions are on lonely paths in the forest by night." Robert H. Nassau, *Fetishism in West Africa* (London: Duckworth, 1904), 65–66.

[f]Kongo Africans believe that some spirit or, temporarily, even the soul of humans, may enter into any animal's body. The animal, "guided by human intelligence and will," exercises its strength for the purposes of the temporary human possessor." The people believe that many murders are committed in this way. Nassau, *Fetishism in West Africa*, 70.

[g]Another manifestation of the spirit-animal is the Uvengwa. Kongo Africans say that it is not simply spiritual, but tangible. It is the self-resurrected spirit and body of a dead human being and an object of dread. "Why it appears is not known. Perhaps it shows itself only in a restless, unquiet, or dissatisfied feeling. It is white in color, but the body is variously changed from the likeness of the original human body. Some say that it has only one eye, placed in the centre of the forehead. Some say that its feet are webbed like an aquatic bird. It does not speak; it only wanders, looking as if with curiosity." Melville Herskovits observed that in Haiti, the term "Baka" referred to one who guarded money which

had been buried in jars. It was said that these jars also had human bones either beside them or under them, "and tradition has it that the slave-owners who are believed to have been strong in magic customarily killed the most evil slave on a plantation that his spirit might keep watch over the jars. If the owner returned, the spirit of the slave, as a 'sold baka,' remained to wreak vengeance upon anyone who dared disturb his charge." Nassau, *Fetishism in West Africa*, 71; Melville J. Herskovits, *Life in a Haitian Valley* (New York: Alfred A. Knopf, 1937), 242–43.

A "Ghost" Story

A certain negro church in the country was noted for its strange procedures during the late hours of the night. It was said that at one time a man was driving down the road about midnight, and as he approached the church he saw to his surprise that it was all lit up and the benches filled with people. Just as he drove up the lights went out, and all the people came out, crossed the road in front of him, and went into the cemetery which was just opposite the church on the other side of the road.

Another man was passing the church one night. Just as he got between the church and the cemetery, a ghost came out, caught his horse by the bit and stopped him.

These and similar stories were repeatedly heard throughout the neighborhood, so a young Negro man was not surprised when passing by the church one night to hear voices in the cemetery.

One would say, "You take this one; I take that one."

Then the other, "I take this one; you take that one."

So on they went over and over. The young Negro ran across the field to the Negro preacher's house. After waking the aged preacher, the young man told him "de good Lord an' de devil are in de cemetery a'dividin' up de people." He insisted that the old man go with him to the cemetery to see about it. Reluctantly, the old man consented.

Sure enough as they reached the gate, they heard, "You take this one; I take that one." "I take this one; you take that one." After this was repeated several times, one voice was heard to say, "Well, is that all?" the answer came, "Yes, all except those two at the gate."

That was enough for the two listening ones. The young Negro tells that the old preacher got away from there so fast that he, who was also running with all his strength—couldn't keep him in sight.

At least this story had its explanation. The next day the old preacher and the young man were told that two Negroes after a fishing trip had stopped under a tree in the cemetery to divide their fish. One had a sack full of fish. The other had only two which he had dropped on the ground as he opened the gate of the cemetery.

Truss Gawd

"Plat Eye? Yas'm. De ole folks is talk about Plat Eye. Dey say dey takes shape ob all kind de critter—dawg, cat, hawg, mule, varmint—and I is hear tell ob Plat Eye taking form of gator. I ain see dem scusing one leetle time. You know dat leetle swampy place hind de Parsenage? Dem does call dat Parsenage Branch. Well, one time I hab meh bloom on me en wuz clamming dem days, en de tide been berry late in de ebenin. Hit wuz dusky dark when I hit de Parsenage Lane—light dusky dark. I wuzn't feared none tall. You see, ez I say, I hab meh bloom on me in dem days. En I pass de Cap'n barn en stable. Dere he wuz wid Allan son milkin. En I say: "Good even, Cap'n Bill!' En he gin me back meh word. En I bawg t'ru dat deep white san en I passes de graveyard entrance en I leabes de [gate] open en enters dem dark woods whey de moss wabe low en bresh in you face. En I bin think about Plat Eye. De mind come ter me it wuz good time ter meet em.

"Den I bresh dem weepin moss aside en I trabble de wet mud in meh bare feets en meh shoe bein tie ter meh girdle string. En, Miss Jin, when I bin come ter de foot lawg I could see same ez I see yo now. I could see de foot lawg—dat same old cypress what been dere now. He blow in dat las big September gale. En I bin see Mr. Bull Frawg hit de water— ker plunk! En a cooter slide offen de lawg at meh feets. En, Miss Jin, clare ter Gawd, I bin fer look up at dat cooter den I turn meh eye up en dere wuz a cat—black cat wid he eye lak balls ob fire en he back all arch up en he tail twissin en er switchin en he hair stan on end. He move backward front ob me cross dat cypress lawg. En he bin big. He bin large es meh leetle yearlin ox. En I talk ter em en try fer draw close. En I say ter em; 'I ain fer fear nuttin!'

"En I'se try fer sing: 'He carry me t'ru many ob danger. Because he fust lub me. He guard gainst hant en Plat Eye. Because he fust lub me!'

"En dat Plat Eye ain gib me back meh word. He mobe forward en he tail swish en swish same lak big moccasin tail when he lash de rushes. En de sound come to me; 'Child ob Gawd, doan you show no fear.'

"En I is brace up. En meh short-handle leetle clamrake been in meh hand en I sing:

'Gawd will take care ob me.
Walkin t'ru many ob dangers,
Gawd will take care ob me.'

"En den de min come ter me; 'De Lawd heps dem what heps demsef.' Den I raise up meh rake en I come right cross dat critter hed. Ef dat had bin real cat, I'd er pin him ter dat lawg. My rake bin bury deep en de lawg hold em. En I clare ter Gawd, Miss Jin, he up en prance right onder meh feets, dem eyes burnin holes in me en he tail swish-swish lak ole Sooky tail when de flies bad. En meh ire bin raise. I fer struggle wid meh rake en de lawg loose em he grip en I fer pray: 'Gib Addie Strength, O Gawd!'

"En down I come straight t'ru dat critter middle. He stummick ball up same lak de leetle puffer toad-fish. But dat critter ain feel meh lick. En I ressel lak Jacob wid de angel. I bin strong en hab meh bloom on me. It ain 'vail nuttin.

"No, man! Mr. Plat Eye jest es peart en frisky ez fore he bin hit. En I buse em en I cuss em en I say: 'You debbil! Clare meh path!'

"En ef dat critter didn't paw de air en jest raise up dat big bamboo vine, en meh fer hit em ebery jump! So, Miss Jin, I tink: 'Sinner leble dat lawg.' Meh mind come ter me: 'Child ob Gawd, trabbel de woods path!'

"En I turn back en meh haste. En I hit dat path. En I ain bin tarry en jest ez I wuz gibbin Gawd he praise fer deliver me, dere dat cat! Dis time he big ez meh middle-size ox, en he eye bin blaze! En I lam en I lam. En dat rake handle bin wire en bin nail on. En jest ez I mek meh las lam, dat critter raise up fore meh eyes, en dis time he bin big ez cousin Andrew full-grown ox. En he vanish up dat ole boxed pine ez you quits de woods. Yas'm. I ain bleeve in Plat Eye twill den, but I minds meh step since dem days.

"En when I trabbles de deep woods whey de moss wabe low en Mr. Cooter lib en Mr. Moccasin crawl in de firefly flicker—meh packet fer load.

"Yas'm. I'm ready fer em. Gunpowder en sulphur. Dey is say Plat Eye can't stan dem smell mix. No'm. Dey ain fer trubble me sense dat one time. Uncle Murphy he witch doctor, en he bin tell me how fer fend em off. Dat man full ob knowledge. He must hap Gawd mind in em. So I totes meh powder en sulphur en I carries stick in meh han en puts meh truss in Gawd."

Notes

Introduction

1. C. J. Calhoun, "History, Anthropology and the Study of Communities: Some Problems in Macfarlane's Proposal," *Social History* 3, no. 3 (1978): 369, and his "Community: Toward a Variable Conceptualization for Comparative Research," *Social History* 5, no. 1 (1980): 109–16. For other views of community, see for instance Thomas Bender, *Community and Social Change in America* (New Brunswick, N. J.: Rutgers University Press, 1978); and Robert Redfield, *The Little Community: Viewpoints for the Study of a Human Whole* (Chicago: University of Chicago Press, 1955).

2. Clifford Geertz, *The Interpretation of Cultures* (New York: Basic Books, 1973), 89; C. J. Calhoun, *The Question of Class Struggle: Foundations of Popular Radicalism during the Industrial Revolution* (Chicago: University of Chicago Press, 1982), 159. While Calhoun's views on community are useful here, we strongly disagree on other issues, especially regarding his anti-E. P. Thompson view of how ideologies affect laboring classes. Calhoun, *Question of Class Struggle*, passim.

3. Geertz, *Interpretation of Cultures*, 90–105, 124.

4. Robert T. Parsons, *Religion in an African Society* (Leiden: E. J. Brill, 1964), 173–76, 179, 183–85; James L. Sibley and D. Westermann, *Liberia Old New* (London: James Clarke 1928), 187–88; John S. Mbiti, *African Religions and Philosophies* (New York: Praeger Publishers, 1959), 2–16; Robert Farris Thompson and Joseph Cornet, *The Four Moments of the Sun: Kongo Art in Two Worlds* (Washington, D. C.: National Gallery of Art, 1981), 85–93.

5. W. E. B. DuBois, *The Souls of Black Folk* in *Three Negro Classics* (New York: Avon Books, 1965, first pub. 1903), 213–21, 337–49; Julius Lester, ed. *The Seventh Son: The Thoughts and Writings of W. E. B. DuBois*, 2 vols. (New York: Random House, 1971) I: 252–62, 277–82; Manning Marable "The Faith of W. E. B DuBois: Sociocultural and Political Dimensions of Black Religion," *The Southern Quarterly* 23, no. 1 (Fall, 1984): 15–33; Sterling Brown, et al., eds., *The Negro Caravan* (New York: Dryden Press, 1941); 6, 412–21; Sterling Stuckey, "Through the Prism of Folklore: The Black Ethos in Slavery," *The Massachusetts Review* 9, Pt. 2 (Summer, 1968) 417–37. Stuckey's newly completed work is an addition to the new scholarship. However it was unavailable when my book went to press. Sterling Stuckey, *Slave Culture: Nationalist Theory and the Foundations of Black America* (New York: Oxford University Press, 1987). Lawrence W. Levine, *Black Culture and Black Consciousness; Afro-American Folk Thought from Slavery to Freedom* (New York: Oxford University Press, 1977), 3–135, 54.

6. Levine, *Black Culture and Consciousness*, 36–37, 43, 49–51, 75–77.

7. Albert J. Raboteau, *Slave Religion: The "Invisible Institution" in the Antebellum South* (New York: Oxford University Press, 1978), ix.

8. August Meier and Elliott Rudwick, *Black History and the Historical Profession, 1915–1980* (Chicago: University of Illinois Press, 1986), 191.

9. Raboteau, *Slave Religion*, 92. For a discussion of how Raboteau's view "minimizes the contribution of African ritual traditions" see Robert Simpson, "The Shout and Shouting in Slave Religion in the United States," *The Southern Quarterly* 23, no. 3 (Spring, 1985): 40–46.

10. Raboteau, *Slave Religion*, 152.

11. Ibid., Chapters 3 and 4.

12. Ibid., x.

13. Edward H. Carr, *What Is History?* (New York: Vintage Books, 1961), 23–35.

14. Raboteau, *Slave Religion*, Chapters 5 and 6.

15. Vincent Harding, *There Is a River: The Black Struggle for Freedom in America* (New York: Vintage Books, 1983). Years ago, Harding explored relationships between religion and resistance among slaves. See his "Religion and Resistance among Antebellum Negroes, 1800–1860," in August Meier and Elliott Rudwick, eds., *The Making of Black America* I (New York: Atheneum, 1969), 179–97.

16. Harding, *There Is a River*, Introduction.

17. Herbert G. Gutman, *The Black Family in Slavery and Freedom, 1750–1925* (New York: Pantheon Books, 1976), passim.

18. Eugene D. Genovese, *Roll, Jordan, Roll: The World the Slaves Made* (New York: Pantheon Books, 1974), passim, but especially xvi–xvii, 3–149, 280–84, 597–98, 658–60.

19. Meier and Rudwick, *Black History*, Chapter 3 and 258–65.

20. See for example Paul D. Escott, *Slavery Remembered: A Record of Twentieth Century Slave Narratives* (Chapel Hill: University of North Carolina Press, 1979) 18–35; E. P. Thompson, "Eighteenth-Century English Society: Class Struggle without Class?" *Social History* 3, no. 2 (1978): 134–37; Eric Perkins, "Roll, Jordan, Roll: A 'Marx' for the Master Class," *Radical History Review* 3, no. 4 (1976): 41–59; Gutman, *Black Family in Slavery and Freedom*, 309–20; For the most recent interpretation in support of paternalism, see Peter Kolchin, *Unfree Labor: American Slavery and Russian Serfdom* (Cambridge, Mass.: Harvard University Press, 1987) 103–57, 195–241.

21. Genovese, *Roll, Jordan, Roll*, 283. According to Elkins, the typical American slave was labeled "Sambo" in Southern lore. "Sambo" was "loyal but lazy, humble but chronically given to lying and stealing: his behavior full of infantile silliness and his talk inflated with childish exaggeration." The "Sambo" of the Old South was compared by Elkins to what he termed a similar personality type, the prisoners of Auschwitz-Birkenau. The author states that they were one and the same historically, both products of a "closed" and "authoritarian" system. This personality type developed in the United States and in Nazi Germany but not in Latin America, according to Elkins, because Latin American institutions protected slaves while American institutions did not protect slaves nor German institutions protect Jews. Stanley Elkins, *Slavery, a Problem in American Institutional and Intellectual Life* (Chicago: University of Chicago Press, 1959), 82, 63–79, 73, 136–37, 175–217.

22. Genovese, *Roll, Jordan, Roll*, 209–232.

23. Ibid., 281.

24. Ibid.

25. Ibid., 212.

26. Ibid., 283–84.

27. Georg Lukács, *History and Class Consciousness, Studies in Marxist Dialectics*, trans. Rodney Livingstone (Cambridge, Mass.: MIT Press, 1973), 46–59.

28. Ibid.; Arthur P. Mendel, ed., *Essential Works of Marxism* (New York: Bantam Books, 1961), 15–16.

29. John Blassingame, *The Slave Community: Plantation Life in the South* (New York: Oxford University Press, 1972 ed.), 200–201.

30. Genovese, *Roll, Jordan, Roll*, 329–88, 441.

31. Ibid., xvii.

32. John M. Janzen and Wyatt MacGaffey, *An Anthology of Kongo Religion: Primary Texts from Lower Zaire* (Lawrence, Kans.: University of Kansas Publications in Anthropology, No. 5, 1974), 2–3.

Prologue

1. Mason Crum, *Gullah, Negro Life in the Carolina Sea Islands* (Durham: Duke University Press, 1940), 3, 19–22, 78; Guion G. Johnson, *A Social History of the Sea Islands* (Chapel Hill: University of North Carolina Press, 1930), 112, 130; Paul Quattlebaum, *The Land Called Chicora* (Gainesville: University of Florida Press, 1958), 86–88.

2. The spelling of Kongo with a K instead of C is used by some Africanists. It refers to the traditional, unitary civilization and way of life of BaKongo peoples. The C spelling represents the political shift that occurred with white colonial penetration and partition in Central Africa. Traditional Kongo civilization includes modern Bas-Zaire, neighboring Cabinda, Congo-Brazzaville, Gabon, and Northern Angola. The ancient civilization was once under the united suzerainty of the kingdom of Kongo. The language is KiKongo, although dialects vary widely in this Bantu-speaking world of Africa. The numerous ethnic groups and some neighboring ones share cultural and religious traditions. They also share memories of the trials and tears left in the wake of centuries of transatlantic trade in slaves. John M. Janzen and Wyatt MacGaffey, *An Anthology of Kongo Religion: Primary Texts from Lower Zaire* (Lawrence, Kans.: University of Kansas Publications in Anthropology, No. 5, 1974), 1–3; Robert Farris Thompson and Joseph Cornet, *The Four Moments of the Sun: Kongo Art in Two Worlds* (Washington, D. C.: National Gallery of Art, 1981), 27; Robert Farris Thompson, *Flash of the Spirit: African and Afro-American Art and Philosophy* (New York: Vintage Books, 1983), 103; Wyatt MacGaffey, *Custom and Government in the Lower Congo* (Berkeley: University of California Press, 1970), 11; Philip D. Curtin, *The Atlantic Slave Trade: A Census* (Madison: University of Wisconsin Press, 1969), 30–36, 44–45, 134–35, 411.

3. *SCG*, March 27, 1742; Reed Smith, "Gullah," *A Reprint of Bulletin #190 of the University of South Carolina* (Columbia: State Printing Co., 1926), 3–4; Winifred Vass, *The Bantu Speaking Heritage of the United States* (Los Angeles: Center for Afro-American Studies, 1979), 31.

4. Smith, "Gullah," 3–4; *SCA*, December 22 and 29, 1843; Elizabeth Hyde Botume, *First Days Amongst the Contrabands* (New York: Arno Press and New York Times, 1968; repr. from 1893 ed.), 54, 57. Peter Wood also suggests that perhaps Gullah derived from a "multiple etymology." See *Black Majority: Negroes in Colonial South Carolina from 1670 through the Stono Rebellion* (New York: Alfred Knopf, 1974), 172, n. 12.

5. Lorenzo D. Turner, *Africanisms in the Gullah Dialect* (New York: Arno Press and New York Times, 1969; repr. from 1949 ed.).

6. See reviews and discussions by Raven I. McDavid, Jr., *Language: Journal of the Linguistic Society of America* 26 (April–June, 1950): 323–32, and Morris Swadish, *Word: Journal*

of the Linguistic Circle of New York 7 (April, 1951): 82–83; P. E. Hair, "Sierra Leone Items in the Gullah Dialect of American English," *Sierra Leone Language Review* no. 4 (1965): 79–84; Frederick G. Cassidy, "The Place of Gullah," *American Speech* 55 no. 1 (Spring, 1980): 3–14.

7. Turner, *Africanisms in Gullah*, 194. Gullahs often referred to themselves as "countrymen," as a way of identifying themselves as African-born. When asked what their language was, they would reply, "the way we talk." Mary A. Twining and Keith E. Baird, "Introduction to Sea Island Folklife," *Journal of Black Studies* 10, no. 4 (June, 1980): 398; Donald R. Kloe, "Buddy Quow: An Anonymous Poem in Gullah-Jamaican Dialect Written Circa 1800," *Southern Folklore Quarterly* 38, no. 2 (June, 1974): 82–84.

8. Hair, "Sierra Leone Items in Gullah," 79–81.

9. Ibid., 83.

10. Turner, *Africanisms in Gullah*, passim; Curtin, *Atlantic Slave Trade*; Wood, *Black Majority*. Wood does suggest, however, that the Windward Coast slaves had a special appeal and significance because South Carolinians recognized their familiarity with rice, the colony's main export. The Windward Coast was also called the Grain Coast and in specific areas the Rice Coast. As Wood observes, "Throughout the era of slave importation in South Carolina references can be found concerning African familiarity with rice." Wood, *Black Majority*, 59–60. Daniel Littlefield further explored Wood's idea and provides an exception to the general emphasis on Kongo-Angolan influences. See his *Rice and Slaves: Ethnicity and the Slave Trade in Colonial South Carolina* (Baton Rouge: Louisiana State University Press, 1981). Another important author, the late Walter Rodney, also early recorded the significance of Upper Guinea in the transatlantic trade, although Rodney was not specifically writing about South Carolina. See his *A History of the Upper Guinea Coast, 1545–1800* (Oxford: Clarendon Press, 1970).

11. Turner, *Africanisms in Gullah*, 91, 194; Twining and Baird, "Introduction to Sea Island Folklife," 397–98.

12. Turner, *Africanisms in Gullah*, 63, 151, 189; see Chapters 2 and 9.

13. Ibid., 136, 138; Wood, *Black Majority*, 131, 302, 334–39; Thompson, *Flash of the Spirit*, Chapter 2, 107, 108; Hair, "Sierra Leone Items in Gullah," 83; Kloe, "Buddy Quow," 87; Cassidy. "Place of Gullah," 7–14. Linguist Ian Hancock believes that KiKongo speech "cannot be counted as a contributing factor to Gullah," despite the large numerical representation, because BaKongo peoples did not go through a creolization process. He argues, even more forcefully than Hair, for Upper Guinea Coast influences since some of these Africans already spoke a creole because of contact with whites on the Guinea Coast. While assessment of Upper Guinea linguistic impact appears sound, Turner, Cassidy and others continue to support significant Kongo and Gold Coast influences. Ian F. Hancock, "Gullah and Barbadian—Origins and Relationships," *American Speech* 55 no. 1 (Spring, 1980): 27–32.

14. Roger Bastide, *African Civilizations in the New World*, trans. Peter Green (New York: Harper & Row, 1971), 106, 154, 161; Melville J. Herskovits, *The Myth of the Negro Past* (Boston: Beacon Press, 1958 repr. from 1941 ed.); Thompson, *Flash of the Spirit*, Chapter 2; Thompson and Cornet, *Four Moments of the Sun*, 151–57, 178–203.

15. Willie Lee Rose, *Rehearsal for Reconstruction: The Port Royal Experiment* (Indianapolis: Bobbs-Merrill, 1964).

16. Arthur Sumner to Lt. Joseph Clark, January 23, 1863, Penn School Papers, vol. 4, SHC.

17. Diary of William F. Allen, 25, 44, 83–84, in William F. Allen Family Papers, 1775–

1937, State Historical Society of Wisconsin, Madison; David Thorpe to John Mooney, January 25, 1863, Thorpe Series, James McBride Dabbs Papers, SHC.

18. Charles Sumner to Nina Hartshorn, July 7, 1862, Penn School Papers, vol. 4 SHC. See also Frances Anne Kemble, *Journal of a Residence on a Georgian Plantation* (New York: Harper & Brothers, 1863), 218–19; Sir Charles Lyell, *A Second Visit to the United States*, 2 vols. (New York: Harper & Brothers, 1859), I: 244–45; *SCA*, July 14, 1863 and December 29, 1843; Allen Diary, 18, 127–28, 151–54.

19. For an extensive bibliography on works about Gullahs and the need for more modern approaches, see Mary A. Twining, "Sources in the Folklore and Folklife of the Sea Islands," *Southern Folklore Quarterly* 39 (1975): 135–50; In 1980 the *Journal of Black Studies* devoted an entire issue to Sea Island culture. Twining and Baird, eds., *Journal of Black Studies*; Rose, *Rehearsal for Reconstruction*, passim; Charles Joyner, *Down by the Riverside: A South Carolina Slave Community* (Urbana & Chicago: University of Illinois Press, 1984), passim.

20. Harriott Pinckney Rutledge to Edward Rutledge, August 5, 1822, Pinckney Papers, SCHS; James Hamilton, *Negro Plot* (Charleston: Joseph W. Ingraham, 1822), 291; Benjamin Elliott, "To Our Northern Brethren," quoted in Edwin C. Holland, *A Refutation of the Calumnies Circulated against the Southern and Western States, Respecting the Institution and Existence of Slavery among Them* (Charleston: A. E. Miller, 1822), 79; Lionel Kennedy and Thomas Parker, *The Trial Record of Denmark Vesey*, Intro. by John Oliver Killens (Boston: Beacon Press, 1970; repr. from 1822 ed. and published under title: *An Official Report of the Trials of Sundry Negroes*), 13–14, 76–79; F. A. Mood, *Methodism in Charleston* (Nashville: E. Stevenson and J. E. Evans, 1856), 130–31; William W. Freehling, *Prelude to Civil War* (New York: Harper & Row. 1965), 72–76; Susan Markey Fickling, "Slave Conversion in South Carolina, 1830–1860" (M. A. thesis, University of South Carolina, 1924), 16–17; Thomas Bennett to Richard Furman, 1822, Furman Papers, SCL; Henry Irving Tragle, *The Southhampton Slave Revolt of 1831: A Compilation of Source Materials* (Amherst: University of Massachusetts Press, 1971); Rev. Leroy F. Beaty, *Work of South Carolina Methodism Among the Slaves: An Address Delivered Before the Historical Society of the South Carolina Conference*, November 26, 1901, HSSCC, 9–10; C. C. Pinckney to William Capers, January 24, 1835, HSSCC; Luther Porter Jackson, "Religious Instruction of Negroes, 1830–1860," *Journal of Negro History* 15 (1930): 79–79.

21. Charles C. Pinckney, *An Address Delivered in Charleston Before the Agricultural Society of South Carolina, At Its Annual Meeting, 18th August, 1829* (Charleston: A. E. Miller, 1829), passim; James O. Andrew, "The Southern Slave Population," *MMQR* 13 (1831): 315–17; Charles C. Jones, *The Religious Instruction of the Negroes in the United States* (New York: Negro Universities Press, 1969; repr. from 1842 ed.), 16–18; 80; *Proceedings of the Meeting in Charleston, South Carolina, May 13–15, 1845 on the Religious Instruction of the Negroes* (Charleston: B. Jenkins, 1845), passim; Beaty, *Work of South Carolina Methodism*, 13–34, HSSCC; Report of the Board of Managers of the South Carolina Missionary Society, in *SCA*, January 3, 1851.

1. Gullah Roots

1. James Pope-Hennessy, *Sins of Our Fathers: A Study of the Atlantic Slave Traders, 1441–1807* (New York: Alfred A. Knopf, 1968), 38; Daniel Littlefield, *Rice and Slaves: Ethnicity and the Slave Trade in Colonial South Carolina* (Baton Rouge: Louisiana State University Press, 1981), 34–36; Basil Davidson, *The African Slave Trade: Precolonial History, 1450–1850*,

originally published as *Black Mother* (Boston: Little, Brown, 1961), 105; Melville J. Herskovits, *The Myth of the Negro Past* (Boston: Beacon Press, 1958; repr. from 1941 ed.), 34–40; Philip D. Curtin, *The Atlantic Slave Trade: A Census* (Madison: University of Wisconsin Press, 1969), passim; Daniel P. Mannix and Malcolm Cowley, *Black Cargoes: A History of the Atlantic Slave Trade, 1518–1865* (New York: Viking Press, 1969), 14–20; The term Upper Guinea Coast has altered over centuries. Here our definition is taken from Walter Rodney, *A History of the Upper Guinea Coast, 1545–1800* (Oxford: Clarendon Press, 1970), 2, 7; Elizabeth Donnan, *Documents Illustrative of the History of the Slave Trade to America*, 4 vols. (Washington, D. C.: Carnegie Institution, 1935), vol. 4, *The Southern Colonies*, passim; Roger Anstey, *The Atlantic Slave Trade and British Abolition, 1760–1810* (Atlantic Highlands, N. J.: Humanities Press, 1975), 58–60.

2. Peter H. Wood, *Black Majority: Negroes in Colonial South Carolina from 1670 through the Stono Rebellion* (New York: Alfred A. Knopf, 1974), 131; Curtin, *Atlantic Slave Trade*, 156; Elizabeth Donnan, "The Slave Trade into South Carolina before the Revolution," *American Historical Review* 33 (1927–28): 816–17; William Snelgrave, *A New Account of Some Parts of Guinea and the Slave Trade* (London: James, John and Paul Knapton, 1734; London: Frank Cass, 1971), 173–74; William Smith, *A Voyage to Guinea* (London: John Nourse, 1744; London: Frank Cass, 1967), 135; William Bosman, *A New and Accurate Description of the Coast of Guinea*, trans. John Ralph Willis (Holland, 1704; 4th English ed., New York: Barnes and Noble, 1967), 56–68; Mannix and Cowley, *Black Cargoes*, 17–18; Herskovits, *Negro Past*, 35; Pope-Hennessy, *Sins of Our Fathers*, 58–59.

3. Donnan, *Documents*, vol. 2, *The Eighteenth Century*, 282.

4. Ibid., II:xxxi–xxxiii, 355; IV:301, 382.

5. Wood, *Black Majority*, 301–4, Appendix C, 333–41.

6. Douglas L. Wheeler and Rene Pelissier, *Angola* (London: Pall Mall Press, 1971), 28–51; Davidson, *African Trade*, 144–52; Donnan, *Documents*, II:xvii–xviii; Herskovits, *Negro Past*, 37. Roger Bastide has written that the official documents concerning the Portuguese trade were burned after slavery was suppressed "in an effort to expunge a blot on the country's escutcheon." See Roger Bastide, *African Religions of Brazil: Toward a Sociology of the Interpretations of Civilizations*, trans. Helen Sebba (Baltimore: Johns Hopkins Press, 1978). 33.

7. Jan Vansina, "Long Distance Trade Routes in Central Africa," *Journal of African History* 3 (1962): 375–90; Walter Rodney, "Slavery and Other Forms of Social Oppression on the Upper Guinea Coast in the Context of the Atlantic Slave Trade," *Journal of African History* 8, no. 3 (1966): 431, 440; Quoted from Herskovits, *Negro Past*, 37–38.

8. Vansina, "Trade Routes," 375–83; Lorenzo D. Turner, *Africanisms in the Gullah Dialect* (New York: Arno Press and New York Times, 1969; repr. from 1949 ed.), passim; Winifred Vass, *The Bantu Speaking Heritage of the United States* (Los Angeles: Center for Afro-American Studies, 1979), 9–19. Wheeler and Pelissier, *Angola*, 6–10; Herskovits, *Negro Past*, 38; Curtin, *Atlantic Slave Trade*, 157, Table 45.

9. Wheeler and Pelissier, *Angola*, 6–10; Placide Tempels, *Bantu Philosophy*, trans. Colin King (Paris: Présence Africaine, 1959), passim; H. P. Junod, *Bantu Heritage* (Johannesburg: Hortors, 1938; Westport, Conn.: Negro University Press, 1970), 59–67, 82–102, 125–33; Robert Farris Thompson, *Flash of the Spirit: African and Afro-American Art and Philosophy* (New York: Vintage Books, 1983), 103; *Gentleman's Magazine* 35 (October 1764): 487; Leila Sellers, *Charleston Business on the Eve of the American Revolution* (Chapel Hill: University of North Carolina Press, 1934), 143; Augustine Smyth et al., *The Carolina Low Country* (New York: Macmillan, 1931) 173; Vass, *Bantu Heritage*, 3–5; Wood, *Black Majority*, 96–130, 195–217, 272–326; Littlefield, *Rice and Slaves*, 11–15.

10. Wood, *Black Majority*, 52–153, 324–35. From 1741 to 1743 a prohibitive duty was imposed. In 1744 four African cargoes arrived. No slave cargoes entered Charleston in 1745 and from 1746 and 1748 another prohibitive duty was in effect. Three African cargoes arrived in 1749 and 1750, respectively. By 1752 the trade was once again in full swing. Donnan, "Slave Trade before the Revolution," 807–8; W. E. B. DuBois, *The Suppression of the African Slave Trade to the United States of America, 1638–1870* (New York: Schocken Books, 1969; repr. from 1896 ed.), 9–10; W. Robert Higgins, "The Geographical Origins of Negro Slaves in Colonial South Carolina," *South Atlantic Quarterly* 70 (1971): 42–43.

11. Wood, *Black Majority*, 148, 323; Frank J. Klingberg, *An Appraisal of the Negro in Colonial South Carolina: A Study in Americanization* (Washington, D. C.: Associated Publishers, 1941), 69–70; 72; Converse D. Clowse, *Economic Beginnings in Colonial South Carolina, 1730–1760* (Columbia: University of South Carolina Press, 1971), 206, 230–32. Rice was never raised to any large extent on the Sea Islands since salt water in poisonous to the rice plant. Some Sea Islands did have a few fresh water ponds where rice was grown, but the amount was small and only for local consumption. Guion G. Johnson, *A Social History of the Sea Islands* (Chapel Hill: University of the North Carolina Press, 1930), 18; Frederick V. Emerson, "Geographical Influences in American Slavery," *Geographical Society Bulletin* 63 (1911): 108–9.

12. William A. Schaper, *Sectionalism and Representation in South Carolina* (New York: DaCapo Press, 1968), 51; Emerson, "Geographical Influences," 108–11; Edward McCrady, *South Carolina under the Royal Government, 1719–1776* (New York: Macmillan, 1899), 386–88; Higgins, "Geographical Origins of Negro Slaves," 35, 37, 46–47; Robert L. Meriwether, *The Expansion of South Carolina, 1728–1765*, (Kingsport, Tenn.: Southern Publishers, 1940), 37–38; Philip D. Morgan, "Black Society in the Lowcountry, 1760–1810," in Ira Berlin and Ronald Hoffman, *Slavery and Freedom in the Age of the American Revolution* (Charlottesville: University of Virginia Press, 1983), 84; Peter Wood offers interesting evidence which points to Africans' immunity to certain diseases, such as malaria. Yet, as he states, this was not "absolute." Moreover, Todd L. Savitt notes that malaria certainly took its toll in human losses among slaves. He maintains that some blacks did possess an inherited immunity to one or another strain of malaria. But adds that even adult African-born slaves had to go through a "seasoning" period because the "strains of malarial parasites in this country differed from those in their native lands." The "acquired" immunity that blacks reportedly developed was "risky," according to Savitt, since this involved repreated, uninterrupted exposure to malaria over a period of years. Furthermore, we must rely heavily on the words of colonial whites with a vested interest in rationalizing that blacks were more suited to labor in the Carolina swamps and marshes. Africans may have had a varied immunity to certain diseases, but it appears unlikely that this determined white attitudes toward black labor. For Wood, See *Black Majority* 85–88, 90–91. See also Todd L. Savitt, *Medicine and Slavery: The Diseases and Health Care of Blacks in Antebellum Virginia* (Urbana, Ill.: University of Illiois Press, 1978), 21–26.

13. Schaper, *Sectionalism* 55–56; Emerson, "Georgraphical Influences," 112; Higgins, "Geographical Origins of Negro Slaves," 40–46; Johnson, *Social History*, 18–19; McCrady, *South Carolina under Royal Government*, 267–69; Donnan, *Documents*, IV: passim; See Appendix A.

14. Ellen Gibson Wilson, *The Loyal Blacks* (New York: G. P. Putnam's Sons, 1976), 48; Philip M. Hamer, et al. eds., *Papers of Henry Laurens*, 10 vols. (Columbia: University of South Carolina Press, 1968), IV: 294–95.

15. *SCG*, July 14, 1759.

16. Hamer, *Laurens Papers*, I:252, 331.

17. Littlefield, *Rice and Slaves*, 74–114, Additionally Ian Hancock partly bases his contention of the prevalence of Upper Guinea influence in Gullah dialect on the introduction of creole-speaking slaves brought to South Carolina from this region of Africa. The number of Africans speaking Guinea Coast creole English was small compared to those who spoke no English. Yet the former could have begun the process of spreading creolized English to the latter. Ian F. Hancock, "Gullah and Barbadian—Origins and Relationships." *American Speech* 55 no. 1 (Spring, 1980): 27–30.

18. Richard Jobson, *The Golden Trade or A Discovery of the River Gambia* (London: Nicholas Okes, 1623), 42, 123–25; Francis Moore, *Travels into the Inland Parts of Africa* (London: J. Stagg, 1739), 17–29, 30–32, 38–39, 47–52, 72–73, 80–82, 105–22; Michel Adanson, *A Voyage to Senegal, the Isle of Goree and the River Gambia* (London: J. Nourse and W. Johnston, 1759), 166; Joseph Corry, *Observations Upon the Windward Coast of Africa* (London: Frank Cass 1958; repr. from 1807 ed.), 64–66; David McPherson, *Annals of Commerce*, 4 vols. (London: Johnson Reprint Co., 1972; repr. from 1805 ed.), IV: 141–42; Harry Gailey, Jr., *A History of the Gambia* (London: Routledge and Kegan Paul, 1964), 6, 11, 13; Sellers, *Charleston Business*, 143; David P. Gamble, *The Wolof of Senegambia* (London: International African Institute, 1957), 31–37; Christopher Fyfe, *A History of Sierra Leone* (London: Oxford University Press, 1962), 1–4; Mannix and Cowley, *Black Cargoes*, 15–16; *SCG*, July 2, 1760, October 11, 1760, August 29, 1761; *South Carolina Gazette and Country Journal*, March 13, 1769, May 8, 1769, June 22, 1769, July 2, 1771, August 13, 1771, December 1, 1772. June 1, 1773, July 18, 1774, January 13, 1785, December 1, 1772.

19. Appendix A; *SCG*, August 19, 1756, June 23, 1756.

20. Donnan, *Documents*, IV: 404 n.; Higgins, "Geographical Origins of Negro Slaves," 41; Morgan, "Black Society in the Lowcountry," 84–85; DuBois, *African Trade*, 90; Schaper, *Sectionalism*, 81–88, 149–62; Sellers, *Charleston Business*, 29–30, 128; Appendix A; Wood, *Black Majority*, 333–41. Higgins states that many slaves, prior to 1775, entered Charleston but were not employed in Carolina. The Sea Island port of Beaufort did some importing as well, although Higgins gives no port-by-port importation breakdown. He believes the "majority of all Negroes in the United States today are descended from blacks brought to North America during the colonial period." This has even stronger implications for the spread of cultural influences by ethnic groups of the middle period of the trade. Higgins, "Geographical Origins of Negro Slaves," 39, 46–47.

21. Rodney, *History of Upper Guinea*, 3–15, 233.

22. Moore, *Travels*, 29–35, 40–51; Jobson, *Golden Trade*, 27–37; Adanson, *Voyage to Senegal*, 57–59; Smith, *Voyage to Guinea*, 32; Rodney, *History of Upper Guinea*, 117; Charlotte Quinn, *Mandingo Kingdoms of the Senegambia* (Evanston: Northwestern University Press, 1972), 1–54; Gailey, *History of Gambia*, 10–17; Henry Fenwick Reeve, *The Gambia: Its History, Ancient, Medieval and Modern* (London: Smith, Elder, 1972), 12, 73, 78–79, 171–79, 180–81, 198–203; Curtin, *Atlantic Slave Trade*, 156–67.

23. Rodney, *History of Upper Guinea*, 112–15, 116–17; Moore, *Travels*, 41–44; Reeve, *Gambia, Ancient Medieval, Modern*, 171–78.

24. Moore, *Travels*, 42–43.

25. Douglas Grant, *The Fortunate Slave* (London: Oxford University Press, 1968), Chapter 4, 156–67; Moore, *Travels*, 205–8; Rodney, *History of Upper Guinea*, 116–17. Curtin, *Atlantic Slave Trade*. For another example of a black nobleman being sold into slavery see Terry Alford, *Prince Among Slaves* (New York: Oxford University Press, 1986; repr. from 1977 ed.).

26. Rodney, *History of Upper Guinea*, 111–17, 236–39.

27. John Matthews, *A Voyage to the River Sierra Leone* (London: Frank Cass, 1966; repr.

from 1788 ed.), 13, 18, 74–75, 91–95, 141–42; Corry, *Windward Coast*, 94–95; Thomas Winterbottom, *An Account of the Native Africans in the Neighborhood of Sierra Leone*, 2 vols. (London: Frank Cass, 1969; repr. from 1803 ed.), I: 3–7; Rodney, *History of Upper Guinea*, 232–39; Fyfe, *Sierra Leone*, 2–3, 5–6, 9, 65; Robert T. Parsons, *Religion in an African Society* (Leiden: E. J. Brill, 1964), xiv. 226.

28. Rodney, *History of Upper Guinea*, 236–53; Appendix A.

29. Kenneth Little, *The Mende of Sierra Leone* (London: Routledge & Kegan Paul, 1951), Paul, 1951), 28–29, 37–39; Fyfe, *Sierra Leone*, 5–6.

30. Higgins, "Georgraphical Origins of Negro Slaves," 41; James L. Sibley and D. Westermann, *Liberia Old and New* (London: James Clarke, 1928), 45–46; Sir Harry Johnston, *Liberia*, 2 vols. (London: Hutchinson, 1906), I: 107–10; II: 921–24, 947–48, 1095–96: Warren L. d'Azevedo, "The Setting of Gola Society and Culture: Some Theoretical Implications of Variation in Time and Space," *Kroeber Anthropological Society Papers* (Berkeley: University of California, 1959), 21, 51.

31. d'Azevedo, "Gola Society and Culture," 55–59; Rodney, *History of Upper Guinea*, 255.

32. Folkways Research Series, *Tribes of the Western Province and the Denwoin People* (Monrovia: Dept. of Interior 1955) 140–42; and *The Traditional History and Folklore of the Gola Tribe in Liberia*, 2 vols. (Monrovia: Dept. of the Interior, 1961) I: 2–3; Rodney, *History of Upper Guinea*, 255.

33. Rodney, *History of Upper Guinea*, 253.

34. Diary of William F. Allen, 63, in William F. Allen Papers, 1775–1937, State Historical Society of Wisconisn, Madison; Donald R. Kloe, "Buddy Quow: An Anonymous Poem in Gullah-Jamaican Dialect Written Circa 1800," *Southern Folklore Quarterly* 38, no. 2 (June, 1974): 82–84, 87; Wilbur Zelinsky, *The Cultural Geography of the United States* (Englewood Cliffs, N. J.: Prentice-Hall, 1973), 20–21.

2. The Socioreligious Heritage

1. Warren L. d'Azevedo, "The Setting of Gola Society and Culture: Some Theoretical Implications of Variation in Time and Space," *Kroeber Anthropological Society Papers* (Berkeley: University of California, 1959), 43–45, 67–68; Walter Rodney, A *History of the Upper Guinea Coast, 1545–1800* (Oxford: Clarendon Press, 1970), 32–33, 65; Kenneth Little, *The Mende of Sierra Leone* (London: Routledge & Kegan Paul, 1951), 7–8, 240–42, and "The Poro Society as Arbiter of Culture," *African Studies* 7 (March, 1948): 1; M. McCulloch, *Peoples of Sierra Leone* (London: International African Institute, 1950), 29–37, 68–69, 81–82, 93; George W. Harley, "Notes on the Poro in Liberia," *Papers of the Peabody Museum of American Archaeology and Ethnology, Harvard University* 19 (1941): 6; James L. Sibley and D. Westermann, *Liberia Old and New* (London: James Clarke, 1928), Chapters 5–9; Folkways Research Series, *Tribes of the Western Province and the Denwoin People* (Monrovia: Dept. of Interior, 1955), 17, 24–32; Robert T. Parsons, *Religion in an African Society* (Leiden: E. J. Brill, 1964), 140–51.

2. Rodney, *History of Upper Guinea*, 32–33, 65–67; Kenneth Little, "The Political Function of the Poro," Part I, *Africa* 35 (October, 1965): 349–50.

3. Nicholas Owen, *Journal of A Slave Dealer, A View of Some Remarkable Axedents in the Life of Nicholas Owen on the Coast of Africa and America From the Year 1746 to the Year 1757* (London: George Routledge, 1930), 30–31.

4. John Matthews, *A Voyage to the River Sierra Leone* (London: Frank Cass, 1966; repr. from 1788 ed.), 82–83.

5. Mark Hanna Watkins, "The West African 'Bush' School," *American Journal of Sociology* 48 (1943): 667–70, 674–75; Harley, "Notes on Poro," 13, 16–18, 27, 28, 32; Little, "Poro as Arbiter of Culture," 5–6, and "Political Function of the Poro," Part I, 349–56, and *Mende*, 240–43; Richard Fulton, "The Political Structures and Functions of Poro in Kpelle Society," *American Anthropologist* 74 (1972): 1222–23; Sibley and Westermann, *Liberia*, 176–86, 217–36; Folkways Research Series, *The Traditional History and Folklore of Gola Tribe in Liberia*, 2 vols. (Monrovia: Dept. of the Interior, 1961) II; 10–12, 16–22.

6. Watkins, " 'Bush' School," 671; Little, "Political Function of the Poro," Part I, 357–58, and "The Role of the Secret Society in Cultural Specialization," *American Anthropologist* 51 (1949): 200–205, and "Poro as Arbiter of Culture," 1, 4–6, 9–10; Harley, "Notes on Poro," 19–20, 6–7, 15, 31; Matthews, *Voyage to Sierra Leone*, 82–83; S. N. Eisenstadt, "Primitive Political Systems: A Preliminary Comparative Analysis," *American Anthropologist* 61 (1959): 202–3, 208.

7. Little, "Secret Society in Cultural Specialization," 199–206, and "Poro as Arbiter of Culture," 3–4 and "Political Function of the Poro," Part I, 350–54; Fulton, "Functions of Poro in Kpelle Society," 1221, 1226–27; Warren L. d'Azevedo, "Common Principles of Variant Kinship Structures among the Golas of Western Liberia," *American Anthropologist* 64, no. 3 (1962): 513–14 and "Gola Society and Culture," 70–76.

8. Little, *Mende*, 226–27, 240–47 and "Poro as Arbiter of Culture," 3 and "Secret Society in Cultural Specialization," 199–201; Fulton, "Functions of Poro in Kpelle Society," 1226–28; Harley, "Notes on Poro," 3–9, 11–12, 29–31.

9. Harley, "Notes on Poro," 7.

10. d'Azevedo, "Gola Society and Culture," 70; Little, "Poro as Arbiter of Culture," 2; Rodney, *History of Upper Guinea*, 67.

11. d'Azevedo, "Gola Society and Culture," 70, and "Gola Poro and Sande: Primal Tasks in Social Custodianship," *Ethnologische Zeitschrift Zürich* I (1980): 15–16 and "Mask Makers and Myth in Western Liberia," in A. Forge, ed., *Primitive Art and Society* (Oxford: Oxford University Press, 1973): 126–130; see also Margaret Washington Creel, "The Significance to Female Diviners in Antebellulm Slave Communities," unpublished paper presented at the Dark Madonna Symposium, November 8–9, 1986, University of California, Los Angeles.

12. Little, "Poro as Arbiter of Culture," 1, and "Secret Society in Cultural Specialization," 210–11; Harley, "Notes on Poro," 5; Dominique Zahan, *The Religion, Spirituality and Thought of Traditional Africa* (Chicago and London: University of Chicago Press, 1979), 53–65; Betty M. Kuyk, "The African Derivation of Black Fraternal Orders in the United States," *Comparative Studies in Societies and History* 25, no. 4 (October, 1983): 559–92; Rodney, *History of Upper Guinea*, 258.

13. Francis Varnod to SPG, January 13, 1723 SPGLL BV 7, reel 7, series B, vol. 4 (2); John S. Trimingham, *A History of Islam in West Africa* (Glasgow: Oxford University Press, 1962), 104–13, 174–76; Kofi Asare Opoku, *West African Traditional Religion* (Jurong, Singapore: FEP International Private, 1978), 14–29; J. B. Danquah, *The Akan Doctrine of God: A Fragment of Gold Coast Ethics and Religion* (London: Lutterworth Press, 1944), 30–42; R. S. Rattray, *Religion and Art in Ashanti* (London: Clarendon Press, 1923), 1–2; Sibley and Westermann, *Liberia*, 192–97; Folkways Research Series, *History of Gola Tribe*, I:5; John H. Weeks, *Among the Primitive BaKongo* (London: Seeley, Service, 1914), 276; Kwabena Amponsah, *Topics on West African Traditional Religion* (Accra, Ghana: McGraw-Hill, 1974), 20–30; H. P. Junod, *Bantu Heritage* (Johannesburg: Hortors, 1938; Westport, Conn.: Negro University Press, 1970), 132–41; Janheinz Jahn, *Muntu: An Outline of Neo-African Culture*, trans. Marjorie Greene (London: Faber and Faber, 1961), 104–8; Geoffrey Parrinder, *Re-*

ligion in Africa (Middlesex, England: Penguin Books, 1969), 39–41, 83–86; Little, *Mende*, 2, 217–18; W. T. Harris and Harry Sawyerr, *The Springs of Mende Belief and Conduct: A Discussion of the Influence of the Belief in the Supernatural Among the Mende* (Freetown: Sierra Leone University Press, 1968), 2–13, 119–20; Parsons, *Religion in an African Society*, 22–24, 163–69; Folkways Research Series, *Traditional History of Folklore of the Glebo Tribe*, 2 vols. (Monrovia: Dept. of Interior, 1955 and 1961) II: 83, 123, and *Tribes of the Western Province*, 18, 21, 25, 27; William Bosman, *A New and Accurate Description of the Coast of Guinea*, trans. John Ralph Willis (Holland, 1704; 4th English ed., New York: Barnes and Noble, 1967), 156; Harry Gailey, Jr., *A History of the Gambia* (London: Routledge and Kegan Paul, 1965), 6–7; Gamble, *Wolof*, 39; Thomas Winterbottom, *An Account of the Native Africans in the Neighborhood of Sierra Leone*, 2 vols., (London: Frank Cass, 1969; repr. from 1803 ed.), I: 222, 226; Joseph Corry, *Observations Upon the Windward Coast of Africa* (London: Frank Cass, 1958, repr. from 1807 ed.), 60–61; Karl Laman, *Kongo*, 5 vols. (Uppsala: Studia Ethnographica Upsaliensia, 1962) III: 1–2, 53–63; Georges Balandier, *Daily Life in the Kingdom of the Kongo, from the Sixteenth to the Eighteenth Century*, trans. Helen Weaver (London: George Allen & Unwin, 1968), 244–45; W. C. Willoughby, *The Soul of the Bantu: A Sympathetic Study of the Magico-Religious Practices and Beliefs of the Bantu Tribes of Africa* (Westport, Conn.: Negro Universities Press, 1970, originally published 1928), 72–76; John S. Mbiti, *African Religions and Philosophies* (New York: Praeger Publishers, 1959), 4–5, 28–38, 159–62; Willie Abraham, *The Mind of Africa* (Chicago: University of Chicago Press, 1962), 52–56; Beryl L. Bellman, *Village of Curers and Assassins; on the Production of Fala Kpelle Cosmological Categories* (The Hague and Paris: Mouton, 1975), 129–30; see also John S. Mbiti, *Concepts of God in Africa* (New York: Praeger Publishers, 1970). This author's approach seems more theological than anthropological or historical. African concepts of God are placed in Christian theological terms rather than discussed and interpreted in their own contextual environments. An older study is Edwin Smith, ed., *African Ideas of God* (London: Edinburgh House Press, 1950). It provides the best information on concepts of God among various African peoples.

14. Jahn, *Muntu*, 109–14; Parsons, *Religion in an African Society*, 167–69, 181; Sibley and Westermann, *Liberia*, 194–96; Little, *Mende*, 218–221; Harris and Sawyerr, *Mende Belief*, 14–18, 30–33; Abraham, *Mind of Africa*, 63–64; Mbiti, *African Religions*, 6–7; John M. Janzen and Wyatt MacGaffey, *An Anthology of Kongo Religion: Primary Texts from Lower Zaire* (Lawrence, Kans.: University of Kansas Publications in Anthropology, No. 5, 1974), 34; Robert Farris Thompson and Joseph Cornet, *The Four Moments of the Sun: Kongo Art in Two Worlds* (Washington, D. C.: National Gallery of Art, 1981), 27–28, 42–47, 134, n. 50, and passim; Robert Farris Thompson, *Flash of the Spirit: African and Afro-American Art and Philosophy* (New York: Vintage Books, 1983), 103–58; Balandier, *Daily Life in Kongo*, 245–49.

15. Parrinder, *Religion in Africa*, 26; Mbiti, *African Religions*, 159–62; Harris and Sawyerr, *Mende Belief*, 88–90; Sibley and Westermann, *Liberia*, 199; Folkways Research Series, *Tribes of the Western Province*, 18, 27, 29; Rattray, *Religion in Ashanti*, 153; Abraham, *Mind of Africa*, 59–60; Danquah, *Akan Doctrine of God*. 153–64.

16. Laman, *Kongo*, III: 1–6, 216–18; Thompson and Cornet, *Four Moments of the Sun*, 43.

17. Willoughby, *Soul of Bantu*, 76–82; Parsons, *Religion in an African Society*, 26–27, 75–76; Harris & Sawyerr, *Mende Belief*, 14–18; Rattray, *Religion in Ashanti*, 216; Abraham, *Mind of Africa*, 63–64; Opoku, *West African Religion*, 35–39; Mbiti, *African Religions*, 11–12; Amponsah, *Topics on African Traditional Religion*, 85–91.

18. Igor Kopytoff, "The Suku of Southwestern Congo," in James L. Gibbs Jr., ed.,

Peoples of Africa (New York: Holt, Rinehart and Winston, 1965), 450–52, 458; Wyatt MacGaffey, *Custom and Government in the Lower Kongo* (Berkeley: University of California Press, 1970), 84; Laman, *Kongo* II: 130–31; Balandier, *Daily Life in Kongo*, 246–47.

19. Laman, *Kongo*, II: 22–23; Balandier, *Daily Life in Kongo*, 217–20, 246–57; Willoughby, *Soul of Bantu*, 71, 77–82, 315; Weeks, *Among the BaKongo*, 158–71.

20. Weeks, *Among the BaKongo*, 266–68, 278; Laman, *Kongo*, II: 92; MacGaffey, *Custom in Lower Kongo*, 148–50; Willoughby, *Soul of Bantu*, 86; Opoku, *West African Religion*, 36–39; Amponsah, *Topics on African Traditional Religion*, 86; Harris and Sawyerr, *Mende Belief*, 30–33; Melville J. Herskovits, *The Myth of the Negro Past* (Boston: Beacon Press, 1958; repr. from 1941 ed.), 206; Roger Bastide, *African Civilizations in the New World*, trans. Peter Green (New York: Harper & Row, 1971), 106, 161; Thompson and Cornet, *Four Moments of the Sun*, 181–203; Thompson, *Flash of the Spirit*, 132–58; John M. Vlach, *The Afro-American Tradition in Decorative Arts* (Cleveland, Ohio: Cleveland Museum of Art, 1978), 139–47; Elizabeth A. Fenn, "Honoring the Ancestors; Kongo-American Graves in the American South," *Southern Exposure* 28 (September–October, 1985): 42–57; "Notes and Documents; Antebellum and War Memories of Mrs. Telfair Hodgson," Sarah Hodgson Torian, ed., *Georgia Historical Quarterly* 27, no. 4 (December, 1953): 352; Albert H. Stoddard, "Origin, Dialect, Beliefs and Characteristics of the Negroes of the South Carolina and Georgia Coasts," *Georgia Historical Quarterly* 28 (September, 1944): 181–93; Irving E. Lowrey, *Life on the Old Plantation* (Columbia: University of South Carolina Press, 1911), 81–86; South Carolina Folklore Project, #1655, D-4-27A, WPA, SCL: Folk-Lore Scrap-Book, "Mortuary Customs and Beliefs of South Carolina Negroes," from an article originally published in the *Atlanta Constitution* by May A. Waring, *Journal of American Folk-Lore* 7 (1894): 318–19.

21. Opoku, *West African Religion*, 147–51; Amponsah, *Topics on African Traditional Religion*, 80–84; Parsons, *Religion in an African Society*, 50–55, 71–72, 186; Harris and Sawyerr, *Mende Belief*, Chapter 4; Sibley and Westermann, *Liberia*, 211–213; Balandier, *Daily Life in Kongo*, 248–50; Laman, *Kongo* III: 81–104; Weeks, *Among the BaKongo*, 214–20, 232–35; Willoughby, *Soul of Bantu*, 192–95; Thompson and Cornet, *Four Moments of the Sun*, 37; Thompson, *Flash of the Spirit*, 106–7, 117–19; E. J. Glave, "Fetishism in Congo Land," *Century* 41 (November–April, 1890–91): 825–26.

22. Parsons, *Religion in an African Society*, 50–55, 71–72, 186; Harris and Sawyerr, *Mende Belief*, Chapter 4; Sibley and Westermann, *Liberia*, 211–13; Laman, *Kongo*, III: 57, 81–104, 157–59; Weeks, *Among the BaKongo*, 231–36; Thompson and Cornet, *Four Moments of the Sun*, 110–14; Thompson, *Flash of the Spirit*, 106–7, 117–21; Janzen and MacGaffey, *Kongo Religion*, 34–35; Mbiti, *African Religions*, 169, Chapters 15–16.

23. Sibley and Westermann, *Liberia*, 213–14; Harris and Sawyerr, *Mende Belief*, 54–59; Rattray, *Religion in Ashanti*, 148–49; Mbiti, *African Religions*, 168–171, Chapters 15–16; Thompson and Cornet, *Four Moments of the Sun*, 37; Janzen and MacGaffey, *Kongo Religion*, 34–35; Laman, *Kongo*, III: 81–105.

24. Mbiti, *African Religions*, 166–67, Rattray, *Religion in Ashanti*, 38–39; Parsons, *Religion in an African Society*, 71–72; Sibley and Westermann, *Liberia*, 211; Folkways Research Series, *History of Gola Tribe*, II: 22–23; Glave, "Fetishism in Congo Land," 828–29; Weeks, *Among the BaKongo*, 214–18; Thompson and Cornet, *Four Moments of the Sun*, 37, 110–14; Laman, *Kongo*, II: 130–32.

25. *SCA*, June 26, 1840, June 26, 1843, October 30, 1847; *Minutes; Beaufort Baptist Church*, "Origin of the Colored Societies," October 7, 1859, Business Meeting in which organization of societies was discussed, 271–72, January 7, 1842 and November 1, 1840, 12, BC; *SCA*, Diary of Laura M. Towne, 52, 162, Penn School Papers, SHC; John L. Field to George W. Moore, March 21, 1833, HSSCC.

26. Folklore Project, #1655 and #1855, D-4-27A, 27B, WPA, SCL; Lowrey, *Old Plantation*, 83–87; Towne Diary, 98; Elsie Clews Parsons, *Folk-lore of the Sea Islands of South Carolina* (Cambridge, Mass.: American Folk-lore Society 1923), 211–13; E. Horace Fitchett, "Superstitions in South Carolina," *The Crisis* 43 (1936): 360–71; Henry F. Davis, "Folklore in South Carolina," *Journal of American Folklore* 27 (1914): 245–49; Leonora Herron and Alice M. Bacon, "Conjuring and Conjure Doctors," *Southern Workman* 24 (1895): 118; Louis Pendleton, "Notes on Negro Folklore and Witchcraft in the South," *Journal of American Folklore* 3 (1890): 301–17; Balandier, *Daily Life in Kongo*, 248–50; Laman, *Kongo*, III: 216–21; Glave, "Fetishism in Congo Land," 834–36; James R. Stuart Recollections, n.d., circa 1850, 2–4, SHC; Charles A. Raymond, "Religious Life of the Negro Slave," *Harpers New Monthly Magazine* 27 (June–November, 1963): Part I, 478–80, Part II, 676, Part III, 821; David Thorpe to John Mooney, January 25, 1863, Thorpe Series, James McBride Dabbs Papers, SHC.

27. Despite the exalted modern application of the term "ontology" in its reference to abstract being, "ontology" originally referred to that which belongs to existent finite being. See Walter Brugger, ed., *Philosophical Dictionary*, trans. Kenneth Baker (Spokane: Gonzaga University Press, 1972), 301–2 ("Ontology"). With regard to African culture and spirituality, the concept of being cannot be restricted to the physiological, as opposed to the psychological or fantastic sphere.

28. MacGaffey, *Custom in Lower Kongo*, 261–62; Parsons, *Religion in an African Society*, 173–76, 179, 183–85; Parrinder, *Religion in Africa*, Chapters 2–6; Placide Tempels, *Bantu Philosophy*, trans. Colin King (Paris: Présence Africaine, 1959), passim; Sibley and Westermann, *Liberia*, 187–88; Abraham, *Mind of Africa*, 52; Harris and Sawyerr, *Mende Belief*, 115–17; Mbiti *African Religions*, 2–16.

29. Michael Welton, "Themes in African Traditional Belief and Ritual," *Practical Anthropology* 18 (1971): 1–8; E. Bolaji Idowu, *African Traditional Religion, A Definition* (London: SMC Press, 1973), 61–68; *CAJ*, January 31, 1834; *SCA*, July 28, 1843, February 16, 1844, October 30, 1846; Charlotte Forten, "Life on the Sea Islands," Part I, *Atlantic Monthly* 13 (June, 1864): 592.

30. Mbiti *African Religions*, 210–13; Abraham, *Mind of Africa*, 106; Sibley and Westermann, *Liberia*, 190–91; Parsons, *Religion in an African Society*, 174, 183–84; Harris and Sawyerr, *Mende Belief*, 103–5; Parrinder, *Religion in Africa*, 41, 81–89; Tempels, *Bantu Philosophy*, Chapters 5–6; Jahn, *Muntu*, 110, 114–17; Amponsah, *Topics on African Traditional Religion*, 70–80; Opoku, *West African Religion*, 152–60.

31. Mbiti, *African Religions*, 16.

32. Harris and Sawyerr, *Mende Belief*, 117–21; Thompson and Cornet, *Four Moments of the Sun*, 84.

33. Tempels, *Bantu Philosophy*, 64–66; Jahn, *Muntu*, 121–27; Sibley and Westermann, *Liberia*, 187–202; Abraham, *Mind of Africa*, 48–49, 52, 59–62; Parsons, *Religion in an African Society*, 174–93; Harris and Sawyerr, *Mende Belief*, 123–24; Mbiti, *African Religions*, 15–16, Chapters 11–14; Parrinder, *Religion in Africa*, 78–83; Thompson and Cornet, *Four Moments of the Sun*, 27–99; Opoku, *West African Religion*, 91–139; Amponsah, *Topics on Traditional Religion*, 48–68.

3. Missionaries and Masters

1. Samuel Thomas to SPG, December 25, 1702, SPGLL, BV 6, reel 1, series A, vol. 1; Faith Vibert, "Society for the Propagation of the Gospel in Foreign Parts: Its work for the Negroes in North America before 1783," *Journal of Negro History* 25 (April, 1933): 171, 182–84, 188–89; John C. Van Horne, ed., *Religious Philanthropy and Colonial Slavery: The*

Correspondence of the Associates of Dr. Bray, 1717–1777 (Urbana and Chicago: University of Illinois Press, 1985), 25; Sidney E. Ahlstrom, *A Religious History of the American People* (New Haven and London: Yale University Press, 1972), 196–97. There was a tendency among some early missionaries to indiscriminately refer to Indians and Africans as "blacks." See Van Horne, *Religious Philanthropy and Colonial Slavery*, 39, n. 20.

2. Peter H. Wood, *Black Majority: Negroes in Colonial South Carolina from 1670 through the Stono Rebellion* (New York: Alfred A. Knopf, 1974), 37–38; Samuel Thomas to Dr. Bray, January 20, 1702, SPGLL, BV 6, reel 1, series A, vol. 1; Francis Varnod to SPG, January 13, 1723, SPGLL, BV 6, reel 6, series B, vol. 4 (1); Thomas Nairne to Dr. Marston, August 20, 1705, SPGLL, BV 6, reel 12, series A, vol. 2.

3. South Carolina Clergy to Gideon Johnston, March 4, 1712, SPGLL, BV 6, reel 6, series A, vol. 8; William Taylor to SPG, May 15, 1716, SPGLL, BV 7, reel 6, series B, vol. 4 (1); Gilbert Jones to SPG, November 16, 1716, SPGLL, BV 6, reel 13, series B, vol. 4 (1).

4. Francis Le Jau to SPG, March 22, 1708–9, SPGLL, BV 6, reel 3, series A, vol. 4; South Carolina Clergy to Gideon Johnston, March 4, 1712, SPGLL.

5. Robert Maule to SPG, Summer, 1710, SPGLL, BV 6, reel 5, series A, vol. 5.

6. Richard Ludlam to SPG, 1725, SPGLL, BV 6, reel 11,series A, vol. 19; Francis Varnod to SPG, April 3, 1728, SPGLL, BV 6, reel 12, series A, vol. 21; Robert Stevens to SPG, February 21, 1705, SPGLL, BV 6, reel 2, series A, vol. 2.

7. Frank Klingberg, ed., *Carolina Chronicle, the Papers of Commissary Gideon Johnston, 1707–1716* (Berkeley and Los Angeles: University of California Press, 1946), 118–19; South Carolina Clergy to Gideon Johnston, March 4, 1712, SPGLL.

8. Thomas Naire to Dr. Marston. August 20, 1705, SPGLL; Lewis Jones to SPG, January 26, 1727–28 SPGLL, BV 6, reel 11, series A, vol. 20; Frank J. Klingberg, *An Appraisal of the Negro in Colonial South Carolina: A Study in Americanization* (Washington, D. C.: Associated Publishers, 1941), 66–68; Wood, *Black Majority*, 127–30; M. Eugene Sirmans, *Colonial South Carolina, A Political History 1663–1763* (Chapel Hill: University of North Carolina Press, 1966), 111–16; Verner W. Crane, *Southern Frontier*, 1670–1732 (Ann Arbor: University of Michigan Press, 1964), 168–69, 184–85.

9. Lewis Jones to SPG, January 26, 1727–28; Sirmans, *Colonial South Carolina*, 81, 99.

10. Lewis Jones to SPG, January 26, 1727–28; Wood. *Black Majority*, 150.

11. Verner W. Crane, "Dr. Thomas Bray and the Charitable Colony Project, 1730," *William and Mary Quarterly* 19, 3d. ser. (January, 1962): 58–61; Sirmans, *Colonial South Carolina*, 168–69; Henry A. M. Smith, "Purrysburgh," *South Carolina Historical and Genealogical Magazine* 10 (October, 1909): 189–91; Van Horne, *Religious Philanthropy and Colonial Slavery*, 1–18.

12. Van Horne, *Religious Philanthropy and Colonial Slavery*, 18–19.

13. Smith, "Purrysburgh," 187–95; Van Horne, *Religious Philanthropy and Colonial Slavery*, 17–18; Arnold Dallimore, *George Whitefield, Life and Times of the Great Evangelist of the Eighteenth Century Revival*, 2 vols. (Guildford and London: Billing and Sons, 1970), I: 506; Walter Brooks, "The Priority of the Silver Bluff Church and its Promoters," *Journal of Negro History* 7 (April, 1922): 172–96; "Letters Showing and Rise and Progress of the Early Negro Churches of Georgia and the West Indies," *Journal of Negro History* 1 (January, 1916): 69–92; Albert J. Raboteau, *Slave Religion: The "Invisible Institution" in the Antebellum South* (New York: Oxford University Press, 1978), 139–42; *CAJ*, January 31, 1834, June 20, 1834.

14. Klingberg, *Appraisal of the Negro*, 66–68, 69–70, 72; Wood, *Black Majority*, 314–26.

15. Klingberg, *Appraisal of the Negro*, 70–74; Van Horne, *Religious Philanthropy and Colo-*

nial Slavery, 72; Sirmans, *Colonial South Carolina*, 231–32; Edward McCrady, *South Carolina under the Royal Government, 1719–1776* (New York: Macmillan, 1899), 238, 240–42; David T. Morgan, "The Great Awakening in South Carolina, 1740–1775," *South Atlantic Quarterly* 70 (Fall, 1971): 595–606.

16. A. S. Salley, ed., *Minutes of the Vestry of St. Helena's Parish, South Carolina, 1726–1812* (Columbia: State Co., 1919), 22–25; Frederick Dalcho, *An Historical Account of the Protestant Episcopal Church in South Carolina* (New York: Arno Press, 1972; repr. from 1820 ed.), 379–81; Klingberg, *Appraisal of the Negro*, 72–74; Morgan, "Great Awakening in South Carolina," 602–3.

17. John Wikhead to SPG, September 26, 1715, SPGLL, BV 6, reel 6, series B, vol. 4 (1); Francis Varnod to SPG, January 13, 1723, SPGLL; South Carolina Clergy to Gideon Johnston, March 4, 1712, SPGLL.

18. Francis Varnod to SPG, January 13, 1723 SPGLL; John Fulton to SPG, December 4, 1730, SPGLL, BV 6, reel 12, series A, vol. 23; Richard Ludlam to SPG, 1725, SPGLL.

19. Samuel Thomas to SPG, December 25, 1702, SPGLL; Thomas Hassell to SPG, August 20, 1712, BV 6, reel 3, series A, vol. 7; Letters of J. Ottolenghe, July 12, 1758, SPG, London Ms. of Dr. Bray's Associates, Letters from the American Colonies, BX 19, reel 10; Klingberg, *Carolina Chronicle*, 118–19.

20. *SCG*, May 4, 1734; Wood, *Black Majority*, Chapter 10; *SCG*, April 16 and 23, 1737; David Barry Gaspar, *Bondmen and Rebels: A Study of Master-Slave Relations in Antigua* (Baltimore: Johns Hopkins University Press, 1985) 342.

21. Wood, *Black Majority*, 314–15, 324–25; For a discussion on the relationship between literacy, rebelliousness and Spanish agitation, see Klingberg, *Appraisal of the Negro*, 69–70; and Sirmans, *Colonial South Carolina*, 207–9.

22. Alexander Garden to SPG, May 6, 1740, Box 20 from Lambeth Palace Library, vol. 941, no. 72, Ms. of Archbishop of Canterbury; Klingberg, *Appraisal of the Negro*, 70–104; Garden attempted to interest the Bray Associates in his plans for a Negro school. He proposed that the two Purrysburgh missionaries alter their arrangement, pointing to the larger, more accessible black population in Charleston and better opportunities for success. The two Moravians presented the proposal to Oglethorpe and the Associates, but to no avail. The Purrysburgh missionaries reluctantly kept their commitment to the Associates. Van Horne, *Religious Philanthropy and Colonial Slavery*, 19.

23. Klingberg, *Appraisal of the Negro*, 66–68; Wood, *Black Majority*, 323–24; Robert Maule to SPG, Summer, 1710, SPGLL; Dalcho, *Episcopal Church of South Carolina*, Chapter 4.

24. Sirmans *Colonial South Carolina*, 14–15, 76–77; Ahlstrom, *Religious History*, 198; George Fox, *A Memoir of the Life, Travels, and Gospel Labours of George Fox* (London: Friends' Book and Track Depository, 1867), 263–65, 270, 279–80; Sidney V. James, *A People Among People: Quaker Benevolence in Eighteenth-Century America* (Cambridge, Mass.: Harvard University Press, 1963), 148–49; William F. Medlin, *Quaker Families in South Carolina and Georgia* (Columbia, S. C.: Ben Franklin Press, 1982), 7–11, 19. As Quakers strengthened their antislavery stand in the colonial era, they were less and less successful in South Carolina. By the time of the War for Independence, the Quakers had left South Carolina. Howard Beeth, "Outside Agitators in Southern History: The Society of Friends, 1650–1800" (Ph.D. dissertation, University of Houston, 1984), 101, 424–51.

25. Sirmans, *Colonial South Carolina*, 36–37; Edward McCrady, *The History of South Carolina under the Proprietary Government, 1670–1719* (New York: Macmillan 1897), 334, 325–26; Joe Madison King, *A History of South Carolina Baptists* (Columbia: General Board, South Carolina Baptist Convention, 1964), 10–13.

26. F. Varnod to SPG, April 3, 1728, SPGLL; H. A. Tupper, ed., *Two Centuries of the*

First Baptish Church of South Carolina, 1683–1883 (Baltimore: R. H. Woodland, 1899), 7, 39, 56–59, 84–86, 94–97; A. H. Newman, *A History of the Baptist Church in the United States* (New York: Christian Literature, 1894), 1–79, 221–26, 242–52; David Benedict, *A General History of the Baptist Denomination in America and Other Parts of the World* (New York: Lewis Colby, 1848), 700–702; Ahlstrom, *Religious History*, 172–73; King, *South Carolina Baptists*, 26–35. There is some controversy over Screven's actual arrival with the largest group of Baptists. The Charleston Baptist Church maintains that the date of its establishment and Screven's arrival is 1683. Baptist historian Joe M. King places it at 1696. Here we use the generally accepted date of 1683. King, *South Carolina Baptists*, 13.

27. Samuel Thomas to SPG, January 25, 1712, SPGLL, BV 6, reel 1, series A, vol. 1; Francis Le Jau to SPG, August 30, 1712, SPGLL BV 6, reel 5, series A, vol. 7.

28. Lewis Jones to SPG, January 26, 1727–28, SPGLL; Francis Varnod to SPG, April 3, 1728, SPGLL; John Fulton to SPG, December 4, 1730, SPGLL; Klingberg, *Appraisal of the Negro*, 74–75; King, *South Carolina Baptists*, 25–35.

29. Francis Le Jau to SPG, February 20, 1711, SPGLL, BV 6, reel 4, series A, vol. 7; William G. McLoughlin and Winthrop D. Jordan, eds., "Baptists Face the Barbarities of Slavery in 1710," *Journal of Southern History* 29 (November, 1963): 497–501.

30. McLoughlin and Jordan, "Baptist Face the Barbarities of Slavery," 496–98; New Jersey prescribed death for slaves convicted of murder, arson, mutilation or rape of a white woman, and castration for attempted rape. The Lords of Trade (in London) denounced such "inhumane penalities on Negroes," and the Privy Council voted to disallow the law. See Edgar McManus, *Black Bondage in the North* (Syracuse: Syracuse University Press, 1973), 84–85; *Documents Relating to the Colonial, Revolutionary, and Post-Revolutionary History of the State of New Jersey* 42 vols. (Newark: New Jersey Historical Society), 3:473–74; W. L. Grant and James Munro, eds. *Acts of the Privy Council: Colonial Series, 1613–1783*, 6 vols. (London: Wyman Publishers), 2:848.

31. McLoughlin and Jordan, "Baptists Face the Barbarities of Slavery," 496–98.

32. King, *South Carolina Baptists*, 14–17, 26–35.

4. Christianity, Bondage, and the Great Awakening

1. Peter H. Wood, *Black Majority: Negroes in Colonial South Carolina from 1670 through the Stono Rebellion* (New York: Alfred A. Knopf, 1974), 77, 81, 308–9; Edward McCrady, *South Carolina under the Royal Government 1719–1776* (New York: Macmillan, 1899), 180, 185–88; Eugene Sirmans, *Colonial South Carolina, A Political History 1663–1763* (Chapel Hill: University of North Carolina Press, 1966), 207–8; David T. Morgan, "The Great Awakening in South Carolina, 1740–1775," *South Atlantic Quarterly* 70 (Fall, 1971): 595–96.

2. William Seward, *Journal of a Voyage from Savannah to Philadelphia and from Philadelphia to England* (London: James Buckland, 1740), 5; Arnold Dallimore, *George Whitefield, Life and Times of the Great Evangelist of the Eighteenth Century Revival*, 2 vols. (Guildford and London: Billing and Sons, 1970), I: 418–19, II: 60, 139–43; John Pollack, *George Whitefield and the Great Awakening* (Garden City: Doubleday, 1972), 3–10, 47–54, 62–68; *George Whitefield's Journals* (Guildford and London: Billing and Sons, 1960; repr. unabridg. from 1905 ed., with unpubl. Journal, first publ. 1938), 82–93, 156–59, 302–11, 571–88; Sir James Stephens, *Essays in Ecclesiastical Biography*, 5th ed. (London: Longmans, Green, Reader, and Dyer, 1837), 382–83, 389–90.

3. Whitefield, *Journals*, 165.

4. Ibid., 302–5; Pollack, *Whitefield and Great Awakening*, 45–50, 63–71.

5. Dallimore, *Whitefield, Great Evangelist*, II: 413–42; Whitefield, *Journals*, 338–62 and passim.

6. Dallimore, *Whitefield, Great Evangelist*, I: 442–43; Whitefield, *Journals*, 384–85.

7. Whitefield, *Journals*, 384–85.

8. Ibid., 386–89.

9. Ibid., 400–401.

10. Dallimore, *Whitefield, Great Evangelist*, I: 482–83; Frank J. Klingberg, *An Appraisal of the Negro in Colonial South Carolina: A Study in Americanization*, (Washington, D. C.: Associated Publishers, 1941), 71–73; Seward, *Journal*, 5; Whitefield, *Journals*, 401, 439–49; Morgan, "Great Awakening in South Carolina," 596–602. Whitefield was preaching to up to 4,000 listeners in Charleston in 1740 on his summer tour. He finally grew tired of listening to Garden bewail against him and no longer attended St. Philip's when he was in the city. Instead he "went to the Baptist and Independent meeting-houses, where Jesus Christ was preached." Whitefield, *Journals*, 449–50.

11. McCrady, *South Carolina under Royal Government*, 246–47; Rev. Alexander Garden to Rev. Samuel Smith, September 24, 1742, in John C. Van Horne, ed., *Religious Philanthropy and Colonial Slavery: the Correspondence of the Associates of Dr. Bray, 1717–1777* (Urbana and Chicago: University of Illinois Press, 1985), 93–94, 338; Klingberg, *Appraisal of the Negro*, 101–17.

12. Klingberg *Appraisal of the Negro*, 113–14, 119–22; McCrady, *South Carolina under Royal Government*, 245–46, 439–40.

13. Klingberg, *Appraisal of the Negro*, 121, n. 56; McCrady, *South Carolina under Royal Government*, 247.

14. Klingberg, *Appraisal of the Negro*, 119–21; Clarke's population estimate was very close to the mark. Philip D. Morgan's recent article places the Lowcountry population at 53,257 in 1760. See his "Black Society in the Lowcountry, 1760–1810," in Ira Berlin and Ronald Hoffman, *Slavery and Freedom in the Age of the American Revolution* (Charlottesville: The University of Virginia Press, 1983), 85, Table 1.

15. Seward, *Journal*, 6, 7, 11; Whitefield, *Journals*, 379; Stephen J. Stein, "George Whitefield on Slavery: Some New Evidence," *Church History* 42, no. 2 (June, 1973): 243, 248.

16. Pollack, *Whitefield and Great Awakening*, 124–26; Dallimore, *Whitefield Great Evangelist*, I: 482–84, 495–501; Seward, *Journal*, 10; Alexander Garden, *Six letters to the Rev. George Whitefield*, 2nd ed. (Boston: T. Fleet, 1740), passim; Stein "George Whitefield on Slavery." 244.

17. Whitefield, *Journals*, 406–7; Seward, *Journal*, 10; Dallimore, *Whitefield, Great Evangelist*, I: 495; *Three Letters from the Reverend Mr. G. Whitefield* (Philadelphia: B. Franklin, 1740), 13. Whitefield's "Letter . . . Concerning . . . Negroes" was written in Savannah in January 1740, *Three Letters from Whitefield*, 16.

18. *Three Letters from Whitefield*, 13–14.

19. Ibid., 14–16.

20. Ibid.

21. Thomas Hassell to SPG, August 30, 1712, SPGLL: Francis Le Jau to SPG, March 22, 1708–9, and February 20, 1711, SPGLL, BV 6, reel 3, series A, vols. 4–7.

22. John Fulton to SPG, May 25, 1734, SPGLL, BV 6, reel 13, series A, vols. 24–25.

23. Francis Le Jau to SPG, June 13, 1710, SPGLL, BV 6, reel 4, series A, vol. 5; John Fulton to SPG, December 4, 1730, SPGLL, BV 6, reel 12, series A, vol. 23; Francis Le Jau to SPG, March 22, 1708–9, and July 18, SPGLL, BV 6, reel 4, series A, vol. 6.

24. Dallimore, *Whitefield, Great Evangelist*, I: 497, 509; Pollack, *Whitefield and Great Awakening*, 130–31; Garden, *Six Letters to Whitefield*, 50–53; *Three Letters from Whitefield*, 16.

25. Dallimore, *Whitefield, Great Evangelist*, I: 497, 509; Pollack, *Whitefield and Great Awakening*, 221–25; Betty Wood, *Slavery in Colonial Georgia, 1730–1775* (Athens: University of Georgia Press, 1984), 66–67; Stein "Whitefield on Slavery," 245; Stephens, *Ecclesiastical Biography*, 391; Stuart C. Henry, *George Whitefield, Wayfaring Witness* (Nashville: Abingdon Press, 1957), 116–17; James Habersham to Countess Dowager of Huntington, December 31, 1770, *Letters of James Habersham 1756–1775*, Collections, Georgia Historical Society, vol. 6, 109–11.

26. Quoted from Henry, *Whitefield, Wayfaring Witness*, 117.

27. Donald Mathews, *Slavery and Methodism: A Chapter in American Morality 1780–1845* (Princeton: Princeton University Press, 1965), 5–6; Whitefield, *Journals*, 446–50; Dallimore, *Whitefield, Great Evangelist*, II: 219; *Hugh Bryan and Mary Hutson, Living Christianity, Delineated in the Diaries and Letters of two Pious Persons lately Deceased; Mr. Hugh Bryan and Mrs. Mary Hutson, both of South Carolina* (London: J. Buckland, 1750), 13, 70, 91, passim; William Maine Hutson, "The Hutson Family of South Carolina," *South Carolina Historical and Genealogical Magazine* 9 (July, 1908): 127; Klingberg, *Appraisal of the Negro*, 70–71; Mrs. J. H. Redding, *Life and Times of Jonathan Bryan, 1708–1788* (Savannah: Morning News Print, 1901), 31–45; Wood, *Slavery in Colonial Georgia*, 19.

28. Bryan and Hutson, *Living Christianity*, 1–4, 13; Redding, *Jonathan Bryan*, 7–9, 32; Whitefield, *Journals*, 446, 440, 502–4; Harvey H. Jackson, "Hugh Bryan and the Evangelical Movement in Colonial South Carolina," *William and Mary Quarterly* 47, 3d ser., no. 4 (October, 1986): 596–98; Henry, *Whitefield, Wayfaring Witness*, 70; Sirmans, *Colonial South Carolina*, 231–32; McCrady, *South Carolina under Royal Government*, 238–43; Klingberg, *Appraisal of the Negro*, 71; Stein, "Whitefield on Slavery," 248–51.

29. Whitefield, *Journals*, 446, 450; Hutson, "Hutson Family," 127; Colonial Records of South Carolina, *Journal of the Commons House of Assembly, 1741–42*, 404, 406–8, and *1742–44*, 72; McCrady, *South Carolina under Royal Government*, 241–43; Jackson, "Hugh Bryan," 594, 605–9; David S. Lovejoy, " 'Desperate Enthusiasm': Early Signs of American Radicalism," in Margaret Jacob and James Jacob, *The Origins of Anglo-American Radicalism* (London: George Allen & Unwin, 1984), 237, 241, n. 24.

30. Whitefield, *Journals*, 502–4; Dallimore, *Whitefield, Great Evangelist*, I: 586; Jackson, "Hugh Bryan," 600–3.

31. Jackson, "Hugh Bryan," 605–10; Lovejoy " 'Desperate Enthusiasm,' " 237; McCrady, *South Carolina under Royal Government*, 240–42; Sirmans, *Colonial South Carolina*, 231–32; *Journal of the Assembly, 1741–42*, 406–8, 461–62.

32. *Journal of the Assembly, 1742–44*, 72–73, 364–368, 394, 398; Bryan and Hutson, *Living Christianity*, 55–126; Jackson, "Hugh Bryan," 604, 609, 613–14.

33. Morgan, "Great Awakening in South Carolina," 599–601; Mrs. R. W. Hutson, "Register kept by the Rev. William Hutson of Stoney Creek Independent Congregational Church and (Circular) Congregational Church in Charles Town, S. C., 1743–1760," *South Carolina Historical and Genealogical Magazine* 38 (January, 1937): 21–33; Klingberg, *Appraisal of the Negro*, 70–71; Jackson, "Hugh Bryan," 606, 612–13.

34. Whitefield, *Journals*, 501; Wood, *Slavery in Colonial Georgia*, 66, 92, 209, n. 12; Redding, *Jonathan Bryan*, 11–20, 29–30, 32–33.

35. Wood, *Slavery in Colonial Georgia*, 84–87, 111, 114–15, 159–66; Walter Brooks, "The Priority of the Silver Bluff Church and its Promoters," *Journal of Negro History* 7 (April, 1922): 172–77; "Letters Showing the Rise and Progress of the Early Negro Churches of Georgia and the West Indies," *Journal of Negro History* 1 (January, 1916): 73, 77–78.

36. Wood, *Slavery in Colonial Georgia*, 164–65, 195; "Early Negro Churches," 77–78, 83–86; Brooks, "Silver Bluff Church," 177, 182–84; William Aldridge, ed., *A Narrative of the Lord's Wonderful Dealings with John Marrant, A Black*, 4th ed. (London: Gilbert and Plummer, 1785).

37. Thomas Hassell to SPG, December 2, 1731 and March 12, 1712, SPGLL, BV 7, reel 6, series A, vol. 4 (2); Francis Varnod to SPG, January 13, 1723, SPGLL BV 7, reel 7, series B, vol. 4 (2); Peter H. Wood, "Jesus Christ Has Got Thee at Last," *Center for the Study of Southern Culture and Religion Bulletin* 3, no. 3 (November, 1979): 2–5.

38. Quoted from James B. Lawrence, "Religious Education of the Negro in the Colony of Georgia," *Georgia Historical Quarterly* 14 (March, 1930): 46–47.

39. Ibid.

40. Donald R. Kloe, "Buddy Quow: An Anonymous Poem in Gullah-Jamaican Dialect Written Circa 1800," *Southern Folklore Quarterly* 38, no. 2 (June, 1974): 82–85, 87–88. For a discussion which denies, incorrectly I think, that there is a distinction between Gullah and "generalized Black English vernacular," see J. L. Dillard, *Lexicon of Black English* (New York: Seabury Press, 1977), 103–4. An interesting discussion of Gullah as a Creole language is found in Charles Joyner, *Down By the Riverside: A South Carolina Slave Community* (Urbana and Chicago: University of Illinois Press, 1984), Chapter 7: see also Wood, *Black Majority*, 172–90. For a discussion of cultural unity joining Gullahs with blacks of the Caribbean, see Velma Pollard. "Cultural Connections in Paule Marshall's *Praise Song for the Widow*," *World Literature Written in English* 25, no. 2 (1985): 285–98. For a fascinating, informative debate over the formulation of Creole and the impact of Upper Guinea versus Gold Coast and Angolan influences see Frederick G. Cassidy, "The Place of Gullah," 3–16, and Ian F. Hancock, "Gullah and Barbadian—Origins and Relationships," *American Speech* 55, no. 1 (Spring, 1980): 17–35.

41. See Chapter 2. Also see Keith Thomas, *Religion and the Decline of Magic* (New York: Charles Scribner and Sons, 1971). Thomas discusses systems of beliefs current in sixteenth- and seventeenth-century England, and retention of some beliefs after that time. As Thomas states, almost every "primitive" religion was for the adherents a means of gaining supernatural power. Yet this does not preclude religion as a means of explanation, decreeing of moral imperatives, or representation of social order.

42. Benjamin Pownall to SPG, October 24, 1723, SPGLL, BV 7, reel 7, series B, vol. 4(2); Alexander Garden to SPG, May 6, 1740, Box 20 from Lambeth Palace Library, vol. 941, no. 72, Ms. of Archbishop of Canterbury; J. Ottolenghe to SPG, July 12, 1758, November 18, 1754, SPG London Mss of Dr. Bray's Associates.

43. Robert Maule to SPG, Summer, 1710, and, Francis Le Jau to SPG, October 20, 1709, SPGLL, BV 6, reel 4, series A, vol. 5.

44. Ibid.; Thomas Hassell to SPG, March 12, 1712, SPGLL, BV 6, reel 5, series A, vol. 7.

45. Whitefield, *Journals*, 382–83, Stein, "Whitefield on Slavery," 246–47.

46. *Three Letters from Whitefield*, 14; Francis Varnod to SPG, April 3, 1728, SPGLL, BV 6, reel 12, series A, vol. 21; John Fulton to SPG, May 25, 1734, SPGLL William Taylor to SPG, May 15, 1716, SPGLL, BV 7, reel 6, series B, vol. 4 (1).

47. Bryan and Hutson, *Living Christianity*, 56, 57, 63, 72, 90, passim; Hutson, "Register of Stoney Creek Church," 22–26; Jackson, "Hugh Bryan," passim.

48. Bryan and Hutson, *Living Christianity*, 70–91.

49. Ibid., 63; *Journal of the Assembly, 1739–1741*, 230, 505.

50. Whitefield, *Journals*, 419, 422, 444, 446; Seward, *Journal*, 6–7; Aldridge, *Marrant Narrative*.

51. Aldridge, *Marrant Narrative*, 6–9; Wood, "Jesus Christ Has Got Thee," 1–2.

52. Aldridge, *Marrant Narrative*, 10–11; Wood, "Jesus Christ Has Got Thee," 2.

53. Aldridge, *Marrant Narrative*, 10–11; Wood, "Jesus Christ Has Got Thee," 2.

54. Aldridge, *Marrant Narrative*, 13.

55. Ibid., 14, 36–37.

56. Ibid., 15–28, 31–33, 36–39.

57. Dallimore, *Whitefield, Great Evangelist*, I: 45–56, 364, n. 3; Henry, *Whitefield, Wayfaring Witness*, 27, 61.

58. Henry, *Whitefield, Wayfaring Witness*, 96–98; Stephens, *Ecclesiastical Biography*, 400.

59. Dallimore, *Whitefield, Great Evangelist*, I: 484, 498–501 and II: 436–38; Anon., probably George Whitefield, *A Letter to the Negroes Lately Converted to Christ in America* (London: J. Hart, 1743), 3–6; Stein, "George Whitefield on Slavery," 243–56.

60. Dallimore, *Whitefield, Great Evangelist*, II: 438; Mathews, *Slavery and Methodism*, 5–6; Wood, *Slavery in Colonial Georgia*, 162.

61. Dallimore, *Whitefield, Great Evangelist*, I: 499–509; Klingberg, *Appraisal of the Negro*, 113–22; Joseph Ottolenghe to SPG, December 4, 1751 and July 12, 1758, SPG, London Mss. of Dr. Bray's Associates; Habersham to William Knox, July 17, 1765 and November 26, 1770, *Habersham Letters*, 38, 95–99, 102, Wood, *Black Majority*, 324–25; W. Robert Higgins, "The Geographical Origins of Negro Slaves in Colonial South Carolina," *South Atlantic Quarterly* 70 (1971): 40; Morgan, "Black Society in the Lowcountry," 83–86.

62. Wood, *Slavery in Colonial Georgia*, 160–65; Darold D. Wax, "Georgia and the Negro Before the American Revolution," *Georgia Historical Quarterly* 51, no. 1 (March, 1967): 73–75.

5. An Almost Chosen People

1. Lionel Kennedy and Thomas Parker, *The Trial Record of Denmark Vesey*, Intro. by John Oliver Killens (Boston: Beacon Press, 1970; repr. from 1822 ed., and published under title: *An Official Report of the Trials of Sundry Negroes*), Bibliographic Note; Edward L. Pierce, "The Freedmen at Port Royal," *Atlantic Monthly* 12 (September, 1863): 295; Willie Lee Rose, *Rehearshal for Reconstruction: The Port Royal Experiment* (Indianapolis: Bobbs-Merrill, 1964), 11–12.

2. Robert Starobin, ed., *Denmark Vesey: The Slave Conspiracy of 1822* (Englewood Cliffs, N. J.: Prentice-Hall, 1970), 11; John Lofton, *Denmark Vesey's Revolt* (Kent, Ohio: Kent State University Press, 1983), 132–37; updated ed. of *Insurrection in South Carolina: The Turbulent World of Denmark Vesey* (Yellow Springs, Ohio: Antioch Press, 1964); Harriott Pinckney Rutledge to Edward Rutledge, August 5, 1822, Pinckney Papers, 1744–1849, SCHS; William Jones to Samuel Jones, Jane Bruce Jones Mss, 1784–1831, SCL; F. A. Mood, *Methodism in Charleston* (Nashville: E. Stevenson and J. E. Evans, 1856), 130–31; Kennedy and Parker, *Trial*, 4–14, 18, 21–22, 57–59, 111; Marina Wikramanayake, *A World in Shadow: The Free Black in Antebellum South Carolina* (Columbia: University of South Carolina Press, 1973), 133–36.

3. Philip D. Morgan, "Colonial South Carolina Runaways: Their Significance for Slave Culture," *Slavery and Abolition* 6 no. 3 (1985): 57–58; Joseph Cepas Carroll, *Slave Insurrections in the United States, 1800–1865* (Boston: Chapman and Grimes, 1938), 17, 19–24; Peter H. Wood. *Black Majority: Negroes in Colonial South Carolina from 1670 through the Stono Rebellion* (New York: Alfred A. Knopf, 1974), 285–307, 314–35; Vincent Harding, *There Is a River: The Black Struggle for Freedom in America* (New York: Vintage Books, 1983), 31–36; Kennedy and Parker, *Trial*, 157. Although Morgan offers no explanation for the discrep-

ancy between the number of runaways in Virginia and South Carolina, he notes the presence of more African-born slaves among the captive runaway population in South Carolina. Thus the numbers of Africans in Carolina's slave population clearly accounts for some of the difference between the two colonies.

4. *SCG*, September 8 to September 15, 1759, October 23, 1751, November 25, 1751, May 28 to June 4, 1754, June 16, 1758.

5. Ibid., September 14 to September 21, 1747, June 25 to July 2, 1750; Eugene D. Genovese, *From Rebellion to Revolution: Afro-American Slave Revolts in the Making of the Modern World* (New York: Vintage Books, 1979), 69; Jill M. Watts, " 'We Do Not Live for Ourselves Only': Seminole Black Perceptions and the Second Seminole War," *UCLA Historical Journal* 7 (1986): 5–7; Herbert Aptheker, *American Negro Slave Revolts* (New York: International Publishers, 1967; repr. from 1943 ed.), 197–98; Philip D. Morgan, "Black Society in the Lowcountry, 1760–1810," in Ira Berlin and Ronald Hoffman, *Slavery and Freedom in the Age of the American Revolution* (Charlottesville: University of Virginia Press, 1983), 92, 138.

6. *SCG*, March 4, 1756, April 29, 1754; Colonial Records of South Carolina, *Journal of the Commons House of Assembly, 1739–1741*, 230, 505; Watts, " 'We Do Not Live For Ourselves Only'," 6–7.

7. Michael P. Johnson, "Runaway Slaves and the Slave Communities in South Carolina, 1799–1820," *William and Mary Quarterly* 38, no. 3 (July, 1981): 3, 418, 433–36, 441. Although Professor Johnson is dealing with a later period, his research is applicable for the eighteenth century; *SCG*, March 17, 1724, April 21, 1759.

8. *SCG*, September 17, 1772. This view of slavery in the Lowcountry, in terms of its harshaness, is different from that of Philip Morgan. He cites, for example, the transition from a period of negative to one of positive increase, as an important indicator of less harsh conditions and more black autonomy. Yet Morgan's table on natural increase shows an annual rate of only 1.9 percent as the highest, from 1770–75. This rate of increase appears far too negligible to tell us much about better contitions. Morgan, "Black Society in the Lowcountry," 83–89.

9. *SCG*, September 17, 1772. For other manifestations of black assertion in urban Charleston see Peter H. Wood, " 'Taking Care of Business' in Revolutionary South Carolina: Republicanism and the Slave Society," in Jeffrey J. Crow and Larry E. Tise, eds., *The Southern Experience in the American Revolution* (Chapel Hill: The University of North Carolina Press, 1978), 268–93.

10. James Oakes, *The Ruling Race: A History of American Slaveholders* (New York: Vintage Books, 1983), 4–34. For paternalistic arguments, see Eugene D. Genovese, *Roll, Jordan Roll, the World the Slaves Made* (New York: Pantheon Books, 1974), xiv–xvii, 3–149, 280–84; also for a more measured discussion of paternalism, see Charles Joyner, *Down By the Riverside: A South Carolina Slave Community* (Urbana and Chicago: University of Illinois Press, 1984), 56, 231–32.

11. Benjamin Quarles, *The Negro in the American Revolution* (New York: W. W. Norton, 1973; first pub. Chapel Hill: University of North Carolina Press: 1961), Preface; Ira Berlin, "The Revolution in Black Life" in Alfred F. Young, ed. *The American Revolution: Explorations in the History of American Radicalism* (De Kalb: Northern Illinois University Press, 1976), 351–52; J. Madison, Jr. to William Bradford, November 26, 1774 and July 10, 1775, William Bradford Collection, HSP; Wood, " 'Taking Care of Business'," 283–87; and his " 'Impatient of Oppression'; Black Freedom Struggles on the Eve of White Independence," *Southern Exposure* 28 (October, 1985): 606, 612–13.

12. Walter Brooks, "The Priority of the Silver Bluff Church and its Promoters," *Journal*

of Negro History 7 (April, 1922): 176–77; Ellen Gibson Wilson, *The Loyal Blacks* (New York: G. P. Putnam's Sons), 22–26, 41–57; James W. St. G. Walker, *The Black Loyalists: The Search for a Promised Land in Nova Scotia and Sierra Leone, 1783–1870* (New York: Delhousie University Press, 1976), 1–5, 10–12; Watts, " 'We Do Not Live For Ourselves Only'," 6–7, 12–13; Quarles, *Negro in the American Revolution*, 19–26, 113–14; Kenneth Coleman, *The American Revolution in Georgia, 1763–1789* (Athens: University of Georgia Press, 1958), 121–29, 130–31, 144; *Papers of the Continental Congress*, Inspection Rolls of Negroes, Book I, April 23–September 13, 1783, Book II, September 22–November 19, 1783, passim. The name "Mellia Marrant" and her two children, listed as slaves of John Marrant, raises the question of whether these were the slaves of Whitefield convert John Marrant. Marrant was born in New York and there is no reason to believe that the family (apparently free) took the surname of a white South Carolinian. Mellia Marrant may be the sister or wife of John who was impressed into the British navy during the war and eventually went to England. His services to the British would enable his family to be given a certificate of freedom, and he related in his narrative that he had family in Nova Scotia. See William Aldridge, ed., *A Narrative of the Lord's Wonderful Dealings with John Marrant, A Black*, 4th ed. (London: Gilbert and Plummer, 1785).

13. Herbert G. Gutman, *The Black Family in Slavery and Freedom, 1750–1925* (New York: Pantheon Books, 1976), 325. For a view which argues that South Carolina blacks did not "take advantage of their owners' predicament during the Revolution," see Michael Mullin, "British Caribbean and North American Slaves in an Era of War and Revolution, 1775–1807," in Crow and Tise, *Southern Experience*, 235–36; this interpretation is also presented in Morgan, "Black Society in the Lowcountry," 108–9. For a discussion of the Afro-American family during the War for Independence, see Mary Beth Norton et al., "The Afro-American Family in the Age of Revolution," in Ira Berlin and Ronald Hoffman, *Slavery and Freedom in the Age of the American Revolution* (Charlottesville: University of Virginia Press, 1983), 157–91. For a discussion of structural manifestations of autonomy in black life during the postwar period, see Berlin, "The Revolution in Black Life," 363–71.

14. Quarles, *Negro in The American Revolution*, 171–72; "Memoirs of the Life of Boston King, a Black Preacher," *London Methodist Magazine*, 21 (1798–99) 105–110, 157–61, hereafter referred to as "Boston King Memoirs"; Wilson, *Loyal Blacks* 13, 30–31; Walker, *Black Loyalists*, 5, 7.

15. "Boston King Memoirs"; Wilson, *Loyal Blacks*, 31–34, 56–66.

16. "Boston King Memoirs"; Aldridge, *Marrant Narrative;* Walker, *Black Loyalists*, 10–12; Quarles, *Negro in the American Revolution*, 156–57, 163–65, 171–77.

17. Ira Berlin, *Slaves Without Masters: The Free Negro in the Antebellum South* (New York: Pantheon Books, 1974), 16–21 and "Revolution in Black Life, 355; Oakes, *Ruling Race*, 28–29; Quarles, *Negro in the American Revolution*, 61, 102–04, 124–26, 163–66, 171–77; Philip S. Foner, *Blacks in the American Revolution* (Westport, Conn.: Greenwood Press, 1975), 46; David Ramsey to Benjamin Rush, June 20, 1779, March 21, 1780, Rush Correspondence, Ramsey Letters, HSP; Wood, *Black Majority*, 124–30; Walker, *Black Loyalists*, 6–10; Quoted from Wilson, *Loyal Blacks*, 31, 41–47. For works on black participation in the War for Independence, see Sidney Kaplan, *The Black Presence in the Era of the American Revolution, 1770–1800* (New York: New York Graphic Society, 1973); Graham R. Hodges, "Black Revolt in New York City and the Neutral Zone, 1775–1783." Unpublished paper presented at the New-York Historical Society Conference on the Constitutional Era in New York, May 15, 1987.

18. Berlin, *Slaves Without Masters*, 30–31, 35–41; Lofton, *Vesey's Revolt*, 38–43, 51–55, 59–64; Richard Wade, *Slavery in the Cities* (New York: Oxford University Press, 1964), 29–

30; William W. Freehling, *Prelude to Civil War* (New York: Harper & Row, 1965), 9–10, 18–19; Guion G. Johnson, *A Social History of the Sea Islands* (Chapel Hill: University of North Carolina Press, 1930), 24–29, 50–54, Wikramanayake, *World in Shadow*, 117–18, 121–22; John Phillips, *An Appeal to Matters of Fact and Common Sense, Recommended to the Serious Consideration of the Inhabitants of Charleston, South Carolina* (New York: T. Kirk, 1798), passim; Morgan, "Black Society in the Lowcountry." Although Morgan does not see much black participation during the War for Independence (a point on which we disagree), he does note the postwar impact on the Lowcountry in terms of an increased sense of autonomy among blacks which was manifested in a number of ways. See especially 108–41.

19. Lofton, *Vesey's Revolt*, 47–51; J. Hector St. John de Crevecoeur, *Letters from an American Farmer* (New York: E. P. Dutton, 1957 repr. from 1782 ed.), 155–161; Johann Schöepf, *Travels in the Confederation, 1783–84*, trans. Alfred Morrison (Philadelphia: W. J. Campbell, 1911), 220–221; Phillips, *Appeal to Inhabitants of Charleston*, 29; Avonor Samuel to William Tilghman, December 30, 1785, William Tilghman Papers, HSP; Benjamin Rush Medical Notes, July 12, 1803, Rush Corr. v. 2: 64, HSP.

20. Major Pierce Butler to Mrs. Izard, February 25, 1797, Butler to John Hoom, January 6, 1803, Butler to John Cooper, February 15, 1818 and March 7, 1818, Wistar Papers, Butler Section, box 31, fol. 7, HSP; Roswell King to Pierce Butler, September 20, 1835, box 33, fol. 5, Pierce Butler to Mr. Taylor, March 28, 1840, Letterbook, 1838–1840, 53–55, and notation of sale of Butler slaves, February 21, 1859, box 41, fol. 5, Wistar Papers, Butler Section, HSP; Frances Ann Kemble, *Journal of a Residence on a Georgian Plantation*, ed. John A. Scott (New York: Alfred A. Knopf, 1970; New York: Harper & Brothers, 1863), 94, 176, 203, 128, 265–66, 273–74.

21. Aptheker, *Slave Revolts*, 207–08; Watts, " 'We Do Not Live for Ourselves Only'," 6–8; Letter of John De Brahn, August 28, 1787, Cox-Parrish Wharton Coll., vol. 4, HSP; Pierce Butler letter, July 4, 1789, Wistar Papers, Butler Section, box 31, fol. 1, HSP; Major Pierce Butler to R. Izard, September 8, 1789, SCL; the full account of the expeditions in Morgan, "Black Society in the Lowcountry," 139.

22. Gerald Mullin, *Flight and Rebellion; Slave Revolts in Eighteenth Century Virginia* (New York: Oxford University Press, 1972), 140–161; Aptheker, *Slave Revolts*, 217–18, 241; Samuel G. Stoney, ed., "The Autobiography of William John Grayson" *South Carolina Historical and Genealogical Magazine* 49, no. 1 (January, 1948): 29–30; Theodore Rosengarten, *Tombee, Portrait of a Cotton Planter, Journal of Thomas B. Chaplin, 1812–1890* (New York: William Morrow 1986), 118; Carroll, *Slave Insurrections*, 66–67; Harding, *There Is a River*, 62–63.

23. Although white Loyalists were never really compensated for their losses in bondspeople during the War for Independence, Americans fared better after the War of 1812. The dispute over losses in slave property raged on after the Treaty of Ghent in 1814. But in 1822, with the Czar of Russia as arbitrator, the dispute was decided in favor of the United States. Britain agreed to pay $1,204,960 for 3,601 slaves, only half of the value claimed by American slave owners. Wilson, *Loyal Blacks*, 56–57; Quarles, *Negro in the American Revolution*, 171–72; Harding, *There Is a River*, 62–63; Aptheker, *Slave Revolts*, 91; November 17, 1862, John Forsyth Mss., SCL.

24. Letter of Rachel Blanding, July 4, 1816, William Blanding Mss., SCL.

25. Ibid.; Trial of Negroes for Insurrection, July 3–17, 1816, Kershaw County Manscripts, SCL.

26. Quoted in Aptheker, *Slave Revolts*, 258–59; Trial of Negroes, SCL; Blanding Letter, July 25, 1816, SCL.

27. Letter of Rachel Blanding, December 2, 1808, July 25, 1813, SCL.

28. Lofton, *Vesey's Revolt*, 118.

29. Ibid., 113–30.

30. "Historical Sketch of the Euhaw Baptist Church," submitted for private reading by church officers, 1928, Euhaw Baptist Church Mss., SCL; David Benedict, *A General History of the Baptist Denomination in America and Other Parts of the World* (New York: Lewis Colby, 1848; repr. from 1813 ed.) 701–3; James W. Busch, "The Beaufort Baptist Church," Beaufort County Historical Society Paper, n.d., 4–5, Beaufort Township Library; John Archibald Armstrong, "Beaufort and the Sea Islands, Their History and Traditions," compiled from newspaper articles in the *Beaufort Republican*, 1867–1873, Beaufort Township Library; Joe Madison King, *A History of South Carolina Baptists* (Columbia: General Board, South Carolina Baptist Convention, 1964), 10–17, 26–38; quoted from James H. Cuthbert, *Life of Richard Fuller*, (New York: Scheldon Co., 1789), 12–13.

31. Lawton Family Papers, SCL: Charlotte Verstille to Nancy Verstille, February 9 and March 2, 1821, Tristram Verstille Papers, SCL: Chalmers D. Davidson, *The Last Foray: The South Carolina Plantations in 1860: A Sociological Study* (Columbia: University of South Carolina Press, 1975), 96–99; Busch, "Beaufort Church," 6; Rosengarten, *Tombee*, 92–96, 146–47; Cuthbert, *Life of Fuller*, 13, 15, 78–79.

32. Brooks, "Silver Bluff Church," 172–82; "Early Negro Churches," 70–71; Wilson, *Loyal Blacks*, 12–13; Albert J. Raboteau, *Slave Religion: The "Invisible Institution" in the Antebellum South* (New York: Oxford University Press, 1978), 139. In the Peedee region, the Welsh Neck Church, formed in 1738, was a large congregation whose extensive black membership was organized into a separate church in 1779. This was a short-lived experiment, ending in 1782. At that time, some whites and a "greater number of blacks" were excommunicated by a new minister who discovered that upon examination, the blacks especially "appeared to be very ignorant of the nature of true religion." King, *South Carolina Baptists*, 39–44.

33. Brooks, "Silver Bluff Church," 174–76, 178, 182, 191; Wilson, *Loyal Blacks*, 29–31.

34. Mrs. J. H. Redding, *Life and Times of Jonathan Bryan 1708–1788* (Savannah: Morning News Print, 1901), 43; "Early Negro Churches," 77–79; Brooks, "Silver Bluff Church," 186–87; John Rippon, ed., *Baptist Annual Register for 1798–1801* (London: Dilly, Button, Thomas, 1802), 366–67; Raboteau, *Slave Religion*. Andrew's church spawned two sister churches in Savannah by the early nineteenth century.

35. Brooks, "Silver Bluff Church," 181–190; "Early Negro Churches," 83–87; Wilson, *Loyal Blacks*, 11.

36. Wilson, *Loyal Blacks*, 10–12, 29–31; Walker, *Black Loyalists*, 4–5; Kathleen Tudor, "David George: Black Loyalist," *Nova Scotia Historical Society* 3, no. 1 (1983): 71–75.

37. Donald Blake Touchstone, "Planters and Slave Religion in the Deep South," (Ph.D. dissertation, Tulane University, 1973), 9–14; Redding, *Jonathan Bryan*, 44–45.

38. Quarles, *Negro in the American Revolution*, 135–40, 44–45; Matthew Tate to Benjamin Rush, October 1, 1792, Benjamin Rush Correspondence, vol. 7: 6, HSP.

39. Diary of John Bartram, 78–79, John Bartram Papers, HSP.

40. U.S. Census Office, *First Census, 1790* (Philadelphia: Childs and Swaine, 1791), 54; "Diary of Timothy Ford," *South Carolina Historical and Genealogical Magazine* 45 (1944): 142–45.

41. Abigail Capers to Eliza Russell, March 25, 1971; James McBride Dabbs Papers, SHC.

42. John Bartram Diary, July 1, 1765–April 10, 1766, John Bartram Papers, HSP; Johnson, *Social History*, 18–26, 115–118; Armstrong, "Sea Islands History," 30; Euhaw Baptist Church Mss., March 14, 1834, SCL; Charlotte Verstille to Nancy Verstille, March 2, 1821, Tristram Verstille Papers, SCL.

43. Richard Furman to Roger Williams, September 10, 1800, Richard Furman Papers, SCL.

44. Charlotte Verstille to Nancy Verstille, February 9 and March 2, 1821, Tristram Verstille Papers, SCL.

45. Charles C. Jones, *The Religious Instruction of the Negroes in the United States* (New York: Negro Universities Press, 1969; repr. from 1842 ed.), 57, 60–61; Reverend Dr. Richard Furman, *Exposition of the Views of the Baptists, Relative to the Coloured Population in the United States, in A Communication to the Governor of South Carolina* (Charleston: A. E. Miller, 1823), 15; Rules and Regulations of the Coloured Ministers, Elders and Members of Baptist Church in Charleston, SCL; Edmund Botsford to Richard Furman, March 10, October 12, 1796, October 15, 1808, Edmund Botsford Letters, BC.

46. Arnold Dallimore, *George Whitefield, Life and Times of the Great Evangelist of the Eighteenth Century Revival*, 2 vols. (Gildford and London: Billing and Sons, 1970), II: 438; Rev. A. M. Chreitzberg, *Early Methodism in the Carolinas* (Nashville: Barbee and Smith, 1897), 32–34; Donald Mathews, *Slavery and Methodism, A Chapter in American Morality 1780–1845* (Princeton: Princeton University Press, 1965), 3–6; Frederick A. Norwood, *The Story of American Methodism: A History of the United Methodists and Their Relations* (Nashville: Abingdon Press, 1974), 59–60, 75; Albert Deems Betts, *History of South Carolina Methodism* (Columbia: Advocate Press, 1952), 192; F. A. Mood, *Methodism in Charleston* (Nashville: E. Stevenson and J. E. Evans, 1856), 23–24, 40, 48, 71, 128.

47. *Journal of the Rev. Francis Asbury, Bishop of the Methodist Episcopal Church*, 3 vols. (New York: N. Bangs and T. Mason, 1821), I: 381–82; Chreitzberg, *Early Methodism*, 39–43; Mathews, *Slavery and Methodism*, 7–9.

48. Phillips, *Appeal to Inhabitants of Charleston*, 22–23; Mood, *Methodism in Charleston* 71, 128; Asbury, *Journals*, II: 28–29.

49. Asbury, *Journals*, II: 241.

50. Norwood, *American Methodism*, 88–93; Albert M. Shipp, *History of Methodism in South Carolina* (Nashville: Southern Methodist Publishing House, 1884), 467–71; "Christmas Agreement," January 2, 1795, HSSCC; James Jenkins, *Experience, Labours and Sufferings of Reverend J. Jenkins of the South Carolina Conference*, printed for the author in 1842, copy found at HSSCC; Mathews, *Slavery and Methodism*, 10–21; H. Shelton Smith, *In His Image, But . . . Racism in Southern Religion, 1780–1910* (Durham: Duke University Press, 1972), 38–43.

51. William Hammett Journal, entries for August 26, 1794, January 15, 1795, February 8, 1795, and February 15, 1795, Wm. Hammett Ms., SCL.

52. Ibid., January 15, 1795.

53. Smith, *In His Image, But*, 129–35.

54. Hammett Journal, entries for January 15, 1795, February 8, 1795, February 15, 1795, SCL; Phillips, *Appeal of Inhabitants of Charleston*, 10–11, 15, 17, 21–22, 29.

55. Chreitzberg, *Early Methodism*, 78, 126; James O. Andrew, "On Methodism in Charleston," *MMQR* 12 (1830): 20–28; A. M. Travis, *Autobiography of the Reverend Joseph M. Travis*, (Nashville: E. Stevenson and F. A. Owens), 1855, 86–87; Mathews, *Slavery and Methodism*, 21–26.

56. William M. Wightman, *Life of William Capers, Including an Autobiography* (Nashville: J. B. McFerrin, 1858), 136–37; Andrew, "Methodism in Charleston," 18–20; Shipp, *Methodism in South Carolina*, 167; Betts, *South Carolina Methodism*, 55–57.

57. Betts, *South Carolina Methodism*, 223–24; Carol George, *Segregated Sabbaths, Richard Allen and the Emergence of Independent Black Churches, 1760–1840* (New York: Oxford University Press, 1973), 14–18, 29–32; Asbury, *Journals*, III: 22–23, 128.

58. Article written by Sancho, a former slave, in the Papers of Hugh A. C. Walker, HSSCC.

59. Phillips, *Appeal to Inhabitants of Charleston*, 10, 22–23; Wikramanayake, *World in Shadow*, 122; Lofton, *Vesey's Revolt*, 79, 91; Wightman Ledger and Notebook, 1801, Papers of William May Wightman, HSSCC; Asbury, *Journals*, III: 9, 14; Jenkins, *Experience, Labours and Sufferings*, 102–3, 105–6.

60. Mathews, *Slavery and Methodism*, 22–26; Shipp, *Methodism in South Carolina*, 467.

61. Chreitzberg, *Early Methodism*, 156; Lofton, *Vesey's Revolt*, 61–62; Jenkins, *Experience, Labours and Sufferings*, 96–97; Wikramanayake, *World in Shadow*, 117; Betts, *South Carolina Methodism*, passim; Jones, *Religious Instruction*, 64.

62. George, *Segregated Sabbaths*, 69–86; Betts, *South Carolina Methodism*, 80; Kennedy and Parker, *Trial*, 14–15; Lofton, *Vesey's Revolt*, 92–93; Wikramanayake, *World in Shadow*, 120–124; Archie Epps, "A Negro Separatist Movement in the Nineteenth Century," *The Harvard Law Review* 4, no. 1 (Summer–Fall, 1966): 70–72.

63. Wikramanayake, *World in Shadow*, 124–26; Lofton, *Vesey's Revolt*, 92–94; Starobin, *Denmark Vesey*, 2–3.

64. Lofton, *Vesey's Revolt*, 93, 145; Epps, "A Negro Separatist Movement," 71, 75; Wikramanayake, *World in Shadow*, 74, 87–88, 125.

65. The most thorough study is Lofton, *Denmark Vesey*; Also see Wikramanayake, *World in Shadow*, 113–153; Richard Wade, "The Vesey Plot: A Reconsideration," *Journal of Social History* (May, 1964); Thomas Wentworth Higginson, *Black Rebellion* (New York: Arno Press, 1969; repr. from 1889 ed.), 215–75; Freehling, *Prelude to Civil War*, 49–86; Starobin, *Denmark Vesey*; Richard Wade has maintained that the conspiracy never really existed. Wade is refuted by Sterling Stuckey in "Remembering Denmark Vesey," *Negro Digest* (February, 1966); and to a lesser extent by Freehling, in *Prelude to Civil War*, 53–61. Yet John Oliver Killens has made objections to Freehling's and Wade's presentations of the conspiracy, describing their interpretations as distorted. Freehling adopts the language of the slaveholders. He portrays Denmark Vesey as "a powerful unscrupulous man who was given to fits of rage and violence," and as a man who employed a "skillful fusion of the high ideals of the Age of Reason with the ruthless savagery of a barbaric chief." Bibliographic note in Kennedy and Parker. (*Trial*, xiv.) Freehling's characterization of Gullah Jack is also taken from the slaveholder's presentation. The author wrote:
Possessed of tiny limbs, which looked *grotesque* despite his small frame, Gullah Jack had enormous whiskers, which seemed monstrous on the *bulking* Denmark Vesey. No witch doctor ever looked more the part . . . a scorcerer whose bizarre appearance, wild gestures and malevolent glances could terrorize the bravest slave. (55–56).

66. Kennedy and Parker, *Trial*, 45, 58, 63–65, 114–15; Starobin, *Denmark Vesey*, 21, 62, 25. The late Professor Starobin's excellent edition of primary sources related to the Vesey Conspiracy was most useful. Testimony not in the official record but part of manuscript collections, contemporary reactions to the plot, and private letters are contained in his volume. Starobin's edition adds to the body of literature on this little-studied rebellion effort and reveals that some sources related to it have yet to be fully utilized.

67. Lofton, *Vesey's Revolt*, 142; Starobin, *Denmark Vesey*, 25, 50, 61, 64; Kennedy and Parker, *Trial*, 46, 58–59.

68. Starobin, *Denmark Vesey*, 66; Kennedy and Parker, *Trial*, 61, 64; Gayraud S. Gilmore, *Black Religion and Black Radicalism: An Interpretation of the Religious History of Afro-American People*, 2nd ed. rev. and enl. (Maryknoll, N. Y.: Orbis Books, 1983), 57–58.

69. Kennedy and Parker, *Trial*, 61, 64.

70. Ibid., 43.

71. C.L.R. James, *The Black Jacobins, Toussaint L'Ouverture and the San Domingo Revolution*, 2nd ed. rev. (New York: Vintage, 1963), 83–89, and passim.

72. Kennedy and Parker, *Trial*, 13–14, 76–79, 89; Starobin, *Denmark Vesey*, 26, 32, 41–42, 45, 46.

73. Robert Farris Thompson, *Flash of the Spirit: African and Afro-American Art and Philosophy* (New York: Vintage Books, 1983), 117, 121; Michael Adas, *Prophets of Rebellion: Millenarian Protest Movements against European Colonial Order* (Chapel Hill: University of North Carolina Press, 1979), passim.

74. See Chapter 2; Starobin, *Denmark Vesey*, 45; Kennedy and Parker, *Trial*, 76–77, 163, 17, 37–38, 81, 85–86, 95–102, 105–6, 125.

75. Kennedy and Parker, *Trial*, 50, 88, 90, 95, 130; John M. Vlach, *The Afro-American Tradition in Decorative Arts* (Cleveland, Ohio: Cleveland Museum of Art, 1978), 144; James, *Black Jacobins*, 86–87.

76. Starobin, *Denmark Vesey*, 39; Killens, *Trial*, 75, 89, 86, 109, 117, 122–23, 125, 134–35, 164–65.

77. Kennedy and Parker, *Trial*, 79, 81–82, 95–96, 140–41; Starobin, *Denmark Vesey*, 52.

78. Starobin, *Denmark Vesey*, 39, 42, 63–64, Killens, *Trial*, 28–38, 42, 74–75, 77, 79, 86, 112–13, 125.

79. Kennedy and Parker, *Trial*, 31–32.

80. Ibid., 38–40, 79.

81. Ibid., 137.

82. Ibid., 94–95, 131; Starobin, *Denmark Vesey*, 38, 40.

83. Among them are Wade, *Slavery in the Cities*. Here Wade argues that the urban environment was "inhospitable to conspiracies because it provided a wider latitude to the slave, a measure of independence within bondage. . . ." According to Wade, this environment served to deflate the insurrectionary impulse, 241–42. Also see Gerald Mullin, *Flight and Rebellion*. Vesey did not make the mistake which Mullin claimed was made by Gabriel, that is, not providing an appealing ideology to country slaves and the African-born. We will never know if indeed Gabriel did make this mistake since the record reveals no spiritual presence in the 1800 revolt. This does not however preclude the existence of a spiritual force undetected by the court.

84. Lofton, *Vesey's Revolt*, 38–53, 96–99; Starobin, *Denmark Vesey*, 64–65, 83.

85. Kennedy and Parker, *Trial*, 26.

86. Starobin, *Denmark Vesey*, 19, 23–25, 39, 47, 65; Kennedy and Parker, *Trial*, 19–22, 50–54, 56, 62, 78, 80–81, 86, 92, 97, 100–5, 109–10, 119, 130–31.

87. Kennedy and Parker, *Trial*, 18, 20–21, 26–27, 62, 78–79, 85; Diary of John Edwin Fripp, 1857–58 and 1865–68, passim, Beaufort Township Library; Dorothy Sterling, *Captain of the Planter, The Story of Robert Smalls* (Garden City, N. Y.: Doubleday, 1958), 24; Mason Crum, *Gullah, Negro Life in the Carolina Sea Islands* (Durham: Duke University Press, 1940), 36–37; Rosengarten, *Tombee*.

88. William Jones to Samuel Jones, July 23, 1822, Jane Bruce Jones Mss., 1784–1834, SCL; Jacob Rapelye to Paul Rapelye, August 5, 1822, Napier, Rapeley and Bennett Papers, SCL; E. M. Starrs to Zalmon Wildman, July 19, 1822, Zalmon Wildman Papers, 1812–1840, SCL; Lofton, *Vesey's Revolt*, 184; James Hamilton, *Negro Plot* (Charleston: Joseph W. Ingraham, 1822), 29.

89. Benjamin Elliott, "To Our Northern Brethren," as quoted by Edwin C. Holland in *A Refutation of the Calumnies Circulated against the Southern and Western States, Respecting the Institutions and Existence of Slavery Among Them* (Charleston: A. E. Miller, 1822), 79.

90. Ibid., 11–12.

91. Kennedy and Parker, *Trial*, 31–32.
92. *Ibid.*
93. Ibid., 132–33; Lofton, *Vesey's Revolt*, 173–75, 182–84.
94. Thomas Bennett to Richard Furman, 1822, Furman Papers, SCL.
95. Richard Furman, *Exposition on the Views of the Baptists*, 15.
96. Fickling, "Slave Conversion," 16–17; Freehling, *Prelude to Civil War*, 60–61, 72–73; Janet Duitsman Cornelius, "God's Schoolmasters: Southern Evangelists to the Slaves, 1830–1860" (Ph.D. dissertation, University of Illinois at Urbana-Champaign, 1977), 27, 33–49; Harding, *There Is a River*, 81–94; Starobin, *Denmark Vesey*, 82, 163–64; Aptheker, *Negro Revolts*, 273, 279; Lofton, *Vesey's Revolt*, 182–85.
97. Cornelius, "God's Schoolmasters," 11–13; Jones, *Religious Instruction*, 64. Cornelius maintains that international events such as Latin American independence movements and West Indian slave revolts were among the factors which hindered religious instruction.

6. *"Religion of the Warm Heart"*: *Plantations Missions and Methodist Impact*

1. Anon., "Letter to the Editor," *Christian Advocate* 4 (January, 1826): 96; Not to be confused with the *Southern Christian Advocate*, a Methodist newspaper.
2. Ibid., 4 (June, 1826): 258–59.
3. See Chapter 5 for references to "Philemon"; *Wesleyan Journal*, July 1, 1826 and July 22, 1826, HSSCC.
4. Luther Porter Jackson, "Religious Instruction of Negroes, 1830–1860," *Journal of Negro History* 15 (1930): 83–84; Donald Mathews, *Slavery and Methodism: A Chapter in American Morality, 1780–1845* (Princeton: Princeton University Press, 1965), 68–69, 71–72; William W. Wightman, *Life of William Capers, Including an Autobiography* (Nashville: J. B. McFerrin, 1858), 291–92; Donald Blake Touchstone, "Planters and Slave Religion in the Deep South," (Ph.D. dissertation, Tulane University, 1973), 46–47; Janet Duitsman Cornelius, "God's Schoolmasters: Southern Evangelists to the Slaves, 1830–1860," (Ph.D. dissertation, University of Illinois at Urbana-Champaign, 1977), 15, 40–42; Charles C. Pinckney, *An Address Delivered in Charleston Before the Agricultural Society of South Carolina at Its Annual Meeting, 18th August, 1829* (Charleston: A. E. Miller, 1829), passim and 1–8, 10.
5. Pinckney, *Address*, 11–12.
6. Ibid., 13.
7. Ibid., passim; Charles C. Jones, *The Religious Instruction of the Negroes in the United States* (New York: Negro Universities Press, 1969; repr. from 1842 ed.), 101–53; Jackson, "Religious Instruction of Negroes," 73, 78; James O. Andrew, "The Southern Slave Population," *MMQR* 13 (1831) 315–17.
8. Mathews, *Slavery and Methodism*, 68–71; Jones, *Religious Instruction*, 70–71; Susan Markey Fickling, "Slave Conversion in South Carolina, 1830–1860," (M. A. thesis, University of South Carolina, 1924), 16, Jackson, "Religious Instruction of Negroes," 81–83; Andrew, "Slave Population," 291–92, 315–17; Albert J. Raboteau, *Slave Religion: The "Invisible Institution in the Antebellum South* (New York: Oxford University Press, 1978), 161–66.
9. Andrew, "Slave Population," 316–19; Wightman, *Life of Capers*, 291–92; Mathews, *Slavery and Methodism*, 68–71.
10. L.J.C. Lambert to Methodist Conference, South Carolina, January 10, 1829, HSSCC; "Statistical Report," *MMQR* (1828): 40; Wightman, *Life of Capers*, 288, 292–293; Mathews, *Slavery and Methodism*, 68; Touchstone, "Planters and Slave Religion," 45–47. Much of the work of religious instruction in coastal Georgia was done by a Presbyterian, Charles Col-

cock Jones. But Jones began about ten years after Capers. See Touchstone, "Planters and Slave Religion," 39–45 and Raboteau, *Slave Religion*, 155–57.

11. Andrew, "Slave Population," 314–15.

12. Ibid., 316–19, 322.

13. David Brion Davis, *The Problem of Slavery in the Age of Revolution, 1770–1823* (Ithaca: Cornell University Press, 1975), 356–61, 365–66, 452–53, 460–62; E. P. Thompson, *The Making of the English Working Class* (New York: Vintage Books, 1963), 350–62. For a different, more sympathetic view of the Methodists, see Sidney G. Diamond, *The Psychology of the Methodist Revival: An Empirical and Descriptive Study* (London: Oxford University Press, 1926), passim, especially 18–41, 87–103, 254–73.

14. Andrew, "Slave Population," 321.

15. Letter about the life of George W. Moore, missionary to the slaves in South Carolina, written at the time of his death in 1863 (name of writer of the letter is illegible), HSSCC; Leroy F. Beaty, *Work of South Carolina Methodism among the Slaves: An Address Delivered Before the Historical Society of the South Carolina Conference*, November 26, 1901, HSSCC, 9–10; *CAJ*, March 16, 1932. Wightman, *Life of Capers*, 291–92; Pinckney, *Address*, 23, (Appendix); Andrew, "Slave Population," 314; Mathews, *Slavery and Methodism*, 66–69. Both Jackson and Fickling take the position that the South Carolina Conference made the first moves toward religious instruction. They probably got this impression from Jones, *Religious Instruction*. In Georgia, two associations were formed by planters for religious instruction in 1830–31. Raboteau, *Slave Religion*, 155.

16. *CAJ*, April 12, 1833, January 22, 1836; "Report of the Missionary Society," *Minutes of the South Carolina Conference of the Methodist Episcopal Church*, January 9, 1839, 14–18, HSSCC; Wightman, *Life of Capers*, 288–91, 295–96; Andrew, "Slave Population," 315–16; Mathews, *Slavery and Methodism*, 72–73.

17. Courtlandt Van Renssalaer letter, n.d. (between 1835 and 1836), SHC; Frances Anne Kemble, *Journal of a Residence on a Georgian Plantation* (New York: Harper & Brothers, 1863), 90–91; Frederick A. Norwood, *The Story of American Methodism: A History of the United Methodists and Their Relations* (Nashville: Abingdon Press, 1974), 93–96; Mathews, *Slavery and Methodism, CAJ*, November 20, 1835, January 22, 1836; Jones, *Religious Instruction*, 86; Wightman, *Life of Capers*, 295–96.

18. Van Renssalaer letter, SHC.

19. "Report of the Missionary Society," *Minutes of South Carolina Conference*, February 10, 1836, 20, HSSCC; Wightman, *Life of Capers*, 295–96; *SCA*, January 26, 1838.

20. Pinckney to Capers, January 24, 1835, HSSCC; Mathews, *Slavery and Methodism*, 78–79; *SCA*, January 26, 1838.

21. Jones, *Religious Instruction*, 74–80; Fickling, "Slave Conversion," 16–18; Jackson, "Religious Instruction of Negroes," 86–87. For an excellent treatment on this surge of activity, see Raboteau, *Slave Religion*, Chapter 4.

22. *CAJ*, May 3, 1833, October 22, 1833.

23. Pinckney to Capers, January 24, 1835, HSSCC; Virginia C. Holmgren, *Hilton Head: A Sea Island Chronicle* (Hilton Head, S. C.: Hilton Head Publishing, 1959) 61–67; James Kirk to William E. Baynard, Esq., January 12, 1833, HSSCC.

24. Holmgren, *Hilton Head*, 130–31; William Pope, Sr. to William E. Baynard, Esq., January 8, 1834, HSSCC.

25. *CAJ*, January 31, 1834: James Sealy to William E. Baynard, Esq., January 8, 1834, HSSCC.

26. *CAJ*, January 31, 1834.

27. George W. Harley, "Notes on the Poro in Liberia," *Papers of the Peabody Museum of*

American Archaeology and Ethnology, Harvard University 19 (1941): 3, 7; Wilfred D. Hambley, "Initiation of Boys in Angola," *American Anthrologist,* 37, ser. 2, (1935): 36–40.

28. *CAJ,* January 31, 1834.

29. Ibid. and June 20, 1934.

30. *CAJ,* January 31, 1834; Raboteau, *Slave Religion,* 189–90. The First African Church's association with white ministers and with the regional Baptist Association was anything but smooth. Because many members were slaves, the African Church was subjected to jurisdictions contrary to Baptist policy. In January 1833, Marshall was barred from preaching in his own pulpit, and the Church expelled from Georgia's Sunbury Association. This struggle and turmoil lasted for five years. The Church managed to keep its status, but lost many members before returning to the good graces of white Baptists. See Raboteau, *Slave Religion,* 189–94.

31. *CAJ,* October 4, 1833.

32. Ibid.

33. John Coburn to the Missionary Society, January 11, 1835, HSSCC; "Report of the Missionary Society," *Minutes of South Carolina Conference,* February 10, 1836, 16, HSSCC.

34. John L. Field to George W. Moore, March 21, 1833, HSSCC; *CAJ,* January 14, 1834, January 31, 1834, June 26, 1835, July 22, 1836. Field to Moore, March 21, 1833, HSSCC; *CAJ,* January 31, 1834, July 29, 1836; Pierce Butler to James Smith; March 19, 1839, Wistar Papers, Butler Section, box 38 Letterbook 1838–1840, HSP; *SCA,* June 26, November 13, 1840.

35. "Report of the Missionary Society," *Minutes of South Carolina Conference,* January 9, 1839, 18 and December 25, 1844, 19, HSSCC.

36. "Pastoral Address," *Minutes of South Carolina Conference,* December 25, 1844, 14, HSSCC; *Proceedings of the Meeting in Charleston, South Carolina, May 13–15, 1845 on the Religious Instruction of the Negroes* (Charleston: B. Jenkins, 1845), 71–72; Norwood, *American Methodism,* 208–9; William W. Barnes, *The Southern Baptist Convention, 1845–1953* (Nashville: Broadman Press, 1954), 35; *SCA,* February 23, 1844; "Report of the Missionary Society," *Minutes of South Carolina Conference of the Methodist Episcopal Church, South,* January 13, 1847, 11, and February 10, 1855, 18, HSSCC; *SCA,* May 25, 1855; *Minutes of South Carolina Conference,* December 13, 1860, HSSCC; Mason Crum, *Gullah, Negro Life in the Carolina Sea Islands* (Durham: Duke University Press, 1940), 188.

37. Eugene D. Genovese, *Roll, Jordan, Roll: The World the Slaves Made* (New York: Pantheon Books, 1974), passim, but see especially 3–7, 91–93, 119–20, 135–36, 89–91, 597–98, 658–59; Records of Coffin Point Plantation, St. Helena Island, 1800–1821, SCHS; John Stapleton Papers, St. Helena, 1790–1839, SCL: Diary of John Edwin Fripp, 1857–58 and 1865–68, Beaufort Township Library; Kemble, *Journal,* 42–45, 75; Theodore Rosengarten, *Tombee, Portrait of A Cotton Planter, Journal of Thomas B. Chaplin, 1812–1890* (New York: William Morrow, 1986) 30, 55; Diary of Laura M. Towne, Penn School Papers, SHC; Guion G. Johnson, *A Social History of the Sea Islands* (Chapel Hill: University of North Carolina Press, 1930), 74–77, 104, 108–12; Major Pierce Butler to John Cooper, March 7, 1818, Wistar Papers, Butler Section, HSP.

38. Jenkins Mikell, *Rumblings of the Chariot Wheels* (Columbia: The State Co., 1923), 134–35; R. King, Jr. "On Management of the Butler Estate and Cultivation of Sugar Cane," *Southern Agriculturalist* (December, 1828): 597; Kemble, *Journal,* 42. For a different version, one which views the power of the driver as representing an enlargement of black autonomy for Lowcountry slaves in general, see Philip D. Morgan, "Black Society in the Lowcountry, 1760–1810," in Ira Berlin and Ronald Hoffman, *Slavery and Freedom in the Age of the*

American Revolution (Charlottesville: University of Virginia Press, 1983), 118–20. See also Genovese, *Roll, Jordan, Roll*, 371–74, 386–88.

39. Towne Diary, 10; Edward Philbrick to Dr. L. B. Russell, June 15, 1863, Edward Atkinson Papers, Massachusetts Historical Society; Thomas Wentworth Higginson, *Army Life in a Black Regiment* (New York: Collier Books, 1962, repr. from 1870 ed.), 210–211; *SCA*, August 11, 1843.

40. Peter H. Wood, *Black Majority: Negroes in Colonial South Carolina from 1769 through the Stono Rebellion* (New York: Alfred A. Knopf, 1974); Johann Schöepf, *Travels in the Confederation, 1783–84*, trans. Alfred Morrison (Philadelphia: W. J. Campbell, 1911), 220–21.

41. Lucius Gaston Moffatt and Joseph Médard Carrière, "A Frenchman Visits Charleston, 1817," *South Carolina Historical and Genealogical Magazine* 49, no. 2 (April, 1948): 141; Johnson, *Social History*, 22–29; Mikell, *Chariot Wheels*, 19–20; R. F. W. Allston, "Sea Coast Crops of the South," *Debow's Review*, XVI (January–June, 1854): 596–98; William Elliot, "On Cultivation of Sea Island Cotton," *Southern Agriculturalist* I (April, 1828): 154; Rosengarten, *Tombee*, 70, 72; Crum, *Gullah*, 233–34, U. B. Phillips, *American Negro Slavery* (Baton Rouge: Louisiana State University Press, 1966, repr. from 1918 ed.), 153–54, 223–25. Philip Morgan takes a different view. He argues that Sea Island cotton cultivation resulted in less arduous slave labor and that the task system augmented black independence and autonomy. See his "Ownership of Property by Slaves in the Mid-Nineteenth-Century Low Country," *Journal of Southern History*, no. 3 (August, 1983): 399–405, and "Black Society in the Low Country," 106–7, 120–21.

42. Mikell, *Chariot Wheels*, 19–20; Allston, "Sea Coast Crops of the South," 596–98; Fripp Diary, passim; J. A. Turner, ed., *The Cotton Planter's Manual* (New York: Negro Universities Press, repr. from 1867 ed.) 135–36; Elliott, "Sea Island Cotton," 154; Thomas Lagare, "Preparation of Sea Island Cotton," *Southern Agriculturalist* II, ser. 2 (December, 1842): 626–27; R. King to P. Butler, October 31, 1824, December 5, 1824, box 33, folder 1, and March 1, 1835, box 33, fol. 5, Wistar Papers, Butler Section, HSP; Whitemarsh B. Seabrook, "A Memoir on the Origin, Cultivation and Uses of Cotton," *Proceedings of the Agricultural Convention and State Agricultural Society of South Carolina* (Charleston: Miller & Browne, 1844), 30; Diary of William F. Allen, 82–83 in William F. Allen Family Papers, 1775–1937, State Historical Society of Wisconsin, Madison; Rosengarten, *Tombee*, 71–73.

43. Fripp Diary, passim; Towne Diary, 10, 20, 24, 32–33; R. King to P. Butler, Oct. 19, 24, and 31, 1824, box 33, fol. 1, Wistar Papers, Butler Section, HSP; Kemble, *Journal* 174–75, 182–83, 189–92, 226–27, 233, 251, 263–64; King, Jr., "Management of Butler Estate," 3–4; Seabrook, "Memoir on Cotton," 30–31; Johnson, *Social History;* Elizabeth Ware Pearson, *Letters From Port Royal* (New York: Arno Press and New York Times, repr., 1969, repr. from 1906 ed.), 13, 31, 114; Willie Lee Rose, *Rehearsal for Reconstruction;* The Port Royal Experiment (Indianapolis: Bobbs-Merrill, 1964), 126–27.

44. Allen Diary, 136, 91; Towne Diary, 33.

45. Kemble, *Journal*, 120–21, 182–83, 189–205, 214, 226–27, 233, 263.

46. Ibid., 135–36, 79–80.

47. Coffin Point Records Overseer report for 1818, SCHS; Fripp Diary, passim; Crum, *Gullah*, 244–45; Wightman, *Life of Capers*, 291; Pinckney, *Address*, 23–24 (Appendix); Johnson, *Social History*, 28–29, 106; W. E. B. DuBois, *The Suppression of the African Slave Trade to the United States of America, 1638–1870* (New York: Schocken Books, 1969; repr. from 1896 ed.), 180–86; James H. Cuthbert, *Life of Richard Fuller* (New York: Sheldon Co., 1878), 198; Federal Writers Program, Georgia, *Drums and Shadows* (Westport, Conn.:

Greenwood Press, 1973; repr. of 1940 ed.), xviii–xix. Civil War missionaries reported seeing Africans in the Sea Islands. Towne Diary, 12, reads: "I saw at church from Gabriel Eddings plantation a woman brought from Africa. Her face was tatooed. She seemed of a more vigorous stock"; Harriett Ware, related an account of her meeting a black steward from the *Wabash* in Port Royal. He had just returned from Africa where a slave ship *Ariel* and its slave-pirate were taken. "He gave us a most interesting account of the whole affair, as he went on board with the Captain when he ordered the hatches to be opened and the nine hundred blacks were discovered." Pearson, *Port Royal*, 225.

48. *SCA*, May 1, 1840; Lorenzo D. Turner, *Africanisms in the Gullah Dialect* (New York: Arno Press and New York Times, 1969; repr. from 1949 ed.), 5, 151; Arthur Sumner to Nina Hartshorn, May 18, 1862, Penn School Papers, v. 4, SHC; David Thorpe to John Mooney, January 25, 1863, Dabbs Papers, Thorpe Series, SHC.

49. Allen Diary, passim and 139.

50. *CAJ*, January 31, 1834; Federal Writers Program, *Drums and Shadows*, Chapter 6; Field to Moore, March 21, 1833, HSSCC.

51. *CAJ*, January 31, 1834, November 20, 1835, January 22, 1836.

52. *CAJ*, July 22, 1836.

53. Ibid., June 26, 1835; *SCA*, June 26, 1840, June 26, 1843.

54. *Proceedings of Charleston Meeting*, 48–49.

55. *SCA*, June 26, 1840; *CAJ*, July 17, 1835.

56. John W. Blassingame, *The Slave Community: Plantation Life in the South* (New York: Oxford University Press, 1972 ed.), 72; Crum, *Gullah*, 189; Kemble, *Journal*, 58; *CAJ*, February 7, 1834, April 25, 1834, September 25, 1835, July 22, 1836; *SCA*, May 24, 1839, June 30, 1843, September 29, 1843.

57. William Capers, *A Catechism for the Use of the Methodist Missions* (Charleston: J. S. Burges, 1833), passim; *SCA*, January 31, 1835.

58. Andrew, "Slave Population," 317–18; "Report of the Missionary Society," *Minutes of South Carolina Conference*, February 10, 1836, 20, HSSCC; *SCA*, January 26, 1838, June 30, 1843; Charles C. Jones, *Suggestions on the Religious Instruction of the Negroes in the Southern States* (Philadelphia: Presbyterian Board of Publication, 1847), 14; Wightman, *Life of Capers*, 295–96. Quoted in John Spencer Bassett, *The Southern Plantation Overseer, as Revealed in His Letters* (Northhampton, Mass: Smith College, 1925), 14–15.

59. John Bunch to Missionary Society, South Carolina Conference, January 11, 1835, HSSCC; Pinckney to Capers, January 24, 1835, HSSCC; *CAJ*, April 10, 1833, September 9, 1833, January 24, 1835, June 26, 1835, July 22, 1836; *SCA*, December 22, 1843, February 23, 1847; Wightman, *Life of Capers*, 298–99.

60. Bunch to Missionary Society, January 11, 1835, HSSCC; *CAJ*, February 7, 1834, June 13, 1834, October 17, 1834, June 26, 1835; *SCA*, April 8, 1842, January 29, 1847, May 6, 1848, March 28, 1851; Crum, *Gullah*, 218.

61. *SCA*, July 7, 1843.

62. Ibid.

63. *SCA*, July 14, 1843, September 15, 1843, September 29, 1843, August 13, 1847, May 18, 1849, September 6, 1850, May 25, 1855.

64. John McKim to Mrs. Wendell Garrison, April 20, 1864. Antislavery Papers, Rare Book Room, Cornell University, Ithaca, N. Y. The most well-known individual who argues that Gullah music came from Methodist hymns is Guy B. Johnson, *Folk Culture on St. Helena Island* (Chapel Hill: University of North Carolina Press, 1930), ix–xi, 6–8, 74–84; Albert Deems Betts, *History of South Carolina Methodism* (Columbia: Advocate Press, 1952), 159–68. Betts provides a history of the camp meetings in South Carolina and lists

the known campgrounds by name, location, and dates of their existence. Crum, *Gullah*, 151. According to Crum, W. A. Massebeau in *Camp Meetings in South Carolina* (1919) records the names of 50 campgrounds. Of these, only one, Black Swamp, is south of Charleston. Black Swamp was in the Beaufort District and is close to Savannah. The area experienced its religious revival in the 1830s; Capers, *Catechism*, 14–16; *SCA*, June 30, 1843, July 14, 1843, December 29, 1843, January 12, 1849; John McKim to Mrs. Wendell Garrison, April 20, 1864, W. Athorp to Mrs. Wendell P. Garrison, April 20, 1867 Antislavery Papers; Allen Diary, 18–19, 127–28, 164; Nicholas George Julius Ballanta, *St. Helena Spirituals* (New York: G. Schirmer Press, 1925), Introduction and Foreword; Higginson, *Army Life*, 187–88; Crum, *Gullah*, 132–34.

65. *SCA*, December 29, 1843.

66. *CAJ*, August 18, 1837.

67. Higginson, *Army Life*, 71–72.

68. *CAJ*, January 31, 1834; *SCA*, June 26, 1840; Archie Epps, "A Negro Separatist Movement in the Nineteenth Century," *The Harvard Law Review* 4, no. 1 (Summer–Fall, 1966): 69–80; *Proceedings of Charleston Meeting*, 48–49; Fripp Diary, 60.

69. *CAJ*, September 7, 1833, November 7, 1834; *SCA*, September 15, 1843, September 6, 1850; Thompson, *English Working Class*, 367–68.

70. "Report of Missionary Society," *Minutes of South Carolina Conference*, January 13, 1847, 11, HSSCC; *SCA*, June 26, 1840, September 15, 1843, September 29, 1843.

71. Albert H. Stoddard, "Origin, Dialect, Beliefs and Characteristics of the Negroes of the South Carolina and Georgia Coasts," *Georgia Historical Quarterly* 28 (September, 1944): 186–95; Geoffrey Parrinder, *Religion in Africa* (Middlesex, England: Penguin Books, 1969), Chapters 2, 3, 5, and especially 7; Views on the "spirit" versus the "letter" of Christian doctrine are based on Friedrich Hegel, *Early Theological Writings* (Chicago: University of Chicago Press, 1948), Chapter 2, ii, "The Moral Teaching of Jesus, (a) The Sermon on the Mount Contrasted with the Mosaic Law and with Kant's Ethics": iv, "The Religious Teaching of Jesus"; E. J. Hobsbawm, *Primitive Rebels*, 2nd ed. (New York: Praeger, 1963), Intro., especially Chapters 1–3.

72. "Pastoral Address," *Minutes of South Carolina Conference*, December 25, 1844, 14–15, HSSCC; *SCA*, January 29, 1847; Norwood, *American Methodism*, 208–9; Barnes, *Southern Baptist Convention*, 40–41; *Proceedings of Charleston Meeting*, 71–72.

7. To Make Them Better Slaves: Baptist Persuasion, 1830–1861

1. *Proceedings of the Meeting in Charleston, South Carolina, May 13–15, 1845 on the Religious Instruction of the Negroes* (Charleston: B. Jenkins, 1845), 49; Theodore Rosengarten, *Tombee, Portrait of a Cotton Planter, Journal of Thomas B. Chaplin, 1812–1890* (New York: William Morrow, 1986), 146–47; *CAJ*, June 20, 1834; Harvey H. Jackson, "Hugh Bryan and the Evangelical Movement in South Carolina," *William and Mary Quarterly* 47, 3rd. ser., no. 4 (October, 1986); 594–95; Albert J. Raboteau, *Slave Religion: The "Invisible Institution" in the Antebellum South* (New York: Oxford University Press, 1978), 152–57; A. H. Newman, *A History of the Baptist Churches in the United States* (New York: Christian Literature, 1894), 4–6, 79; David Benedict, *A General History of The Baptist Denomination in America and Other Parts of the World* (New York: Lewis Colby, 1848 repr. from 1813 ed.), 701–3; Joe Madison King, *A History of South Carolina Baptists* (Columbia: General Board, South Carolina Baptist Convention, 1964) 212–14; H. A. Tupper, ed., *Two Centuries of the First Baptist Church in South Carolina, 1663–1833* (Baltimore: R. H. Wooland, 1899), 224–25; Euhaw Baptist Church Mss., March 14, 1834, Lawton Family Papers, SCL; Charlotte Verstille to Nancy Ver-

stille, March 2, 1831, Tristram Verstille Papers, SCL; *Minutes of the Savannah River Baptist Association*, 1802, October 17, 1817, November 27, 1830, BC.

2. James Busch, "The Beaufort Baptist Church," Beaufort County Historical Society Paper, n.d., 13, Beaufort Township Library, Beaufort, South Carolina; *CAJ*, January 6, 1832; William M. Baker, *The Life and Labours of the Reverend Daniel Baker, D. D., Pastor & Evangelist* (Philadelphia: William & Alfred Martien, 1859), 145–56; James H. Cuthbert, *Life of Richard Fuller* (New York: Sheldon Co., 1879), 67–68; *Minutes, Savannah River Baptist Association*, November 22, 1831, 24, November 26, 1831, 18, 20, November 23, 1833, 10, BC; see Appendix C. Table C.1 lists the churches within the Savannah River Baptist Association in 1833, and indicates the number of baptisms for that year.

3. *Minutes of the Euhaw Baptist Church, 1831–1875*, December 21, 1831, 11, February 18, 1832, 12, June 23, 1832, 16, August, 1832, 18, SCL; James W. Busch, "Beaufort Church," 15; Cuthbert, *Life of Fuller*, 79–82, 104–5; Rosengarten, *Tombee*, 147. Some Episcopalian planters participating in the 1831 revival subsequently became liberal contributors to the Methodist cause of religious instruction of the slaves. *Minutes of the South Carolina Conference of the Methodist Episcopal Church*, February 10, 1836, 22, January 9, 1839, 18–19, HSSCC; *CAJ*, January 26, 1838. *Minutes, Savannah River Baptist Association*, November 20, 1834, BC.

4. Appendix C, see tables C.1 and C.2. The fluctuation noticeable in the membership of mainland churches occurred because new churches drew members away from older congregations. *Minutes, Savannah River Baptist Association*, November, 1834, taken from the pages of the *Southern Baptist and General Intelligencer*, January 3, 1835, BC.

5. *Minutes, Savannah River Baptist Association*, November 21, 1835, 4, BC; Busch, "Beaufort Church," 16; Charles C. Jones, *The Religious Instruction of the Negroes of the United States* (New York: Negro Universities Press, 1969; repr. from 1842 ed.), 96–98; Chalmers D. Davidson, *The Last Foray: The South Carolina Plantations in 1860: A Sociogical Study* (Columbia: University of South Carolina Press, 1975), 96–98.

6. Bynum Shaw, *Divided We Stand: The Baptists in American Life* (Durham: Moore Publishing, 1874), 113–14; Newman, *Baptist Church in the United States*, 304–6; Guion G. Johnson, *A Social History of the Sea Islands* (Chapel Hill: University of North Carolina Press, 1930), 45, 103–4, 117; Cuthbert, *Life of Fuller*, 15; *Minutes, Savannah River Baptist Association*, November 24, 1849, BC. William W. Barnes, *The Southern Baptist Convention, 1845– 1953* (Nashville: Broadman Press, 1954), 19; H. Shelton Smith, *In His Image, But . . . Racism in Southern Religion, 1780–1910* (Durham: Duke University Press, 1972), 53–55; Reverend Dr. Richard Furman, *Exposition of the Views of the Baptists, Relative to the Colored Population in the United States, in A Communication to the Governor of South Carolina* (Charleston: A. E. Miller, 1823), 6.

7. Shaw, *Divided We Stand*, 113–16; Barnes, *Southern Baptist Convention*, 20–21; Smith, *In His Image, But*, 117–21, 127–28; Cuthbert, *Life of Fuller*, 227; *Minutes, Beaufort Baptist Church*, September 12, 1840, 9, BC; *Minutes, Savannah River Baptist Association*, November 21, 1835, 4, November 25, 1837, 5, October 24, 1840, 3, BC.

8. *Minutes, Savannah River Baptist Association*, November 24, 1838, 6, November 23, 1839, 11, October 23, 1841, 12, November 26, 1842, 4–5.

9. Cuthbert, *Life of Fuller*, 153, 227; Busch, "Beaufort Church," 16; *Minutes, Savannah River Baptist Association*, November 21, 1835, 4, BC.

10. *Minutes, Savannah River Baptist Association*, November 25, 1841, BC.

11. Jones, *Religious Instruction*, 210–11; John B. Adger, D. D., *My Life and Times, 1810– 1899* (Richmond, Va.: Presbyterian Committee of Publication, 1899), 198–99; *Proceedings*

of Charleston Meeting, 5–6, 14; *Minutes, Savannah River Baptist Association,* October 21, 1841, 4, BC.

12. Thomas Bennett to Richard Furman, 1822, Furman Papers, SCL; Charles C. Pinckney, *An Address Delivered in Charleston Before the Agricultural Society of South Carolina, At Its Annual Meeting, 18th August, 1829* (Charleston: A. E. Miller, 1829), passim; James O. Andrew, "The Southern Slave Population," *MMQR* 13 (1831): 315–17; *Proceedings of Charleston Meeting,* 14–15.

13. "South Carolina through New England Eyes, Almira Coffin's Visit to the Low Country in 1851," John H. Tucker to T. D. Grimke, n.d., early in 1845, SCHS; *Proceedings of Charleston Meeting,* 71–72; "Pastoral Address," *Minutes of the South Carolina Conference of the Methodist Episcopal Church,* December 25, 1844, 14–15, HSSCC; *Minutes, Savannah River Baptist Association,* November 25, 1848, 6, November 24, 1849, 7–8, BC; *SCA,* January 29, 1847; John B. Adger, *A Sermon Preached by the Rev. J. B. Adger of the Second Presbyterian Church, Charleston, S. C.,* May 9, 1847 (Charleston: T. W. Haynes, 1847), 12–13, and *Life and Times,* 164–99; Reverend Alexander Glennie, *Sermons Preached on Plantations to Congregations of Negroes* (Charleston: A. E. Miller, 1844), passim; Charles Colcock Jones, *Suggestions on the Religious Instruction of the Negroes in the Southern States* (Philadelphia: Presbyterian Board of Publication, 1847, 27–33; and *A Catechism of Scripture Doctrine and Practice* (Savannah: T. Purse, 1844), passim; Reverend A. F. Dickson, *Plantation Sermons* (Philadelphia: Presbyterian Board of Publication, 1855), passim; Tupper, *Baptist Church of South Carolina,* 317–18; Donald Blake Touchstone, "Planters and Slave Religion in the Deep South," (Ph.D. dissertation, Tulane University, 1973), 71–85; Raboteau, *Slave Religion,* Chapter 4; Rev. J. H. Thornwell, *The Rights and Duties of Masters. A Sermon Preached at the Dedication of A Church Erected in Charleston, S. C., For the Benefit and Instruction of the Colored Population* (Charleston: Steam-Power Press, 1850), 48–51.

14. *Minutes, Savannah River Baptist Association,* November 25, 1848, 6–7, November 24, November 26, 1853, 10–11, November 25, 1854, 19, November 23, 1855, 12, November 14, 1857, BC; *Minutes, Beaufort Baptist Church,* April 9, 1841, 15, November 11, 1843, 66, BC; Benedict, *Fifty Years among the Baptists,* 39.

15. *Minutes, Savannah River Baptist Association,* passim, BC; see Appendix C, tables C.1 and C.2; *Minutes, Beaufort Baptist Church,* August 7, 1853, 179, BC; Fred Jones, "Report on Church History: A Historical Sketch of the Old Black Swamp Church," Lawton Family Papers, SCL.

16. See Chapters 3 and 4.

17. Busch, "Beaufort Church," 13; Jones, "Old Black Swamp Church"; *Minutes, Savannah River Baptist Association,* November 26, 1831, 18–20, BC; *CAJ,* January 6, 1832; Diary of William P. Hill, 1833–39, SHC (Hill was a Universalist from Maine who went South for health reasons and became a Baptist preacher); Cuthbert, *Life of Fuller,* 67–68; W. H. Dowling, "Black Swamp Church," n.d., SCL; Baker, *Life and Labours,* 144–45, 157, 169–73.

18. Baker, *Life and Labours,* 153; Samuel Gaillard Stoney, ed. "The Autobiography of William John Grayson," *South Carolina Historical and Genealogical Magazine* 49, no. 1 (January, 1948): 34–36.

19. Baker, *Life and Labours,* 153; Stoney, "Autobiography of Grayson," 34–36.

20. *CAJ,* January 6, 1832; Stoney, *"Autobiography of Grayson,"* 34–37.

21.Baker, *Life and Labours,* 154–55.

22. Racial designations were not yet indicated nor names of slaves included on membership rolls. But the slaves' acceptance into the church was recorded in the Minutes. *Minutes,*

Beaufort Baptist Church, Membership Rolls, and see Appendix C, tables C.1 and C.2; *Minutes, Euhaw Baptist Church*, 11–12, 14, 16, 18–19, 32, 55–56, 58, 66–68, 70; Jones, "Old Black Swamp Church."

23. Cuthbert, *Life of Fuller*, 79–82; Stoney, "Autobiography of Grayson," 36; *Minutes, Beaufort Baptist Church*, passim, BC; Busch, "Beaufort Church," 13–17. Within this same article is a section entitled "Richard Fuller and Slavery," 11; and see Appendix C, tables C.1 and C.2.

24. Johnson, *Social History*, 103; Cuthbert, *Life of Fuller*, 15–20, 67–79; Busch, "Beaufort Church," 14–16.

25. *Minutes, Beaufort Baptist Church*, passim, BC; Cuthbert, *Life of Fuller*, 81–106; Busch, "Beaufort Church," 14–16.

26. "Former Slaves Recollect Fuller," in Cuthbert, *Life of Fuller*, 106–113; Charlotte Forten, "Life on the Sea Islands," Part I, *Atlantic Monthly* 13 (May, 1864): 589–90.

27. *Minutes, Savannah River Baptist Association*, November 26, 1853, 10–11; November 25, 1854, 16; November 14, 1857, 10–11, BC; *Minutes, Beaufort Baptist Church*, July 12, 1857, 2–3, 35; November 7, 1857, 241–43, BC.

28. This is an estimate and represents population based on the 1830 census returns. U.S. Census Office, *Sixth Census, 1840* (Washington: T. Allen, 1841), 95; see Appendix C. tables C.1 and C.3.

29. See Appendix C, table C.2; U.S. Census, *Sixth Census*, 95–96, 226–27; *Minutes, Savannah River Baptist Association*, November 22, 1845, 16, BC; *Proceedings of Charleston Meeting*, 48–50; *Minutes, Beaufort Baptist Church*, 273, BC.

30. *Minutes, Savannah River Baptist Association*, November 25, 1848, 5, November 1859, BC; see Appendix C, table C.3.

31. Baker, *Life of Labours*, 155–56; Busch, "Beaufort Church," 13; Cuthbert, *Life of Fuller*, 15–16, 64–65, 67–75; John Stapleton Papers, SCL, have information on the Rhetts, who bought Frogmore Plantation, St. Helena, from Stapleton in 1836; Jones, "Old Black Swamp Church"; Charlotte Verstille to Nancy Verstille, March 2, 1821, Tristram Verstille Papers, SCL; Diary of John Edwin Fripp, Beaufort Township Library; For Princeton preference see "Notes and Documents; Antebellum and War Memories of Mrs. Telfair Hodgson," Sarah Hodgson Torian, ed., *Georgia Historical Quarterly* 27, no. 4 (December, 1953): 352; Rosengarten, *Tombee*, 88–91; Johnson, *Social History*, 103–11; Hill Diary, SHC; Baptist Church at Black Swamp Mss., Lawton Family Papers, SCL; George P. Rawick, *The American Slave: A Composite Autobiography*, 19 vols., *South Carolina Narratives*, vols. 2 and 3 in 4 Parts (Westport, Conn.: Greenwood Publishing), II (1) 155–58, 161–62; Jenkins Mikell, *Rumblings of the Chariot Wheels* (Columbia: The State Co., 1923), 201; Johnson, *Social History*, 114–15; Henry Noble Sherwood, ed., Introduction, "Journal of Miss Susan Walker, March 3d to June 6, 1862," *Historical and Philosophical Society of Ohio* 7 (January–March, 1912): 5.

32. Mikell, *Chariot Wheels*, 201–2; Frank Moore, ed., *The Rebellion Record*, Supp. I (New York: D. Van Nostrand, 1871), 197–202; William W. Freehling, *Prelude to Civil War* (New York: Harper & Row, 1965), 353–56; Rosengarten, *Tombee*, 140–43, 203–11; Mason Crum, *Gullah, Negro Life in the Carolina Sea Islands* (Durham: Duke University Press, 1940), 35–54.

33. Edward L. Pierce, "The Freedmen at Port Royal," *Atlantic Monthly*, 12 (September, 1863): 295.

34. Janet Duitsman Cornelius, "God's Schoolmaster: Southern Evangelists to the Slaves, 1830–1860," (Ph.D. dissertation, University of Illinois at Urbana-Champaign), 16–22; Cuthbert, *Life of Fuller*, 140–58.

35. Cuthbert, *Life of Fuller, 140–58;* Smith, *In His Image, But,* 133–36, 138–39; King, *South Carolina Baptists,* 211–12.

36. David Donald, ed., *Inside Lincoln's Cabinet* (New York: Longmans, Green, 1954), 69–70.

37. William Howard Russell, *My Diary North and South,* Fletcher Pratt, ed. (New York: Harper Brothers, 1854), 76–77; Busch, "Beaufort Church," sections entitled "Work among the Negroes," 3 and "Richard Fuller and Slavery," 1; *Minutes, Beaufort Baptist Church,* October 9, 1840, 11, October 8, 1841, 23, October 8, 1842, 39, BC; *Minutes, Euhaw Baptist Church,* October 9, 1836, 59; September 24, 1838, 66, SCL; Cuthbert, *Life of Fuller,* 104–6; C. C. Pinckney to William Capers, January 24, 1835, HSSCC; *SCA,* September 29, 1843; Rawick, *American Slave, South Carolina* II (2) 72–73, 184–85, 279, III (3) 202, 274.

38. *Proceedings of Charleston Meeting,* 49.

39. *Minutes, Beaufort Baptist Church,* "Origin of the Colored Societies," October 7, 1859, Business Meeting in which the organization of the societies is discussed, 271–74, January 7, 1842 and November 11, 1840, 12, BC; Cuthbert, *Life of Fuller,* 83–104; *CAJ,* January 31, 1834; Field to Moore, March 21, 1833, HSSCC.

40. See Chapter 6.

41. *Minutes, Beaufort Baptist Church,* 12, BC.

42. Ibid., 271–72.

43. Ibid., 271–74; Rawick, *American Slave, South Carolina,* II: (2) 185.

44. *Proceedings of Charleston Meeting,* 48–49; *Minutes, Beaufort Baptist Church,* April 9, 1847, 111, passim, BC; Rawick, *American Slave, South Carolina,* II (2) 184–85; Rev. Mansfield French to Revs. Whipple and Jocelyn in Elizabeth Ware Pearson, *Letters from Port Royal* (New York: Arno Press and New York Times, 1969; repr. from 1906 ed.), 20. The spelling generally is *Praise* House. Black and white Northerners living among the Gullahs during the Civil War spelled the word thusly. But Samuel Lawton did research in the Sea Islands in the 1920s and indicates the word was "Prays," named for its function as a place of prayer. According to Lawton, Gullah pronunciation of the flat "a" and dropping of the final syllable on many words explain why no difference was noted between "prays" and ':'praise." Lawton interviewed former Sea Island slaves in the 1920s who referred to the plantation meetinghouse as "Pray House" without the "s" sound, or they pronounced two syllables very distinctly, "pray-ers house." Informants stated it was "Way ooner go fur pray." Gullahs changed verbs into nouns without adding the extra ending. Thus, at the meetinghouse, "One pray"—Den Anudder lead a pray'—Dat make two prays." Lawton's argument is reinforced by Patricia Guthrie's more recent fieldwork in the 1970s. According to Guthrie, "Praise houses are also known locally and in the literature as prayer and pray houses." The Gullahs' mastering of double meaning however may also inform the discussion. They often asked white Northerners to "jine praise wid we." Also their anthem, "New Jerasulem," stated, "Sing God praise both night and day." Thus the Gullahs went to the meetinghouse to *praise* and *pray.* Samuel Lawton, "The Religious Life of Coastal and Sea Island Negroes," (Ph.D. dissertation, George Peabody College for Teachers, 1939), 54–56; Patricia Guthrie, "Praise House Worship and Litigation Among Afro-Americans on a South Carolina Sea Island," Paper, Sixth Annual Martin Luther King Lecture Series, Purdue University, February 21, 1980, 1.

45. Rawick *American Slave, South Carolina* II (2) 279–80, III (3) 200–202; Diary of John Edwin Fripp, 1857–58 and 1865–68, 24, Beaufort Township Library; Russell, *My Diary North and South,* 71–77; Cuthbert, *Life of Fuller,* 15–20; Minutes, *Beaufort Baptist Church,* April 9, 1841, 15, May 14, 1842, 34, BC. August 12, 1843, 61–62; October 1, 1853, 180,

BC. A good example of how little attention some masters paid to slaves is provided in the T. B. Chaplin Journal, edited by Theodore Rosengarten. Chaplin probably spent more time supervising his property than most Sea Island planters. However Rosengarten writes: "Because Chaplin had very little to do with his slaves outside of work, we seldom see them in their quarters and only then when peace is disturbed." T. B. Chaplin was on the Episcopalian side of the family and "appears to have invested nothing in the spiritual welfare of his slaves." Some of his slaves did join the Island Baptist church through the "praise house." Rosengarten, *Tombee*, 145, 147, 151.

46. *Minutes, Savannah River Baptist Association*, November 25, 1854, November 23, 1855, BC; *Minutes, Beaufort Baptist Church*, June 10, 1843, 61–62, September 4, 1852, 171, September 12, 1854, 197, November 7, 1857, 241–42, BC; Rosengarten, *Tombee*, 147; Pierce Butler to A. Marvin, March 19, 1839, Letterbook, 1838–1840, box 38, Wistar Papers, Butler Section, HSP.

47. James Leo Garrett, Jr., *Baptist Church Discipline: An Historical Introduction to the Practices of Baptist Churches, with Particular Attention to the Summary of Church Discipline Adopted in 1773 by the Charleston Association* (Nashville: Broadman Press, 1962), 3–4, 10–18, 28; King, *South Carolina Baptists*, 62–63. The Baptist religion as it developed in the Lowcountry from Georgetown southward to the Beaufort District was considerably different from that planted in the upcountry. The latter was closer to the frontier Baptist tradition. Unlike "Regular" Baptists of the Lowcountry, the "frontier theology" was a compromise of Arminian and Calvinist views. King, *South Carolina Baptists*, 38, 148; Sidney E. Ahlstrom, *A Religious History of the American People* (New Haven and London: Yale University Press, 1972), 440–43.

48. Garrett, *Baptist Church Discipline*, 39–44; J. William Harris, *Plain Folk and Gentry in a Slave Society* (Middletown, Conn.: Wesleyan University Press, 1985), 100–04; Raboteau, *Slave Religion*, 180–81; King, *South Carolina Baptists*, 38, 148–55; Daniel W. Hollis, "The Role of the Church in South Carolina History," *Journal of the South Carolina Baptist Historical Society* 4 (November, 1978): 11–13; Smith, *In His Image, But*, Chapter 2.

49. *Minutes, Euhaw Baptist Church*, passim, SCL; *Minutes, Baptist Church at Black Creek*, 1828–1922, 15–59, SCL; Jones, "Old Black Swamp Church"; *Minutes, Beaufort Baptist Church*, October 9, 1840, 10–11, BC; For information about discipline of slaves in other churches, see Cornelius, "God's Schoolmasters," 228–40; Harris, *Plain Folk and Gentry*, 48–52.

50. *Minutes, Beaufort Baptist Church*, August 12, 1843, 61–62.

51. Ibid., November 11, 1840, 12, April 5, 1852, 166, October 7, 1859, 272–73.

52. Ibid., October 8, 1840, 11, July 9, 1841, 19, July 8, 1842, 34; September 8, 1843, 63; April 5, 1855, 203–4.

53. Rawick, *American Slave, South Carolina*, II (2) 184; Allen Diary, 23, 57.

54. *Minutes, Beaufort Baptist Church*, November 9, 1844, 83, April 5, 1852, 166, October 7, 1859, 272–73, BC; *Minutes, Euhaw Baptist Church*, February 5, 1832, 11, September 1848, 75, SCL.

55. Fripp Diary, 60, Beaufort Township Library; Johnson, *Social History:* 47, 54; Rawick, *American Slave, South Carolina*, III (3) 200–201, 272; Diary of William F. Allen, 62, in William F. Allen Family Papers, 1775–1937, State Historical Society of Wisconsin, Madison.

56. John W. Blassingame, ed., *Slave Testimony: Two Centuries of Letters, Speeches, Interviews and Autobiographies* (Baton Rouge: Louisiana State University Press, 1977), 374, 381; Forten, "Sea Islands," Part I, 668; Diary of Laura M. Towne, 15, Penn School Papers, SHC.

57. *CAJ*, January 31, 1834; Allen Diary, 37, 71, 87–88; Rev. W. T. Richardson to Rev. Whipple, July 3, 1863, AMA; Sherwood, "Walker Journal," 32–33, 40–41.

58. Blassingame, *Slave Testimony*, 377; Charlotte Forten, "Life on the Sea Islands," Part II, *Atlantic Monthly* 13 (June, 1864): 674; Allen Diary, 32, 143; Rawick, *American Slave, South Carolina*, II (1) 158–59, 162, 179–81, III (3) 273–75.

59. Allen Diary, 47–48, 103, 118, 136; Rosengarten, *Tombee*, 150–54, 164–65.

60. Allen Diary, 48, 62, 72, 84.

61. Rosengarten, *Tombee*, 456–58.

62. Ibid., 124.

63. *Minutes, Beaufort Baptist Church*, March 31, 1849, 133, May 5, 1849, 134, June 30, 1849, 135, BC.

64. Thomas Wentworth Higginson to Louisa Higginson, October 23, 1863, Papers of Thomas Wentworth Higginson, Houghton Library, Harvard University; Allen Diary, 91–92; Typescript copy of Diary of Laura M. Towne (varies from Ms. Diary), April 3, 1862, Penn School Papers, vol. I, SHC. Theodore Rosengarten perhaps in support of arguments favoring paternalism on the Sea Islands (a point on which we disagree), maintains that black sentiments toward masters "were sometimes not always understood or accurately rendered by the people who solicited information." He cites by example, Laura Towne's reaction to Clarence Fripp's relationship with his slave Rachel. They lived together openly, and during the war, Fripp deeded over his plantation to Rachel. Towne said Fripp "led an infamous life, too bad to write of, to vile to speak of." Rosengarten implies that Towne's disgust toward Fripp centered on his living with Rachel. Yet Laura Towne was not so naive as to condemn Fripp for this alone, However, she was very upset upon learning that Clarence and his two brothers passed Rachel around for sexual favors. "She lived with her master and his two brothers infamously and her children are almost white," wrote Towne. Thus Towne reacted to the wanton license exercised by the Fripps toward slave women. Rosengarten, *Tombee*, 166; Towne Diary Typescript, February 14, 1864, Penn School Papers, vol. 2, SHC.

65. *Minutes, Beaufort Baptist Church*, 162–274; Blassingame, *Slave Testimony*, 358–61, 450–53; Sherwood, "Walker Journal," 34; Fripp Diary, 60; Allen Diary, 103; Towne Diary, 14, 20.

66. Rosengarten, *Tombee*, 214–20; Towne Diary Typescript, April 3, 1862; Forten, "Sea Islands," Part I, 593.

67. *Minutes, Prince William Baptist Church*, May 20, 1865, 107, SCL.

68. March 14, 1824, in Lawton Family Papers, SCL; Black Swamp Church Mss., SCL; Rawick, *American Slave, South Carolina*, II (1) 158; William Tillinghast, *Address to Baptist Ministers of the U. S. Who Hold Slaves by A Minister of the Ministeral Conference of the Black River Association* (Antwerp:, 1845), New-York Historical Society.

69. *Minutes, Savannah River Baptist Association*, November 21, 1835, 3–4; November 25, 1849, 9, BC; *Minutes, Beaufort Baptist Church*, September 12, 1840, 9, April 9, 1841, 15, BC.

70. *Minutes, Savannah River Baptist Association*, November 25, 1839, 9, BC.

71. Elizabeth Hyde Botume, *First Days Amongst the Contrabands* (New York: Arno Press and New York Times, 1968; repr. from 1893 ed.), 158–61; Rawick, *American Slave, South Carolina*, III (3) 201; Blassingame, *Slave Testimony*, 381.

72. Blassingame, *Slave Testimony*, 374–76.

73. Rosengarten, *Tombee*, 155; Laura M, Towne to Wendell Phillips Garrison, June 8, 1867, Antislavery Papers, Rare Book Room Cornell University.

74. Forten, "Sea Islands," Part I, 594; Botume, *Amongst the Contrabands*, 157–58.

75. *CAJ*, August 18, 1837; *SCA*, July 7, 1843, August 21, 1840, February 3, 1841, September 29, 1843.

76. As far as total immersion was concerned, Methodist missionaries were willing to baptize slaves in this manner if the slaves so desired. *CAJ*, February 7, 1834; John L. Field to George W. Moore, March 21, 1833 HSSCC; *Minutes, Beaufort Baptist Church*, passim, BC; Rawick, *American Slave, South Carolina*, II (2) 184–85; III (3) 202.

77. Towne Diary, 26, 54; Pearson, *Letters from Port Royal*, 26–28; *CAJ*, January 31, 1834, November 20, 1835, July 22, 1836; *SCA*, May 1, 1840, April 8, 1842, June 26, 1843, July 28, 1843.

78. *SCA*, February 16, 1844, October 30, 1846.

79. *SCA*, July 28, 1843; *Proceedings of Charleston Meeting*, 29–50; Russell, *My Diary*, 77; James R. Stuart Recollections, n.d. (around 1850), SHC; *SCA*, March 30, 1849, May 12, 1849, September 6, 1850, July 5, 1855.

80. *SCA*, May 18, 1849; Rosengarten, *Tombee*, 145–47; Fripp Diary, 9, 18, 40, 47, Towne Diary, 22.

8. *Elements of the Head and the Heart: Gullah Interpretations of Christianity*

1. "The Long Look," 2–3, undated sketch of a former slave, Sam Polite, who lived to be over 100 years old, Penn School Papers, vol. 1, SHC. For discussions on the Union victory at Port Royal see Willie Lee Rose, *Rehearsal for Reconstruction: The Port Royal Experiment* (Indianapolis: Bobbs-Merrill, 1964), 3–12; Theodore Rosengarten, *Tombee: Portrait of a Cotton Planter, Journal of Thomas B. Chaplin, 1812–1890* (New York: William Morrow, 1986), 202–22.

2. Randall Hunt, "Journal of a Traveller from Charleston, S. C. to New Haven, Conn., 1832," SCHS; "South Carolina through New England Eyes, Elmira Coffin's Visit to the Low Country in 1851," SCHS; William Howard Russell, *My Diary North and South*, ed. Fletcher Pratt (New York: Harper Brothers, 1854), Charles Joyner, *Down By the Riverside: A South Carolina Slave Community* (Urbana and Chicago: University of Illinois Press, 1984), 154–59, 161–63, 229–30; "All Saints, Waccamaw, the Parish, the Place, the People, 1739–1948," Beaufort Township Library, South Carolina, Society of Colonial Dames of America, 22–24, 30–33, 38–43. Joyner's book is a reconstruction of black life in All Saints Parish.

3. W. T. Richardson to Rev. S. S. Jocelyn, June 19, 1863, Lydia Fuller to Rev. S. S. Jocelyn, July 5, 1864, AMA; Diary of William F. Allen in William F. Allen Family Papers, 1775–1937, State Historical Society of Wisconsin, Madison, 144; Elizabeth Hyde Botume, *First Days Amongst the Contrabands* (New York: Arno Press and New York Times, 1968; repr. from 1893 ed.), 91–92, 112–14.

4. Edward L. Pierce, "The Freedom at Port Royal," *Atlantic Monthly*, 12 (September, 1863): 304; Laura M. Towne to James McKim, February 1, 1862, Antislavery Papers, Rare Book Room, Cornell University; Allen Diary, 96, 127–28, 151–52.

5. Mary Ames, *From a New England Woman's Diary in Dixie* (New York: Negro Universities Press, 1969; repr. from 1906 ed.), 68; Botume, *Amongst the Contrabands*, 74–75.

6. Lawrence W. Levine, *Black Culture and Black Consciousness: Afro-American Folk Thought from Slavery to Freedom* (New York: Oxford University Press, 1977), 43; Albert J. Raboteau, *Slave Religion: The "Invisible Institution" in the Antebellum South* (New York: Oxford University Press, 1978), 320–21; Thomas Wentworth Higginson, *Army Life in a Black Regiment* (New York: Collier Books, 1962, repr. from 1870 ed.), 49; Joyner, *Down by the Riverside*,

164–66; Edwin S. Williams to Rev. S. S. Jocelyn, January 28, 1863, AMA. For an interesting discussion of the fusion of Old and New Testament figures, see Eugene Genovese, *Roll, Jordan, Roll: The World the Slaves Made* (New York: Pantheon Books, 1974), 252–55.

7. George P. Rawick, *The American Slave: A Composite Autobiography*, 19 vols., *South Carolina Narratives*, vols. 2 & 3, in 4 parts (Westport, Conn.: Greenwood Publishing, 1972), II (2) 180–81.

8. Charlotte Forten, "Life on the Sea Islands," Part II, *Atlantic Monthly* 13 (June, 1864): 672.

9. Mansfield French to Revs. Whipple and Jocelyn, n.d., AMA; Ira Berlin, ed., *Freedom: A Documentary History of Emancipation, 1861–1867, Series II* (Cambridge: Cambridge University Press, 1982), 49–50; Allen Diary, 57–58; Rose, *Rehearsal for Reconstruction*, 145–48; Diary of Laura M. Towne, 26, Penn School Papers, SHC. It is interesting to note that "Old Marcus' " "Massa" was Daniel Pope of the Oaks Plantation. Pope was an important individual in St. Helena's Baptist Church. The Oaks was one of the plantations where Northerners saw so many signs of "Ill-treatment," and was referred to as "de cruelest place." Towne Diary, 32–33.

10. Arthur Sumner to Lt. Joseph Clark, January 23, 1863, Penn School Papers, vol. 4 SHC: Botume, *Amongst the Contrabands*, 218; Higginson, *Army Life*, 231–39.

11. Paul Radin, "Status, Phantasy, and the Christian Dogma," in Clifton Johnson, ed., *God Struck Me Dead: Religious Conversion Experiences and Autobiographies of Negro Ex-Slaves* (Nashville: Social Science Institute, Fisk University, 1945), Foreword, i–ix.

12. There is much that is interesting and convincing in Radin's analysis of slave religion. But he does not take into account fully, the effects of slave religion on social cohesion in the quarters. Radin ignores the cultural and communal components of slave religion—its most progressive elements. He apparently views slave religion in mainly Christian terms, referring to the slaves' "sin" and desire for cleanliness and rebirth. The self-doubt and vacillation which he maintains the Christian conversion experience dispelled represents an analysis of the role of Christianity only on one level. It does not take full cognizance of other influences on the development of black religion. Perhaps Radin attributes too much to Christianity, and views the slaves' perception of Christianity too simply. The Gullahs' conception of sin differed from that which the masters attempted to instill. The slaves looked beyond the concept of a personal God, an "other world," a "rebirth," and beyond an attitude toward sin that worked against their interests. We agree with Radin that religion helped the slaves escape "demoralization" and "neurosis." Radin credits this "escape" from the degrading features of enslavement to Christianity. But communal and cultural development also provided that extra layer of faith. His interpretation of the psychological features and effects of the conversion experience would be even more insightful if a broader approach to slave religion were taken. Ibid.

13. John W. Blassingame, ed., *Slave Testimony: Two Centuries of Letters, Speeches, Interviews and Autobiographies* (Baton Rouge: Louisiana State University Press, 1977), 377; Rose, *Rehearsal for Reconstruction*, 132; Dorothy Sterling, *Captain of the Planter: The Story of Robert Smalls*, (New York: Doubleday, 1958) 32–33; Ames, *Dixie Diary*, 45; Towne Diary, passim. Northern teachers related that the Gullahs sometimes found ways to gain some literacy during slavery. Two house servants "picked it up from their master's children," letter by letter. Several other people learned from hymn books. Some were never taught but picked up letters "here and there," which enabled them to read "easy sentences." Allen Diary, 62.

14. Berlin, *Freedom: Black Military Experience*, 46–54; Allen Diary, 155; Leon F. Litwack, *Been in the Storm So Long: The Aftermath of Slavery* (New York: Alfred A. Knopf, 1979), 68–70, 75–76, 93–97; Higginson, *Army Life*, 39–40.

15. Berlin, *Freedom: Black Military Experience*, 54–55; Higginson, *Army Life*, 63, 72, 86–105, 149–50; H. G. Spaulding, "Under the Palmetto," *Continental Monthly* 4 (August, 1963): 202–3; Litwack, *Been in the Storm So Long*, 64, 87–93.

16. Higginson, *Army Life*, 46–48, 70–71, 240–41; Spaulding, "Under the Palmetto," 196.

17. Allen Diary, 82–83; Pearson, *Port Royal*, 99, n. 1, 102, 114, 181–82; Charles Nordhoff, "The Freedmen of South Carolina," in Frank Moore, ed., *Papers of the Day* (New York: C. T. Evans, 1863), 4–5; Towne Diary, 14, 21; Botume, *Amongst the Contrabands*, 143–56.

18. Forten, "Sea Islands, Part I, 588.

19. Rupert Holland, ed. *Letters and Diary of Laura M. Towne* (New York: Negro Universities Press, 1969; Cambridge, Mass.: Riverside Press, 1912), 26.

20. Higginson, *Army Life*, 192; Tilden G. Edelstein, *Strange Enthusiasm: A Life of Thomas Wentworth Higginson* (New York: Atheneum, 1970; repr. from 1968 ed.) 257–60.

21. Botume, *Amongst the Contrabands*, 204; Forten, "Sea Islands," Part II, 672; Allen Diary, 164.

22. Botume, *Amongst the Contrabands*, 204.

23. Higginson, *Army Life*, 208.

24. Edelstein, *Strange Enthusiasm*, 257–60 For an enlightening and provoking treatment of "romantic racialism" see George M. Frederickson, *Black Image in the White Mind: The Debate on Afro-American Character and Destiny, 1817–1914* (New York: Harper & Row, 1971), Chapter 4; William Francis Allen, Charles P. Ware, and Lucy M. Garrison, *Slave Songs of the United States* (New York: Peter Smith, 1951; repr. from 1867 ed.), 48; Higginson, *Army Life*, 208–9.

25. Rev. Mansfied French to Revs, Whipple and Jocelyn, n. d., AMA.

26. Higginson, *Army Life*, 235.

27. Ibid., 71, 236–38, and his Appendix D, 267–76.

28. Litwack, *Been in the Storm So Long*, 457.

9. Folk Religion in the Slave Quarters

1. Mrs. William R. Wister, "Recollections of a Southern Plantation and School," Penn School Papers, vol. 5, 19, SHC; Rosa B. Cooley, *School Acres*, (New Haven: Yale University Press, 1930), 148–49; Diary of Laura M. Towne, 52, Penn School Papers, SHC; "The Long Look," 2–3, undated sketch of a former slave, Sam Polite, who lived to be over 100 years old, Penn School Papers, vol. 1, SHC.

2. *Minutes, Beaufort Baptist Church*, November 11, 1840 and January 7, 1842, 12; October 7, 1859, 271–74, BC; James H. Cuthbert, *Life of Richard Fuller* (New York: Sheldon Co., 1879), 104–5.

3. Cooley, *School Acres*, 148–49; Towne Diary, 52, Samuel Lawton, "The Religious Life of Coastal and Sea Island Negroes," (Ph.D. dissertation, George Peabody College for Teachers, 1939), 61, 69–72; William F. Allen et al., *Slave Songs of the Untied States* (New York: Peter Smith, 1951; repr. from 1867 ed.) xviii.

4. Thomas J. Woofter, *Black Yeomanry* (New York: Henry Hold, 1930), 243–54; Towne Diary 26, 42; Charlotte Forten, "Life on the Sea Islands," Part II, *Atlantic Monthly* 13 (June, 1864): 672; Edward L. Pierce, "The Negroes at Port Royal, S. C.," Doc. 51 in *Rebellion Record*, ed. Frank Moore, Suppl. 1 (New York: D. Van Nostrand, 1871) 305; Lawton, "Religious Life," 54–57, 60–62; Patricia Guthrie, "Catching Sense: The Meaning

of Plantation Membership on St. Helena Island, South Carolina," (Ph.D. dissertation, University of Rochester, 1977).

5. SCA, July 28, 1843; Rupert Holland, ed. Letters and Diary of Laura M. Towne (New York: Negro Universities Press, 1969; repr. from 1912 ed.) 162; Rev. Augustine Roots to Rev. Jocelyn, February 8, 1863, AMA; Woofter, Black Yeomanry, 243–54; Jenkins Mikell, Rumblings of the Chariot Wheels (Columbia: The State Co., 1923), 138; Lawton, "Religious Life," 62–63, 69–72; Guthrie, "Catching Sense," Chapters 4 and 5.

6. Towne Diary, passim; Guthrie, "Catching Sense," 95–97, 117–18; Elsie Clews Parsons, Folk-lore of the Sea Islands of South Carolina (Cambridge, Mass: American Folk-lore Society, 1923), 205–6; Lawton, "Religious Life," 61–23, 69–70.

7. Lawton, "Religious Life," 61–63; Guthrie, "Catching Sense," 95–118. The Praise House membership consisted of households. These units were not always filial and might consist of several "outside children." Yet if these children "caught sense" in that household, they were members of that plantation. They were also members of the Praise House, could be buried in the plantation graveyard, and after slavery, could use the land. Plantation members tried to keep nonmembers off the land. Guthrie, "Catching Sense," 116–22.

8. Pierce, "Negroes at Port Royal," 305; Towne Diary, 55; Frances Anne Kemble, Journal of a Residence on a Georgian Plantation (New York: Harper & Brothers, 1863), 167–68; Rev. W. T. Richardson to Rev. Jocelyn, August 7, 1863, AMA; Arthur Sumner to Nina Hartshorn, May 18, 1862, Penn School Papers, vol. 4, SHC.

9. Diary of William F. Allen, William F. Allen Family Papers, 1775–1937, State Historical Society of Wisconsin, Madison, 106–7, 145, 164; Elizabeth Hyde Botume, First Days Amongst the Contrabands (New York: Arno Press and New York Times, 1968, repr. from 1893 ed.), 125–26; Thomas Wentworth Higginson, Army Life in a Black Regiment (New York: Collier Books, 1962, repr. from 1870 ed.), 48; Elizabeth Ware Pearson, Letters from Port Royal (New York: Arno Press and New York Times, 1969, repr. from 1906 ed.), 198; Charlotte Forten "Life on the Sea Islands," Part I, Atlantic Monthly 13 (May, 1864): 592.

10. Guthrie, "Catching Sense," 55–57, 119–23; Grace Bigelow House, "The Little Foe of All the World," Southern Workman 35 (1906): 603; Wister, "Recollections," 14; Allen Diary, 45; Towne Diary, 13.

11. Ruth Finnegan, Survey of the Limba People of Northern Sierra Leone (London: HMS, 1965), 69–80; Robert T. Parsons, Religion in an African Society, 99–100; Folkways Research Series, The Traditional History and Folklore of the Gola Tribe in Liberia, 2 vols. (Monrovia: Dept. of the Interior, 1961) II: 55–56; Thomas Winterbottom, An Account of the Native Africans in the Neighborhood of Sierra Leone, 2 vols. (London: Frank Cass, 1969; repr. from 1803 ed.) I: 211; Wyatt MacGaffey, Custom and Government in the Lower Congo (Berkeley: University of California Press, 1970), 103.

12. Mikell, Chariot Wheels, 139–41.

13. W. T. Harris and Harry Sawyerr, The Springs of Mende Belief and Conduct: A Discussion of the Influence of the Belief in the Supernatural among the Mende (Freetown: Sierra Leone University Press) 103; W. C. Willoughby, The Soul of the Bantu: A Sympathetic Study of the Magico-Religious Practices and Beliefs of the Bantu Tribes of Africa (Newport, Conn.: Negro Universities Press, 1970, originally published 1928), 393.

14. Minutes, Beaufort Baptist Church, 271–72, BC; James R. Stuart Recollections, n.d., circa 1850, 2–4, SHC; SCA, June 26, 1843; Holland, Towne Letters and Diary, 162, 145; Cooley, School Acres, 148–49; Charles A. Raymond "The Religious Life of the Negro Slave," Harper's New Monthly Magazine 27 (September, 1863): Part I, 479.

15. *Minutes, Beaufort Baptist Church*, May 14, 1842, 34, BC; "Religious Life," Part I, 478; Lawton, "Religious Life," 71–72.

16. David Thorpe to John Mooney, January 25, 1863, Dabbs Papers, Thorpe Series, SHC; Raymond, "Religious Life," Part I, 479–80; Towne Diary, 52, 162; Lawton, "Religious Life," 36–37.

17. *Minutes, Beaufort Baptist Church*, 272–73, BC; Guthrie, "Catching Sense," 93–94; Towne Diary, 52, 162.

18. Towne Diary, 52, 162: John L. Field to George W. Moore, March 21, 1833, HSSCC; *SCA*, June 26, 1840; Pearson, *Port Royal*, 43–44; Guthrie, "Catching Sense," 88–89, 93–94.

19. *SCA*, April 18, 1843, July 28, 1843, September 6, 1859.

20. *Minutes, Beaufort Baptist Church*, October 7, 1849, 271–74, BC; *SCA*, October 30, 1846, October 30, 1847. "Seekin' " was practiced among other African-American slaves. See Charles A. Raymond, "The Religious Life of the Negro Slave," *Harper's New Monthly Magazine* 27 (October, 1863); Part II, 680–82.

21. Mikell, *Chariot Wheels*, 137–39; Raymond, "Religious Life," Part II, 680–81; Higginson, *Army Life*, 194–95; Cooley, *School Acres*, 151–53; Lawton, "Religious Life," 143–45; Parsons, *Folk-lore of the Sea Islands*, 204–5; Allen Diary, 155; Botume, *Amongst the Contrabands*, 254–55.

22. John W. Blamagame, ed., *Slave Testimony: Two Centuries of Letters, Speeches, Interviews and Autobiographies* (Baton Rouge: Louisiana State University Press, 1977), 373; Lawton, "Religious Life," 170–80; Parsons, *Folk-lore of the Sea Islands*, 204–5; Cooley, *School Acres*, 151–53; Mikell, *Chariot Wheels*; Guthrie, "Catching Sense," Chapter 5; Raymond, "Religious Life," Part II, 680–82.

23. *SCA*, August 11, 1843.

24. Mark Hanna Watkins, "The West African 'Bush' School," *Journal of Sociology* 48 (1943): 66–67; Warren L. d'Azevedo, "Common Principles of Variant Kinship Structures among the Golas of Western Liberia," *American Anthropologist* 64 no. 3, 505; James L. Gibbs, Jr. "The Kpelle of Liberia," in James L. Gibbs, Jr. ed., *Peoples of Africa* (New York: Holt, Rinehart & Winston, 1965), 219–22; Ruth Finnegan, *Limba Stories and Story Telling* (London: Oxford University Press, 1967), 21–23; Michael Jackson, *The Kuranko: Dimensions of Social Reality in a West African Society* (London: C. Hurst, 1977), 34, 182–84, 202–3; George Harley and George Schwab, "The Mano of Liberia," in Carleton S. Coon, ed., *A Reader in General Anthropology* (New York: Henry Holt, 1960), 348–49, 359–60, 364–65, 369; Folkways Research Series, *Tribes of the Western Province and the Denwoin People* (Monrovia: Dept of Interior, 1955), 11–22; *Traditional History and Folklore of the Glebo Tribe*, 2 vols. (Monrovia: Dept. of Interior, 1955 and 1961) II: 83; Harris and Sawyerr, *Mende Belief*, 47–49; Warren L. d'Azevedo, *Gola of Liberia*, 2 vols. (New Haven: Human Relations Area Files, 1972) II: 312–13; and "Gola Poro and Sande: Primal Tasks in Social Custodianship," 98–104; M. C. Jedrej, "Structural Aspects of a West African Secret Society," 136; Carolina H. Bledsoe, "Stratification and Sande Politics," 143–45; and Svend Holsoe, "Notes on the Vai Sande Society in Liberia," 97–107, all in *Ethnologische Zeitschrift Zürich* I (1980). For a discussion of the relationship between African-American fraternal orders and West African secret societies, see Betty M. Kuyk, "The African Derivation of Black Fraternal Orders in the United States," *Comparative Studies in Societies and History* 25, no. 4 (October, 1983): 559–94.

25. Jackson, *The Kuranko*, 34, 204, 206–7, 211, 221; Finnegan, *Limba Stories*, 23–33; Harley and Schwab, "The Mano," 348–49, 360–69; Little, *Mende*, 225–27, and "The Role of the Secret Society in Cultural Specialization," *American Anthropologist* 51 (1949): 199–

202, 210–12; Gibbs, "The Kpelle," 221–22; Watkins, " 'Bush' School," 666–68, 670–72. The fact that initiation into society was not peculiar to Windward Coast and Gambia groups has been mentioned in Chapter 2. Yet its existence elsewhere could reinforce the Poro and Sande influence since no initiation process was as pervasive and germane to sacred and secret life as these associations and their equivalents under different names. In other African-American societies, such as Jamaica, there is evidence of Poro power in socialization and group authority. This is reflected through the Jonkonnu masquerade tradition. Masks were central to some African Poro and Sande means of expression, leadership concealment, and instilling obedience through intimidation. The masquerade and other apparent manifestations of Poro power have been discussed by researchers of Jamaican history and culture. The mask-wearing conveys "supernatural authority" in the Jamaican Jonkonnu, but appears in a "secular/entertainment context." Mask-wearing has no part in Gullah culture but this may be the result of Gullah incorporation of secret society elements into Christianity. In Jamaica, where little Christian instruction of slaves was conducted, the masquerade and festive aspects of the association could continue, whereas there was no base upon which the religious element could remain. Also, covering the face with ash, as done by Gullahs, may be a substitute for the mask and for clay, since both are used in African supernatural and spiritual rituals. For an account of the relationship of Poro and Jamaican culture, see Cheryl Ryman, "Jonkonnu, A Neo-African Form," Part I, *Jamaica Journal* 17, no. 2 (May, 1984): 50–56.

26. Folkways Research Series, *History of Gola Tribe*, II: 2–5, 21–22; James L. Sibley and D. Westermann, *Liberia Old and New* (London: James Clarke, 1928), 219–20, 231–32, Harley and Schwab, "The Mano," 351; Jackson, *The Kuranko*, 201–14; Little, *Mende*, 121; Watkins, " 'Bush' School," 669–674; Holsoe, "Notes on Vai Sande," 97–100.

27. *SCA*, June 26, 1840, June 26, 1843, October 30, 1846; Pearson, *Port Royal*, 43–44; Holland, *Towne Letters and Diary*, 145, 162; Cooley, *School Acres*, 152; Kemble, *Journal*, 84.

28. Harris and Sawyerr, *Mende Belief*, 103–16; Little, *Mende*, 183–85, and "Secret Society in Cultural Specialization," 204–5; Harley and Schwab, "The Mano," 355; Folkways Research Series, *History of Gola Tribe*, II: 5; John H. Weeks, *Among the Primitive BaKongo* (London: Seeley, Service, 1914), 100–102; E. J. Glave, "Fetishism in Congo Land," *Century* 71 (November–April, 1890–91): 826–27.

29. Sibley and Westermann, *Liberia*, 176–86, 222–26; Little, "Secret Society in Cultural Specialization," 199–200; Watkins, " 'Bush' School," 670–71; *SCA*, June 26, 1843, October 30, 1847; Lawton, "Religious Life," 138–43; Cooley, *School Acres*, 152.

30. Watkins, " 'Bush' School," 673–74; Jackson, *The Kuranko*, 214, n. 1; Folkways Research Series, *History of Gola Tribe*, II: 15–21; Sibley and Westermann, *Liberia*, 228–29; Holsoe, "Notes on Vai Sande," 103.

31. Towne Diary, 52.

32. Thorpe to Mooney, January 25, 1863, Dabbs Papers, Thorpe Series, SHC.

33. Folkways Research Series, *History of Gola Tribe*, II: 17; Watkins, " 'Bush' School," 671–73; Holsoe, "Notes on Vai Sande," 97–104.

34. Sir Charles Lyell, *A Second Visit to the United States*, 2 vols. (New York; Harper & Brothers, 1849), I: 231; *SCA*, August 111, 1843.

35. Pearson, *Port Royal*, 145–46; Rev. Augustine Roots to Rev. Jocelyn, February 8, 1863, and March 6, 1863, AMA; Laura Towne to J. M. McKim, July 1 and August 2, 1862, Antislavery Papers, Rarebook Room, Cornell University, AMA; Towne Diary, 75, 104.

36. Lyell, *Second Visit*, I: 269–70; Robert Simpson, "The Shout and Shouting in Slave Religion of the United States," *The Southern Quarterly* 23, no. 3 (Spring, 1985): 34–37.

37. *SCA*, April 18, 1843.

38. Forten, "Sea Islands," Part II, 672; Holland, *Towne Letters and Diary*, 20–22; Lawton, "Religious Life," 77–79; Spaulding, "Under the Palmetto," 195–99.

39. Spaulding, "Under the Palmetto," 195–99; 199; Holland, *Towne Letters and Diary*, 22–23; Higginson, *Army Life*, 41; Forten, "Sea Islands," Part II, 672.

40. Allen Diary, 155; Spaulding, "Under the Palmetto," 199; Allen et al., *Slave Songs*, xii; Wister, "Recollections," 17.

41. Holland, *Towne Letters and Diary*, 20; Wister, "Recollections"; Sumner to Clark, July 7, 1862, Penn School Papers, SHC; Allen et al., *Slave Songs*, xii; Cooley, *School Acres*, 150–51; Towne Diary, 83.

42. John Beattie, *Other Cultures* (New York: Free Press of Glencoe, 1964), 229; Anthony F. C. Wallace, *Religion: An Anthropological View* (New York: Random House, 1966), 190; Simpson, "The Shout and Shouting," 36.

43. Erika Bourguignon, "Ritual Dissociation and Possession Belief in Caribbean Negro Religion," in Norman E. Whitten, Jr. and John F. Szwed, eds., *Afro-American Anthropology, Contemporary Perspectives* (New York: Free Press, 1970), 96–97; Jackson, *The Kuranko*, 201–3; Harley and Schwab, "The Mano," 349–50, 359–65; Sciela S. Walker, *Ceremonial Spirit Possession in Africa and Afro-America* (Leiden: E. J. Brill, 1972), 3–9, 52–58.

44. Lawton, "Religious Life," 77–79; Simpson, "The Shout and Shouting," 36–40.

45. Stuart Recollections, 2–3, SHC.

10. Gullah Attitudes Toward Death and the Supernatural

1. Robert Farris Thompson and Joseph Cornet, *The Four Moments of the Sun: Kongo Art in Two Worlds* (Washington, D. C.: National Gallery of Art, 1981), 27; Diary of William F. Allen, 96, in William F. Allen Family Papers, 1775–1937, State Historical Society of Wisconsin, Madison; Charlotte Forten, "Life on the Sea Islands," Part II, Atlantic Monthly 13 (June, 1864): 666.

2. Charles Nordhoff, "The Freedmen of South Carolina," in Frank Moore, ed., *Papers of the Day* (New York: C. T. Evans, 1863), 4.

3. *SCA*, July 7, 1843, August 11, 1843, January 19, 1844, August 20, 1847, May 5, 1844.

4. South Carolina Folklore Project, #1655, D-4-27, WPA, SCL.

5. James Ball, *Fifty Years in Chains, or the Life of an American Slave* (New York: H. Dayton, 1860), 150.

6. *SCA*, July 7, 1843.

7. Elizabeth Ware Pearson, *Letters from Port Royal*, (New York: Arno Press and New York Times, repr. from 1906 ed.), 253–54; Diary of Laura M. Towne, 64, 75, Penn School Papers, SHC; Folklore Project, #1655, D-4-27, WPA, SCL.

8. Pearson, *Port Royal*, 252; Irving E. Lowrey, *Life on the Old Plantation* (Columbia: University of South Carolina Press, 1911), 81–83; Folklore Project, #1655 and #1855, D-4-27, WPA, SCL; T. W. Richardson to Rev. George Whipple, September 14, 1863, AMA.

9. W. T. Harris and Harry Sawyerr, *Springs of Mende Belief and Conduct: A Discussion of the Influence of the Belief in the Supernatural Among the Mende* (Freetown: Sierra Leone University Press, 1968), 31–32; George W. Ellis, *Negro Culture in West Africa* (New York: Neale Publishing, 1914), 70; Thomas Winterbottom, *An Account of the Native Africans in the Neighborhood of Sierra Leone*, 2 vols. (London: Frank Cass, 1969, repr. from 1803 ed.), I: 236–37; Dennis Benjamin, *The Gbandes, A People of the Liberian Hinterland* (Chicago: Nelson-

Hall, 1922), 173–74; Karl Laman, *Kongo*, 5 vols. (Uppsala: Studia Ethnographica Upsaliensia, 1962), II: 85.

10. Folklore Project #1655 and #1855, D-4-27A, 27B, WPA, SCL: Janie G. Moore, "Africanisms Among Blacks of the Sea Islands," *Journal of Black Studies* 10, no. 41 (June, 1980): 476–77; John M. Vlach, *The Afro-American Tradition in Decorative Arts* (Cleveland, Ohio: Cleveland Museum of Art, 1978), 139–40; Elsie Clews Parsons, *Folk-lore of the Sea Islands of South Carolina* (Cambridge, Mass: American Folk-lore Society, 1923), 213–14.

11. Parsons, *Folk-lore of the Sea Islands*, 213–14.

12. Harris and Sawyerr, *Mende Belief*, 31–32, 89; M. McCulloch, *Peoples of Sierra Leone* (London: International African Institute, 1950), 74; W. C. Willoughby, *The Soul of the Bantu: A Sympathetic Study of the Magico-Religious Practices and Beliefs of the Bantu Tribes of Africa* (Westport, Conn: Negro Universities Press, 1970, originally published 1928), 86–87; Laman, *Kongo*, II: 84.

13. Lowrey, *Old Plantation*, 83–87; Laman, *Kongo*, II: 88–92; Moore, Africanisms in the Sea Islands," 473–76; Parsons, *Folk-lore of the Sea Islands*, 213; Robert Farris Thompson, *Flash of the Spirit: African and Afro-American Art and Philosophy* (New York: Vintage Books, 1983), 117; John H. Weeks, *Among the Primitive BaKongo* (London: Seeley, Service, 1914), 267–68.

14. Towne Diary, 98; Charles A. Raymond, "The Religious Life of the Negro Slave," *Harpers New Monthly Magazine* 28 (November, 1863): Part III, 821.

15. John S. Mbiti, *African Religions and Philosophies* (New York: Praeger Publishers, 1959), 149; Ellis, *Negro Culture in West Africa*, 70–71; Harris and Sawyerr, *Mende Belief*, 14, 50; Laman, *Kongo*, II: 95–96.

16. Harris and Sawyerr, *Mende Belief*, 14.

17. Lowrey, *Old Plantation*, 85–86; Folklore Project, #1655 and #1855, D-4-27 and #1655, D-4-27A, WPA, SCL; Vlach, *Afro-American Decorative Arts*, 139–40; H. Corrington Bolton, "Decoration of Graves of Negroes in South Carolina," *Journal of American Folklore* 4 (July–September, 1891): 214; "Notes and Documents: Antebellum and War Memories of Mrs. Telfair Hodgson," Sarah Hodgson Torian, ed., *Georgia Historical Quarterly* 27, no. 4 (December, 1953): 352; Virginia C. Holmgren, *Hilton Head: A Sea Island Chronicle* (Hilton Head, S. C.: Hilton Head Publishing, 1959), 63; Samuel Lawton, "The Religious Life of Coastal and Sea Island Negroes," (Ph.D. dissertation, George Peabody College for Teachers, 1939), 196.

18. Wilfred Hambly, *The Ovimbundu of Angola* (Chicago: University of Chicago Press, 1934, 288; Laman, *Kongo*, II: 92, 95; Bolton, "Decoration of Graves," 214; Thompson, *Four Moments of the Sun*, 181–91; Folkways Research Series, *Tribes of the Western Province and the Denwoin People* (Monrovia: Dept. of Interior, 1955), 25, 27; Ellis, *Negro Culture in West Africa*, 87; McCulloch, *Peoples of Sierra Leone*, 74.

19. Lawton, "Religious Life," 212–213.

20. Edward G. Brinder, *West African Psychology* (London: Butterworth Press, 1951), 17–18; Vlach, *Afro-American Decorative Arts*, 139–43; Lawton, "Religious Life," 213.

21. Lawton, "Religious Life," 214.

22. Daniel Brinton, *Religions of Primitive Peoples* (New York: G. P. Putnam's Sons, 1899), 208. Harris and Sawyerr, *Mende Belief*, 33.

23. Lawton, "Religious Life," 217; Vlach, *Afro-American Decorative Arts*, 143; Thompson, *Flash of the Spirit*, 132–46; Elizabeth A. Fenn, "Honoring the Ancestors: Kongo-American Graves in the American South," *Southern Exposure* 28 (September–October, 1985): 44–45; Hodgson, "Antebellum and War Memories," 352.

24. Vlach, *Afro-American Decorative Arts*, 143; Laman, *Kongo*, III: 21, 37; Thompson, *Four Moments of the Sun*, 198.

25. Thompson, *Flash of the Spirit*, 139–42, and *Four Moments of the Sun*, 183; Vlach, *Afro-American Decorative Arts*, 141. Laman writes that "the porcelain articles may comprise mugs (with holes knocked in bottom), to prevent their being stolen," *Kongo*, II: 95.

26. Vlach, *Afro-American Decorative Arts*, 147; Parsons, *Folk-lore of the Sea Islands*, 215; Thomas Wentworth Higginson, *Army Life in a Black Regiment* (New York: Collier Books, 1962, repr. from 1870 ed.).

27. See Appendix E.

28. Folklore Project, #1655, D-4-27, 27A, 27B WPA, SCL.

29. Ibid.

30. See Appendix E.

31. Maxim Gorky, *A Confession*, trans. William Frederick Harvey (London: Everett, 1910).

Epilogue

1. Stephen B. Oates, *With Malice Toward None: The Life of Abraham Lincoln* (New York: Mentor Books, 1977) 421–22, 439–41; Elizabeth Ware Pearson, *Letters from Port Royal* (New York: Arno Press and New York Times, 1969; repr. from 1906 ed.), 128–31; Thomas Wentworth Higginson, *Army Life in a Black Regiment* (New York: Collier Books, 1962, repr. from 1870 ed.), 59–60; Tilden G. Edelstein, *Strange Enthusiasm: A Life of Thomas Wentworth Higginson* (New York: Atheneum, 1970; repr. from 1968 ed.), 261.

2. Anna Carter to Rev. S. S. Jocelyn, January 22, 1863, AMA.

3. Lawrence W. Levine, *Black Culture and Black Consciousness: Afro-American Folk Thought from Slavery to Freedom* (New York: Oxford University Press, 1977), Chapter 3.

Appendix D: The Deity

1. Samuel Lawton, "The Religious Life of Coastal and Sea Island Negroes," (Ph.D. dissertation, George Peabody College for Teachers, 1939), 116–26.

2. Rosa B. Cooley, *School Acres* (New Haven: Yale University Press, 1930), 157–58.

Index

Kpelle, 42, 46
Kromanti. *See* Akan; Ashanti
Kru(s), 41-46
Kuranko, 40, 288
Kwa, *See* Kru(s)

Labor
and Health, 191
and slave trading, 34
black, 34, 36
cotton, 125, 190-93, 237, 241
indentured servants, 79
Indian, 67-68, 78
Urban, 124-25
Lane, Lunsford, 198-99
Lauren(s),
Henry, 35-36, 121, 123
John, 123
Lawton, Samuel, 317, 319
Lawton(s)
affluency of, 132, 225
and Black Swamp Church, 132
and Christian instruction, 219
Joseph, 245
migration to South Carolina, 132
religious background, 132
See also Roberts family
Ledbetter, T. E., 195
Le Jau, Francis, 70, 78-79, 88-89, 101
Lee, Jessie, 139
Liele, Reverend George, 133
Levine, Lawrence, 5-6, 325
Liberia, 2
and secret societies, 48, 288
as Gola homeland, 17
linguistic groups, 41
Limba(s), 40, 46, 282, 288
Lincoln, President Abraham, 323
Little, Kenneth, 48
Littlefield, Daniel, 36, 358n10
Litwack, Leon, 275
Lofton, John, 131
Lokkos, 40, 46
Loma, 42
"Long Look, The." *See* Polite, Sam
Lower Guinea, 29, 57
Lucas, Eliza, 34. *See also* Pinckney(s)
Lyell, Charles, 297-98

MacGaffey, Wyatt, 59

McCrea, James, 239
McKim, J. Miller, 277
McMillan, Harry, 238
McLoughlin, William, 80
Malaguetta pepper, 36
Mande language, 42, 208
Mandinga(s), 17, 37-42
Mano, 42, 46, 288-89, 300
Maroons
aiding British, 126
early national evidence of, 130
in Colonial era, 110
in post-Independence era, 126-27
Marrant, John
among Indians, 106
and "Book of Negroes," 376n12
call to ministry, 123
conversion of, 104-5
in British navy, 106
in Sierra Leone, 106
Marshall, Reverend Abraham, 134-35
Marshall, Reverend Andrew, 183-84, 384n30
Marx, Karl, 11
Masks in Poro-Sande, 19, 49-50
Matthews, John, 47
Maule, Reverend Robert, 101
Mayombe, 31
Mazowo, (Grand Lady of Sande), 288, 290
Mbiti, John, 56, 59, 61, 365n13
Mbundu, 15, 31
Medicine specialists (white magic), 56-58, 60, 181-82
Mende, 17, 19, 42, 46, 283
and death, 52
and Poro-Sande, 50, 288
deity, 52
Methodism
and antislavery sentiment, 177, 213
and black insurrection, 23, 148
and black leadership, 148, 181-82, 184-85, 187-88, 248-55
and Camden Conspiracy, 129-30
and class meeting, 200, 202
and Great Awakening, 82
and Vesey Conspiracy, 148-53, 161, 166
appeal to blacks, 13, 145-47
doctrinal position, 145
early black participation, 144-47
emotionalism, 298